FOUNDATIONS OF UTILITY AND RISK THEORY WITH APPLICATIONS

THEORY AND DECISION LIBRARY

AN INTERNATIONAL SERIES
IN THE PHILOSOPHY AND METHODOLOGY OF THE
SOCIAL AND BEHAVIORAL SCIENCES

Editors

GERALD EBERLEIN, *University of Technology, Munich*
WERNER LEINFELLNER, *University of Nebraska*

Editorial Advisory Board

VOLUME 37

FOUNDATIONS OF UTILITY AND RISK THEORY WITH APPLICATIONS

Edited by

BERNT P. STIGUM
University of Olso, Norway

and

FRED WENSTØP
Norwegian School of Management, Bekkestua, Norway

D. REIDEL PUBLISHING COMPANY

A MEMBER OF THE KLUWER ✱ ACADEMIC PUBLISHERS GROUP

DORDRECHT / BOSTON / LANCASTER

Library of Congress Cataloging in Publication Data

Main entry under title:

Foundations of utility and risk theory with applications.

    (Theory and decision library ; v. 37)
    Includes indexes.
    1. Utility theory—Addresses, essays, lectures. 2. Risk—Addresses, essays,
lectures. I. Stigum, Bernt P. II. Wenstøp, Fred, 1945–   . III. Series.
HB201.F58   1983   330.15′7   83–13774
ISBN 90–277–1239–5

Published by D. Reidel Publishing Company,
P.O. Box 17, 3300 AA Dordrecht, Holland

Sold and distributed in the U.S.A. and Canada
by Kluwer Academic Publishers
190 Old Derby Street, Hingham, MA 02043, U.S.A.

In all other countries, sold and distributed
by Kluwer Academic Publishers Group,
P.O. Box 322, 3300 AA Dordrecht, Holland.

Printed in The Netherlands

TABLE OF CONTENTS

EDITORIAL PREFACE

In this volume we present some of the papers that were delivered at FUR-82 – the First International Conference on Foundations of Utility and Risk Theory in Oslo, June 1982. The purpose of the conference was to provide a forum within which scientists could report on interesting applications of modern decision theory and exchange ideas about controversial issues in the foundations of the theory of choice under uncertainty. With that purpose in mind we have selected a mixture of applied and theoretical papers that we hope will appeal to a wide spectrum of readers from graduate students in social science departments and business schools to people involved in making hardheaded decisions in business and government. In an introductory article Ole Hagen gives an overview of various paradoxes in utility and risk theory and discusses these in the light of scientific methodology. He concludes the article by calling for joint efforts to provide decision makers with <u>workable</u> theories. Kenneth Arrow takes up the same issue on a broad basis in his paper where he discusses the implications of behavior under uncertainty for policy.

In the theoretical papers the reader will find attempts at definitive statements of the meaning of old concepts and suggestions for the adoption of new concepts. For instance, Maurice Allais discusses four different interpretations of the axioms of probability and explains the need for an empirical characterization of the concept of chance. In a commentatory paper, Herman Wold asserts that it is absolutely necessary to keep apart theoretical and empirical knowledge when discussing the concepts of utility and chance. Nils-Eric Sahlin argues that second-order probabilities are measures of *epistemic reliability*. The set of such measures that an agent uses in a given decision-theoretic situation reflects his attitude towards a form of risk taking that Sahlin designates by *epistemic risk*. And Roman Krzysztofowicz and Sten Thore respectively introduce the concept of a *relative risk attitude* and the idea of a *Hotelling utility function*.

B. P. Stigum and F. Wenstøp (eds.), Foundations of Utility and Risk Theory with Applications, vii–ix.
© 1983 by D. Reidel Publishing Company.

In the theoretical papers the reader will also find discussions of the status of controversial axioms in various theories of choice under uncertainty and proposals for new axiom systems. For instance, Edward McClennen discusses L.J. Savage's sure-thing principle and the validity of the arguments that have been directed against it. George Wright and Peter Whalley question the additivity of subjective probabilities and describe situations in which they tend to be supra-additive. Knut Midgaard uses John Harsanyi's rationality postulates as a basis for ascertaining the significance of Zeuten's principle in bargaining situations. Hector Munera and Richard de Neufville suggest a characterization of an agent's risk preference when they do not satisfy R.D. Luce and H. Raiffa's substitution principle. And Mark Machina shows that the basic concepts and results of expected utility theory do not depend on P. Samuelson's independence axiom, but may be derived from weaker assumptions concerning the smoothness of preferences over alternative probability distributions.

The theoretical papers also include Hans Gottinger's discussion of the economics of organizational design as seen from the point of view of a graph theorist and Frank Milne and H.M. Shefrin's examples of second-best problems of resource allocation that result from changes in the markets for securities. Finally, they include J.M. Blatt's description of a class of individuals whose behavior under uncertainty cannot be rationalized by expected-utility theory, and Maurice De Groot's analysis of problems that arise in decision theory when an agent is forced to choose an act without complete knowledge of his utility function.

The applied papers present empirical tests of controversial axioms, suggest new uses for subjective probabilities, propose new ways of interpreting and constructing cardinal utility indices, and describe problems that decision makers in large organizations and government face. For instance, Mark McCord and R. de Neufville present tests of the independence axiom, John Harsanyi discusses the use of subjective probabilities in game theory. Also Peter Farquhar and Peter Fishburn discuss indifference spanning methods for practical assessments of multiattribute utility functions and Fred Wenstøp describes how multiattribute utility theory can be applied to problems that arise in the exploration and development of North Sea oil. Finally, A. Camacho presents a new way of interpreting and constructing measurable utility indices, Robin Pope discusses the necessity of inter-

preting uncertainty as a flow-concept, and Andrew MacKinnon
and Alexander Wearing describe some experimental findings
concerning the nature of problems faced by human beings in
managing dynamic systems.

Acknowledgements

The First International Conference on the Foundations of
Utility and Risk Theory would never have come about had it
not been for the driving forces of Ole Hagen and Werner
Leinfellner. The Board of Advisors consisted of Maurice
Allais, Helmut Frisch, Werner Leinfellner, Amartya Sen,
Ingolf Ståhl and Herman Wold. The executive committee was
chaired by Ole Hagen with Jon Elster, Jan-Erik Fenstad,
Aanund Hylland, Bernt Stigum, Jan Smedslund and Fred Wenstøp
as members. Mrs. Lise Fog was secretary for the committee.
    The financial support from the following institutions
made the conference possible and is gratefully acknowledged:
- the Norwegian Ministry of Culture and Science
- the Norwegian Research Council for Science and the
    Humanitites
- the International Union of History and Philosophy of Science
- the Bank of Norway's fund to further research in economics
- the Embassy of the Federal Republic of Germany
- the University of Nebraska
- the Norwegian School of Management

    Both during the conference and in the preparation of
this volume, Mrs. Lise Fog has been indispensable by maintaining order in the face of imminent chaos.
    Finally we want to thank all those who participated at
the conference and contributed to what we think is a step
forward in this area of research.

Oslo, April 26, 1983.
Bernt Stigum
Fred Wenstøp

PART I

INTRODUCTION

Maurice Allais

OPENING ADDRESS

Mister Chairman, Ladies and Gentlemen,

First, I would like, in the name of all the participants, to express the most grateful thanks to Professor Leinfellner, Ole Hagen, the members of the executive Committee, and its very efficient secretary, Mrs Fog, as well as the Norwegian School of Management of Oslo, for the organisation of this First International Conference on the Foundations of the Theory of Risk and Utility.

From the viewpoint of both fundamental and applied science, this is an especially happy initiative for reconsidering the foundations of the Theory of Decision and its applications in a world which is heavily dependent on the uncertainty of the future.

Professor Leinfellner and Ole Hagen did me the honour of naming me to the Board of Advisors. However, I want to say that my own contribution was almost non-existent, and that the whole merit of the initiative and organisation of this Conference is theirs alone.

Even greater value attaches to this Conference because it is multi-disciplinary and covers a very wide field, namely, the individual or collective decisions, in which both utility and risk ought to be taken into account.

Given the extremely wide range of the Theory of Decision, may be it is preferable to present a few examples illustrating the need to put on solid foundations the two basic concepts of this Theory, namely, probability and utility.

If for instance the problem is to determine the height of Dutch dykes, what is the optimum solution in the light of the frequency distribution of the height of tides, the cost of different heights of dykes, the probability of them being insufficient some day, and the perceived utility of dykes as an instrument of safety in relation to their cost ?

In the field of minerals exploration, what is the best strategy to adopt if we consider at the same time the probability of existence of workable deposits, the cost of pros-

B. P. Stigum and F. Wenstøp (eds.), Foundations of Utility and Risk Theory with Applications, 3–4.
© 1983 by D. Reidel Publishing Company.

pection, the profits to be made, and the utility function which will allow a choice to be made between these various elements ?

In the area of economic policy, how can we take into account the uncertainty of the future, the latent variables influencing the economic conjunctural situation, and the utility or disutility of the measures which should be taken ?

Whether the aim is to judge statistical goodness of fit or to compare a theoretical model in a certain field with the observed data, there is always the need to take a decision, and it is necessary to specify clearly the considerations which should be taken into account.

Similarly, when research leads to numerical concordance, the question which immediately comes to the mind is whether this corresponds to an intrinsic reality or whether it is only a fortuitous regularity. And indeed in any case we must decide whether the research should be continued or not.

But in all theses cases on what criteria should our decisions be based ? Whether we consider utility or probability, the heated, and sometimes sharp and polemical, discussions to which the Theory of Decision has given rise over the last thirty years appear mostly to be the result of semantic confusion between entirely different concepts. Whether the Theory of Decision is viewed as a fundamental or an applied science, no real progress is conceivable until both concepts have been clarified.

How can one conceive that it is possible to interpret observed data ; how can the future be predicted in the light of all the uncertainties it involves ; how can our knowledge be used to take the best decisions, *if the fog of vagueness shrouding the two concepts underlying the whole Theory of Decision is not cleared away ?*

Here appears the vast interest of this Conference : the confrontation of different viewpoints, of approaches which overlap in part, but yet preserve their own identity, with each shedding light on the others.

Papers and books have an irreplaceable utility, but direct exchange of ideas and views is no less indispensable. Thus there is no doubt that this Conference will be very fruitful, and of benefit to each of us. This is why I wish again to thank Professor Leinfellner, Ole Hagen and the organising Committee in your name for their initiative in convening the Conference, and through considerable and very efficient effort, for having organised it in the best possible conditions.

Ole Hagen

PARADOXES AND THEIR SOLUTIONS

A. WHAT IS A PARADOX

Much of the discussions of the subject of FUR-82 has centered
around "paradoxes". Just to make sure that we know what we
are talking about, I have consulted (1) Encyclopedia Brit-
annica, (2) The Concise Oxford Dictionary, and (3) Colin's
National Dictionary. The result of my research is that we
don't know. In (1) there is no explicit definition of "paradox", but it is said to be approximately the same as antinomy,
which is a pair of (seemingly) correct but contradictory implications from the same base. In (2) we find a similar definition, but also: "statement contrary to received opinion".
In (3) less neutrally: "statement seemingly absurd or self-
contradictory, but really founded on truth".

Ethymologically, para means against and doxa means
opinion, so the definition quoted under (2) seems to be least
contaminated by abuse of language.

In this article I try to give a survey of which paradoxes,
mainly observations contrary to received opinion, have played
or are likely to play an important role in the development of
decision theory. The conclusion seems to be that we still
don't have an uncontroversial theory, free of paradoxes, that
can show the decision maker a narrow path to wise decisions.

It is suggested that failing this we may offer a decision
technique which we hope can produce a ranking of games with
a high rank correlation with the ranking that would result
from direct evaluation of the complex games we meet in reality,
if this were within the capacity of the decision maker's in-
tellect.

B. P. Stigum and F. Wenstøp (eds.), Foundations of Utility and Risk Theory with Applications,
5–17.
© 1983 *by D. Reidel Publishing Company.*

B. CLASSICAL PARADOXES

1. The St. Petersburgh Paradox

Bernoulli described a game for which a person would only pay
a limited amount of money, although the game had an infinite
monetary expectation (Bernoulli, Translation 1954). In the
20th century, K. Menger (1934) pointed out that no such game
could exist, but also that a similar game with limited monetary expectation could only be sold for a much lower price
than its monetary expectation.

     This is, or rather was, paradoxical to the received
opinion, namely the belief in expected monetary value maxi-
mixation, and was, therefore, in reference to the place where
it was presented, named the St. Petersburgh Paradox.

     Bernoulli's solution to this paradox was to reject the
"received opinion" and adopt a new hypothesis. People maximise the expectation of a function of monetary wealth. That
he considered this function to be the logarithm, is immaterial.
Mark that he changed the received opinion as little as possible to accommodate the discovered fact. The remaining implication of the St. Petersburgh Paradox is the negative
conclusion: People do not maximise the expectation of monetary value of the outcome. Bernoulli himself pointed to an
alternative hypothesis: that people maximise the expectation
of a function of wealth, e.g. the logarithm. The best known
axiomatic base of a theorem to this effect was presented by
von Neumann and Morgenstern.

2. Allais Paradoxes

Let four games be arranged in such a manner that when EU
means expected utility:
     $EU(A) > EU(B) \Leftrightarrow EU(X) > EU(Y)$
A respondent is asked to choose between A and B and between
X and Y. He prefers A and Y:
     APfB and YPfX

     Many adherents of the expected utility theory would now
say that the person in one case implies that $EU(A) > EU(B)$ and
in the other $EU(Y) > EU(X)$, so this pair of statements is inconsistent and shows that he is irrational. His pair of
choices is therefore inadmissible as evidence.

But this is a <u>non sequitur</u>.   The (so they claim) refutable EU-hypothesis has been used to prove that an observation is inadmissible and can not disprove the EU-hypothesis.

An alternative interpretation would be that in his first choice he implies that <u>if he maximises EU</u>, then EU(A)>EU(B), and in his second choice that <u>if he maximises EU</u>, then EU(Y)>EU(X).   If this interpretation is applied, we cannot avoid Allais' conclusion, that the respondent does not maximise expected utility.   That is the negative part of any solution to the Allais type of paradox: <u>People do not maximise the expectation of utility of the outcome</u>.

C.   OTHER PARADOXES

1.   A refutable theorem?

Let us take a problem from agriculture, which agriculturists are not expected to find interesting, but may demonstrate a logical point: Are all potatoes of equal size?

> Axiom 1: All potatoes have the same mass (content of
>   matter)
> Axiom 2: All potatoes have the same density (mass/
>   volume)

> Theorem I: All potatoes have the same volume

> Proof: Omitted

Theorem (I) is formulated as a statement of fact, just as the theorem of expected utility maximising.   Further, if this statement is tested against observations, it will soon be rejected.   But given the axioms and logic, it is true. This is a paradox, but easy to solve.   What we really mean is:

> Theorem (II):   If all potatoes have the same mass and
>   the same density, then all potatoes have
>   the same volume.

This is undeniably true, which shows the importance of the distinction between the two formulations.

Easy as it is in this case, it is not always so simple:

"- the subject of criticism should not be the expected
    utility proposition - which is a well proven
    theorem - but its underlying axioms".
    (Amihud, 1979, p. 150).

What each author proves is that if his axioms are true,
the expectation of some function of wealth is maximised, which
corresponds to formulation II above. This may be valid even
if the axioms are wrong. But insofar as n authors build
their proofs on n·different and mutually independent sets
of axioms, we have as many different theorems in the sense
of formulation II. These theorems may all be true (logically
compelling), and still the proposition that people maximise
expected utility (formulation I) may be wrong. It can be refuted by empirical evidence.

Now Amihud goes on (loc.cit.) to refer to authors with
alternative sets of axioms. In fact, he is then referring to
as many expected utility theorems (type II), but he speaks of
"a" theorem, which must then be of type I. This is not particular for Amihud, he is quoted because he is fairly representative.

2. Is a refuted theory still refutable?

Another paradox in argument is that of stressing refutability
as a virtue, and on the other hand explain away all evidence
presented as refutation, without ever explaining positively
how the hypothesis could be refuted. One possible exception:
Morgenstern (1979, p.178) may be interpreted as indicating
how my experiment of 1971 (Hagen, 1979, pp. 288-293) should
have been arranged. I arranged a new experiment in 1975,
profiting from his critisism (loc.cit., pp. 293-296). The
result was still a refutation of expected utility maximisa-
tion.

There is no place here for discussing the allegation
that Allais' theory and others following his lead are all
presenting untestable and, therefore, unscientific non-
theories. My contribution to Allais/Hagen (eds.) 1979
(Hagen, 1979 a) consists mainly of refutable propositions,
where it is shown what "counter paradoxes" could refute
them (1). I also think that papers presented in this volume
may speak for themselves. It is up to anybody to refute them.

3. Prospect theory and stochastic dominance

The type of theory presented by Allais and others, based on the assumption that the value of a prospect depends (not only on expectation, but on) the general shape of the probability distribution over utilities, has got a competing group under the heading of prospect theory, used by Kahneman and Tversky (1979), but of which a special case was already presented by Bernard (1974). What is common to them, is (1) that they consider utility of change rather than of wealth, and (2) that they weight utilities by a function of probability.

The last point is the weakness of that approach

$$U = \Sigma w_i u_i$$

not even

$$U = \Sigma W_i u_i / \Sigma w_i$$

where

U = utility of game

and the weight w of each utility is a simple function of the probability p

$$w_i = f(p)$$

This function is such that

$w_i > p_i$ when p_i is small

$w_i < p_i$ when p_i is close to unity

Assume for instance that

$w_i(p_i) = p_i$ when $0.10 \quad p_i < 0.90$

$w_i(p_i) > p_i$ when $p_i < 0.10$

$w_i(p_i) < p_i$ when $0.90 < p_i$

and specifically
$$w(0.01) = 0.011$$

Compare the prospect

    p($9900)   =   0.01
    p($9910)   =   0.01
    . . . .
    . . . .
    p($9990   =   0.01
    p($10000)   =   0.90

with the certainty of $ 10000 which obviously dominates the game.

If we assume the utility of $x to be:

$$u(x) = \sqrt{x}$$

then the value of the game is

$u = 0.011 \cdot 997.25 + 90 = 10.96975 + 90 = 100.96975$

The utility of $10000 is 100, so the game has a higher value than the certainty of $10000, contrary to "preference absolue" or stochastic dominance 1. order. This example of the possibilities of the model is very moderate compared to the weight functions indicated graphically by Kahneman and Tversky.

Even if the product-sum is divided by the sum of the weights, such anomalies can be shown.

If the utility of a game is to be a weighted mean of utilities of outcomes, weights must be as indicated by Allais:

$$w_i = f(p_1, p_2, \ldots p_n, u_1, u_2 \ldots u_n)$$

On the other hand, the nucleus of prospect theory, that the utility of the outcome of a game is not only a function of wealth, but also of past history, may be true.

D. A NEW PARADOX

But we must go further. Also, what would have happened had we made a different decision, may be relevant. Ingolf Ståhl (1980) has pointed this out in a book review and maintains

that this may lead to results contradicting Allais' and
Hagens axioms. He is right as far as Hagen is concerned.

It is not so difficult for me to admit this, because in
an earlier presentation of my model (Hagen, 1972)[1] I put in
certain restrictions on its validity, one being that the
decision maker must be indifferent as to how a given probability distribution over outcomes is distributed over numbered
events.

Let two rich men both be willing to enter a double or
nothing game over $100 000 if the chance is slightly more
than even. Put them in the same boat. One thinks the probability of their being saved (Event 1) is 0.6 and of both
dying (Event 2) is 0.4. The other has the reverse probability
distribution. Assume that a bet can be made legally binding
also for their estates. They have no relatives or close
friends. Can a bet be made? Not very likely. Both would
probably prefer to bet on being saved.

Another example, which I referred to in 1972, was of
how Savage corrected his mistake when he had first preferred
Y: Probability of winning 500 mill. old Fr.fr. = 0.10 to X:
Probability of winning 100 mill. old Fr.fr. = 0.11. When
Allais pointed out that he had committed the Allais Paradox,
he arranged the two games over 100 numbers like this:

    X. No. 1-89 : Nothing.   No. 90-100 : 100 million
    Y. No. 1-90 : Nothing.   No. 91-100 : 500 million

Since the numbers 1-89 would yield the same in both games,
by the sure thing principle, the choice could be reduced to:

    X' : No. 1-11 : 100 million
    Y' : No. 1   : Nothing. No. 2-11 : 500 million

Savage would then prefer X'. Or, as he put it, convinced
himself that his preference for Y was "wrong".

I rearranged the games in this manner (Hagen, 1972):

    X : No. 1-89 : Nothing.   No. 90-100 : 100 million
    Y : No. 1-10 : 500 million. No. 11-100 : Nothing

If the sure thing principle is applied, we ignore No. 11-89

and reduce to 21 events:

    X " : No. 1-10 : Nothing.   No. 11-21 : 100 million
    Y " : No. 1-10 : 500 million No. 11-21 : Nothing

Most people will find Y more attractive in this arrangement.
Comment supporting my view in MacCrimmon and Larsson, 1979.

    Please note that the minimax regret principle favours X
in Savage's arrangement, and Y in my arrangement. Further to
this in Hagen, 1979b, where (p. 256) I specifically named it
a paradox distinct from the Allais paradox. We have here
indeed a paradox: <u>Given the arrangement of X, the ranking
of Y above or below X may not depend on the probability
distribution over utilities alone.</u> This applies to people
whose preferences obey the sure thing principle disregarding
states of the world that will yield the same payoff regardless of their choice, and are influenced by a wish to minimize regret. See also Loomes and Sugden 1982.

    It may be that after (1) the St. Petersburgh Paradox,
showing that ranking is not determined by expected monetary
value, and (2) the Allais Paradox, showing that ranking is
not determined by expected utility, comes (3) this paradox
showing that <u>the probability distribution over utilities does
not always determine the ranking of games</u>.

D. THE PROBLEM OF A NORMATIVE DEVICE

1. Does expected utility theory provide a useful decision
    technique?

Let us clarify the practical implications of this question.

    Assume that in constructing a utility index to be used
for ranking actual games we want to establish the ratios
between the utilities of winning $50 and $100. Our questions
to the decision maker could now aim at determining equivalent
two outcome games between 0 and $50 and $100 respectively.
From previous experience we would not be surprised if it
turned out that the certainty of getting $50 would be equiva-
lent to a probability of winning $100 of more than 0.5, say
0.6, and we have established a utility index u for three
points: $u(0) = 0$, $u(\$50) = 0.6$, $u(\$100) = 1$.

Suppose now we had the choice between A and B:

A: Pr(0)=0.30, Pr($50)=0.45, Pr($100)=0.25 with $\bar{u}$ = 0.52
B: Pr(0)=0.50, Pr($50)= 0 , Pr($100)=0.50 with $\bar{u}$ = 0.50

The preference should be for A if the decision maker is "rational".

If the outcomes included $1.000.000, the lottery effect might well give the following utility index values when in each case comparing with the highest outcome:

u(0) = 0,u($50) = 0.00004,u($100) = 0.00008,u($1000000) = 1
or: u(0)=0,u($50)=0.5,u($100)=1,u($1000000)=12500

The "constant ratio paradox", see MacCrimmon and Larsson (1979) and Hagen (1979), indicates that if the probabilities of $50 and $100 were to be reduced by retaining the ratio 1 to 0.6, the game with the prize $100 would be preferred, so to maintain indifference, the ratio must change in favor of the $50 game, e.g. to 1 to 0.5, thus changing u($50) from $0.6 \cdot u(\$100)$ to $0.5 \cdot u(\$100)$.

The two games above, taken out of this context, would give these expected utilities:

A :.0.475
B : 0.500

So now the "rational" preference should be for B.

But why include $1.000.000 if that is not one of the prizes in either A or B? Suppose we had a third game C:
C: Pr(0) = 0.99997, Pr($1 000 000) = 0.00003 with u=0.375.

We would then obviously include $1.000.000 in our quest for a utility index. Otherwise, we could not evaluate C at all. When we have done so, and ranked it last, it turns out that we have the ranking B, A, C. The existence of C, which does not qualify for the finale, has reversed the ranking of A and B. Whether this should be allowed, is a well known problem from the theory of games. We could cut out the prize that occurs only in the game ranked last and form a new index.

But even if we did that, we could still use the probabi-

lity 0.00008 of winning (instead of certainty) the prize to
be evaluated and seek the equilibrating probability of $100
in full accordance with the expected utility theory.

So to get a unique utility index, we must specify that
it is the certainty of the prize to be evaluated that is to
be compared to the equilibrating probability of the highest
of the remaining prizes.

When it is claimed that "the" expected utility model
is being used as a device in practical decision making, I
suspect that what is maximised is one out of the infinite
number of utility indexes that agrees with the expected
utility theory but not with one another, chosen by principles
or ad hoc methods as hinted at above.

Going back again to the ranking A, B, let us introduce
the probability p of $1.000.000 in A and reduce the two other
probabilities by the factor (1-p). This should increase the
utility of A, but if p is sufficiently small, it will reverse
the preference order to B,A. From this dilemma I see no way
to save any version of the expected utility theory if the
model is expected to generate the utility index endogeneously.

An alternative procedure could be: Determine the
decision maker's cardinal utility function independent of
risk, as indicated by Allais and others, Neufville/MacCord
and Krystofovitsch, and maximise the expectation of that.

2. A simple non-dogmatic aid for portfolio selection under risk

Portfolio is here to be understood as the composition of the
balance sheet including contracts.

I will presume that the existence of the Markowitz rule
and other methods of simplifying the task of the decision
makers, their virtues and shortcomings are known, and proceed
to present my suggestion.

We start at a point where all dominated alternatives
and alternatives violating restrictions are excluded, and
assume that some alternatives are left.

We know that they cannot be ranked by expectation (E) and

variance (S^2) alone. Still, reasonable men accept the Markowitz rule as a rule of thumb, and rightly so. But there is
a psychological difficulty. What does the E and S^2 of the
elements in the efficient set really tell the decision maker
(who needs consultation)?

We further know that including the third moment (M_3) does
not give a general ranking, but obviously more information than
E and S^2 alone. The psychological difficulty, however, becomes
greater.

Any game with a discrete probability distribution over n
outcomes is fully determined if we know E and S^2 a.s.o. up to
central moment No. 2n − 1, since this is the number of degrees
of freedom for n outcomes and n probabilities adding up to
unity.

If including the third moment is an advantage, and we can
avoid the psychological difficulty of interpreting the statistics and yet avoid the greater difficulty of direct evaluation of complex games, we have achieved something useful.

If we are satisfied with the degree of accuracy that can
be obtained by including the third moment, we should be prepared to accept the ranking of the original games following
from a ranking of "proxies", each having the same E, S^2 and
M_3 as the original game it represents.

In short, the suggested method is this:

(1) For each alternative, substitute a "proxie", a two-
     outcome game with the same E, S^2, M_3

(2) Ask the decision maker which of these proxies he
     prefers

(3) Recommend the corresponding portfolio

Please note that we do not require the decision maker to
know anything about utility or moments. All we ask is that
he can rank two-outcome games according to his subjective
preferences.

Since my model postulates u'>0, u''<o, u'''>0 and
positive/negative/positive effects of expectation/standard

deviation/skewness in utility, it would be roughly approximated with some function of these three measures referring to money. Judging from Amihud, 1979, expected utility maximisers might also accept it.

What if we tried to offer something to the decision makers that we could jointly recommend.

Norwegian School of Management
P.O. Box 69
1341 Bekkestua
Norway

NOTES

1. The gist of the underlying model is that the utility of a unique game is influenced in positive direction by expectation of utility, negative by even number moments and positive/negative by positive/negative skewness (odd numbers moments) approximated by third moment/variance.

REFERENCES

Allais, M.: "The Foundations of a Positive Theory of Choice involving Risk and a Criticism of the Postulates and Axioms of the American Shool" (1979a) in Allais, M. and Hagen, O. (Eds.), q.v.

Allais, M.: "The So-Called Allais Paradox and Rational Decisions under Uncertainty" (1979b), in Allais, M. and Hagen, O. (Eds.), q.v.

Allais, M. and Hagen, O. (Eds.): Expected Utility and the Allais Paradox, D. Reidel, 1979.

Amihud, Y.: "Critical Examination of the New Foundation of Utility" in Allais, M. and Hagen, O. (Eds.), q.v.

Bernard, G.: "On Utility Functions" in Theory and Decision, (1974), pp. 205-242.

Friedman, M. and Savage, J.: "The Utility Analysis of Choices Involving Risk", The Journal of Political Economy, LVI 279.304, Aug. 1948.

Hagen, O.: "Separation of Cardinal Utility and Specific Utility of Risk in Theory of Choices under Uncertainty", Statsøkonomisk Tidsskrift, No. 3, (1969).

Hagen, O.: "A New Axiomatization of Utility under Risk", Teorie A Metoda, IV/2, (1972).

Hagen, O.: "Towards a Positive Theory of Decsion under Risk", in Allais, M. and Hagen, O. (Eds.), q.v. 1979a

Hagen, O.: "Ambiguity in Normative Decision Theory" in Forskning, utbildning, praxis, ed. by Ingolf Ståhl, Stockholm School of Economics, 1979b.

Kahneman, D. and Tversky, A.: "Prospect Theory: An Analysis of Decision under Risk", Econometrica 47 (1979), pp. 263-291.

Loomes, G. and Sugden, R.: "Regret Theory: An Alternative Theory of Rational Choice under Uncertainty" in The Economic Journal, pp. 805-824, 1982.

Machina, M.J.: "Generalized Expected Utility Analysis and the Nature of Observed Violations of the Independence Axiom" in Foundations of Utility and Risk Theory with Applications, pp. 263-293 (this volume).

de Neufville, R. and McCord, M.R.: "Empirical Demonstration that Expected Utility Decision Analysis is not Operational" in Foundations of Utility and Risk Theory with Applications, pp. 181-199 (this volume).

de Neufville, R. and Múnera, H.A.: "A Decision Analysis Model when the Substitution Principle is not Acceptable" in Foundations of Utility and Risk Theory with Applications, pp. 247-262 (this volume).

Ståhl, I.: "Review of Allais/Hagen (Eds)" in Scandinavian Journal of Economics, (1980), pp. 413-417.

Kenneth J. Arrow

BEHAVIOR UNDER UNCERTAINTY AND ITS IMPLICATIONS
FOR POLICY

A key tool in the modern analysis of policy is benefit-
cost analysis. Though its origin goes back to the remarkably prescient paper of Dupuit, 1844, its theoretical development came much later, after the "marginal revolution" of
the 1870's, and its practical application really dates only
from the period after 1950. The underlying theory is that
of notion of economic surplus, to which, after Dupuit, such
major figures as Marshall, Pareto, Hotelling, Allais, and
Debreu have contributed: for a remarkable synthesis, see
Allais, 1981.

Without going into technical details, the essential
steps in the actual calculation of a surplus depend on using
choices made in one context to infer choices that might be
made in different contexts. If we find how much individuals
are willing to pay to reduce time spent in going to work by
one method, e.g., buying automobiles or moving closer to
work, we infer that another method of achieving the same
saving of time, e.g., mass transit or wider roads, will be
worth the same amount. Frequently, indeed, we extrapolate,
or interpolate; if it can be shown that the average individual will pay $1,000 a year more in rent to reduce his or her
transit time by 30 minutes, we infer that a reduction of 15
minutes is worth $500. This is all very much according to
Dupuit's reasoning; he would value an aqueduct by the amount
that individuals would be willing to pay for the water to be
transported in it (and vice versa, if the opposite inference
is useful).

The assumption that choices made under different conditions are consistent with each other is then essential to
the practice of benefit-cost analysis. The elaboration of
these consistency conditions leads to the rationality postulates of standard economic theory. In the usual formulation,
we postulate that all choices are consistent with an ordering, a transitive and complete relation, and both our theory

B. P. Stigum and F. Wenstøp (eds.), Foundations of Utility and Risk Theory with Applications,
19–32.

and our practice are based on this assumption. We know, of
course, that even with these assumptions there are ambiguities
in the inferences that can be drawn from empirical observations to policy choices, mostly because of the so-called income effects, a point on which Walras already criticized
Dupuit. But in this paper, I will not be concerned with this
last set of issues.

We now have a new kind of benefit-cost analysis, namely,
benefit-risk analysis. The risk of a disutility is itself a
cost and a proper subject for measurement along with the direct costs of the usual resource-using type. Similarly, a
reduction in risk is to be counted as a benefit. This is
true even if individuals are risk-neutral, since we would
still want to count the expected value of the risk; in the
presence of risk aversion, there is still an additional cost
or benefit, as the case may be.

Our current interest in risk-benefit analysis has been
largely stimulated by concern with health hazards. In terms
of public attention, though not in actuality, it is the risks
associated with the operation of nuclear power plants that
have appeared at the forefront. At a fundamental level, the
issues in benefit-risk analysis are not different from those
in more familiar welfare comparisons. Again, willingness to
pay either for benefits (reduced risks) or to avoid costs
(increased risks) is a crucial element. Again, it can in
principle be measured by seeking out comparable situations.
Thus, if air pollution control results in decreased probability of death, then one way of measuring the benefit is to
find out what individuals are willing to pay to decrease
this probability in other contexts. A standard method is to
compare wages in industries with different occupational risks.
After controlling for other factors, we find that in general
hazardous occupations have higher wage rates. In equilibrium,
this means that workers are indifferent at the margin between
the two occupations at the given wage levels. Hence, the
difference in wages can be regarded as compensation for the
difference in probability of death. (Needless to say, I am
ignoring many obvious complications, for example, the risks
of non-fatal injury.) This provides a measure of willingness
to pay for reduced probability of death, to be used in evaluating the reduction in risk due to air pollution (or auto-
mobile safety measures or anything similar).

The similarity in principle can be accepted to justify similarity in practice provided we accept some theory of rationality in individual behavior under uncertainty, which is precisely what is frequently questioned. It is this theme, the implications of current research on decision-making in the presence of risk for benefit-risk analysis, that I want to pursue today.

It is necessary to call attention to one important matter on which the analogy to the case of certainty is necessarily loose, that is, the establishment of probability judgments. Benefit-cost analysis under certainty of course requires not only measures of willingness to pay but also measures of the costs of alternative policies. The analogue under uncertainty is measurement of the probabilities of different possible outcomes for each possible policy. Thus, we need the probability of death associated with each possible level of atmospheric pollution or for each possible siting and design of nuclear reactors.

Now no probability can, strictly speaking, be known from a finite sample. In many cases, the evidence is very limited indeed, so that this condition is a practical as well as a theoretical limitation. In many of the most difficult situations, those with high risks but very low probabilities, such as the possibility of a nuclear core meltdown, the evidence on the relevant uncertainty is extremely small. It may all be indirect.

This raises a new and philosophically difficult problem of rationality. Just as we need some kind of rationality hypotheses for measuring willingness to pay, under uncertainty as under certainty, we need rationality hypotheses about probability judgments. These are usually supplied in theory by the theory of subjective probabilities and applications of Bayes's Theorem. But what if individuals do not make their probability judgments in this manner?

One last orientation is needed. Who is doing the benefit-risk analysis? I want to ignore all the additional complications due to the difficulties of social choice, so I will suppose that there is a representative individual. Equally, however, I do not want to reduce the solution to the uninteresting proposition that the individual should do what he or she wants. Instead, I will suppose that the

analyst is a professional adviser to the individual. Both
the client and the economist expect that the latter will
have something to contribute by way of clarification, even
though ultimately it is the client's interests that are to
be served--but the client's interests as properly interpreted,
not mere expression of first thoughts.

A little intellectual history will be helpful. In 1952,
at a conference on the foundations of risk-bearing held by
the Centre National de la Recherche Scientifique of France,
Allais, 1953, and I (Arrow, 1953) presented independently
formulated models incorporating risk-bearing into the theory
of general equilibrium (Allais had also presented his theory
a year earlier at a meeting of the Econometric Society). As
a good Paretian, Allais followed the lead of his earlier work
on welfare economics, Allais, 1945, and perceived and expressed the welfare optimality that necessarily underlies any
general competitive equilibrium. This is an essential first
step in a benefit-risk analysis. Properly applied, it can
be used to derive the shadow prices which yield the first
approximations to the appropriate measures of surplus.

There are several differences between Allais' model and
mine, most not very relevant to the present discussion. One
that was much discussed at the conference later turned out
to be irrelevant. In my paper, I assumed that individuals
maximize expected utility. I accepted the Bernoulli, 1738,
theory as it had been updated by von Neumann and Morgenstern,
1947, and by Savage, 1954. Allais, as is well known, subjected that theory to very strong attack. His own view
amounted to a general ordinalist position; there was on
ordering on probability distributions, not necessarily linear in probabilities. This position had been advanced earlier by Hicks, 1931, though he had done little with it.[1]

A few years later, Gerard Debreu, 1959, Chapter 7,
showed that the two models could be synthesized. A theory
of general equilibrium in contingent contracts did not require the Bernoulli hypothesis; it was consistent with any
utility function over the outcomes. Debreu also extended
the theory to paths over time, in which the uncertainties
are realized successively.

Policy analysis with regard to risk, as in the case of
certainty, is necessitated by failures of the competitive

mechanism, that is, externalities and public goods. An individual living near a nuclear plant cannot buy safety for himself or herself alone; only collective safety can be obtained.
Similarly, air pollution cannot for well-known reasons be
obtained without collective action; no assignment of property
rights will permit the market to achieve an optimal allocation.
We use the general equilibrium model to simulate a market;
what would individuals be willing to pay at the margin for
changes in the externalities if they could be implemented as
commodities?

I will consider four doubts about rational behavior in
the presence of uncertainty which have arisen from recent
empirical research and ask about their implications for the
practice of benefit-risk analysis: (1) questions about the
expected-utility theory; (2) miscalculations of probabilities;
(3) preference reversals; and (4) framing.

1. THE EXPECTED UTILITY HYPOTHESIS

To be concrete, let us consider the expected utility hypothesis applied to policies aimed at affecting mortality. To
bring out the essence, I consider only the simplest possible
case. A living individual receives a utility from consumption if alive but zero utility if dead. Let,

   p = probability of survival,
   U = utility,
   c = consumption.

Then expected utility is,

   $pU(c)$.   (1)

We may think of some policy which increases p but requires
resources and therefore reduces c. The willingness-to-pay
(WTP) is then the slope of the curves on which (1) is constant, that is, the amount of consumption that an individual
is willing to give up per unit probability of survival while
keeping expected utility constant. We see easily that,

   $WTP = U(c)/pU'(c)$.   (2)

This expression has the dimensions of consumption per unit
life and therefore can be and is frequently referred to as

the "value of life." However, it is not what an individual
would pay for the certainty of life as against the certainty
of death; it is a marginal evaluation of a small change in
the probability of life. Since what an individual would pay
for the certainty of life is limited by initial wealth, the
WTP is apt to be a good deal larger.

Suppose the Bernoulli hypothesis is false, but individuals are rational in the weaker sense of Allais and Hicks;
there is an ordering of probability distributions. In the
present simple context, this means that there is a utility
function which depends on c and p (and is defined only
up to monotone transformations):

$$U(c, p). \tag{3}$$

Again, there is a trade-off between the two variables,

$$WTP = U_p/U_c. \tag{4}$$

When a real benefit-risk analysis is done, what data are
used? Suppose, as suggested above, that willingness to pay
is estimated from the wage differentials to be found in riskier jobs, as in Thaler and Rosen, 1976, or Viscusi, 1979.
Now, the probability of survival for one more year (which is
what is to be compared with annual wages) depends on many
factors, of which occupational safety is only one and not a
major one. The observed risk differential is therefore small,
so that the observed ratio of wage differential to risk differential is really a measure of (4). In fact, when one looks
closely, the empirical material made no real use of the Bernoulli hypothesis as embodied in (1) and (2).

What in fact is gained by the stronger expected-utility
hypothesis? It is really the ability to extrapolate over
large changes in p. But in practice, any feasible policy,
whether in nuclear power safety, biomedical research, or
occupational safety, will have only a relatively slight effect
on the probability of survival over a year or other relevant
period. Therefore, the strength of the Bernoulli hypothesis
is never employed in practice.

The argument amounts to saying that even a general utility functional for probability distributions, if differentiable, can be regarded as approximately linear in the

probabilities, if we are not considering large changes in them. This is precisely the idea so beautifully and richly developed by Machina, 1982.

I cannot however, leave this subject without another re-statement of the Allais problem. It is hard to believe that the paradox will occur when the alternatives are laid out in a sufficiently transparent fashion. Let us introduce a more specific temporal structure.

Suppose there are 3 time periods. At time 0, there is a chance move; it yields a payment of 1 monetary unit with probability .89. If the complementary event occurs, then at time 1 the subject is offered a choice. He or she can take 1 unit (with certainty), to be paid at time 2, or go on to time 2 and face a gamble yielding 2.5 with probability 10/11 and 0 with probability 1/11. At time 1, the possibility of an immediate payment of 1 with termination is now in the past, and there can be no question that the individual faces and considers only the second gamble, as against certainty. Presumably, the individual will usually choose the gamble. Now suppose at time 0, the individual is asked: <u>if</u> the com-plementary event were to occur at the chance move coming up, <u>would</u> you choose the certainty or the gamble? This is clearly the same decision as in the first story; it requires only a certain immagination. Yet in this form, a hypothetical choice of certainty amounts to choosing 1 with certainty as against a distribution of 2.5 with probability .10, 1 with probability .89, and 0 with probability .01.

In other words, all that is required is understanding a hypothetical choice and calculating probabilities correctly.

Now it may be that rendering the decision tree transpar-ent may be all that is involved, in which case it suggests that the real issue is one of framing, a point to which I will return below.

2. MISCALCULATION OF PROBABILITIES

A more serious problem than the nonlinearity of the utility function is the calculation of the probabilities to be used in estimating the risk. There are two issues here. One is not deep conceptually; it is simply that an individual will in general simply not possess all the information available

to society as a whole. The probabilities used should of
course be conditional on all the information available, if
the information can be assembled at a cost which is negligible compared with the improved expected benefits. Hence,
there is an externality with regard to information-gathering.
Therefore, if the information is assembled, the expert opinion
should be used to form probabilities. Presumably, any rational
individual would agree to this and would voluntarily defer,
as he or she does to a physician or other professional.

This observation does create some problems, not at the
normative level but at that of interpreting observed choice
behavior as a measure of willingness to pay to avoid risks.
What is relevant is the ratio of wage difference to difference in probability of death or injury as perceived by the
individuals involved. If they act not on the probabilities
as estimated by a national collection of statistics but on
those estimated by themselves from much more limited data,
it is the latter probabilities that should be used as a di-
visor. There is considerable theoretical and empirical evidence in the case of occupational hazards that individuals
are influenced by their own experiences (Viscusi, 1979, Chapters 4 and 13). This is consistent with the view that they
have little knowledge of general injury rates and therefore
condition their probabilities heavily on their own experiences.

A deeper question is raised by the well known observations mostly by psychologists that even in situations where
Bayes' Theorem is clearly applicable, individuals do not use
it correctly; for reports on such studies, see Tversky and
Kahneman, 1974. In most of their experiments, too little
weight was given by subjects to the prior information; individuals were overly influenced by the current data. This
result is consistent with other studies in different fields.
Eddy, 1980, showed that physicians in relying on diagnostic
tests did not take adequate account of the underlying prevalence of the disease in forming their judgments. Thus, if a
test gave a probability .9 of detecting cancer if it were
there and a probability .9 of a negative response if there
were no cancer, it would be regarded as highly reliable. Yet
the prevalence of cancer is only about .1, which is thus the
prior probability of cancer in a random choice from the population. A simple application of Bayes' Theorem shows that
the probability of cancer given a positive response on the
test is .5, far less than most physicians would believe.

The misuse of Bayes' Theorem is at least compatible with the evidence for volatility in the securities and futures markets. Since the value of a long-lived bond, stock, or futures contract is ultimately dependent upon a great many events which will occur in the future, it should be unresponsive to any particular piece of new information. These markets, however, are notoriously volatile, with large movements in a single day. This has been argued many times for the futures markets; for a summary of the evidence, see Cagan, 1981. A very rigorous analysis for the bond and stock markets (Shiller, 1979, 1981) has shown the incompatibility of observed behavior with rational expectations models, at least in a simple form. For more extended discussion of these misperceptions, see Arrow, 1982.

The extent to which the average person exaggerates the risks in a possible accident to nuclear power plants is of course well known. (I hasten to add that I am not an unreserved admirer of nuclear power. The risks to the plant itself, as exemplified by the Brown's Ferry and Three Mile Island accidents, plus the costs of construction, themselves increased by safety precautions, make the economics of nuclear power very doubtful. Indeed, the main case for nuclear power are the social costs of coal-fired power plants in the form of atmospheric pollution caused by combustion and carbon dioxide effects on the world's climate.)

What is the normative or policy implication of this propensity to irrational judgments about uncertainty? Here, I feel strongly we must invoke the appropriate role of the expert. I have postulated a relation of professional to client, and it is certainly in judgments of reality and probability that this professional concern is most appropriate. The normative judgment may and should respect the utility functions (linear or nonlinear) of the public being advised, but it should certainly use probability judgments based both on the maximum of information and the maximum of correct statistical and probabilistic logic.

The two problems discussed thus far, the more general ordinal theory of choice among probability distributions as against the expected-utility hypothesis and the miscalculation of probabilities, have been made much of by those, for example at the conference at which this paper is presented, who think of themselves as revolutionaries against an

established (though rather recently established) orthodoxy.
Beware! These arguments are those of the moderate revolutionaries, the Girondins or the Mensheviks. The cognitive psychologists have found evidence for worse traps; if the implications are as they seem, it is hard to see how any form of
benefit-risk analysis can survive.

3. PREFERENCE REVERSAL

So far, transitivity has been unquestioned; and transitivity
is essential to any type of benefit-cost analysis; the substitution of compensations for costs or risks depends essentially on the (usually unstated) transitivity of indifference. I have not checked the literature, but I believe that
experiments do not even verify transitivity fully even in the
case of certainty. It was for this reason that economists
and psychologists developed notions of stochastic orderings
(see, e.g., Davidson and Marschak, 1959). But experimental
studies of choice under uncertainty has revealed what at the
present appear to be a less remedial form of intransitivity.

I refer to the well-known phenomenon of preference reversal, first identified by Lichtenstein and Slovic, 1971.
Suitably chosen pairs of gambles can be found with the following characteristics: When subjects are asked to choose
between the two, they express a preference for one. But
when asked to state the amount of money which, if given with
certainty, would be indifferent to each gamble, the amounts
chosen are in opposite order to the expressed preferences.

This result is so upsetting, indeed to almost any theory
of choice under uncertainty, that the experiments were carefully replicated by Grether and Plott, 1979. They varied the
experiments in ways designed to test various explanations
(e.g., cost of information processing) which would preserve
transitivity. Not only were the original results confirmed,
but no simple rational explanation could be found.

This work does seem to be a major barrier to the use of
risk-cost tradeoffs from one area in measuring benefits and
costs in another. I can only offer some observations derived
from earlier work in consumer demand theory as a partial
solution.

The comparisons in the preference reversal experiments

are global or long-range rather than local. The identification of certainty equivalents requires comparison of two alternatives, one risky, one certain, which are far from each
other in any reasonable metric. This distinction was considered also in the theory of consumer's choice under certainty;
it is the essence of what has been called the integrability
problem. There are many variations in the literature. One
is the proposed theory advanced by Hicks and Allen, 1934, and
Georgescu-Roegen, 1936: At each point in commodity space,
there is a local indifference map (hence, transitive and complete ordering), but it is an additional assumption that the
local indifference maps integrate into a global indifference
map permitting indifference judgments across large differences
in alternatives.

The very meaning of optimality and therewith the meaning of a benefit-risk analysis as a basis for policy is in
principle undermined if comparisons are only local. One might
conceivably have a series of local improvements which cycle.

In practice, though, it could be argued, though not with
entire conviction, that the possibilities of paradox do not
really arise. As we have already argued with relation to
policies which affect the probability of death, any feasible
changes are apt to be small. Hence, only the local indifference maps are relevant. In that case, the theoretical possibility of cycling will not be realized. To put the matter
another way, the willingness-to-pay data used in benefit-risk
analysis does not really measure comparison of gambles with
certainties. Rather, it compares gambles with small differences in probabilities and stakes. Therefore, the preference
reversal phenomenon need not occur in the choices which are
the basis for benefit-risk analysis.

4. FRAMING

The most damning criticism of risk-benefit analysis from experiments is the evidence for what Tversky and Kahneman, 1981,
have called, "framing." An element of rationality, so obvious
to the analyst as to pass almost unnoticed, is its extension-
ality, to use the language of logic. That is, if a choice
is to be made from a set of alternatives, the choice should
depend only on the membership in the set and not on how the
set is described. If I have to choose which night of next
week I will go to a play, it should not matter if each

alternative is labeled by the day of the week or the numbered
day of the month. If my budget permits me to divide $1,000
between housing costs and other expenditures, my alternatives
can be identified indifferently in terms of either of the two
kinds of costs.

    Yet the lesson of the framing experiments is precisely
that these invariances do not hold. How the choice question
is framed affects the choice made.[2] Let me draw a dramatic
illustration from a paper on the choice of medical therapy
by McNeil, Pauker, Sox, and Tversky, 1982. McNeil and some
of her colleagues have had a program, which economists and
decision theorists should applaud, of letting the patients'
values affect medical decision-making. In this study, a comparison was being made between two therapies, surgery and
radiation therapy, for the treatment of certain forms of cancer. A therapy defines a probability distribution of length
of survival. In general, surgery has a positive risk of mortality during the operation, for which there is no counter-
part in radiation therapy, but it has a longer expected survival even when this risk is taken into account. Different
groups of individuals, including a group of physicians, were
presented with the probabilities of survival during treatment,
for one year, and for five years for each of the two therapies. With these data, 84% of the physicians preferred surgery, 16% radiation therapy. Then another group was presented
with the same data presented differently: the probabilities
of dying at each stage were given instead of the probabilities
of survival. At each stage, the probability of dying is 1
minus the probability of survival, so the two formulations
are not merely logically equivalent but can be transformed
into each other by a trivial calculation. Yet the proportion of psysicians choosing surgery over radiation therapy
dropped from 84% to 50%.

    I leave the implications of framing for benefit-risk
analysis as an open problem. Economists would tend to argue
that the choices made in the market, where the stakes to the
individual are high, reflect the correct choice of frame.
But this is probably too complacent a view. It may well be
true that the individual makes different trade-offs in contexts which, to the analyst, appear to be identical. But
this is a deep topic for further study.

NOTES

1. In the development of his specific general equilibrium model, Allais assumed that all distributions were normal, and therefore individuals were assumed to order distributions according to their means and variances. However, I take this to be a particular application, not the underlying general principle.

2. The rest of this paragraph is drawn, with slight modification, from Arrow, 1982.

REFERENCES

Allais, M.: 1945, Économie pure et Rendement Social, Sirey, Paris.

Allais, M.: 1953, 'Généralisation des theories de l'équilibre économique general et du rendement social au cas de risque,' in Économetrie, Colloques Internationaux de Centre National de la Recherche Scientifique, XL, Paris, pp. 81-109.

Allais, M.: 1981, La Théorie Génerale des Surplus, Institut des Sciences Mathematiques et Economiques Appliquées, Paris.

Arrow, K.J.: 1953, 'Rôle des valeurs boursières pour la répartition la meilleure des risques,' in Économetrie, Colloques Internationaux du Centre National de la Recherche Scientifique, XL, Paris, pp. 41-47.

Arrow, K.J.: 1982, 'Risk Perception in Psychology and Economics,' Economic Inquiry, 20, 1-9.

Bernoulli, D.: 1738, 'Specimen theoriae novae de mensura sortis,' Commentarii academiae scientiarum imperiales Petropolitanae 5, 175-192.

Cagan, P.: 1981, 'Financial Futures Markets: Is More Regulation Needed?', Journal of Futures Markets, 1, 169-190.

Davidson, D., and J. Marschak: 1959, 'Experimental Tests of a Stochastic Decision Theory,' in C.W. Churchman and P. Ratoosh (eds.) Mathematical Models of Human Behavior. Dunlap and Associates, Stamford, Conn. Reprinted in J. Marschak, Economic Information, Decision, and Prediction, Volume I, pp. 133-171. Reidel, Dordrecht, The Netherlands, and Boston, Mass., 1974.

Debreu, G.: 1959: Theory of Value, Wiley, New York.

Dupuit, J.: 1844, 'De la Mesure de l'Utilité des Travaux Publics,' Annales des ponts et Chaussées, 2ième Série, 8.

Eddy, D.: 1980, Screening for Cancer: Theory, Analysis, and Design. Prentice-Hall, Englewood Cliffs, N.J.

Georgescu-Roegen, N.: 1936, 'The Pure Theory of Consumer's Behavior,' Quarterly Journal of Economics, 50, 545-593.

Grether, D., and C. Plott: 1979, 'Economic Theory of Choice and the Preference Reversal Phenomenon,' American Economic Review, 69, 623-638.

Hicks, J.R.: 1931, 'The Theory of Uncertainty and Profit,' Economica, 11, 170-189.

Hicks, J.R., and R.G.D. Allen: 1934, 'A Reconsideration of the Theory of Value,' Economica, 1, 52-76.

Lichtenstein, S., and P. Slovic: 1971, 'Reversal of Preferences between Bids and Choices in Gambling Decisions,' Journal of Experimental Psychology, 89, 46-55.

Machina, M.: 1982, '"Expected Utility" Analysis without the Independence Axiom,' Econometrica 50, 277-324.

McNeil, B.J., S.G. Pauker, H.C. Sox, Jr., and A. Tversky: 1982, 'On the Elicitation of Preferences for Alternative Therapies,' New England Journal of Medicine, 306, 1259-1262.

Savage, L.J.: 1954, The Foundations of Statistics, Wiley, New York

Shiller, R.J.: 1979, 'The Volatitility of Long-term Interest Rates and Expectations Models of the Term Structure,' Journal of Political Economy 87, 1190-1213.

Shiller, R.J.: 1981, 'Do Stock Prices Move Too Much to Be Justified by Subsequent Changes in Dividends?', American Economic Review, 71, 421-436.

Thaler, R., and S. Rosen: 1976, 'The Value of Saving a Life,' in N. Terleckyj (ed.) Household Production and Consumption, National Bureau of Economic Research, pp. 265-298.

Tversky, A., and D. Kahneman: 1974, 'Judgement under Uncertainty: Heuristics and Biases,' Science, 185, 1124-1131.

Tversky, A., and D. Kahneman: 1981, 'The Framing of Decisions and the Psychology of Choice,' Science, 211, 453-458.

Viscusi, W.K.: 1979, Employment Hazards: An Investigation of Market Performance. Harvard University Press, Cambridge, Mass.

von Neumann, J., and O. Morgenstern: 1947, Theory of Games and Economic Behavior, 2nd edition, Princeton University Press.

PART II

CONCEPTS OF PROBABILITY

Maurice Allais

FREQUENCY, PROBABILITY AND CHANCE

> *Fundamental ideas play an essential role in the formation of a theory. Books are full of complex mathematical formulae, but the creation of any theory is governed by thought and ideas.*
> *Albert EINSTEIN and Leopold INFELD* [1]

> *The history of science shows that the progress of science has always been hampered by the tyrannical influence of some conceptions which are finally adopted as dogma. The principles which are now taken for granted should therefore be reviewed thoroughly from time to time.*
> *Louis de BROGLIE* [2]

> *It would be vain presumption to try to solve one of the scientific problems which so many minds, several of them great, have wrestled with fruitlessly, and to lay down a doctrine to deal with a problem which has remained pending over the centuries ; by contrast, it is possible to propose a little fresh illumination without offending either wisdom or modesty, in the form of attempts at a new approach to co-ordination, which to the contrary, resolutely avoid any pretence of doctrinal decision-taking and absolute dogmatism.*
> *Augustin COURNOT* [3]

The heated and sometimes sharply polemical discussions which the Decision Theory has caused over the last thirty years as regards the two basic concepts on which it is based, utility and probability, appear in most instances to stem from semantic confusion between entirely different concepts.

B. P. Stigum and F. Wenstøp (eds.), Foundations of Utility and Risk Theory with Applications,
35–86.
© 1983 *by D. Reidel Publishing Company.*

The present Memoir will be limited to a critical appraisal
of the concept of probability and the associated concepts [4,5]

1. THE CONCEPT OF PROBABILITY

The theory of probability dates back over three centuries.
Its creators and their successors have always included highly
intelligent minds within their ranks. Nevertheless, the word
probability has unceasingly been used by all the authors *with
incompatible meanings relating to entirely different realities.*

To some, probability is objective, and corresponds to a
physical reality in the case of repeated events. Others believe
that probability is basically subjective, but that it corresponds to a physical reality in the case of repeated events,
and is then identified with objective probability. For still
others, there is no such thing as objective probability. For
all three groups, probability can be defined independently
of the consideration of random choice. For a fourth group,
the existence of subjective probability is demonstrated at
the same time as the existence of an index of utility on the
basis of a set of axioms on random choice. For a last group,
probability is a purely mathematical concept the study of
which is developed in the framework of axiomatic theories,
independently of any concrete reality.

*Much confusion stems from this situation, as well as
endless debate on the nature of the concept of probability
and its relationship with the data observed in the natural
sciences, the sciences of life and the sciences of man.*

To be convinced of this, one needs only to read the com-
mentaries on the concepts of probability, chance, and the so-
called law of large numbers in the major works published
over the last three centuries. Very deep statements are indeed often to be found, but they generally leave one's mind
unsatisfied *as to the relationship which should be established
between the rigorous calculations of the theory and the empirical regularities which emerge from the analysis of reality,
and as to the criteria to be applied to establish this relationship.*

The difficulties do not stem from the mathematical calculations which are made, and whose consistency is common
ground. *They relate fundamentally to the relationship to be
established between theory and experience,* the interpretation
of observed data, and the *applicability* of calculations to
forecasting, and the interpretation of the elements of a
forecast in the light of earlier experience.

It is obviously not the purpose of this memoir to present an exhaustive critical analysis of all the theories of probability, nor *a fortiori* to propose a general positive theory of probability free of any contradiction and confusion.

It will be limited to different observations on the definition, meaning and utilisation of the concept of probability which will, I hope, shed some light on the different approaches, which oppose themselves so radically, holding that part of each which appears to be basically valid.

Needless to say, I make no claim to exhaust such a wide, difficult and fascinating subject, which many others have already had an opportunity to analyse in depth. But I should perhaps set out some of the guidelines which can get the various theories off the artificial dead end in which they appear to be confined. Some of the following considerations may seem statements of the obvious, but I believe that they can help to dispel much confusion and avoid much specious and useless controversy.

In sum, as I will try to show, *the only real difficulties encountered by the various theories stem from their use of the same word "probability" to represent four entirely different concepts : mathematical frequency, empirical frequency, objective probability, and the coefficient of plausibility*[6]

2. MATHEMATICAL FREQUENCY

The starting point of any mathematical theory of probability is to take the three principles of total probability, compound probability, and inverse probability (or probability of causes) as either theorems, or axioms, or definitions. *From that they yield the same group of propositions*.

As regards their meaning for purposes of analysing real phenomena, authors are at variance on only two points : *What is the definition and interpretation which should be given to the concept of probability ? How can theory be applied to concrete reality ?*

Close scrutiny of these mathematical theories shows that their development is *totally independent of concrete reality throughout*. There is no uncertainty at all, and *chance, whose mathematical definition it has never been possible to give, enters nowhere*. These are *fully deterministic* theories, and the quantities used in the associated calculations *are not "probabilities"*, a word which is indisociably attached to uncertain events, *but purely mathematical frequencies*.

The basic concept at the root of all these theories is

the concept of *mathematical frequency*. These theories should
thus be referred to as *"Mathematical Frequency Theories"*, the
only appropriate title, *and not* to the traditional expression
"Probability Theories", which is totally improper in this
field. The variables which are considered by all these mathematical theories *are not at all random variables,* but frequential variables.

For discrete sets, all these theories are based on the
expansion of the multinomial expression $(a_1 + a_2 + \ldots + a_k)^n$
and the analysis of the properties of the various subsets
which can be derived from this expansion. For continuous sets,
the analysis becomes more abstract, but the process is basically the same when the equality of measure of two elements
has been defined, and *fundamentally the nature of calculations
is always and only that of combinatorial analysis.*

All the fundamental theorems of the mathematical theories
of the so-called *"Probability Theory"*, the Bernoulli law of
large numbers, or the central limit theorem of convergence to
the normal law, the law of iterated logarithm , the arc sine
laws, etc..., *are only asymptotic properties of frequency
distributions fundamentally based on calculations of combinatorial analysis.*

Take the expansion of the binomial $(1-1)^n$ as a simple
illustration. For a given value n of the exponent, there
are 2^n possible trajectories. At the end of the different
trajectories, the frequency of the different possible cases
is proportional to the binomial coefficients, and when n
increases to infinity, their distribution tends to the normal
distribution. *This convergence occurs in the sense given to
it in mathematical analysis.*

Each trajectory is characterised by a certain frequency
of +1 values with a certain order of successions of +1 and
−1, but with each can be associated a trajectory with an
equal frequency of −1 values, in which the order of succession
is the same, the +1 replacing the −1 and vice versa. There is
a single trajectory with only +1, and a single trajectory with
only −1.

·However, if the various trajectories T_i are distributed
according to the frequency f_i of +1, the frequency of the
trajectories for which the absolute value of the difference
$(f_i - 1/2)$ exceeds a certain threshold tends to zero as n
increases to infinity. This convergence is a convergence *in
terms of mathematical analysis.*

Similarly, whatever the exponent n , the average of all
+1 and −1 values for the whole set of trajectories is always

zero. All +1 and -1 values appear in equal number. *From the mathematical viewpoint, they all appear to be equally possible.*

Once more chance is totally absent from all these mathematical theories. All are characterised by purely deterministic counts of configurations corresponding basically to a multinomial expansion with determinate characteristics. When the exponent increases to infinity, all the distributions which can be derived from the multinomial expansion tend to their asymptotic expressions *in terms of mathematical analysis*.

Uncertainty does not enter the picture. All mathematical models of frequencies are *fully deterministic* and based on combinatorial calculations free of uncertainty. All the configurations they consider *are assumed to be simultaneously realized.* To call these models *"probabilistic or probability models" is entirely improper.* It can only lead to redoubtable confusion and erroneous thinking, since these words inevitably convey the interpretation attached to them in everyday parlance.

Again, contrary to the assertion of many very reputable probabilitists, the so-called *"probability theory"* can in no way be viewed as a theory of *"chance"*. *"Chance"* is absolutely excluded from it.

Actually the so-called mathematical theories of probability could all be presented without ever using the words chance, probable, random, or any term from the same family. These words are only used because the mathematicians were pleased to introduce and maintain them, possibly to render their theories more attractive, but most likely through habit or tradition. Nothing would be changed if the word *"probability"* were replaced by *"magnitude M"*. At least the underlying meaning of the calculations would then become much clearer. At all events, the expression *"mathematical frequency"* is the only term which corresponds *specifically* to the considered matter.

These models are of course purely mathematical and cannot in themselves teach us anything about concrete reality.

It is symptomatic that although many eminent mathematicians have spoken of *the mathematical laws governing chance*, very few of them underlined the absence of the concept of chance from the *"Probability Theory"*. Still fewer – perhaps none – have drawn the right conclusions as to the full consequences implied [7].

3. EMPIRICAL FREQUENCY

When studying certain phenomena and grouping a large enough
number of results, many permanent features are observed :
thus the frequency of the various figures drawn in a lottery,
of the faces of a die, the frequency of road accidents, the
frequency of suicides, etc..., are almost constant. Further,
not only do average frequencies not vary much, but the empirical distributions of the considered magnitudes remain relatively stable.

Two classes of empirical distributions can be observed :
distributions over space at a given time, such as the distribution of a population according to size ; and distributions over time, such as the distribution of stock exchange
quotations over a given period.

It has been observed that these distributions are generally well represented by frequential mathematical models
deduced from combinatorial analysis. For example the size and
weight of individuals are well represented by the lognormal
distribution ; similarly successive drawings from an urn
containing white and black balls can be closely represented
by the binomial law.

Each empirical distribution can be interpreted as revealing *an underlying regularity* corresponding to the frequential
mathematical model representing it. Of course, as is true of
all laws of nature, for instance celestial mechanics or elec-
tromagnetism, each distribution is represented by its theoretical model only with a certain degree of approximation. The
parameters of the model are chosen to give the closest possible
representation, unless earlier experience indicates that *a
priori* values should be assigned.

To simplify the discussion, consider an urn containing
black and white balls, which are as alike as they can be made.
Different people make successive drawings with replacement.
Suppose that   s series S_i of n drawings are made to each
of which corresponds an empirical frequency $f_{i,n}$ of white balls
drawn.

Experience shows that the results are what they should
be if there was a frequency f , equal to 1/2, such that the
frequency $F_{\delta,n,\varepsilon}$ of series S_i for which the absolute value
of the difference $f_{i,n} - f$ is higher than a determinate positive
value ε , becomes smaller and smaller as the number n of
drawings in each series and the number s of series increase.
This can be referred to as *the empirical law of large numbers.*

The different empirical frequencies f_i corresponding to

the s series considered can be interpreted *as experimental measurements of a same physical constant f* which characterises the process of drawing from the urn considered ; it can be called the *"intrinsic frequency"*. If relevant conditions of symmetry are met, it is possible to assign an *a priori* determinate value to this intrinsic frequency.

It is essential to underline that nothing permits to infer from observed data that for a given series S_i of n drawings, the frequency $f_{i,n}$ converges to the intrinsic frequency, in the sense of mathematical analysis, when n takes on growingly higher values. The only thing that can be said is that the observation shows that *on average,* the frequency $F_{\delta,n}$ of the series of drawings for which the empirical frequencies $f_{i,n}$ differ markedly from the intrinsic frequency f , becomes lower and lower when the number of drawings n increases in each series S_i , and the number s of series increases.

Just as, in making measurements of a given length, similar results are expected, so we can expect that similar frequencies will be found from many series of drawings.

In fact, too many authors derive this empirical law of large numbers from Bernoulli's mathematical law of large numbers, whereas the Bernoulli law is merely a mathematical asymptotic property of the binomial distribution, and cannot provide any information about concrete reality.

It would be not so *only if* it is postulated that on average white and black balls have an equal possibility to be drawn. *If this axiom of equal possibility on average is admitted the frequential mathematical model not only gives a representation but also "an explanation" of the phenomenon observed.*

It we admit the axiom of equal possibility on average, the intrinsic frequency of the frequential model can be estimated a priori in the case considered of drawings from an urn by taking it as equal to the ratio of the number of white balls to the total number of balls, all assumed to have an equal possibility of being drawn.

To the extent that the process of successive drawings from an urn is assimilated to the frequential mathematical model, this assimilation *to be perfect* would reduce to the assumption that if $s = 2^n$ series of n drawings were performed, these s series of drawings would be distributed exactly as in the frequential mathematical model. *This would be equivalent to saying that what occurs is what one would expect if there were an equal possibility of drawing white or black balls.*

If we reflect on the matter, it can be concluded that whenever a statistical distribution can be represented by a frequential mathematical model, *what is observed is what would be expected if an axiom of equal possibility could be admitted somewhere. This axiom, like the corresponding frequential mathematical models and the concept of intrinsic frequency, is basically an "idealisation" of experience.*

In fact *all* frequential mathematical models are *necessarily* based on a hypothesis of equal possibility. The explicit formulation of this hypothesis is particularily evident in Joseph Bertrand's discussion of the *"probability of a chord being longer than the side of the equilateral triangle inscribed in a circle".* Depending on how the hypothesis of equal possibility is formulated different *"probabilities"* are found.

If the frequential mathematical models may be applied to the empirical distributions of concrete reality, this hypothesis of equal possibility must be also met in the structure of the empirical data.

An axiom of *"representability"* must thus be admitted to allow this application. The basis of this axiom is *the axiom of equal possibility on average.* This axiom, which allows theory to be applied to reality, *must be enounced explicitly.*

When the frequential mathematical models used represent reality efficiently, the quality of this representation raises no more, and no fewer, problems than does the representation of the movements of planets by the laws of celestial mechanics.

If we consider a sufficiently long sequence of lottery drawings, dice throws or tosses of coins, *we can only marvel at the almost rigorous concordance between the empirical distributions found and the frequential mathematical models which represent them. This concordance is the more remarkable in that there is no a priori reason for postulating that frequential deterministic models are adequate to depict the random processes considered in which "chance" plays a determinant role.*

Unfortunately, there is a very regrettable disproportion between the number of studies devoted to the elaboration of theoretical models and the number of empirical studies devoted to the confrontation of these models with experimental data. Yet this is an essential task, the *necessity of which has been felt by all those who are rightly preoccupied by the link between theory and concrete reality.* The first known research was by Buffon who analysed a series of 4040 tosses of a coin. In the 19th century, the Swiss astronomer Wolf analysed a series of over 280.000 casts of a pair of dice, and a few years ago, Herman Wold analysed series simulating 600.000 drawings. In all cases, it was found that everything occurs as if the frequential mathematical models represented reality correctly, which *leads to the conclusion that the axiom of "equal possibility on average"* may be considered as admissible.

Even more rare are the authors who have attempted to explain *why* empirical frequencies approximately reproduce mathematical frequencies ; *why* successive drawings from an urn or similar processes, lead to distributions which are never very far from the normal law ; *why* nature thus appears to obey the normal law. *This is obviously a fundamental question.* Henri Poincaré, in remarkable analyses, was the first to perceive its interest, and to open some very suggestive approaches on the basis of the use of arbitrary frequency functions.

To illustrate the empirical generation of the normal law Francis Galton built a machine and described its operating results in his *"Natural Inheritance"*. In his device, small balls fell vertically into a space fitted with a set of regularly spaced pegs in successive rows, a layout still used today in some slot machines. At the bottom of the apparatus were containers in which the balls finally lodged. It is observed that their distribution pattern follows the normal law, and the approximation is the better, the greater the number of balls.

Galton's apparatus process is a physically deterministic one. How can the fact that it follows the so-called law of "chance" then be explained ? This can only occur if the *axiom of "equal possibility"* is effectively satisfied on average when each ball hits with the pegs on its path. The resulting actions are distributed according to frequency functions – Poincaré's arbitrary functions – so that the axiom of equal possibility is effectively verified on average.

The question which Galton's experimental apparatus raises is the following : *why do the balls precisely fall into places where they should fall so that their distribution is approximately normal ?*

Probability does not intervene in Galton's apparatus as regards the action of the ball hitting the pegs ; what does intervene are frequencies, which can be represented by Poincaré's arbitrary functions, so that they combined according to the central limit theorem applicable to frequencies. This combination yields an accurate representation of the observed frequencies.

By itself the mathematical theory of deterministic frequency models cannot reveal anything about nature. All it can do is to define the deterministic laws of the frequential models which can be confronted with the data of experience. As mentioned earlier, scientists such as Buffon, Weldon, Wolf, Galton and Wold have undertaken this confrontation.

At all events, what are referred to as the laws of chance are merely properties of the binomial or multinomial expansion, or the corresponding formulations in the continuous case. In the last analysis, what experience verifies when it appears that these laws provide an accurate representation of concrete reality,that is the validity of the axiom of equal possibility on average.

A frequential mathematical model generally provides *only an approximate representation of reality, however accurate this representation may be over a very wide range.* For instance it can be asserted that no individual human being has a height of several meters. Similarly, in Maxwell's theory of the distribution of speeds, the foundation of the kinetic theory of gases, it can be stated that no particle can reach a speed equal to a thousand times the speed of light.

In fact extreme values can be very important in the Theory of Decision, and the distributions generally envisaged can only be accepted with great caution if high values of variables are to be considered.

In itself statistical analysis of empirical frequencies relates only to events *which have already occurred.* It implies no consideration of the future. *It does not involve any uncertainty,* the distributions it studies being perfectly determined. It is based on the representation and eventually the *"explanation"* of empirical distributions of frequencies *by fully deterministic frequential mathematical models.* Here again "chance" does not intervene at all and the use of terms such as "probability" or "random" is totally inappropriate as it implies a subjective judgment on the future or suggests interpretations the validity of which nothing can prove. In fact all the propositions we are accustomed to remain valid providing the word *"probability"* is replaced by *"empirical frequency".* This is true in particular of the correlation theory the bases of which have been elaborated by Bravais independently of any use of the probability concept.

4. OBJECTIVE PROBABILITY AND THE COEFFICIENT OF PLAUSIBILITY

In contrast to the deterministic concept of mathematical

frequency and the concept of empirical frequency which pertains to events which have already occurred, *the concept of probability relates basically to the forecasting of an uncertain future.*

When this forecast is based on the consideration of already observed statistical distributions, the best expression to use is *"objective probability"*. If the forecast covers events which have not previously been subjected to statistical analysis, it is an attempt to foretell the future, an estimate of the plausibility of occurrence of such or such an event, the characteristics of which differ completely from those of objective probability as defined above. The most adequate term here is *"coefficient of plausibility"* [6]. *However, in both cases, the forecast of the future is basically subjective in character.*

In the first case (objective probability) two hypotheses are put forward which are *fundamentally subjective* : - the first hypothesis admits *the validity of the representation of empirical distributions by deterministic frequential mathematical models* that are actually *fully deterministic* in character ; - the second one admits implicitly *a postulate of invariance of the laws of nature,* according to which events regularly observed in the past will continue to recur in the future.

In the second case (plausibility) the forecast of the future is virtually detached from any objective component, namely, from any element independent of the person who makes the forecast. In this case the use of the word *"subjective probability"* might be envisaged to describe what I refer to as the *"coefficient of plausibility"*. However, this denomination would be unfortunate for at least two reasons. First it would tend to veil *the subjective nature of the concept of objective probability.* Secondly it would suggest that the probability models derived from earlier findings in the analysis of observed data are just as suitable for the appraisal of the plausibility of events for which there are no objective, that it commonly accepted data ; and this would not be true.

In any case it should be underlined that *the concept of probability, which is indissociably associated with human forecasting of the future, does not exist in nature. It exists only in men's minds. Nature knows only frequencies ; it does not know probabilities.*

5. OBJECTIVE PROBABILITY

Forecasting of the future using statistical distributions

observed in the past is founded essentially on *objective pro-bability,* itself based on the estimation of what I have called *intrinsic frequency* which characterises the process conside-red.

Two very different cases should be envisaged. *In the first,* there is no decisive information as to the respective possibility of occurrence of the various events *in the speci-fic case under study.* The value deduced from the analysis of earlier distributions for similar cases can thus be taken as intrinsic frequency. This applies for instance to dice throws, *for which there is no special information,* even if it may be legitimately expected *a priori* that they will be bia-sed to some extent. *In the second case,* if the distribution corresponding to throws already made *of these same dice* is available, a better course is to adopt as probability the value of the intrinsic frequency which provides the best representation of the distribution observed in the past by the corresponding frequential mathematical model.

However, this may well not be the best principle to apply. As an illustration consider an urn containing an equal number of white and black balls and ensuring optimum conditions of symmetry. In this case one will consider that there are *a priori* equal possibilities of drawing either a black or a white ball ; the value 1/2 will be taken *a priori* as the objective probability, *and that even if in a previous series of fifteen drawings one has just seen that fifteen white balls were drawn. This inference stems from the teachings of long earlier experience that when conditions of symmetry are ful-filled, it is reasonable to assume a priori that all cases are equally possible.* This is the approach used in the clas-sical theory of probability, which culminated in Laplace's theory and which was developed by admitting more or less explicitly *the axiom of equal possibility in frequential ma-thematical models, and the axiom of "equal possibility on average" in empirical applications.*

A probabilistic model can naturally be made to correspond with each frequential mathematical model, but in all cases, the fact that the whole mathematical theory of probability can be identified with combinatorial analysis calculations *proves that the axiom of equal possibility is introduced one way or another. The axiom of equal possibility should thus be viewed as the simplest idealisation of concrete reality.*

A probability model can be used to forecast a single event or a series of events. In the case of the urn, one drawing can be performed or a series of drawings. What it is

essential to underline, is the fact that *the results observed
will never be incompatible with the model considered.*

To draw a white ball from an urn containing an equal
number of white and black balls can neither confirm nor disprove the model used, as this model is based on the axiom of
equal possibility on average, and either a black or a white
ball must be drawn.

Neither will drawing n white balls in a series of n
drawings disprove the model, as each of the 2^n trajectories
must *a priori* be taken as equally possible, and therefore,
equally probable.

Thus the fundamental character of the analysis of objective probability is that it can never provide a certain forecast nor be disproved by experience. *Whatever event occurs
can always be considered in agreement with a previously formulated judgement as to its objective probability of occurence.*

However, if one takes an empirical distribution observed
in the past and if it is possible to represent it with some
approximation by a frequential mathematical model, nothing
prevents us from making *after the event* a calculation of the
probability which could have been assigned to that approximation *before* knowing the empirical distribution, considering
the validity of the frequential mathematical model *as a cri-
terium* ; and in the light of this probability, from taking
the decision to discard or retain this model, when the empirical distribution has become known. This is effectively the
approach followed in all significance tests.

The essential point in any case is that *any probability
model applied to reality is based on a deterministic frequential model whose use is justified by its earlier success.* In
sum, it is *on earlier experience* that the application of probability models to reality is based. *Mathematical theory alone
cannot reveal anything about reality.*

In any case just as frequential mathematical models can
provide an accurate representation of empirical statistical
distributions only when the phenomena under study satisfy somewhere *the axiom of equal possibility on average* at least approximately, so also, probability mathematical models cannot be
used to forecast the future accurately unless *this same hypothesis of equal possibility on average* is made somewhere.

To the extent that empirical distributions are accurately represented by frequential mathematical models and that
this datum of experience is used to forecast the future, it
is sufficient to replace in frequential mathematical models
the term *"mathematical frequency"* by *"mathematical probability"*,

to transpose frequential mathematical models to probability
mathematical models. *However, this transposition should not
mask the nature of the operation which is made and which is
essentially subjective in character.*

*Although it is based on empirical frequency, objective
probability does not exist in nature ; it only exists in the
human mind. Nature knows only frequencies.* The concept of
probability corresponds to a human judgement made in advance
by a human mind. *This judgement does not have any intrinsic
physical meaning as regards the occurrence of the event considered. Nature never makes forecasts on the future.*

6. THE CONCEPT OF PLAUSIBILITY

In ordinary language the word *"probable"* most often relates
to a concept that differs from the concept of objective probability corresponding to events which are susceptible to
repeat themselves and which appear with frequencies which
have an objective character. Rather than probability, it is
better in this case to speak of *"coefficient of plausibility"*[6]
        Coefficients of plausibility can be determined by refe-
rence to and comparison with objective probabilities. For instance it is possible to say that the occurrence of a certain
event is more or less plausible than the drawing of three
white balls in succession from an urn, with an *a priori* probability of 1/8, if the urn contains an equal number of black
and white balls.
        Use of the concept of greater or lesser plaubility is
unavoidable. For, *in the last analysis, and for instance, all
applications of statistical analysis to the real world are
based on judgements as to the greater or lesser plausibility
with which the deterministic frequential models considered
can represent concrete reality.*
        R.A. Fisher's *principle of maximum likelihood,* which
was earlier used systematically by Laplace, is only an illustration of this proposition. It may seem convenient, if not
attractive, to adopt it, but *it cannot be demonstrated.*
        Bayes' principle constitutes a second illustration. If
no information is available on the *a priori* probability, is
it nevertheless legitimate to take all values between 0 and 1
as equally probable, whereas the conditions of total ignorance are never realized ? *That is an indemonstrable principle*
to which only more or less plausibility can be attached according to the particular case considered, and which has been
rightly criticized in the past. In the absence of conditions

of symmetry the arbitrary character of the estimation of *a priori probability* can disappear *only if* the number of observations becomes high enough. In addition, these observations should effectively be independent. In any case it is somewhat strange that apparently no one remarks that if we admit *Laplace's principle, R.A. Fisher's principle* is mathematically tantamount to admitting the validity of the *Baye's principle*.

Likewise, again, the adoption of a given statistical significance threshold can only be justified by a judgement on the greater or lesser plausibility tò be attached to the models considered when, according to these models, the probability of a given deviation of the observed from the theoretical distribution is below a given value.

This is also true of the - *very arbitrary* - principle according to which events with a very low degree of *"probability"* can be considered as virtually impossible. This principle is often adopted, but it is really contestable and logically indefensible. Thus Buffon considered that probabilities of the order 10^{-4} can be neglected, and Borel set the threshold for negligible probability in human affairs at 10^{-6} In his Treatise, Laplace, without setting specific limits, made several applications of this principle to astronomy, considering as unlikely the fact that some very striking regularities could not be explained, whereas their probability calculated on the hypothesis of chance was very low.

Borel made this principle even as the *"unique law of chance"*. This principle simply translates the fact that in all empirical frequency distributions the extreme values of the Laplace-Gauss law *are never observed*. Thus, in distributions of individuals' height, the extremes have determinate limits and the normal law can thus be considered only as an approximation.

In general, the acceptance of the *axiom of equal possibility a priori, or of a hypothesis of symmetry* over all possible cases, which are both simply idealisations of experience, *derives solely from a judgement of plausibility.*

If the concept of greater or lesser plausibility were to be discarded, it would be impossible to confront the theory of probability whith reality without introducing new postulates

In the last analysis, to assess the validity of a model - deterministic or not - *eminently subjective considerations* of the greater or lesser degree of plausibility cannot be avoided. Thus, when a research work leads to some numerical concordance, the immediate questions to come to mind is whether one is in the presence of an intrinsic reality or

simply a fortuitous regularity. An evaluation of the plausibility of the result obtained is unavoidable, and its character
is naturally *fundamentally subjective.*

7. THE CONCEPT OF CHANCE AND REALITY

In its everyday sense, chance is commonly characterised by
such factors as uncertainty, unpredictability, the fortuitous
or unaccountable nature of events, or their dependence on a
large number of causes, unknown or too complex to be analysed.
      Just as the only way, in my opinion, to define *probabi-
lity in its pure state* is to refer to drawing of balls from
a reference urn according to a process providing as perfect
as possible conditions of symmetry, so, similarly, *pure chance
can only be defined by referring to this type of drawing. Pure
chance is characterised by total unpredictability.*
      Pure chance, as probability in the pure state, is a *pri-
mordial conceptual notion* which is only a subjective creation
of our mind, linked to the impossibility of forecasting the
result of a given drawing. *Chance, like probability, stems
from purely subjective judgments existing only in our minds
and unknown in nature.* In fact the two concepts cannot be
dissociated ; they could not be considered independently one
from the other.
      Nature does not attempt to foresee or explain. Because
as a result *the concepts of probability and chance are completely foreign to nature,* an objective definition of these concepts cannot be given ; the only feasible definition involves
subjective reference to drawings from an urn.
      *Actually, the absolute impossibility of forecasting a
drawing from an urn is linked to the fact that we consider a
priori that all alternatives are equally possible.* This judgement can naturally only apply on average, as we are sure
that one ball will be drawn, and that it will be privileged
with respect to the others.
      *This judgment on equal possibility a priori is thus equi-
valent to the axiom of equal possibility on average,* which
axiom permits to explain why the multinomial frequency distribution generally allows the distribution of observed frequencies to be represented remarkably well.
      This leads to the paradox, which is only an apparent one,
that the inability to forecast the outcome *of a particular
drawing* generally makes possible to forecast with an almost
certainty the distribution of the results of a very large
number of drawings. In this regards, the most pure chance

enables the *"laws of chance"* to be specified and "explained".
Pure chance thus finds its logical outcome in the most abso-
lute determinism.

In some cases, the explanation of this paradoxical conclusion should be sought in Henri Poincaré's approach, based
on the consideration of arbitrary frequency functions, and the
use of the central limit theorem, which allows the overall
effect of these arbitrary frequency functions to be forecast.

In fact what we should consider, in the last analysis,
as astonishing, and indeed absolutely astonishing, is the way
in which some events seem to obey the axiom of equal possibi-
lity on average, the only possible explanation of the agreement
between empirical distributions, which we too easily attribute
to chance, and frequential mathematical models that are basi-
cally deterministic in character.

That is this paradox over which the literature generally
passes in silence which it is precisely necessary to explain ;
and by itself this explanation is as important, *if not more*
so, than all the theorems on deterministic frequency models.

For instance, to observe such an agreement, it is necessary that in the long run *some "compensation"* does occur between the number of white balls and the number of black balls
drawn during successive drawings from an urn. That is precisely the very principle of compensation in which all gamblers
believe, but in all logic it has to be rejected *a priori* since any series of white and black balls should be considered
a priori as equally possible. It is nevertheless still true
that if we consider *the mathematical deterministic frequency*
model which represents the process for a number of n drawings
increasing to infinity, we verify that *there is indeed an*
infinite number of trajectories for which there is never any
compensation, but that their frequency tends to zero when n
tends to infinity. Indeed this result implies that *there is*
compensation on average in concrete reality *to the extent*
precisely that the corresponding mathematical frequency model
yields an accurate representation of this reality.

Like nature, but for other reasons, the mathematical
theories which many call *"mathematical theories of chance"*
ignore the concepts of chance, uncertainty, and probability.
As underlined earlier, the models that these theories consider
are *purely deterministic models,* and in fact, in the last analysis, the quantities they study are nothing else than the
frequencies of special configurations in the set of equally
possible configurations, whose calculation is based on combinatorial analysis. *The often very complex and abstract mathe-*

*matical apparatus in the framework of which these theories
are developed cannot hide this fundamental reality.*

Finally, the concept of chance cannot be dissociated from
the psychological concepts of probability and plausibility.
*No axiomatic definition of chance is conceivable. The axio-
matic theory of "probability" does not call on the concept
of chance and it is inconceivable that it could.*

8. FREQUENCY, PROBABILITY AND CHANCE

The above discussion shows that *in the whole literature, the
word probability covers four fundamentally different concepts :
mathematical frequency, empirical frequency, objective probability, and the degree of plausibility.*

When the four concepts are differentiated all the difficulties, contradictions, obscurities disappear. If they are
not, the incompatibilities become irreducible when one en-
deavours to link abstract theory with the analysis of real
or subjective phenomena.

*The models of the mathematical theories are frequential
models which do ignore chance and are completely deterministic.*
In the final analysis, all their theorems whether they apply
to discrete or continuous sets, are merely theorems in combinatorial analysis. The quantities studied are mathematical
frequencies, *which are referred to most improperly as probabilities.*

There is indeed *a real abuse* to use the word probability
in this context. It is in particular responsible for the general belief that Bernoulli demonstrated the *empirical* law
of large numbers, whereas this proof can only be given by
associating Bernoulli's *mathematical* law of large numbers
*with an axiom of equal possibility on average, an axiom the
demonstration of which is impossible, an axiom the validity
of which can be derived only from observation .*

In all the fields where they are applied, whether in the
sciences of nature, the sciences of life, or the sciences of
man, statistical theories *are considering only empirical
frequencies,* and they study only *past* distributions. The reason for the successfull use of frequential deterministic mathematical models is that *nature seems to obey mechanisms
whose effects in practice justify the validity of the axiom
of equal possibility on average.*

*The concepts of probability and chance, by contrast, do
appear to be associated to the forecast of the future, with
its contingencies and uncertainties. They are human constructs*

unknown to nature and mathematics. That is why they appear totally absent from mathematical theories and statistical analysis, *once we examine their substance, and not the semantics they unjustifiably use*.

It is thus not surprising to observe basic contradictions between the different theories since their propositions apply to *entirely different* realities.

In all this analysis we are always finally confronted with only one question, *a fundamental one indeed,* on which depend both the interpretation of theories as regards concrete reality and their *"applicability"* to the study of reality : *how does it happen that nature when it is considered as random can be represented, at least approximately and often with great precision, by mathematical models which are implicitly based on an axiom of equal possibility, and which are in fact fundamentally deterministic models ?* Unfortunately, in almost all books, the question is not even raised.

My own conviction is that *nature itself it totally deterministic,* but that as a first approximation, the sums of small deterministic effects, if present in sufficient numbers and in relative terms not too different in size, are distributed according to mathematical frequential models, whose validity is attributed, wrongly in my view, to purely random causes. This point will be illustrated later[8].

In fact, the *absolutely fundamental* axiom of equal possibility presents itself in the form of *three different aspects* closely linked together : *the axiom of equal possibility of frequential mathematical models* whose theorems are all based on *simultaneous consideration* of all possible cases, which are assumed, at least implicitly, to occur *simultaneously ; the axiom of equal possibility on average relating to empirical processes ; and the axiom of equal a priori possibility* relating to the forecasts of drawings from an urn made *a priori,* or similar processes for which conditions of symmetry are realized.

The general approach presented here is in reverse historical chronological order. The history of thought started with the concept of lesser or greater plausibility of the combinations with which players were confronted. From there it moved to probability theory using the generally unexplicited and in any event inadequately discussed *axiom of the equal a priori possibility* of possible cases. Research then went on to the study of empirical distributions. And finally the mathematicians drew up rigorous axiomatic theories which allowed the development of formal frequential mathematical models appli-

cable to the analysis of real phenomena and the making of
forecasts relating to uncertainty of the future.

There has obviously always been interpenetration of these
four approaches, but at each epoch the importance ascribed
to each approach corresponds approximately to the overall
process just described. This explains why the theorists and
research workers have been imprisoned in a conceptual and
semantic framework dominated by the terms *"probability"*,
"random", and *"chance"*, originating from games of chance,
even where these concepts were altogether alien to the ultimate nature of their research.

In fact had research first concentrated on frequential
models representing past events, and only later on games of
chance characterised by the uncertainty of the future, the
semantics today would certainly have been different. But it
must be acknowledged that it is now somewhat difficult to
renounce deeply rooted habits of speech and thought. Does it
not remain true, however, that inappropriate semantics can
only be very dangerous, as suggesting almost irresistibly
many ideas which are altogether unfounded ?

9. THE SIMULATION OF "CHANCE"

In the light of the above, what should be understood by *"random choice"*, *"simulation of chance"*, *"series of random numbers"*, *"random variables"* and *"random processes"* ?

There is *only one* valid answer to this question. *To make
a random choice, this choice must be derived from a drawing
from a reference urn.* A series of random numbers can be defined
only by a series of drawings according to an experimental
process *guaranteeing conditions of real symmetry.*

However such processes are toilsome, and this leads to
recourse to processes which are believed able to simulate
chance. Two classes of processes are used ; mechanical or
physical processes, and the properties of irrational numbers.

These processes may at first sight appear to be suitable.
They may lead to at least approximately satisfactory series
for the main tests characterising what are referred to as
"random series". But they are not free of biases which, in
certain cases, can produce unacceptable effects.

Consider for instance the process based on a count of
radioactive particles. It is generally admitted that there is
no regularity at all in the resulting series. However, the
experiments performed by Jean Thibaud and his collaborators
have shown *the existence of periodic disturbances* which cannot

be represented validly by the currently accepted laws of probability. Mechanical processes could well be influenced by
similar effects.

Now consider the use of irrational numbers to make a deterministic simulation of chance. At the outset, the idea is
that, in contrast to rational numbers whose decimals recur at
regular intervals beyond a certain rank, irrational numbers,
whose decimal sequence cannot present any periodicity of this
type, can be used to imitate chance. However, and for instance, contrary to the suggestions made by some authors, Franel
has proven that when n increases to infinity, the average
of the n decimals of order i of the decimal logarithms of
the successive integers 1, 2, ..., n does not tend to 4.5,
but fluctuates around a value, indeed very close to 4.5, but
which is a function of the order i , and that the order of
magnitude of the amplitude of the fluctuation is itself function of i . The frequency of the decimal ℓ (equal to one of
the digits 0, 1, 2, ..., 9) increases with ℓ . It is thus
inexact to state, as Joseph Bertrand does, that the distribution of the i.th decimals of the decimal logarithms of integers follows the *"laws of chance"*, that the ten figures 0, 1,
2, ..., 9 are equally probable, and above all, that their
order of succession obeys no law. I myself have found that the
decimals of the fourth order or more of the napierian logarithms of successive integers present remarkable and unexpected
regularities. I have also shown that the decimal parts of
other series of irrational numbers present similar regularities [9]. These results show that the simulation of chance by
decimal of irrational numbers may be *at most only approximate.*

At all events the terms to be used here is *frequency and
not probability,* for the succession of the ith decimal digits
of the decimal logarithms of integers for instance is an
*entirely deterministic phenomenon which cannot be assimilated
to a random phenomenon governed by chance.* Joseph Bertrand
displays here the same semantic confusion between the two
concepts of frequency and probability that contaminates the
literature at large.

Indeed *no mathematical process can imitate chance* since
the essential characteristic of chance is unpredictability
whereas *the essence of any mathematical process is fundamentally deterministic.*

The fact that, *in some cases, and within certain limits,*
sheer determinism can appear as imitating the properties of
the frequencies observed in series of drawings from an urn,
should in no circumstances lead to the conclusion that this
is a manifestation of *so-called chance.*

10. ALMOST PERIODIC FUNCTIONS, CHANCE, AND THE X FACTOR HYPO-THESIS

In the analysis of the results of experiments on the movement
of a paraconical pendulum which I have undertaken between 1954
and 1960, I observed that the successive values of the sum of
thirteen sinusoids,whose periods corresponded to those considered for tidal analysis and whose amplitudes and phases were
given by a least square fit of this sum to the observed series
of the azimuths of the plane of oscillation of the pendulum,
were remarkably well distributed according to the normal law.

These findings led me to study the distribution of the
value X_n of almost periodic functions considered at regularly
spaced times t_n. Such functions are the sum of sinusoidal
components some periods of which are incommensurable. The
main results of this study, the principle of which I have established in 1959, are set out in *Appendix B* of this Memoir
and have been presented as a Communication during the Conference.

It can be shown by applying the central limit theorem
that the distribution of the values X_n of the function considered is very close to the normal distribution, providing
that amplitudes a_i of the various components are of similar
order of magnitude ; that the length N of the series analysed
is sufficiently large, and that the same is true of the number
ℓ of sinusoidal components ; and that the frequencies f_i =
$1/T_i$ are irrational, and that there is no linear relation
with integer coefficients between these frequencies. The distribution considered comes closer to the normal law, the
better these four conditions are fulfilled [10].

It can be seen that when the number ℓ of sinusoidal components increases, convergence to the normal law is rapid,
even for relatively short series.

It can further be observed that under the same conditions
the values ℓ_q of the coefficient of auto-correlation of order
q of the series of values X_n are also approximately normally
distributed, and that *for a given value of N* and under very
general conditions, the series of X_n *may present all the
appearances of a sequence of independent terms*.

For such almost periodic functions, the distribution
according to the length of series of values X_n of the same
sign differs little from that corresponding to a binomial
model with an intrinsic frequency equal to 1/2 for a series
of N drawings. This is also true of the series of coefficients
of auto-correlation of the series of X_n.

Thus, for such series of a given length, there is a near-perfect simulation of what is generally referred to as chance.

Not only can this remarkable properties of some almost periodic functions easily provide artificial series of random numbers, but they also support the hypothesis, which I will call the *"X Factor"* hypothesis for simplicity, according to which the fluctuations of the time series observed in phenomena relating to the sciences of nature, the sciences of life, and the sciences of man could result from the resonance effect of the influence of the innumerable vibrations passing through the space in which we live, whose existence has now been proven with certainty. *This could explain the quasi-periodic structure* [11] *observed in a very large number of time series.*

As these fluctuations manifest themselves by stationary series all the appearances of which simulate what is commonly called chance, *they are generally considered as random.* Thus many economists, for example, view the normal distribution of fluctuations of stock exchange quotations as perfectly random fluctuations which are not produced by systematic causes through a deterministic process. The value of this inference is naturally contradicted by the properties I have just stated of almost periodic functions when they fulfil very general conditions.

In the present state of advancement of science, the existence of the "X Factor" is, of course, just a hypothesis. However for a long time many research workers have come to the more or less explicit, and more often implicit, conclusion that this hypothesis can be taken. As far as I am concerned, this hypothesis has appeared to me more and more plausible over these last thirty years. *At all events this is an hypothesis which it would be antiscientific to discard on the basis only of a priori dogmatic positions.*

11. CHANCE AND DETERMINISM

For the past half century, there has been a tendency for all sciences to abandon the 19th century deterministic ideas, replacing in large part the concept of causality by the concept of chance.

This crisis of determinism can be observed for instance in disciplines as far removed from each other as quantum physics, or economics with the spectral theory of time series considered as having continuous spectra.

Some authors have even maintained that it would be possi-

ble to reduce the interpretation of all real phenomena to the
principle of an entirely random universe. According to this
contemporary tendency, chance would be no longer as viewed
by 19th century theorists and physicists *"an appearance due
to our inability to analyse fully causes which are too small,
too numerous or too complicated, and to take them correctly
into consideration"*, to quote Louis de Broglie. *"On the contrary, chance would be the result of some disruption of causality allowing the independent occurrence of differents
events, without it being possible to do more than assign
their respective probabilities. This would definitely correspond to veritable pure chance. It would not stem from our
inability to foresee, but from the very nature of things"*.

   *Laplace's conception that the so-called chance simply
covers the deterministic order of all that we do not know,
would thus be replaced by the operation of "pure contingency",
to quote Louis de Broglie again.*

   Indeed I do find it hard to understand what could be
"pure contingency" : *it seems to be purely metaphysical in
essence.* Does this concept not stem from the many confusions,
discussed earlier, proliferating in the literature on probability and chance ?

   An exhaustive study of this topic is naturally impossible
here. I will restrict myself to a few remarks.

   First, when a mathematician of the reputation of Emile
Borel states that the analysis of the distribution of the
prime numbers *"confirms the hypothesis of chance"*, such a
statement is merely absurd. What it is about can only be deterministic, and the reference should not be to probability
but to frequencies. *The phenomenon undeniably simulates "chance", but this does not make it a random phenomenon*. In reality
this simulation of chance cannot stem from a fortuitous cause ;
it should be and can be explained.

   This example, at all events, offers many teachings. We
have here a distribution which could rightfully be attributed
to chance if we had no information available on its origin.
*Does this simple fact not suggest that many phenomena which
are attributed to chance could well be characterised in reality by total determinism ?*

   From this perspective reality would merely imitate chance.
Frequential mathematical models would be only approximations,
and Borel's *"unique law of chance"* would become fully justified.

   Remarkable, *indeed extraordinary* regularities can be
observed in the frequency distributions found in the real

world. Certainly they are as remarkable as the regularities observed for instance in the movement of planets, which is considered as fully deterministic. However, going deeper into the matter, these regularities are *even more surprising*. For if it is possible to understand that specific laws govern phenomena in the framework of a deterministic conception of the universe, it is then less easy to understand how *"pure chance"*, which by definition has nothing to do with determinism, can obey perfectly defined laws. *To the extent that they are constantly verified, do they not take on the character of deterministic laws themselves, and should the conclusion not then be that they conceal a hidden order ?* The fact is that the laws governing what is conventionally called *"chance"* allow the results of repeated events to be predicted with a degree of certainty similar to that attaching to the most deterministic physical phenomena. However, in the light of the considerations raised earlier, there is in truth nothing here which could not be explained.

If we consider the quality of the fit of normal distributions by Karl Pearson in his studies on heredity, there is also nothing here which could not be explained by the action of a large number of small causes, in a deterministic framework, if the central limit theorem is enounced in terms of frequencies and not in terms of probabilities.

The same observation can be made of Maxwell's distribution of velocities of atoms, which is the basis of the kinetic theory of gases : the word *"probability"* needs only be replaced by the word *"frequency"* to draw out the foundations of a deterministic approach. *To explain the statistical order suggested by the kinetic theory of gases, there is no need at all to refer to some metaphysical idea of chance* ; this can be viewed as the outcome of a process involving many causes whose simultaneous effects result in the substitution of a frequential regularity in place of chaos. This is also true of Planck's law of the distribution of light quanta, and, as a general rule, of the whole theory of quanta.

As to the stationary time series a theorem of Wold dating back to 1938 states that they can be considered as the sum of a fully deterministic process and a completely non-deterministic process, if we neglect the singular part of the spectrum, which it is generally possible to do. The component of the deterministic process in the most general case is an almost periodic function, some periods of which are incommensurable, and the component of the non-deterministic process derives from the moving summation of the realizations over time of a purely random process.

Theorists presently tend to neglect the deterministic
component and to concentrate their analysis on the non-
deterministic component. However, can doubt not be cast on
this belief in the light of the simulation of chance by almost
periodic functions discussed above ? *Should this conception
and the postulates on which it is based not be revised* ? The
fact is that the outward manifestations of chance and periodicity occur in very similar fashion. Chance may present quasi-
periodic aspects, and periodicity can simulate chance.

Is not the simulation of *"chance"* by almost periodic
functions capable of bringing phenomena considered as random
into an intelligible deterministic framework that would be in
fundamental harmony with the vibrational structure of the
universe of which we have only an inkling ?

Everywhere the evidence shows that the most absolute determinism can produce effects that are distributed according
to the normal law, and which at first sight seem attribuable
to *"chance"*.

Whenever the process according to which the regularities
observed occur is not known, *"chance"* is called upon to explain
them. But this is patently just an easy way of avoiding the
real, and often very difficult problem of explaining the so-
called *"chance"* by determinism.

In fact the basic role attributed to *"chance"* in certain
contemporary theories is in a sense a conception *which trans-
cends the intelligible*. In the last analysis it reduces purely
and simply to a refusal to explain. This is too comfortable
and too simplistic a position.

"Chance" considered as the only process of the ultimate
mechanism governing the universe is a mythical concept, really
incomprehensible if it is viewed as a prime cause which could
not be derived from any other, a law that all other laws would
be derived from. There is indeed no statement of how nature
could choose among the different possible eventualities *or
rather how it would abstain from choosing, since everything
would remain indeterminate and would be governed by pure
chance.*

To call on *"chance"*, *a pure creation of the human mind,*
to explain the reality of the world, is nothing but some resi-
gnation of intelligence, a mythical principle like that of
primitive peoples who explain everything by surnatural causes.
"Chance" is a pseudo-explanation ; the phenomena which are
generally viewed as random are effects, not causes.

The concepts of chance and probability are purely crea-
tions of our mind, totally unknown to nature. Consequently,

to explain concrete reality by chance is to subject it to a
mechanism which finally reduces to an anthropomorphic view
of the world. It reduces to replacing the perfectly clear
notion of causality suggested by all our direct and tangible
experience of the physical world by a mythical concept which
exists only in our mind. ·

12. CONDITIONS FOR PROGRESS

The concept of probability, in parallel with the concept of
utility, is one of the two pillars of the Decision Theory
viewed as either a fundamental or an applied science. However
progress is impossible as long as these two concepts have not
been clarified.

How can it be conceived that it is possible to interpret
observed data, how can the future be forecast in the light
of all the uncertainties it involves, how can our knowledge
be used to take the best decisions, if the very foundations
of the Decision Theory remain *in their present blurred state* ?

As regards the concept of probability, I have just tried
to dispel the confusion flowing from the use of a single
word *"probability"* to represent four entirely different
concepts : - *mathematical frequency,* which is a deterministic
concept relating to combinatorial analysis ; - *empirical
frequency,* which is a datum of observation and can be viewed
as an approximate measure of *intrinsic frequency,* when this
cannot be determined *a priori* by conditions of symmetry ;
- *objective probability, which is a subjective estimate of
the intrinsic frequency* from earlier data of observation to
use for inferences for the future ; - *the degree of plausibility,* which is an eminently subjective concept, and on which
in the final analysis depend the interpretation of our models
and their extrapolation to the future.

In fact the continuing stream of discussion on the concept of probability stems chiefly from efforts of all authors
to reserve the use of the word probability for only one of the
four concepts, eliminating the others. This is obviously
impossible, *as each concept effectively represents a certain
basic aspect of reality which can neither be eliminated nor
reduced to one of the others.*

As in every science only reality is important as our
only source of knowledge, and *what is fundamentally the major
issue is the relationship between theory and observation, the
elaboration and interpretation of our models in the light of
empirical data.* The weakness of the theories of probability

is the absence of the necessary relationship between theory
and concrete reality, *since it is on precisely this point that
they conflict.* It is undeniable that without the consideration
of observed data, the so-called mathematical law of large
numbers could explain nothing, and that by itself it could
not give any basis for a forecast of the occurrence of real
events in the universe. In all disciplines there is a stri-
kingly large number of theorists who endeavour at all costs
to force reality into their models instead of subjecting them
to reality, placing too much weight, in so doing, on *a priori*
ideas instead of considering *first* data of observation. It
may seem strange that I insist on such an obvious point, but
too many theorists tend to forget it.

Incontestably, it is necessary today to forewarn against
certain dangers that are emerging in western european and
american literature. Mathematics is not and cannot be an end
in itself except for a few score of professional mathematicians. Mathematics is an indispensable tool, but only a tool.
It should be used only when it can serve to analyse the real.
*The confrontation of theories with observed data is its neces-
sary outcome.* No theory can be considered as valid unless it
has been verified by experience. Whatever its rigour or aes-
thetic beauty, no theory can be maintained if it is invalidated
by the data. *This is the golden rule of and the fundamental
condition for any science.*

We often tend to forget the teachings of the great mathematicians of the past, as Newton, Bernoulli, Euler, Lagrange,
Laplace, Gauss, Poincaré, all of whom were *particularly concerned* about the application of their mathematical theories
to observed data. In his time Keynes in his remarkable *"Treatise on Probability",* denounced with ruthless criticism the
"mathematical charlatanry" which impaired the progress of
science. What would he say about some of the works that are
published today ?

*That is precisely the unreasonably abusive abstraction
in the teaching of mathematics which today jeopardizes the
future development of scientific thought.* This teaching of
mathematics is totally detached from reality and no longer
pays attention to applications, whether applied mathematics
or numerical calculations. It diverts intelligent minds from
the use of mathematics and it results in a reverse selection
process for the training of those who will use mathematics
for the advancement of the sciences of nature, the sciences
of life, and the sciences of man.

For instance, what view can one take of the teaching of

the probability theory which only considers the concept of
mathematical probability and its axiomatic theory, which takes
as an axiom the principle of compound probability, almost
without reference to empirical frequency, the only data of
observation ? Yet who does not see that all probability theory
boil down to combinatorial analysis, and that chance, which is
a basic and undissociable datum of our probability judgment,
is *totally excluded* from this theory. *As long as they them-*
selves have never tossed a coin or drawn a ball from an urn,
how could students perceive the basic problem set by the
extraordinary matching of fully deterministic frequential
mathematical models to the empirical distributions of observed
data, which are commonly accepted to be determined by "chance".

Actually, the only real danger for the progress of knowledge is dogmatism - the acceptance as gospel of conceptions
inherited from the past whatever they are and considered as
definitively established. It is worth thinking over Pareto's
quip : *"The history of science reduces to the history of the*
mistakes of competent men", and Ernst Mach's statement :
"Thought should always be adapted to the facts and thoughts
to each other".

To conclude this analysis, I will simply say that may be
I have raised more problems than I have solved. Nevertheless,
I hope that this overall presentation and interpretation can
help to renew thinking on questions on which debate has gone
on endlessly. If so, my aim has been achieved.

Centre National de la Recherche Scientifique
and Ecole Nationale Supérieure des Mines de Paris

NOTES

1. Albert Einstein and Leopold Infeld, 1938, *The Evolution of*
   Ideas in Physics.
2. Louis de Broglie, 1953, *La Physique quantique restera-t-elle*
   indéterministe ? (Will Quantum Physics remain Indeterminis-
   tic ?).
3. Augustin Cournot, 1851, *Essai sur les Fondements de nos*
   Connaissances (Essay on the Foundations of our Knowledge).
4. My initial intention had been to devote the Adress, which
   I have been asked for on the occasion of *the First Inter-*
   national Conference on Foundations of Utility and Risk
   Theory, to a critical analysis of utility and probability,
   the two fundamental concepts which are at the root of the
   Decision Theory. It rapidly became clear that it would be

impossible to make a valid overall critical analysis in a
short adress. Thus I decided to limit the discussion to
some observations on the concept of probability.

The reader who may already be familiar with the dis-
cussions of the concept of probability in my 1978 Memoir,
*"The so-called Allais Paradox and Rational Decisions under
Uncertainty"* published in the book *"Expected Utility Hypo-
theses and the Allais Paradox"* (Section 29, and Appendix
D, p. 510-514 and 655-663) will observe that the present
Memoir diverges even further from currently accepted ideas.

Two Appendices have been joined to this Memoir : *"Empirical Frequencies and Mathematical Frequencies"* and
"Simulation of Chance by Almost Periodic Functions". These
two Appendices have been submitted to the Conference in
separate communications of which only the essential parts
are presented below.

Appendix A is presented to justify the viewpoints
expressed in Section 2, *"Mathematical Frequency"*, so as
to precise them and to leave no doubt as to their meaning.
Appendix B justifies some of the points of view presented
in Section 10, *"Almost Periodic Functions, Chance and the
X Factor Hypothesis"*. It may shed a new light on the
structure of the time series observed in nature and in
economics.

The present Memoir and its two Appendices undoubtedly
include many propositions which require justifications.
These justifications will be fully given in a forthcoming
book published by Reidel under the title : *"Frequency,
Probability and Chance"*.

This book will include an extensive *Bibliography* on
the most significant contributions of the literature corresponding to the topics covered in the present Memoir.

5. *On the translation from french into english* some comments
are necessary.

Semantic difficulties - whatever the language used -
can shroud full grasp of the essential distinctions which
this Memoir attempts to present.

The reader must be on his guard whatever his mother
tongue, and even more so if he thinks in a third language :
the connotation his subconscious assigns to a term in
translating mentally into his native tongue can engender
the blurring of concepts which this Memoir precisely attempts
to dispel.

Thus, for instance, for the translation of the french
expression *"Coefficient de vraisemblance"* a choice was

necessary between *"likelihood"* and *"plausibility"* for *"vraisemblance"*. To avoid any confusion with its current meaning, likelihood was felt to be avoided and *"vraisemblance"* is accordingly rendered throughout as *"plausibility"*.

6. French text : "coefficient de vraisemblance". See footnote (5).

7. On all these points see Appendix A , *Empirical Frequencies and Mathematical Frequencies*.

8. See Section 10 below.

9. In fact I have studied the decimal parts of the following series : $\sqrt[4]{23}\,\sqrt{n}$ and $n^2\sqrt{2}$ where n represents successive integers : 1, 2, ..., n, ...

10. See *Theorem (T)* of Appendix B, *Simulation of Chance by Almost Periodic Functions*.

11. The term *"quasi-periodic"* is used here to designate a structure which presents the appearance of an almost periodic function.

REFERENCES

The appropriate references to the literature are too numerous (about five hundreds) to be presented here. They will be given in the Bibliography of the forthcoming book *"Frequency, Probability and Chance"* (See note 4 above).

This *Bibliography* is divided into fourteen sections as follows : - 1. The concept of probability and the theories of probability ; - 2. Classical theories, 1650-1914 ; - 3. Frequency theories ; - 4. Subjectivist theories ; - 5. Axiomatic theories and the central limit theorem ; - 6. Statistical analysis ; - 7. Analysis of time series ; - 8. Applications of the probability theory ; - 9. Probability, chance and physical theories ; - 10. Periodic and almost periodic functions ; - 11. Periodicity and chance ; - 12. Simulation of chance and tests of normality, independence, and local randomness ; - 13. Quasi-periodic structures in physical phenomena ; - 14. Quasi-periodic structures in economic and social phenomena.

APPENDIX A

EMPIRICAL FREQUENCIES AND MATHEMATICAL FREQUENCIES
ILLUSTRATION

I thought it necessary to add this Appendix A to clarify the
propositions on the concept of probability set out in the
Memoir, especially those of Sections 1-5.
    In this context the point in question is not to present
new calculations, but simply to show that the calculations
which are *effectively* presented in the books on the *"Probability Theory"* do not take into account any uncertainty,
chance or probability, or any related concept ; that they
are based only on the calculation of mathematical frequencies
in situations *in which all the possible cases occur simultaneously ;* and that they do not in any way correspond to the
semantics used, nor *a fortiori* to the interpretation which
in general inevitably follows.
    To illustrate this proposition while simplifying the
discussion, I will comment on the basic propositions of the
so-called probability theory only in the case of the binomial
distribution. The conclusions drawn from these comments remain
valid in the most complex cases.

A.1. CONCRETE RANDOM PROCEDURE FOR DRAWINGS FROM AN URN. EMPI-
RICAL FREQUENCIES

To illustrate the deterministic character of the computations
of the *"Theory of Probability"*, let us consider the case of
successive *drawings* from an urn with replacement.

A.1.1. *Case of an intrinsic frequency equal to 1/2*

The urn considered contains an equal number of white and black
balls. A series of n drawings is performed with replacement
of each ball drawn. The ratio of white balls to the total
number of balls is :

$$f = 1/2 \qquad\qquad\qquad (1)$$

In the process considered, intrinsic frequency (Section 3
above) is equal to f.

There is *an equal a priori possibility of drawing a white or a black ball before each drawing*. This process characterises *"pure chance"*.

A.1.2. *Representation of a trajectory of a series of n drawings with replacement*

A player wins + 1 if a white ball is drawn and 0 when a black ball appears. For the considered series of n drawings, the number of drawings is plotted against the abscissa, and the quantity :

$$u_n = 2 X_n - n \qquad (2)$$

with

$$X_n = x_1 + \cdots + x_k + \cdots + x_n \qquad (3)$$

against the ordinate. We take x_k = + 1 or 0 according to the ball drawn, white or black. If we draw m white balls over n drawings we have

$$X_n = m \qquad (4)$$

The points M_1, M_2, ..., M_n corresponding to the ordinates u_1, u_2, ..., u_n on *Graph 1* represent the trajectory T corresponding to a series of n drawings. The frequency of appearance of m white balls on this trajectory is designated as f_n.

There were 2^n trajectories *a priori equally possible* before undertaking this series of n drawings. After completion of n drawings a single trajectory was obtained which so was privileged.

If s series S_i of n drawings are then undertaken, the result will be s successive trajectories which can be graphed in the same way, as illustrated by *Graph (1*)*, in which, to simplify, only two trajectories T_i and T_j are shown.

A.2. FREQUENTIAL MATHEMATICAL MODEL. MATHEMATICAL FREQUENCIES

Let us consider now the *frequential mathematical model* corresponding to the random process of Section A.1 . It is represented by *Graph 2* which shows all possible trajectories, all being *equally possible*.

CONCRETE RANDOM PROCESS

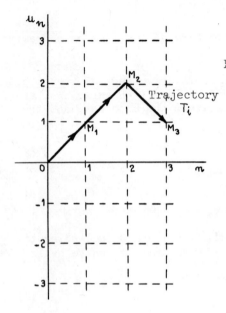

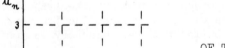

Graph 1

REPRESENTATION OF A TRAJECTORY
CORRESPONDING TO
A SERIES OF n DRAWINGS

Case : f = 1/2

$$X_n = m$$

$$u_n = 2X_n - n = 2m - n$$

$$f_n = \frac{m}{n}$$

$$f_n - f = \frac{1}{2} \frac{u_n}{n}$$

Graph 1[*]

REPRESENTATION
OF THE BUNDLE OF TRAJECTORIES
CORRESPONDING TO δ SERIES S_i
OF n DRAWINGS

Case : f = 1/2

$$f_{i,n} = \frac{m_i}{n}$$

$$f_{j,n} = \frac{m_j}{n}$$

MATHEMATICAL FREQUENTIAL MODEL

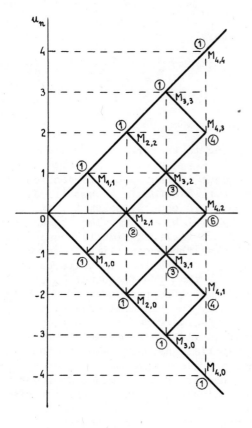

Graph 2

REPRESENTATION
OF ALL FREQUENTIAL
TRAJECTORIES

Case : f = 1/2

$$X_n = m$$

$$u_n = 2X_n - n = 2m - n$$

$M_{n,m}$ = point corresponding
to m white balls
on the trajectory
considered

$$C_n^m = \frac{n!}{m! \, \overline{n-m}!}$$
= number of trajectories
ending at point $M_{n,m}$
(circled number)

$$\sum_{m=0}^{m=n} C_n^m = (1+1)^n = 2^n$$

$$f_{n,m} = \frac{C_n^m}{2^n}$$

A.2.1. *Frequency of the trajectories corresponding to drawing*
        m   white balls in a series of   n   drawings

There are 2^n possible trajectories in all, and among them
C_n^m trajectories end at point $M_{n,m}$, which corresponds to the
presence of m white balls along the considered trajectories
(Graph 2). The corresponding frequency is :

$$f_{n,m} = \frac{C_n^m}{2^n} = \frac{1}{2^n} \frac{n!}{m! \; \overline{n-m}!} \qquad\qquad (5)$$

Naturally for each trajectory we have

$$u_n = 2X_n - n \qquad\qquad (6)$$

with

$$X_n = x_1 + \ldots + x_\ell + \ldots + x_n \qquad\qquad (7)$$

where x_ℓ = + 1 or zero according to the presence of a white
or black ball.
    The calculation which is made is tantamount to conside-
ring that, *as all balls present themselves in a symmetrical
way,* each of the 2^n trajectories is equally possible, and
so is considered simultaneously, which is equivalent to assuming that all the trajectories are *realized simultaneously.*
    It can thus be seen that what the probability theory
refers to as the probability $p_{n,m}$ of drawing m white balls
in n drawings, is nothing other than the frequency $f_{n,m}$
of the trajectories corresponding to the presence of m white
balls, frequency which is given by the binomial expansion.
    *Thus one verifies on this special case that the theory
of the so-called "probability" as a whole rests on deterministic calculations of combinatorial analysis.* Whereas the
concrete process of urns does privilege *only one* trajectory
in a series S_i of drawings, the frequential model *does not
privilege anyone* and considers *simultaneously* all trajectories
equally possible.
    It is *essential* to underline that if the frequency of
white balls along a trajectory varies from one trajectory to
the next, its average for all trajectories corresponds to
the intrinsic frequency f .
    This model can naturally be extended to more and more
complex cases.

A.2.2. *The binomial expansion in the general case*

Graphs similar to the preceding ones can be used when the characteristic frequency f is not equal to 1/2 while remaining equal to the ratio of two integers. This yields :

$$f_{n,m} = \frac{n!}{m! \, \overline{n-m}!} \frac{K_1^m \, K_2^{n-m}}{K^n} \tag{8}$$

in which K_1 and K_2 are the respective numbers of white and black balls with :

$$K = K_1 + K_2 \tag{9}$$

A.2.3. *The multinomial expansion*

Taking an urn containing K_1 , ..., K_i , ..., K_ℓ balls of different types 1,..., i ,..., ℓ with :

$$K_1 + \cdots + K_i + \cdots + K_\ell = K \tag{10}$$

there are K^n trajectories, and the *"probability"* theory is also based on combinatorial analysis using the properties of the multinomial expansion :

$$\left[K_1 + \cdots + K_i + \cdots + K_\ell \right]^n = \sum \frac{n!}{m_1! \ldots m_2! \ldots m_\ell!} K_1^{m_1} \ldots K_i^{m_i} \ldots K_\ell^{m_\ell} = K^n \tag{11}$$

with

$$m_1 + \cdots + m_i + \cdots + m_\ell = n \tag{12}$$

The frequency of presence of m_1 ,..., m_i ,..., m_ℓ balls of types 1,.., i ,.., ℓ on a trajectory is

$$f_n (m_1, \ldots, m_i, \ldots, m_\ell) = \frac{n!}{m_1! \ldots m_i! \ldots m_\ell!} \ell_1^{m_1} \ldots \ell_i^{m_i} \ldots \ell_\ell^{m_\ell} \tag{13}$$

ℓ_i representing the intrinsic frequencies

$$\ell_i = K_i / K \tag{14}$$

It can again be seen immediately that what is commonly referred to as the *"probability"* of drawing m_1 , m_2 ,..., m_ℓ balls of types 1, 2 , ..., ℓ is nothing but the *frequency* of the corresponding trajectories based on the multinomial expansion. It should be underlined here again that although

the frequencies of the different types of balls vary from one
trajectory to the next, their *average values* for all trajectories are exactly equal to $k_1, .., k_i, .., k_g$.

It can be observed *that chance does not enter the matter
in any form whatsoever, and that all possible cases are considered as realised simultaneously. This model is fully deterministic.*

It should again be stressed that *in the case of concrete
drawings from an urn only one* ball comes out at each drawing.
There is thus a *fundamental difference* of nature between the
concrete process of *successive* drawings from an urn and the
corresponding frequential model for which *all* trajectories
are considered at the same time. *In this model no trajectory
is privileged ; all trajectories are considered simultaneously.*

A.2.4. *The case of continuous probability*

In the case of continuous *"probability"* the calculation is
more complex, but it always reduces to calculating frequencies using fully deterministic models. *To the number of trajectories satisfying certain conditions corresponds the measures of some subsets.*

Fundamentally nothing of what has just been said really
needs to be changed : *all "probability" calculations in reality are only calculations of mathematical frequencies excluding any chance in deterministic models in which, instead
of excluding each other, all possibilities are considered as
realized simultaneously.*

A.2.5. *Theorems of total and compound frequencies*

In the multinomial as in the binomial case, the propositions
commonly called *"the principle of total probability"* and
"the principle of compound probability" do result from two
theorems deduced *at once* from the numbering of trajectories,
and which should be called : *the theorems of total frequencies*
and *the theorem of compound frequencies.*

A.3. MEANING OF THE CALCULATIONS OF THE SO-CALLED THEORY OF
PROBABILITY

These few remarks permit to verify that *what is referred to
as "chance" does not intervene in any way in the so-called
theory of probability, for which all the calculations are
fundamentally based on totally deterministic models.* Mathe-

matics can only be developed in the field of certainty.

All *"probability"* calculations boil down to making a count of the number of configurations with certain characteristics by application of combinatorial analysis. *These are only deterministic calculations of frequencies, and nothing more,* for situations in which all the possibilities are *simultaneously realized,* as shown in the chart on *Graph 2* above.

These calculations *cannot, by themselves, teach anything about reality. Their applicability to reality can only derive from a postulate.*

A.4. RANDOM PROCESSES AND DETERMINISTIC FREQUENCY MODELS

The fundamental difference of nature between random processes and the corresponding frequential deterministic models is illustrated in *Graphs 1 and 1*[*] representing the random process and *Graph 2* representing the associated frequential deterministic model.

To avoid any confusion, it is preferable to use the term *random variable* to designate the variable corresponding to a series of successive drawings, such as the process examined in Section A.1 above, to which the variable x_k of this Section corresponds, and to use the term *"frequential variable"* to designate a variable corresponding to a model in which all possible trajectories occur at the same time, such as the model studied above in Section A.2 above to which the variable x_k of this section corresponds.

Random variables correspond to random processes in which chance effectively arises and frequential variables correspond to the deterministic frequential models which exclude any sort of chance. Random variables represent reality and frequential variables describe theoretical deterministic frequency models.

APPENDIX B

SIMULATION OF CHANCE BY ALMOST PERIODIC FUNCTIONS

The aim of this *Appendix B* is to present briefly some particularly suggestive results and some essential comments on the
simulation of chance by almost periodic functions.

B.1. APPLICATION OF THE CENTRAL LIMIT THEOREM TO THE DISTRI-
BUTIONS OF ALMOST PERIODIC FUNCTIONS

Since de Moivre and Laplace the idea has grown in the literature, and finally taken over, that subject to very general
conditions, the sum of independent random variables is distributed according to the normal law.

    In reality, *the central limit theorem underlying this
theory is completely independent of any consideration of chance and the variables in question are not really random variables but frequential variables* (Appendix A, Section 4, above).
In fact the theorem can be applied to the analysis of the
properties of almost periodic functions.

    Effectively, if the frequencies $f_i = 1/T_i$ are irratio-
nal and if there is no linear relation with integer coefficients between the frequencies, it can be shown under very
general conditions that the sums of sinusoids (which define
an almost periodic function)

$$X_n = \sum_{i=1}^{\ell} x_{in} = \sum_{i=1}^{\ell} a_i \cos\frac{2\pi}{T_i}(n - n_i) \qquad (a_i > 0 \,;\, 1 \leqslant n \leqslant N) \qquad (1)$$

are the more normally distributed the higher the numbers **N**
and **ℓ** are. The considered conditions are Liapounoff's
conditions. They imply in particular that the square of each
amplitude is small compared with the sum of the squares of
all the amplitudes. This proposition corresponds to the Theorem (T) below.

B.2. CLASSICAL FORMULATION OF THE CENTRAL LIMIT THEOREM

The presentation of the central limit theorem is set out as
follows in the literature:

"Set

$$X = x_1 + x_2 + \cdots + x_i + \cdots + x_\ell \qquad (2)$$

be the sum of ℓ independent random variables whose distribution functions may be very different and whose averages and standard deviations are m_1 , m_2 , $\ldots$, m_ℓ and σ_1 , σ_2 , $\ldots$, σ_ℓ .
Let

$$m = m_1 + m_2 + \cdots + m_\ell \qquad (3)$$

$$\sigma^2 = \sigma_1^2 + \sigma_2^2 + \cdots + \sigma_\ell^2 \qquad (4)$$

Under very general conditions relating to the distributions of x_i , we have

$$\lim_{\ell \to \infty} P = \text{Probability}\left[\frac{X - m}{\sigma} \leqslant u\right] = \frac{1}{\sqrt{2\pi}} \int_{-\infty}^{u} e^{-\frac{t^2}{2}} \, dt \qquad (5)$$

which reduces to saying that the distribution of the random variable X approaches more and more closely to the normal distribution as ℓ increases to infinity".

Liapounoff has given a sufficient but not necessary condition for the validity of the central limit theorem. This is as follows :

$$\lim_{\ell \to \infty} \frac{\rho}{\sigma} = 0 \qquad (6)$$

σ being defined by relation (4) and ρ by the condition

$$\rho^3 = \rho_1^3 + \rho_2^3 + \cdots + \rho_\ell^3 \qquad (7)$$

$$\rho_i^3 = E\left(|x_i - m_i|^3\right) \qquad (8)$$

in which E represents the average value. Condition (6) means that each single x_i should, on the average, only give a relatively insignificant contribution to the total X.

B.3. FREQUENTIAL REFORMULATION OF THE CENTRAL LIMIT THEOREM

If we carefully scrutinize what are *effectively* the calculations which are made to demonstrate the central limit theorem, we

realize that their meaning is completely different from that
suggested by the usual formulation of this theorem and its
terminology.

a) The use of the expression *"random variables"* suggests
that the values of variables x_i *stem from a random drawing.*
This is not true, as *all* possible realizations of x_i are
considered *simultaneously.*

b) The proof of the central limit theorem *nowhere* involves the consideration of the concepts of *chance* or *random
choice.*

c) Demonstrations result from the calculation of the
frequencies of configurations which are considered as *simultaneously* realized.

In the proofs presented, these three propositions do not
appear explicitly and they are more or less concealed by the
complexity of calculations in the case of continuous probabilities.

In fact, rather than the wording *"random variables"*, the
expression *"frequential variables"* is the only suitable one,
frequential variables being defined as variables *whose all
values are taken into consideration simultaneously* (Section
A.4 above), and the central limit theorem should then states
as follows :

*If X is the sum of ℓ independent frequential varia-
bles,then, under very general conditions :*

$$\lim_{\ell \to \infty} F = \text{Frequency}\left[\frac{X-m}{\sigma} \leqslant u\right] = \frac{1}{\sqrt{2\pi}} \int_{-\infty}^{u} e^{-\frac{t^2}{2}} dt \qquad (9)$$

The calculation corresponding to the proof of this theorem *requires the assumption* that *all* possible trajectories
(Section A.2 above) are *simultaneously* realized, and the
frequency F is the frequency of these trajectories for
which

$$\frac{X-m}{\sigma} \leqslant u \qquad (10)$$

The distributions considered are deterministic distributions of frequential variables of which *all possible values
are considered simultaneously.*

In the most general case corresponding to the central
limit theorem, *the concept of chance does not enter at all
into consideration ;* all values of *all* variables are conside-

red as occuring *simultaneously,* and one considers nothing else than the frequency of configurations which satisfy condition (10). *In fact this is a fully deterministic calculation of combinatorial analysis.*

B.4. THEOREM (T)

By applying the central limit theorem for frequencies the following *Theorem (T)* can be proved.

HYPOTHESES

$$X_n = \sum_{i=1}^{\ell} x_{in} = \sum_{i=1}^{\ell} a_i \cos \frac{2\pi}{T_i} (n - n_i)$$

$$a_i > 0 \qquad 1 \leqslant n \leqslant N \qquad 1 \leqslant i \leqslant \ell \tag{11}$$

$$m_x = \text{ average of } X_n \qquad \sigma_x^2 = \text{ variance of } X_n$$

$$f_i = 1/T_i = \text{ irrational number} \tag{12}$$

- there exists no linear relation $\sum_i \frac{\alpha_i}{T_i} = \lambda$ with integer coefficients α_i, λ $\tag{13}$

$$\lim_{\ell \to \infty} \left[\sqrt[3]{\Sigma a_i^3} \Big/ \sqrt[2]{\Sigma a_i^2} \right] = 0 \tag{14}$$

THEOREM (T)

$$\lim_{\ell \to \infty} \left[\lim_{N \to \infty} F_n = \text{Frequency} \left[\frac{X_n - m_x}{\sigma_x} \leqslant u \right] \right] = \frac{1}{\sqrt{2\pi}} \int_{-\infty}^{u} e^{-\frac{t^2}{2}} dt \tag{15}$$

B.5. LEMMAS

A certain number of *Lemmas* will be established for this purpose.

LEMMA I

The values of t/T being assumed to be uniformly distributed, the frequency density f(x) of the values of

$$x = a \cos \frac{2\pi}{T} (t - t_0) \qquad -\frac{T}{2} \leqslant t - t_0 \leqslant \frac{T}{2} \tag{16}$$

is

$$f(x) = \frac{1}{\pi \sqrt{a^2 - x^2}} \qquad\qquad -a \leqslant x \leqslant a \qquad\qquad (17)$$

Figure 1

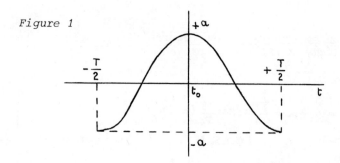

Consider the values of x in the interval $-T/2 < t - t_o < T/2$. In the interval $-T/2 \leqslant t - t_o \leqslant 0$ the density $f(x)$ is defined by the condition

$$f(x)\,dx = 2\,dt/T \qquad -a \leqslant x \leqslant a \qquad -T/2 \leqslant t - t_o \leqslant 0 \qquad (18)$$

This relation defines the *correspondance* between x and t securing the equality of the measures of sub-sets of *equally possible* cases. To two equal intervals on the axis of t correspond two sub-sets of equally possible values of x . From (18) we have

$$f(x) = \frac{2}{T} \frac{1}{dx/dt} = \frac{1}{-\pi a \sin\left[2\pi(t - t_o)/T\right]} = \frac{1}{\pi \sqrt{a^2 - x^2}} \qquad (19)$$

As the $x(t)$ curve is symmetrical with respect to $t = t_o$, the expression (17) effectively represents the frequency density over the whole interval $-T/2 \leqslant t - t_o \leqslant T/2$. We have

$$F(x) = \int_x^a f(x)\,dx = \frac{1}{2} - \frac{1}{\pi} \arcsin \frac{x}{a} \qquad (-a \leqslant x \leqslant a) \qquad (20)$$

with

$$F(-a) = 1 \qquad\qquad\qquad F(a) = 0 \qquad\qquad (21)$$

The curves of $f(x)$ and $F(x)$ are as below :

Figures 2

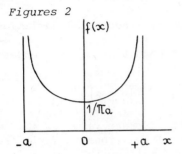
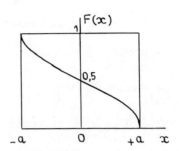

LEMMA II

We have

$$m = \int_{-a}^{+a} x \, f(x) \, dx = 0 \tag{22}$$

$$\sigma^2 = \int_{-a}^{+a} x^2 f(x) \, dx = a^2/2 \tag{23}$$

$$\rho^3 = \int_{-a}^{+a} |x^3| \, f(x) \, dx = 4 \, a^3/3\pi \tag{24}$$

LEMMA III

When N increases to infinity, the frequency density $f(x_i)$ of

$$x_i = a_i \cos \frac{2\pi}{T_i} (n - n_i) \qquad\qquad 1 \leqslant n \leqslant N \tag{25}$$

in which n takes the successive integer values 1, 2, ..., N, tends to

$$f(x_i) \underset{\lim N \to \infty}{=} \frac{1}{\pi} \frac{1}{\sqrt{a_i^2 - x_i^2}} \tag{26}$$

As $1/T_i$ is assumed to be irrational, all the values of x_i appear with the same frequency when N increases to infinity as in the case of the continuous function $x(t)$ defined by relation (16) above. Hence according to LEMMA I we have (26).

LEMMA IV

The frequency variables x_{in} are independent.

   Condition of independence of frequential variables

a - The necessary and sufficient condition of independence
of variables u , v , ..., w is

$$E\left[e^{it(u+v+\cdots+w)}\right] = E\left[e^{itu}\right] E\left[e^{itv}\right] \dots E\left[e^{itw}\right] \tag{27}$$

the symbol $E\left[y\right]$ representing the average value of y .
   If we develop the exponential functions in Taylor's
series, it can be seen that the condition (27) is equivalent
to the conditions

$$E\left[u^p v^q \dots w^t\right] = E\left[u^p\right] E\left[v^q\right] \dots E\left[w^t\right] \tag{28}$$

p , q , ..., t taking all possible integer values, or
zero values.

   Conditions of absence of asymptotic correlation of x_{in}
   and x_{jn}

b - To simplify the discussion of *the implications of the
conditions of asymptotic independence of the* x_{in} consider
first the case p = 1 q = 1, the other exponents t being
equal to zero. Then equation (28) represents *the condition
of absence of asymptotic correlation*:

$$\lim_{N \to \infty} E\left[x_{in} \, x_{jn}\right] = 0 \tag{29}$$

We have

$$E\left[x_{in} \, x_{jn}\right] = \frac{a_i a_j}{N} \sum_{n=1}^{N} \cos \frac{2\pi}{T_i} (n - n_i) \cos \frac{2\pi}{T_j} (n - n_j) \tag{30}$$

$$1 \leqslant n \leqslant N$$

and

$$2 \cos \frac{2\pi}{T_i} (n - n_i) \cos \frac{2\pi}{T_j} (n - n_j)$$

$$= \cos\left[2\pi\left(\frac{1}{T_i} + \frac{1}{T_j}\right)n - 2\pi\left(\frac{n_i}{T_i} + \frac{n_j}{T_j}\right)\right] + \cos\left[2\pi\left(\frac{1}{T_i} - \frac{1}{T_j}\right)n - 2\pi\left(\frac{n_i}{T_i} - \frac{n_j}{T_j}\right)\right] \tag{31}$$

It is known that

$$\cos(a+h) + \cos(a+2h) + \ldots + \cos(a+Nh)$$

$$= \frac{\cos\left(a+\frac{Nh}{2}\right)\sin\left(N+1\right)\frac{h}{2}}{\sin\frac{h}{2}} - \cos a \tag{32}$$

If the sums and differences of frequencies are neither nil or equal to positive or negative integers we have

$$\sin\frac{h}{2} = \sin\pi\left(\frac{1}{T_i} \pm \frac{1}{T_j}\right) \neq 0 \tag{33}$$

Thus from (30), (31) and (32), we deduce condition (29) according to which there is no asymptotic correlation between x_{in} and x_{jn}.

Condition of asymptotic independence of x_{in} and x_{jn}

c - Consider now the case where p and q have any integer values with $l = 0$. We have

$$E\left[x_{in}^{p}\, x_{jn}^{q}\right] = a_i^{p}\, a_j^{q}\, E\left[\left(\cos\frac{2\pi}{T_i}\left(n-n_i\right)\right)^{p}\left(\cos\frac{2\pi}{T_j}\left(n-n_j\right)\right)^{q}\right] \tag{34}$$

$$E\left[x_{in}^{p}\right] = a_i^{p}\, E\left[\left(\cos\frac{2\pi}{T_i}\left(n-n_i\right)\right)^{p}\right] \tag{35}$$

$$E\left[x_{jn}^{q}\right] = a_j^{q}\, E\left[\left(\cos\frac{2\pi}{T_j}\left(n-n_j\right)\right)^{q}\right] \tag{36}$$

For p *even* we have

$$\cos^{p}\alpha = \frac{1}{2^{p-1}}\left\{\cos p\alpha + p\cos(p-2)\alpha + \frac{p(p-1)}{2!}\cos(p-4)\alpha\right.$$

$$\left. + \ldots + \frac{1}{2}\frac{p!}{\left(\frac{p}{2}\right)!\left(\frac{p}{2}\right)!}\right\} \tag{37}$$

and for p *uneven*

$$\cos^{p}\alpha = \frac{1}{2^{p-1}}\left\{\cos p\alpha + p\cos(p-2)\alpha + \frac{p(p-1)}{2!}\cos(p-4)\alpha\right.$$

$$\left. + \ldots + \frac{p!}{\left(\frac{p-1}{2}\right)!\left(\frac{p-1}{2}\right)!}\cos\alpha\right\} \tag{38}$$

According to (37) and (38) the calculation of the three quantities (34), (35) and (36) is *similar* to the calculation of expression (29). For all the sums of cosinus we have thus in the case of (35) or (36)

$$\sin k/2 = \sin k\pi/T_i \tag{39}$$

where k is integer, and in the case of (34)

$$\sin k/2 = \sin \pi\left[\ell/T_i + m/T_j\right] \tag{40}$$

where ℓ and m are integers. Thus according to the hypotheses (12) and (13) we have for (39) and (40)

$$\sin k/2 \neq 0 \tag{41}$$

Then if *one* of the integers p and q is *uneven*, it results from the relations similar to (30), (31) and (32), and from relations (37), (38) and (41) that

$$\lim_{N\to\infty} E\left[x_{in}^{p}\, x_{jn}^{q}\right] = 0 \qquad\qquad \lim_{N\to\infty} E\left[x_{in}^{p}\right] E\left[x_{jn}^{q}\right] = 0 \tag{42}$$

If p and q are *both even* we have

$$\lim_{N\to\infty} E\left[x_{in}^{p}\, x_{jn}^{q}\right] = \left[\frac{1}{2^{p}}\, \frac{p!}{\left(\frac{p}{2}\right)!\left(\frac{p}{2}\right)!}\, a_i^{p}\right]\left[\frac{1}{2^{q}}\, \frac{q!}{\left(\frac{q}{2}\right)!\left(\frac{q}{2}\right)!}\, a_j^{q}\right] \tag{43}$$

$$\lim_{N\to\infty} E\left[x_{in}^{p}\right] = \frac{1}{2^{p}}\, \frac{p!}{\left(\frac{p}{2}\right)!\left(\frac{p}{2}\right)!}\, a_i^{p} \qquad \lim_{N\to\infty} E\left[x_{jn}^{q}\right] = \frac{1}{2^{q}}\, \frac{q!}{\left(\frac{q}{2}\right)!\left(\frac{q}{2}\right)!}\, a_j^{q} \tag{44}$$

Thus under the hypothesis (13) the conditions (28) are asymptotically effectively satisfied.

General case

d – In the general case the same reasoning shows that under hypotheses (12) and (13) we have (conditions 28)

$$E\left[x_{in}^{p}\, x_{jn}^{q} \ldots x_{kn}^{\ell}\right] = E\left[x_{in}^{p}\right] E\left[x_{jn}^{q}\right] \ldots E\left[x_{kn}^{\ell}\right] \tag{45}$$

Finally we see that *if the frequencies* $1/T_i$ *are irrational and if there is no linear relation with integer coefficients between the frequencies*, the frequential variables x_{in} are asymptotically independent.

LEMMA V

When N increases to infinity, the distribution of the X_n tends to the distribution of the

$$X = \sum_{i=1}^{\ell} a_i \cos \frac{2\pi}{T_i}(t - n_i) \qquad -\frac{T_i}{2} \leqslant t - n_i \leqslant \frac{T_i}{2} \qquad (46)$$

This proposition flows directly from *Lemma III*.

LEMMA VI

Condition (14) entails the validity of Liapounoff's condition (Section B.2)

$$\lim_{\ell \to \infty} \frac{\rho}{\sigma} = 0 \qquad (47)$$

When N tends to infinity we have, according to *Lemmas II, III and IV* for asymptotic values σ_x^* and ρ_x^* of σ_x and ρ_x

$$\sigma_x^{*2} = \sum_i \sigma_i^2 = \frac{1}{2} \sum_i a_i^2 \qquad (48)$$

$$\rho_x^{*3} = \sum_i \rho_i^3 = \frac{4}{3\pi} \sum_i a_i^3 \qquad (49)$$

and consequently

$$\mathcal{L} = \rho_x^*/\sigma_x^* = \delta \sqrt[3]{\Sigma a_i^3} / \sqrt[2]{\Sigma a_i^2} \qquad \delta = 2^{7/6}/\sqrt[3]{3\pi} = 1,0628.. \quad (50)$$

Thus condition (14) implies condition (47).

B.6. PROOF OF THE CENTRAL LIMIT THEOREM FOR X_n

It results : – from *Lemma III* that the frequency densities of variables x_i are defined by relation (26) ; – from *Lemma IV* that these variables are effectively independent ; – from *Lemma V* that the distribution of the X_n is identical with that of the X when N increases to infinity, and especially that m_x and σ_x tend respectively to

$$m_x^* = 0 \qquad \sigma_x^* = \sqrt{\sum_i a_i^2 / 2} \qquad (51)$$

- and from *Lemma VI* that condition (14) entails the validity of Liapounoff's condition (47).

Consequently, *Theorem (T) of Section B.4 is only a consequence of the central limit theorem of Section B.3 above associated with Liapounoff's condition.*

Thus Theorem T is an illustration of the fact that *the central limit theorem can be applied to fully deterministic phenomena.*

It should be underlined that the *Theorem (T)* does not imply that the standard deviation σ of X_n remains finite when the number ℓ of sinusoids increases to infinity.

The proof of *Theorem (T)* and the conditions it implies call for the following comments.

B.7. THE AUTO-CORRELATION OF THE $x_{i,n}$

It should first be underlined that the validity of the central limit theorem for a time series X_n *is not subordinated* to the condition of the independance of two *successive* values of the variables x_{in}.

The proof of the central limit theorem considers *frequency variables* of which *all* equally possible values are considered simultaneously *(Section B.3 above). The order in which they are written does not matter.* The *only* condition is that for an infinite value of N, the frequency of their occurence in this order should correspond to that of the distribution function which characterises them. Indeed the distributions of the values of x_{in} and X_n are considered *independently of their succession order.*

From this viewpoint, the only essential condition to which the validity of the central limit theorem is subordinated is that the frequency variables considered be *independent,* namely, that condition (28) of *Lemma IV* be effectively met. It is this condition which allows for the proposition that the characteristic function of X_n is equal to the product of the characteristic functions of the x_{in} (relation 27 above).

As a result, the central limit theorem is applicable when the series of the x_{in} are auto-correlated, if the conditions corresponding to *Lemmas III, IV, V and VI* are met, the conditions of *Lemmas III and IV* being essential in this regard.

B.8. LIAPOUNOFF'S COEFFICIENT

Liapounoff's condition (47), which in fact is *a sufficient but not necessary condition, implies that the amplitudes* a_i

*do not differ too much from each other, but at all event,
this is a general condition of the central limit theorem.*

For a given value of σ_x^* and according to (48) and (49),
the minimum value of the ratio ρ_x^*/σ_x^* is attained when all
the a_i have the same value. Its maximum is reached when all
the a_i are nil except one. According to (50), we then have
whatever the a_i

$$\delta/\sqrt[6]{\ell} \leqslant \mathcal{L} = \rho_x^*/\sigma_x^* \leqslant \delta \qquad\qquad \delta = 2^{7/6}/\sqrt[3]{3\pi} = 1,0628\ldots \quad (52)$$

Let

$$a_i = (1+\alpha_i)a \qquad\qquad a = \sum_i a_i/\ell \qquad\qquad (53)$$

we have

$$\sum_i \alpha_i = 0 \qquad\qquad\qquad\qquad (54)$$

and consequently

$$\mathcal{L}/\delta = \sqrt[3]{\sum_i a_i^3}\Big/\sqrt[2]{\sum_i a_i^2} = \sqrt[3]{\ell + 3\sum_i \alpha_i^2 + \sum_i \alpha_i^3}\Big/\sqrt[2]{\ell + \sum_i \alpha_i^2} \qquad (55)$$

whence

$$\mathcal{L}/\delta = \sqrt[3]{1 + \tfrac{3}{\ell}\sum_i \alpha_i^2 + \tfrac{1}{\ell}\sum_i \alpha_i^3}\Big/\sqrt[6]{\ell}\;\sqrt[2]{1 + \tfrac{1}{\ell}\sum_i \alpha_i^2} \qquad (56)$$

so that

$$\mathcal{L}/\delta \leqslant K/\sqrt[6]{\ell} \qquad\qquad K = \sqrt[3]{1 + 3\sum \alpha_i^2/\ell + \sum \alpha_i^3/\ell} \qquad (57)$$

Thus it is sufficient that the quantity K be bounded
from above for $\mathcal{L}$ to decrease indefinitely with ℓ. This
will be the case if $\sum \alpha_i^2$ and $\sum \alpha_i^3$ rise more slowly than ℓ.
It can also be said that it is sufficient than the mean values
of α_i^2 and α_i^3 be bounded from above.

Given the homogeneity of the expression of Liapounoff's
coefficient, it can always be assumed without loss of generality that the average a of the a_i is equal to one. Liapounoff's condition then implies than no a_i differs greatly from
one.

B.9. POSSIBILITY OF A DETERMINISTIC EXPLANATION OF THE RANDOM
APPEARANCE OF THE TIME SERIES OBSERVED IN NATURE

It results from Theorem (T) that *even if a time series is*

normally distributed, this does not prove that it is necessarily generated by chance, since this distribution can be perfectly well explained by the conjugated action of periodic components.

It is thus established that the deterministic vibrational structure of the universe can produce apparently random effects and that determinism can imitate chance.

We find also that *the analysis of the sums of periodic elements enables all possible circumstances to be illustrated,* from the case of highly auto-correlated series to the case of series *of a limited length* devoid apparently of any auto-correlation, but all having the general characteristic of being approximately normally distributed.

In fact what one generally finds in nature are auto-correlated time series relating to physical, biological and economic phenomena, and *very seldom series of independent terms are observed. In every case the number of terms in a series is finite, and it is rarely high.*

Herman Wold

UTILITY ANALYSIS FROM THE POINT OF VIEW OF
MODEL BUILDING

Professor Ole Hagen kindly asked me to write up my contributions to the discussions from the floor during the conference
week. My comments focussed on the principles of model building
as the general framework for scientific research, scientific
method.

   Utility theory is of old standing as a branch of socio-
economic science. The current principles of scientific model
building in terms of hypothesis specification and hypothesis
testing took shape in the decades 1930-1950, shortly after
R.A. Fisher's bold raise of aspiration levels of statistical
inference in controlled experiments, and as econometrics pion-
eered in the extension to nonexperimental data of his aims at
optimal accuracy in the statistical inference.[1] In consequence, and this is the main point I wish to make, utility analysis as set forth at this conference is not altogether in keeping with the general principles of model building, and is
therefore to some extent confused or obsolete. For illustration I shall take up two cases in point, quoting from Maurice
Allais, namely one statement and one question:
   (i) Cardinal utility exists;
   (ii) How to define chance? A satisfactory definition
        is lacking!
   To repeat what I emphasized during the conference, my
comments on (i)-(ii) do not at all interfere with the tremendous importance of Maurice Allais's substantive contributions
to economic science.[2]

   Speaking broadly, a scientific model involves theoretical knowledge T and empirical knowledge E. To paraphrase, T
is hypothesis specification, is a set of more or less well-
founded theoretical assumptions; E is hypothesis testing, is
a set of empirical observations and tests that shed light on
the real-world relevance of T. The theoretical knowledge T
provides deductive inference on E; conversely, E provides inductive inference on T. In customary symbols,

$$T \overset{\rightarrow}{\underset{\leftarrow}{}} E \qquad\qquad\qquad (1)$$

B. P. Stigum and F. Wenstøp (eds.), Foundations of Utility and Risk Theory with Applications,
87–93.
© 1983 *by D. Reidel Publishing Company.*

In the debate on model building it has been argued by some philosophers that it is impossible to make sharp distinction between theoretical and empirical knowledge; in the realm of human knowledge T and E are so intertwined that they cannot be separated. Against this criticism I argued that to every scientific model belongs a frame of reference that in nontechnical language indicates the scope and purpose of the model; the frame of reference is a mixture of theoretical and empirical knowledge; within the frame of reference, however, it is clear what is theoretical and what is empirical knowledge. Graphically I illustrated the frame of reference by a rectangle around T and E and the matching of T and E by a double arrow for deductive-inductive inference, as follows:[3]

$$\boxed{T \Longleftrightarrow E} \tag{2}$$

For example, in the model for a controlled experiment the frame of reference sets forth the general purpose of the experiment; the model specifies a null hypothesis, say T_0, and within the frame of reference it is perfectly clear what is the theoretical T_0 and what is the empirical outcome of the experiment, say E. Contemporary statistics has general methods for exploring whether or to what extent the empirical outcome E supports the null hypothesis T_0.

As is clear from the above, it is a key feature of scientific method to keep apart T and E, theoretical and empirical knowledge. Hence it is something of a paradox that the evolution of scientific method gives examples of a contrasting fallacy, the fallacy of not keeping apart theoretical and empirical knowledge. A typical case in point is the notion of probability. In the calculus of probabilities that emerged in the late 17th century from the games of chance, the probability p of an event H is defined as the ratio

$$p(H) = \frac{\text{number of cases favourable to H}}{\text{total number of (equally possible) cases}} \tag{3}$$

Letting $f_N(H)$ denote the relative frequency of event H in N realizations of a game of chance, the law of large numbers allows the deductive inference:

$$\plim_{N \to \infty} f_N(H) = p \tag{4}$$

In words, as N increases indefinitely, $f_N(H)$ will almost certainly tend to p. Conversely, the observed relative frequency $f_N(p)$ provides inductive estimation of p:

$$p = \plim f_N(H) . \tag{5}$$

In words, for large N the relative frequency $f_N(H)$ gives a close estimate of p.[4]

Briefly stated, p and f are theoretical and empirical knowledge, and thereby conceptually different; by deduction (3) and induction (4) they are nearly the same for N large,

$$p \approx f_N(H) \tag{6}$$

The definition of probability was subject to a large literature in the 19th century. It was realized that the classical definition (3) in terms of equally possible cases is of limited scope, and many attempts were made to give a more general definition; more precisely, attempts were made to find a definition which at the same time establishes its empirical validity. However, these attempts were in vain because of the fallacy to identify theoretical and empirical knowledge. The Gordian knot was cut by André Kolmogorov (1932) in his general theory of events and probabilities as sets and additive set functions in a probability field.[5] Kolmogorov's theory keeps apart probabilities and frequencies, and provides general proofs of the deductive and inductive inferences (3) and (4).

In the light of Kolmogorov's theory the answer to Allais's question (ii) is that chance is a synonym for probability. For every chance problem the solution takes the form of a set of events and a probability field with probabilities as an additive set function.

Causality joins probability as a much-discussed concept in the philosophy of science, and at bottom of the controversies is the fallacy of not keeping apart theoretical and empirical knowledge. Hume argued that causality cannot be seen; we can only see the before and after sequence of events. This is a subtle way of keeping apart theoretical and empirical knowledge, but in echoing Hume's argument Bertrand Russell (1913) ran into the fallacy at issue, and dramatized the argument by rejecting causality from the scientific vocabulary.[6] Russell's anathema on causality had tremendous impact in philosophy, and in the behavioural and socioeconomic sciences the word causality became taboo for several decades. The natural sciences were less effected; for example, in the design of controlled experiments R.A. Fisher used the terms stimulus-response as equivalent to cause-effect.[1]

The early and mid-1950's brought a comeback of causality in the socioeconomic sciences, by the writings of three largely independent authors.[7] The comeback honoured the principles

of model building, distinction being made on the one hand on
the one hand between cause-effect relations as belonging under the specification of theoretical hypotheses, and on the
other their testing by appropriate compilation and analysis
of empirical observations. In this context I adduced a general two-stage definition of cause-effect relationships:[3]
(i) the relation between stimulus x and response y in a controlled experiment is a special case of cause-effect relationships, say

$$y = f(x) + \varepsilon , \qquad\qquad\qquad\qquad (7)$$

and the outcome of the experiment provides an empirical test
of the causal hypothesis; (ii) If (7) is posed as a theoretical hypothesis in the analysis of nonexperimental data the
investigator may or may not assume that the data under analysis are the outcome of a ficticious controlled experiment
with x as stimulus and y as response variable; if the investigator adopts this assumption (7) is by definition a cause-
effect relation. However, the definition of the cause-effect
relation does not provide or constitute a verification.
Speaking broadly, the empirical testing of a nonexperimental
causal hypothesis is more difficult than in controlled experiments, since y as observed may be influenced by other causal variables than x.

   We are now in a position to return to Allais's statement
(i): Cardinal utility exists. As I see it, this statement is
another fallacy of not keeping apart theoretical and empirical knowledge. Cardinal utility is a theoretical hypothesis,
and it is well supported by empirical measurements in terms
of sure-equivalencies. To regard the measurement by sure-
equivalencies as a proof of the existence of cardinal utility is a fallacy of the same type as trying to give probability a definition that also constitutes its empirical measurement. However, theoretical concepts do not possess real-world
existence - - nobody has seen a theoretical concept, be it a
probability, a cause, or a utility, ordinal or cardinal.

   Vilfredo Pareto's "open cycles of utility" is another
version of the same fallacy.[8] Considering a consumer's choice
between baskets containing three or more commodities, let us
follow the consumer in the consumption space as he changes
the commodity amounts one by one so as to form a cycle in the
space, say A B C ... G H A*, and adjusts the consecutive
amounts so that A is equivalent to B, B is equivalent to C,
..., G is equivalent to H, H is equivalent to A*. Then, accor-

ding as the final A* is or is not equivalent to the initial
A, Pareto says that the integrability condition is or is not
fulfilled. Reviewing Pareto's argument I argued[9], Wold (1944),
that to make the initial choice A the consumer must make a
simultaneous comparison of the baskets A, B, ..., G, H, A*
and they must all be equivalent to the initial A. Thus when
accepting the case of nonintegrability as a meaningful hypothesis Pareto makes the fallacy of not keeping apart theoretical and empirical knowledge. Analytically, the shortcoming
of Pareto's "open cycles" is that he limits the study of the
utility comparisons to the immediate neighbourhood of the
commodity at issue.

In conclusion I wish to refer to the factor analysis of
psychometrics, where the notion of factor as a latent variable
indirectly observed by multiple manifest variables, called
indicators, opened new vistas in substantive analysis, and
brought new problems of statistical estimation. Specific reference is made to the pioneering work of Lee J. Cronbach
(1951) on testing factor models w.r.t. validity and reliability;[10] a factor has validity if its empirical measurement
is in keeping with the hypothesis specification of the model,
and it has reliability if it is stable in the empirical measurement. Cronbach's work is all the more remarkable as it
belongs to the period of formation of the principles of contemporary model building. Validity vs. reliability thus refers to theoretical vs. empirical aspects of a factor, a
variable indirectly observed. At the same time Cronbach's
exposition is influenced by the phenomenological, anti-theo-
retical tendency that adheres psychometrics since its infan-
cy. For example, any theoretical concept -- say a factor --
is not called a concept, but is called a construct. In this
respect there is an apparent but not real fallacy in psychometrics in not keeping apart theoretical and empirical knowledge. Later on when sociology in the 1960's introduced path
models with latent variables as a merger of econometrics
(path models with manifest variables) and psychometrics (modeling with latent variables), the terminological differences
of econometric and psychometric model building have come into
the melting pot of the merger.[11] This is however another story.

NOTES

1. R.A. Fisher, 1935, The Design of Experiments, Edinburgh;
   Oliver & Boyd. A key reference in econometrics: W.C. Hood

& T.C. Koopmans, eds., 1953, Studies in Econometric Method, New York; Wiley.

2. Special reference is made to four of Maurice Allais's major contributions; 1) General theory of economic equilibrium. 2) Capital theory. 3) Theory of utility under uncertainty. 4) Monetary dynamics.

3. H. Wold, 1967, Nonexperimental statistical analysis from the general point of view of scientific method, International Statistical Institute, Sydney session, 28/9-7/9 1967. Reedited for Bulletin of the International Statistical Institute 42 (1) 1969:391-424.
   H. Wold, 1969, Mergers of economics and philosophy of science. A cruise in deep seas and shallow waters, Synthese 20:427:482. Spanish translation in Metodología y Crítica Económica, ed. C.Dagum, Mexico City: Fondo de Cultura Economica.

4. For a recent review and elaboration, see D.V. Lindley,1982, Scoring rules and the inevitability of probability, International Statistical Review 50:1-20.

5. A. Kolmogoroff, 1932, Grundbegriffe der Wahrscheinlichkeitsrechnung, Berlin: Springer.

6. B. Russell, 1913, On the notion of cause, with application to the free-will problem, In: Our Knowledge of the External World, London: Norton,1914.

7. P.F. Lazarsfeld, H. Simon, H. Wold. Early references:
   P.L. Kendall & P.F. Lazarsfeld, 1950, Problems of survey analysis, Pages 133-196 in R.K. Merton & P.L. Lazarsfeld, eds., Continuities in Social Research: Studies in the Scope and Method of 'The American Soldier', Glencoe, Ill.: Free Press.
   H.A. Simon, 1953, Causal ordering and identifiability, Pages 49-74 in [1], Hood & Koopmans.
   H. Wold, 1954, Causality and econometrics, Econometrica 22:162-177.
   Cf. P.F. Lazarsfeld, 1970, A memoir in honor of Professor Wold, Pages 78-103 in T. Dalenius, G. Karlsson & S. Malmquist, eds., Scientists at Work, Festschrift in Honour of Herman Wold, Stockholm: Almqvist & Wiksell. See also two review articles in International Encyclopedia of Statistics, I-II, 1978, eds. W.H. Kruskal & J.M. Tanur, New York: The Free Press: H.A. Simon, Pages 35-41, Causation. J.S. Coleman, Pages 505-507, Lazarsfeld, Paul F.

8. V. Pareto, 1906, Manuale di Economia Politica, French ed.
    1909, Paris: Giard.
9. H. Wold, 1943, A synthesis of pure demand analysis, I,
    Skandinavisk Aktuarietidskrift 26: 85-118. See § 25, The
    integrability condition: 109-112. The argument is reviewed
    on Pages 90 - 93 in: H. Wold in association with L. Juréen,
    1952, Demand Analysis. A Study in Econometrics, Stock-
    holm: Almqvist & Wiksell, 3rd reprint ed. 1982, Westport,
    Connecticut: Greenwood Press.
10. L.J. Cronbach, 1951, Coefficient Alpha and the internal
    structure of tests, Psychometrika 16; 297-334.
11. K.G. Jöreskog & H. Wold, eds., 1982, Systems under In-
    direct Observation. Causality x Structure x Prediction,
    I-II, Amsterdam: North-Holland Publ. See also: H. Wold,
    1982, Comments (on four conference papers) with a brie-
    fing of PLS soft modeling, Forthcoming in Applied Time
    Series Analysis of Economic Data, published by The Ameri-
    can Statistical Association.

Nils-Eric Sahlin

ON SECOND ORDER PROBABILITIES AND THE NOTION OF
EPISTEMIC RISK

0.

Second or higher order probabilities have commonly been viewed
with scepticism by those working within the realm of probability and decision theory. The aim of the present note is to show
how the notion of second order probabilities can add to our
understanding of judgmental and decision processes and how the
traditional framework of Bayesian decision theory can be extended in a fruitful way by taking such entities into account.
Section one consists of a brief account of arguments put forth
against higher order probabilities as well as of counterargu-
ments. In order to provide an example of the applicability of
second order probabilities a decision theory encompassing such
probabilities will be presented in section two. In section
three I will try to emphasize the value of second order probabilities for a deeper and more complete understanding of the
notion of risk.

1.

An early attempt to find a conclusive and definite argument
showing the meaninglessness of assigning a degree of uncertainty to an uncertainty can be found in Hume's A Treatise of
Human Nature. The idea behind Hume's argument is that uncertainty about uncertainties will lead to a hierarchy of such
uncertainties and that the product of the resulting series of
probabilities will converge to zero. It seems unnecessary to
mention that there exist series of products which do not converge to zero. According to Lehrer, Hume seems to have discovered the defect in his argument here since he abandoned it.
However, it is interesting to note that arguments and scepticism more recently put forth against the validity of higher
order uncertainties are closely related to Hume's thoughts on
the subject. Let us consider two of them.[1]
      Hume toyed with the idea that one way of eliminating high-
er order uncertainties is by multiplying them out, i.e. by us-

B. P. Stigum and F. Wenstøp (eds.), Foundations of Utility and Risk Theory with Applications,
95–104.
© 1983 by D. Reidel Publishing Company.

ing higher order probabilities as weights. However, he seems
not to have taken into consideration the fact that for such a
process to be effective the entire second order distribution
has to be employed. What is known today as Savage's (or
Woodbury's) argument against higher order probabilities is
simply an improvement on Hume's basic ideas on this point: If
the event probability (first order probability) appears uncertain then one should employ a weighted average with second order probabilities as weights to obtain a new point estimate,
where the latter estimate then expresses all uncertainty of
relevance in the situation. Against this view one could argue
that the shape of the second order probability distribution
may be of importance. The second order distribution can, for
example, be skewed or bimodal and in such cases the second
order uncertainties seem to play an important role in the
decision making. Thus a mean does not appear as an obviously
adequate solution since it does not preserve all relevant information expressed by the second order distribution. It is
also worth noting that some researchers have taken Savage's
argument as an argument to a certain extent for the introduction of higher order probabilities. If one obtains, for
example, incoherent first order probability estimates one
can by way of eliciting second (or higher) order probability
estimates obtain a coherent set of first order estimates.
Thus, as a way of reconciling incoherent first order probability estimates, higher order probabilities appear advan-
tageous.[2]
      Another frequent argument, also in compliance with Hume's
original idea, is that second order uncertainties or probabilities lead to third order uncertainties or probabilities,
and so on ad infinitum, so that an infinite regress thwarts
any attempt to draw practical conclusions from higher order
probability assessments. To meet this argument one can take
a pragmatic standpoint and observe that the utility of using
successively higher orders of probability would diminish rapidly. In most situations very little would be gained by considering higher than second order probabilities. It should also be
noted that such a hierarchy of probabilities assumes that the
same probability interpretation be given to each level in the
infinite regress. On the other hand, if one starts off with
objective probabilities, as for example in some fields of
physics, it appears reasonable to ask oneself how certain,
likely, probable or reliable one considers such probabilities
to be. Is there really any need then to climb further up the
ladder? A different approach, both interesting and illumina-

ting, is to interpret first order (viz. event) probabilities as ordinary subjective probabilities, i.e. as probabilities qua basis for action, and second order probabilities as epistemic probabilities, i.e. as measures of the quality of knowledge. If the question of interpretation is carefully dealt with here, there is hardly any need to climb more than a few rungs up the ladder. Thus, it is argued that if each level in the hierarchy be given an interpretation different from those given to previous levels, the number of probability interpretations which seem reasonable will effectively stop any unnecessary climbing.

It can also be argued that none of the standard methods for eliciting probability estimates are applicable. By a standard method I mean an operational method making use of gambles or some similar procedure, such as Ramsey and de Finetti employ. The problem is that in the realm of second order estimates we are dealing with "unverifiable" events, i.e. we do not know, and will never know, which first order estimate is the "true" one. However, there seems to be no particular disadvantage in using direct probability assessments on the second order level. The results of a series of experiment carried out together with Robert Goldsmith can be viewed as supporting this assumption.[3]

2.

There are several examples of decision situations in which one's knowledge is rather limited and where it seems to be almost impossible to give a unique primary probability estimate for a given state of nature. For example, what is the probability that if one takes the night train to Oslo one will be able to catch the last bus to be in time for the opening of this conference? I, for one, do not know much about the bus system in Oslo. I can well believe that the probability of being there in time can be .2 or .7, or any value in between. However, in a situation like this, one also seems to be able to discriminate between the reliabilities of the different possible first order probability estimates, i.e. one assigns somewhat greater second order probability to some of these estimates than to others. For example, the probability that the primary probability is .6 might be regarded as somewhat greater than that it is .2. In the general case this type of reasoning leads to the introduction of a second order probability measure. Our question is how this measure can be built into the Bayesian framework of decision theory. Here is one

possible theory. The theory has been developed together with
Peter Gärdenfors.[4]

The theory is based on the assumption that there exists
a finite set of actions, {a1,...,an}, and a set of states of
nature (or states, for brevity), {s1,...,sn}. The outcome of
choosing ai, if the true state of nature is sj, will be denoted oij. It will further be assumed that there exists a utility
function u(.) mirroring the agent's valuation of possible outcomes. However, the ordinary Bayesian assumption that the
agent's state of belief concerning which state is the true
one can be represented by a unique probability measure is
relaxed. The theory assumes that the agent's knowledge and
beliefs about the relevant states can be represented by a class
Π of probability measures, the set of all epistemically possible measures, i.e. those measures which do not contradict the
knowledge which the agent possesses. According to this theory
each state of nature will then be associated with a set of
possible values P(si), where P(.)$\epsilon\Pi$. Here a second order probability measure $\rho(.)$, a measure of epistemic reliability, is
introduced, defined over the set Π of epistemically possible
probability measures. Even though several probability distributions are considered to be epistemically possible some of
them are more reliable than others. some distributions are,
for example, backed up by more information than others. This
measure of epistemic reliability thus reflects how complete
or adequate the knowledge is assessed to be upon which one's
first order probability is based.

The theory has an ordered set of rules for reaching a
decision, i.e. picking one of the action alternatives available. Firstly, the set Π is restricted to a set Π/ρ_0 of probability measures for which the level of epistemic reliability is deemed satisfactory, i.e. a subset Π/ρ_0 of the set Π is
selected such that for all $P\epsilon\Pi/\rho_0$, $\rho(P){\geq}\rho_0$. Secondly, the expected utility of each alternative ai and of each distribu-
tion P in Π/ρ_0 is computed and the minimal expected utility
of each alternative is determined. Finally the action alternative with the largest minimal expected utility is selected.

In order to see how this abstract machinery works let us
examine how the theory provides an intuitively plausible interpretation of Ellsberg's paradox. Ellsberg asks us to consider
an urn known to contain 30 red balls and 60 black balls and
yellow balls, the latter in an unknown proportion. A single
ball is to be drawn from the urn. The paradox consists of two
situations of this type. In the first situation the choice is
between a1; receiving $100 if a red ball, $0 if a black, and

$0 if a yellow ball is drawn, and a2; receiving $0 if a red
ball, $100 if a black, and $0 if a yellow ball is drawn. The
second situation is identical to the first one with the exception that the yellow ball now gives a prize of $100. Let us
denote the action alternatives in the latter case a3 and a4.
Ellsberg observes that most persons he tested preferred a1 to
a2 and a4 to a3 and that this behaviour violates Savage's sure
thing principle.[5]

Applying the present decision theory one observes that
the important task is to determine the set Π/ρ_0 from Π. The
set Π of all epistemically possible distributions should be
the same in the two situations and it seems reasonable to
assume that Π is the class of distributions $(1/3, x, 2/3-x)$,
where x varies from 0 to 2/3.

Let us assume that the agent puts $\Pi/\rho_0 = \Pi$ by choosing an
extremely low ρ_0. In this case the theory recommends choosing
a1 to a2 and a4 to a3, which accords with Ellsberg's findings.
However, if the agent chooses another level of desired reliability, the recommended preference ranking may be different.
For example, if only the distribution $(1/3, 1/3, 1/3)$ is included in Π/ρ_0, the agent would be advised not to violate
Savage's sure thing principle.

3.

In the previous section we assumed that the agent chooses a
satisfactory level of epistemic reliability and thus determines the set Π/ρ_0 upon which the decision is to be based. In
this section I will try to show how this choice is reflective
of an agent's attitude towards one form of risk taking which
will here be called epistemic risk, and contrast it with the
more familiar notion of outcome risk. This new concept, it will
be seen, provides a deeper understanding of the entire notion
of risk.

I will make a distinction between perceived outcome risk
and preferred outcome risk. The notion of perceived risk is
the same as the concept of risk employed within risk-percep-
tion theories. Within these theories one tries to find an
appropriate ordering of the decision situations or action
alternatives with regard to riskiness but also an adequate
measure of an action's or decision situation's riskiness.
Some such theories have, for example, provided arguments for
using variance or semivariance as reasonable measures of risk,
others have suggested that a linear combination of variance
and expected value is an intelligible measure of perceived

outcome risk. In a somewhat simplified way such measures can
be said to be all aimed at pinpointing how "likely" one considers it to be that "bad" or "negative" outcomes, o_{ij}, will
result. A measure of perceived outcome risk can thus be viewed
as expressing all information of relevance to how risky an
agent feels an action to be, based purely on consideration of
the possible outcomes and the relevant probability estimates.
Thus, since the outcomes, o_{ij}, here play such a vital role,
the term outcome risk appears reasonable.

In what follows it is not necessary to use any specific
measure of perceived outcome risk and we thus do not need to
commit ourselves to one specific theory. It may be worth noting, however, that theories of perceived risk have to be
generalized in order to be applicable in connection with a
decision theory making use of second order probabilities. Here
it appears meaningful to consider, along the lines of the
decision theory outlined above, the maximal perceived outcome
risk with respect to the set of all epistemically possible
distributions.

When one has a measure of perceived outcome risk or even
simply the possibility of qualitatively ordering the action
alternatives with regard to outcome riskiness, the basis for
a discussion of risk preference has been established. Does
an agent prefer action alternatives with high outcome risk
to those with low outcome risk, vice versa, or is there some
other conceivable ordering of the alternatives? For example,
two agents may well agree upon the outcome riskiness of a
set of alternatives but still order them differently in terms
of risk preference. The observation that some people buy
lottery tickets and others don't provides informal support
for the assumption that people differ in their risk preferences.[6]

There is another aspect of risk not contained by these
concepts. If in the bus example all possible probability
values between .2 and .7 are taken into account or if before
making any definite decision one considers all 61 possible
compositions of the urn in the Ellsberg example, one is
playing it safe. However, if one only considers the possible
probability value .5 or the distribution (1/3,1/3,1/3), one
is taking a risk, not an outcome risk but an epistemic risk.
The term epistemic risk is chosen since we are interested
here in risk taking on the level of knowledge.

The concept of epistemic risk can in the same way as for
outcome risk be split up into two parts; perceived epistemic
risk and preferred epistemic risk.

The perceived epistemic risk concerns the restriction of the set of all epistemically possible probability measures, Π, to the set of reasonable reliable measures, Π/ρ_0. An agent who took all epistemically possible measures into consideration before making any decision would feel that he or she was taking no epistemic risk at all. Since one cannot play it safer than such an agent does, taking all one knows into account gives no room for further considerations. If instead all distributions with an epistemic reliability of less than ρ_0 are discarded the agent would perceive a degree of risk in any case. The following measure, based on the concept of epistemic reliability, is reflective of how great this perceived risk is:[7]

(i) $\underline{R}(\rho_0) = 1 - \rho(\Pi/\rho_0)/\rho(\Pi)$,

where $\rho(\Pi)$ is equal to $\underset{P\epsilon\Pi}{\Sigma\rho(P)}$ and similar for $\rho(\Pi/\rho_0)$.

It should be noted that this measure is rather naive as it stands since it does not take account of all personal idiosyncrasies and it thus seems necessary that a person-specific parameter be added. However, it serves well for our purposes since it accounts in a general way for risk perception when the set Π is restricted. By discarding some of the epistemically possible measures one is certainly taking a risk, and as the epistemic reliability of those measures discarded increases, the epistemic risk one takes increases as well.

In the same way as two agents can perceive the same outcome risk but have entirely different outcome risk preferences, they can be in identical epistemic situations, here identified by Π and $\rho(.)$, and thus according to (i) have the same view of perceived epistemic risk and yet have entirely different epistemic risk preferences. If, for example, one of the agents chooses a higher ρ_0-level than the other, then we know that his or her epsitemic risk preferences are different (he or she prefers a higher level of epistemic risk).

In the light of the Ellsberg example, this becomes quite clear. Assume that persons A and B are in identical epistemic states. Both consider the set of epistemically possible distributions Π to be the class of distributions $(1/3,x,2/3-x)$, where x varies from 0 to 2/3, and both assign the same epistemic reliability to each of the distributions in Π, i.e. $\rho A(.)=\rho B(.)$, person A's measure of epsitemic reliability being identical to person B's. Consequently person A and B will have the same degree of epsitemic risk taking perception

when restricting the set Π to a subset Π/ρ_0. With this in mind,
let us assume that person A prefers a lower degree of epistemic
risk than person B. Furthermore, person A prefers minimal epistemic risk while B prefers taking maximal epistemic risk. In
this case person A would base his or her decision on the set
Π, i.e. he or she whould take $\Pi/\rho_0=\Pi$ by minimizing the epistemic risk and would thus choose a low ρ_0-level. Person B, on
the other hand, would select a narrow subset of Π as a basis
for action. If the distribution $(1/3,1/3,1/3)$ has been assigned
the highest degree of epsitemic reliability it is likely that
only this distribution will be chosen, i.e. if the epistemic
risk preferred is high, then a high ρ_0-level will be selected.
This type of reasoning also accords with Ellsberg's findings.
It is the epistemic-risk-aversive subject who violates Savage's
sure thing principle!

Since the argument presented shows how the choice of ρ_0-
level is reflective of an agent's epsitemic risk preferences
the aim of this note has been achieved. However, before closing
this section, I would like to point out some links between what
has been said and the experimental findings concerning higher
order probabilities mentioned earlier. In the experiments we
found that in choosing among several equal-valued prospects,
agents were able to consider their epsitemic reliabilty assignments in a consistent and coherent way. For example, two distinct and consistent preference patterns for epistemic reliability were observed. The results can also be viewed in the
light of the present discussion of epistemic risk. The results
support the hypothesis that people have different epistemic
risk preferences and that these preferences follow a fairly
consistent pattern.

The results also raise some new questions. Is there any
interesting relation to be found between, for example, perceived outcome risk and preferred epistemic risk or between
perceived epistemic risk and preferred outcome risk? I will
not be able, unfortunately, to pursue these and related questions within the limits of the present note.

4.

It has been argued that arguments directed against second
order probabilities can be dealt with and that such probabilities provide us with the possibility of generalizing the traditional Bayesian decision model in a fruitful way. Introducing such higher order beliefs into our system of beliefs
allows us to make a distinction between epistemic risk and

outcome risk, i.e. between risk with respect to the amount and quality of information and knowledge, on one hand, and the valuation of outcomes and probabilities, on the other hand. It has likewise been argued that the notion of epistemic risk provides us with a deeper understanding of the general notion of risk and that since questions of epistemic risk are directed at the level of knowledge they cannot be contained in the ordinary concept of outcome risk.

Department of Philosophy
University of Lund

NOTES

I am indebted to my collaborators Robert Goldsmith and Peter Gärdenfors for their comments on and criticisms of the manuscript. I also wish to thank the National Defence Research Institute, section 541 in Stockholm, in particular Jan Fröberg, and the Swedish Acadamy of Science for support of the project.

1. Hume, D., A Treatise of Human Nature, London: Clarendon Press, (1739) 1978, book I, part IV, section I. See also Lehrer, K., "The Evaluation of Method: A Hierarchy of Probabilities Among Probabilities", in Grazer, Philosophische Studien, vol. 12113, 1981. For a more detailed discussion of the arguments presented in this section and for further references see Goldsmith, R.W. and Sahlin N.-E., "The Role of Second Order Probabilities in Decision Making", in Humphreys, P.C., Svenson, O. and Vari, A. (eds.), Analysing and Aiding Decision Processes, Amsterdam: North-Holland, 1982.
2. See Brown, R.W. and Lindley, D.V., "Improving Judgments by Reconciling Incoherence", Theory and Decision, 1981. See also Lehrer, op. cit.
3. See Goldsmith and Sahlin, op. cit. For an interesting discussion of second order probabilities, see Marschak, J., "Do Personal Probabilities of Probabilities have an Operational Meaning?", Theory and Decision, vol. 6, 1975.
4. For a detailed presentation of this theory see Gärdenfors, P. and Sahlin, N.-E., "Unreliable Probabilities, Risk Taking, and Decision Making", Synthese, 1982, and "Decision Making With Unreliable Probabilities", forthcoming. For a discussion of the theory see Levi, I., "Ignorance, Probability and Rational Choice", Synthese, 1982.
5. See Ellsberg, D., "Risk, Ambiguity and the Savage Axioms", Quarterly Journal of Economics, vol. 75, 1961.

6. For a discussion of several outcome risk theories see
   Schaefer, R.E., "What are We Talking About When We Talk
   About "Risk"?", IIASA Research Memorandum, 1978.
7. See also Gärdenfors and Sahlin, op. cit.

PART III

ARGUMENTS AGAINST EXPECTED UTILITY

J. M. Blatt

EXPECTED UTILITY THEORY DOES NOT APPLY
TO ALL RATIONAL MEN

1. INTRODUCTION

Expected utility theory is claimed to apply to all rational
persons. It is the purpose of this paper to disprove this
claim, by exhibiting a class of rational persons whose
preference ordering between uncertain prospects conflicts
with expected utility.

Our example is very simple, and some may consider it
trivial. But its very triviality is its strength: It shows
that one does not need to think up complicated, intricate
counterexamples to disprove the assertions of expected
utility theory. Simple, almost trivial examples suffice.

The usual approach to expected utility theory (we take
this from Borch 1968) is to start from some axioms, which
are supposed to be so self-evident that any rational person
must adopt them; any person who fails to adopt these axioms
is asserted to be obviously irrational. From these axioms,
one then deduces expected utility theory by a mathematical
argument.

This approach is inherently faulty. In the eighteenth
century philosophers attempted to deduce psychological
reactions of people by a combination of abstract reasoning
and introspection. It is most unfortunate that some economists today still seem to use such "theories" of two hundred
years ago, including a utilitarian calculus which has long
since been discarded by professional psychologists.

A pure mathematician may invent axioms based on his own
concepts of rationality, and then declare all people who
disagree with his acioms to be irrational. Considered as
exercises in abstract pure mathematics, one cannot argue
against this procedure.

But a social science such as economics cannot take such
an attitude. If there exist groups of actual people who have
preferences in disagreement with the axioms, people of relevance to economic affairs, then nothing whatever is gained
by calling them uncomplimentary names like "irrational". If
the axioms do not apply to actual economic men, then they

B. P. Stigum and F. Wenstøp (eds.), Foundations of Utility and Risk Theory with Applications,
107–116.
© 1983 by D. Reidel Publishing Company.

are unsuitable for the study of economics.

If economics claims to be a science, it must take real people as they are, with their actual preferences, and study the economic consequences which result from their actions in the market place. The most perfectly consistent system of mathematical axioms is useless if real people do not behave in the way that the axioms assert. In such a situation, a true science must discard the axioms and proceed to develop new axioms, in better accord with the real world. Mere name calling, such as declaring businessmen to be "irrational", is not the response of a true scientist!

In a series of works, Allais and his collaborators have shown that businessmen exhibit preferences in direct conflict with expected utility theory (Allais 1953, 1979, and references quoted there). In our opinion, this evidence is convincing, and proves that the axioms of expected utility theory must be discarded. However, some theoretical economists have argued that the businessmen of Allais are simply "mistaken" in their evaluation of the alternative prospects and may be persuaded to alter their responses after a period of being taught the "correct" (expected utility) way.

Although we consider this attitude quite wrong and even irrational[1], we do not wish to get into that argument in any detail. Rather, it is the purpose of this paper to support Allais' contentions by exhibiting yet another class of economic men whose preferences conflict, clearly and demonstrably, with expected utility theory. There is no need for interview studies, since the people in question have acted and continue to act on these preferences.

The logic of this paper should be stated at the outset. We wish to establish a reductio ad absurdum. To do so, we proceed from the assumption that expected utility theory does apply to these people. We draw consequences from this assumption, and eventually arrive at a clear contradiction. At this point, the initial assumption must be abandoned; that is, expected utility theory does not describe how these people react. There we rest our case.

Our argument is a more formal version of an earlier work (Blatt 1979), taking into account certain criticisms which have been made of that paper. Discussion of some of these criticisms is contained in the final section as well as in Blatt (1982, 1983).

2. GREEDY BUT CAUTIOUS CRIMINALS

In this section, we introduce our class of economic men, by

defining the essentials of their preference scale towards a
certain class of uncertain prospects.

First of all, our people are "greedy", in the sense
that their <u>utility of money is unbounded</u>.[2] No matter how
much money they already have, they always assign a finite
(bounded away from zero) utility to, let us say, doubling
their wealth. Mathematically, if $u(M)$ is the utility
assigned to possession of an amount of money M , the first
defining property of our class is:

<u>Property 1</u>: Given any number U , no matter how large,
there exists an amount of money M_1 (depending on U) such
that $u(M_1) > U$.

We do not assert that all men are greedy; but it is
common knowledge that many people fall into this class.
Nor is there any excuse for calling them "irrational".
They are certainly eager for wealth and in many cases they
are unpleasant or disagreeable. But they are only too
rational.

It may be objected that we are talking of the "utility
of money" in a paper intended to disprove expected utility
theory. This, however, is consistent with our <u>reductio ad</u>
<u>absurdum</u>: for the time being, we pretend that the people
in question have preferences described correctly by expected
utility theory, and therefore possess a measurable utility
of money. The contradiction will come in due course, later
on.

Next, let us introduce our projects. These are highly
illegal ventures, such as smuggling addictive drugs, which
promise large money gains if successful, but the death
penalty upon discovery. Each project has two possible outcomes:

1. Discovery, with probability p , followed by
   immediate execution on the gallows.
2. Success, with probability $1-p$, leading to a
   money gain M.

The projects differ from each other by the values of p and
M.

Properties 2 and 3 below further delimit the reactions
of our class of men to the various possibilities. We motivate our definitions first, then state them formally.

It is a matter of common experience that the death
penalty by itself is <u>not</u> an absolute deterrent to crime.

The (subjective) probability of getting caught is a very
important factor. If there is enough to be gained, and if
the probability of discovery is small enough, some people
will accept the risk. Indeed, the risk of death is faced
by all of us in our everyday life, for example when crossing
a city street, and is ignored when we judge it to be sufficiently small. Otherwise it would be impossible to conduct normal life. Of course, many people refuse illegal
ventures simply because they are law-abiding people. Such
people display no interest in the probability of detection
or in the penalty. However, other people do exist, and
(like everyone else) they ignore the probability of death if
that probability is small enough. We refer to these other
people as "criminals", meaning only that their attitude
towards projects involving a breach of law is not one of
total and immediate rejection.
     We shall describe this mathematically by:

Property 2: There exists a sum of money M_0 and a probability value $p_0 > 0$ such that persons in our class accept
the prospect if $M > M_0$ and $p < p_0$.
     For example, if M_0 is one million dollars and $p_0 = 10^{-8}$,
it is not at all hard to find people willing to accept the
venture. Not the majority of people, for they are law-
abiding on principle. But with a probability of 10^{-8} of
being caught, the death penalty is hardly a deterrent at all:
otherwise no one would ever cross a city street!
     So far, we have defined precisely what we mean by
"greedy" and by "criminal". It remains to define what we
shall mean by "cautious".
     Just as it is well-known that the death penalty by
itself is not an absolute deterrent to crime, it is also
well-known that most people are deterred if the probability
of being hanged, p, is high enough. There may exist religious
martyrs who positively welcome the prospect of a horrible
death, but these are not the people we wish to talk about
here.[3] Our drug smugglers, by and large, have very different
preferences. With the majority of them, a probability of
being caught large enough to amount to virtual certainty in
their own minds is enough to make them lose all interest in
the venture, no matter how much money is being offered in the
unlikely event of not being caught. We shall formalize this
mathematically as:

Property 3: There exists a probability value $p_m < 1$ such

that the prospect is rejected whenever $p > p_m$, no matter
how much the money gain M is.

If we take $p_m = 0.999$, say, so that the criminal has
only one chance in a thousand of escaping the gallows, it is
reasonable to expect <u>most</u> actual criminals to reject the
prospect, i.e., they accept our property 3 in their actual
behaviour. That is all we need: We do not require <u>all</u> men
to possess our properties; indeed, we hope that the
majority of men do not possess them. What we require is
only that the class of "greedy but cautious criminals",
<u>defined</u> by properties 1 to 3, is non-empty.

3.   THE INCONSISTENCY THEOREM

<u>THEOREM</u>: The preference scale of a greedy but cautious
criminal is inconsistent with expected utility theory.

<u>Proof</u>: Assume the contrary. Let $u(M)$ be the utility of
the money gain M , and let $u(G)$ be the utility of being
hanged on the gallows with certainty. The expected utility
of the project then equals:

$$E(U) = (1 - p)u(M) + pu(G) .\tag{1}$$

Let u_0 be the utility level associated with rejecting
the prospect, i.e., with doing nothing. (This may be taken
to be $u_0 = 0$ without loss of generality. Since the value
assigned to u_0 makes no difference subsequently, we leave
this value open). According to expected utility theory, the
prospect is accepted if $E(U) > u_0$ and is rejected if
$E(U) < u_0$. The "critical probability" p_c is obtained by
setting $E(U) = u_0$ and solving the resulting linear equation
for p . This yields:

$$p_c = \frac{u(M) - u_0}{u(M) - u(G)} .\tag{2}$$

The prospect is accepted if $p < p_c$, and is rejected if
$p > p_c$.
For most people $u(G)$, the utility of being hanged on
the gallows, is negative and large. For our purposes, we
need not worry about its precise value; rather, we need to
distinguish only two cases, $u(G)$ large but finite, and

$u(G) = -\infty$.[4]

Case 1: $u(G)$ is negative but finite. It follows that
p_c, equation (2), is also finite, and is a function
of the promised money gain M . By property 1, we
can make $u(M)$ arbitrarily large by making M
sufficiently large. In particular, then, there
exists a promised money gain M_1 large enough so
that p_c, computed from (2), is larger than the
value p_m in assumption 3. This however, is a
contradiction! Expected utility theory asserts that
we can persuade the criminal to accept the risk by
making the promised money gain big enough, whereas
property 3 says that no such money gain exists once
p exceeds p_m.

Case 2: $u(g) = -\infty$. This gives $p_c = 0$. The prospect
is rejected as soon as there is any non-zero probability p of getting caught. This conflicts with
property 2.

This establishes the theorem. Q.E.D.
    There exists a considerable literature on "the value of
human life", summarized in Jones-Lee (1976) and Linnerooth
(1979). This literature has a rather different emphasis to
ours, first, because it is concerned entirely with events of
small probabilities (of the sort relevant to life insurance
and/or cost benefit studies of development projects), and
second, because expected utility theory is taken for granted
as being the one and only correct and rational way.
    Professor Hirshleifer (private communication) believes
that the correct approach to decision problems involving
both income and life-versus-death variables is to make utility state-dependent, allowing explicitly for "living utility"
$u_L(M)$ and "bequest utility" $u_B(M)$ (Hirshleifer 1979, see
pages 1387-1389). We point out that our formula (1) above
already contains this approach: What we have called $u(M)$
is called $u_L(M)$ by Hirshleifer; what we have called $u(G)$
is called $u_B(0)$ by Hirshleifer. The argument of u_B is
zero, because under the postulated conditions the money gain
M is realized only if the criminal is not caught. There is
no "bequest utility": if he is caught and hanged, he has
nothing to bequeath! It follows that the state-dependent
utility approach does not provide a way out of the dilemma,
since just this approach has already been incorporated into

the proof of the basic theorem.

We emphasize that our theorem does not <u>assume</u> anything whatever. Our three properties are used to <u>define</u> a class of people (called "greedy but cautious criminals"). The theorem establishes that people within this class have a preference scale which is inconsistent with expected utility theory. There is <u>no</u> assumption here: rather, there is a mathematical theorem. Let us now turn to a discussion of the relevance of this theorem to the real world.

4. DISCUSSION

The theorem of section 3 asserts that the preference scale of greedy but cautious criminals cannot be described by expected utility theory. The expected utility theorists wish to assert that their theory describes, correctly, the behaviour of <u>all</u> rational men.

To reconcile these two assertions, one of two things must happen:

Either   (1)   there are no greedy but cautious
                     criminals in the real world;
or   (2)   all greedy but cautious criminals are
                     irrational men.

However, (1) is clearly out of the question, by common observation and the sad experience of any number of police departments. When it comes to (2), this amounts to nothing but unjustified and unsupported name calling: On what grounds are these people declared to be "irrational"?[5] Indeed, if you assume for a moment, contrary to fact, that you have lost your inhibitions in principle against illegal behaviour, are you so sure that you, a rational person, should have preferences violating any of these three properties? Which property would not apply to you? There is nothing obviously irrational about properties 2 or 3; and while the "greediness" implied by property 1 is undoubtedly an unpleasant character trait disapproved by the Church as a mortal sin, few of us can be perfectly sure that, given a billion dollars, we would really assign negligible further utility to a second billion!

Thus, both avenues (1) and (2) are closed. There exists a non-empty class of rational persons with a preference scale inconsistent with expected utility theory. The theory therefore does <u>not</u> apply to all rational persons.

Let us dispose quickly of another objection: "What does all this have to do with economics? A businessman who stays

within the law need not fear the gallows. The worst that
can happen to him is bankruptcy, and this is not such an
ultimate disaster."

If you think so, listen to Adam Smith (1937 reprint,
page 325): "Bankruptcy is perhaps the greatest and most
humiliating calamity which can befall an innocent man. The
greater part of men, therefore, are sufficiently careful to
avoid it. Some, indeed, do not avoid it; as some do not
avoid the gallows." It is Adam Smith himself who draws the
analogy between bankruptcy and the gallows; it is not our
invention.

When Charles Dickens was a child, his father became
bankrupt. Young Charles' education was terminated instantly
and he had to go to work in one of those dreadful sweatshops
where children laboured fourteen hours a day, under utterly
inhuman conditions. Charles' father went to jail and never
recovered from the blow; Charles himself was marked for life
by the experience. How many other children, in similar
circumstances, were worked to death?

The examples we have given, hanging on the gallows and
bankruptcy, have this in common: They are disasters from
which it is difficult (or impossible) to recover. For such
eventualities, a preference scale which is non-linear in the
probability p of occurrence of the disaster is eminently
rational. Pure mathematicians like John von Neumann may
choose axioms that lead to formulas linear in p , such as
equation (1). But it is these formulas and the axioms on
which they rest, not the behaviour and preference scales of
real men, which must be declared irrational.

One reason that all this is not perfectly obvious in
the usual discussions is that they "consider only prospects
where all gains are non-negative and finite" (Borch 1968,
page 25). By this simple proviso, all true disasters are
excluded "for simplicity". Would that we could do so in
real life!
Another reason is the neglect of the finite and limited
lifetime of real people. People know that they cannot live
for ever, no matter what happens. Hence the probability of
a disaster leading to death can be ignored if it is small
enough (less than or of the order of 10^{-8}, say), but cannot
be ignored (and is not ignored by real people) once it
becomes sizable. This situation may be messy, mathematically
speaking. But people are messy, mathematically speaking!

We rest our case. For further discussion, we refer to
some papers (Blatt 1979, 1980, 1982) as well as a forthcoming

book (Blatt 1983). For application of these ideas to the strictly economic problem of investment evaluation under uncertainty, leading to results quite different from the usual approach but (unlike it) in good agreement with what businessmen actually are known to do, see Blatt (1979a) and the same book.

In conclusion, we are happy to express our thanks to Dr. J. Hirshleifer of U.C.L.A., Dr. Neil Laing of Adelaide University, and Professor Malcolm Fisher and Mrs. Robin Pope of the University of New South Wales for some extremely helpful comments and discussions.

Department of Applied Mathematics,
University of New South Wales,
Kensington, Sydney, Australia.'

NOTES

1. Briefly, the reasons are: (1) The responses of the businessmen are not in fact mistaken or irrational. On the contrary, the responses are eminently sensible and rational. Only a person blinded by an irrational faith in expected utility theory could possibly fail to understand and appreciate what motivates the respondents. (2) In economics, real businessmen who continue to survive in the hard world of practical affairs are our "economic men" par excellence. If <u>their</u> responses disagree with the theories of some "academic scribblers", it is the latter who must revise their axioms. Any other reaction on the part of economic theorists is unscientific and irrational.
2. Those who dislike "emotive" terms (even when applied to drug smugglers!), may substitute "unbounded" in place of "greedy".
3. No matter how rational religious martyrs may be in fact, they are of very little, if any, importance in economic matters and may <u>therefore</u> be left out of account in economic science.
4. If the reader believes that an (negatively) infinite utility is nonsense, then this case may be ignored. The only possible case is then finite $u(G)$. All this does is to shorten the proof of the theorem.
5. They are of course immoral, but if all immoral (or not perfectly moral) people are called irrational, there should be mighty few rational people left in the business world.

116 J. M. BLATT

REFERENCES

Allais, M.: 1953, 'L'Extension des Theories de l'Equilibre
    Economique Général et du Rendement Social au Cas du
    Risque', Econometrica 21, pp. 269-290.
_____ and O. Hagen (eds.): 1979, Expected Utility
    Hypotheses and the Allais Paradox: Contemporary Dis-
    cussions of Decisions under Uncertainty with Allais' Re-
    joinder, Reidel, Holland.
Blatt, J.M.: 1979, 'The Utility of Being Hanged on the
    Gallows', Journal of Post Keynesian Economy 2(2), pp.
    231-239.
_____ : 1979, 'Investment Evaluation under Uncertainty',
    Financial Management 8, pp. 61-81.
_____ : 1980, 'The Utility of Being Hanged on the
    Gallows - Reply', Journal of Post Keynesian Economy 3(1),
    pp. 132-134.
_____ : 1982, 'The Utility of Being Hanged on the
    Gallows - Some Replies', Journal of Post Keynesian Economy
    4(2), pp. 322-329.
_____ : 1983, Dynamic Economic Systems, M.E. Sharpe,
    New York.
Borsch, K.: 1968, The Economics of Uncertainty, Princeton
    University Press, Princeton, p. 25.
Hirshleifer, J., and J.G. Riley: 1979, 'The Analytics of
    Uncertainty and Information - An Expository Survey',
    Journal of Economic Literature 17(4), pp. 1375-1421.
Jones-Lee, M.W.: 1976, The Value of Life, Martin Robertson,
    London.
Linnerooth, J.: 1979, 'The Value of Human Life: A Review of
    the Models', Economic Inquiry 17(1), pp. 52-76.
Smith, A.: 1937, Inquiry into the Nature and Causes of the
    Wealth of Nations (1776), The Modern Library, New York,
    p. 325.

Edward F. McClennen

SURE-THING DOUBTS*

> If, after thorough deliberation, anyone maintains
> a pair of distinct preferences that are in con-
> flict with the sure-thing principle, he must aban-
> don, or modify, the principle; for that kind of
> discrepancy seems intolerable in a normative theo-
> ry. Analogous circumstances forced D. Bernoulli
> to abandon the theory of mathematical expectation
> for that of utility. In general, a person who has
> tentatively accepted a normative theory must con-
> scientiously study situations in which the theory
> seems to lead him astray; he must decide for each
> by reflection--deduction will typically be of lit-
> tle relevance-- whether to retain his initial im-
> pression of the situation or to accept the impli-
> cations of the theory for it.
>
> L. J. Savage, Foundations
> of Statistics[1]

1. INTRODUCTION

Consider the problem of choosing from among the following
four gambles:

	(66) RED	(33) YELLOW	(01) BLACK
A	$2400	2500	0
B	2400	2400	2400
C	0	2500	0
D	0	2400	2400,

FIGURE 1

B. P. Stigum and F. Wenstøp (eds.), Foundations of Utility and Risk Theory with Applications,
117–136.
© 1983 by D. Reidel Publishing Company.

with monetary prizes based on the color ball drawn from an urn containing balls in the stated proportions. Recent studies show that in cases of this sort a significant number of persons will choose B in preference to A, and C in preference to D, in pairwise choice situations.[2] Such a pattern of preference is in violation of the sure-thing principle, which, as an axiom of rational choice, is ubiquitous in one form or other to contemporary treatments of utility theory and the theory of subjective probability.[3] For contexts in which well-defined probabilities are presupposed, one particularly clear way in which this principle can be formulated, following Samuelson, is as the strong independence axiom, which requires that: for all X, Y, Z, and $p > 0$,

$$X \succeq Y \text{ iff } [X, p; Z, 1-p] \succeq [Y, p; Z, 1-p],$$

where X, Y, Z, are lotteries (gambles), p is a probability, and [X, p; Z, 1-p] is a compound or multistage gamble in which one has p probability of playing X and 1-p probability of playing Z, etc.[4]

What is one to make of preference patterns which violate this axiom? The prevailing view is that while such violations may limit somewhat the predictive power of the sure-thing principle, the principle as normative for preference remains quite secure.[5] Oddly enough, one finds very little by way of systematic defense of this view. A survey of the literature does suggest, however, at least four distinct lines of argument. The first adopts the strategy of a reductio and seeks to show that preference patterns in violation of the sure-thing principle have implications which even the persons exhibiting such preferences would find unacceptable. The second builds on the consideration that a gamble is properly interpreted as a "disjunctive" as distinct from a "conjunctive" bundle of goods, and is not, as such, subject to the kind of complementarity problem which frustrates the use of independence principles in the scaling of consumer preferences for (conjunctive) bundles of commodities. The third treats the axiom as a commutivity principle governing sequential choice and requiring the agent to be indifferent between the temporal order in which certain choice and chance events take place. The fourth treats the principle as a dominance principle and thereby seeks to ground it in what seems to be a secure intuition, namely, that rational choice is choice which maximizes the preferences of the agent with respect to consequences.

I propose to consider the merits of each of these arguments.   My conclusions are negative.   The first two arguments must, I believe, be dismissed.   The first begs the
question and the second involves a non sequitur.   The third
is much more substantial, but I think that when it is carefully examined, the restriction which it places on rational
choice is excessive, and by no means as intuitive as its
supporters have supposed.   The last argument is clearly the
most powerful.   I shall argue, however, that the reserva-
tions expressed in regard to the third argument carry over
here.   I am forced to conclude, then, that the sure-thing
cornerstone to the modern theory of utility and subjective
probability is less secure than one would like.

2. THE UNACCEPTABLE IMPLICATIONS ARGUMENT

Suppose that B is chosen in preference to A and C is chosen
in preference to D. It seems reasonable to assume that this
preference pattern would still obtain if the two inferior
options, A and D, were improved marginally, by the addition
of a small constant amount, say $10, to each possible pay-
off. We would then have:

	(66)R	(33)Y	(01)B
A+	$2410	2510	10
B	2400	2400	2400
C	0	2500	0
D+	10	2410	2410

FIGURE 2

If B is chosen in preference to A+, and C is chosen in preference to D+, then it seems reasonable to suppose that in
the event one is offered the opportunity to choose between
A+ and B, if a fair coin lands heads, and the opportunity to
choose between D+ and C, if the same coin lands tails, the
contingency plan, [Choose B, if heads; C, if tails] would be
preferred to the contingency plan [Choose A+, if heads; D+,
if tails].   The notion here is that the contingency plan
[B/C] gives one a fifty-fifty chance to play each of the two
preferred strategies, while the contingency plan [A+,D+]
gives one a fifty-fifty chance to play each of the two dis-
preferred strategies. The payoffs for these two strategies,

as a function of what color ball is drawn from the urn, is given by:

	R	Y	B
B/C	[2400/ 0]	[2400/2500]	[2400/ 0]
A+/D+	[2410/ 10]	[2410/2510]	[2410/ 10]

FIGURE 3

where [$x/ $y] is a lottery in which one has .5 probabili-ty of getting $x and .5 probability of getting $y. But pre-ference for [B/C] over [A+/D+] now seems quite unaccept-able, since in terms of final payoffs and compounded pro-babilities, [A+/D+] gives one the same probabilities over each of four possible payoffs as [B/C], but the payoffs for [A+/D+] are in each case superior to the corresponding payoffs in [B/C]. Something, then, has to give.[6]

Far from serving as an effective reductio, the argument simply begs the question. It goes through smoothly only on the assumption that the agent who chooses B in preference to A+ and C in preference to D+ must rank [B/C] in preference to [A+/D+]. But this assumption, as Samuelson reminds us, simply invokes another version of the strong independence axiom.[7] Those who want to insist on preference for B over A and C over D, and thereby reject the independence axiom, have only to be on their guard and reject the appeal to an-other version of the same axiom.[8]

3. INDEPENDENCE AND COMPLEMENTARITY

Another defense of the independence axiom proceeds by re-ference to the concept of complementarity. Samuelson, for example, argues that while in the domain of non-stochastic goods an independence axiom would be "empirically absurd," in the domain of stochastic goods such an axiom makes sense, since the possible outcomes of a lottery or gamble are dis-junctive: just one of the possible outcomes can occur.[9] This argument is first alluded to, as a matter of fact, by Von Neumann and Morgenstern in Theory of Games and Economic Be-havior:

By a combination of two events we mean this: Let the two events be denoted by B and C and use, for the sake

of simplicity, the probability 50%-50%. Then the "combination" is the prospect of seeing B occur with probability 50% and (if B does not occur) C with the (remaining) probability of 50%.   We stress that the two
alternatives are mutually exclusive, so no possibility
of complementarity and the like exists.[10]

Although the distinction between stochastic and non-
stochastic goods is obviously important, the argument hardly
suffices to establish the legitimacy of the independence
axiom.   As it stands, the intended argument is a non sequitur.   Since the theory of choice under conditions of uncertainty and risk is concerned with disjunctive bundles of
goods, one does not expect to encounter here the sort of
complementarity problem which arises in the case of conjunctive bundles of goods.   But that serves only to remove one
possible objection to the independence axiom; it does not
show the axiom to be acceptable as a normative principle.[11]

4.   THE ORDER OF CHOICE AND CHANCE

The interpretation of the independence axiom as a commutivity principle was first suggested by Rubin.[12] According to
him the axiom states that:

> ....it is immaterial in which order choice or a random
> event occur, provided that a decision can be made be-
> fore the random event occurs which corresponds to an
> arbitrary decision made afterward.

More recently, Raiffa has made use of this interpretation as part of an analysis of a sequential version of the
decision problem given in Figure 1 above.[13] One is to imagine a story such as this: At 9:00 a.m. a (friendly) experimenter draws a ball from an urn containing red and white
balls in proportion 66:34.   In the event a red ball is
drawn, one gets the prize specified at point Q (In Figure
4). In the event a white ball is drawn, one gets a choice to
make, which must be executed by 9:05 a.m., between (G) receiving $2400 for certain, or (H) participating in a gamble
in which one has 33/34 probability of getting $2500 and 1/34
probability of getting $0.   Note that if Q is set at $2400,
then H is equivalent to A (as defined in our original problem) and G is equivalent to B; alternatively, if Q is set at
$0, then H is equivalent to C and G is equivalent to D.

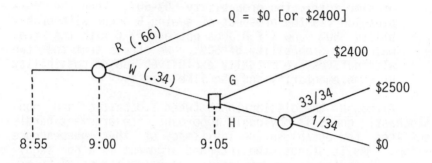

Figure 4

Raiffa now poses the following questions:

(1) If you obtain a white ball, would your choice between alternatives G and H depend on the detailed description of prize Q?

(2) If at 8:55 a.m. the experimenter asks you to announce which alternative you will choose if you draw a
white ball, will your decision depend on Q?   Would it
differ from the choice you would actually make at 9:05
when the chips are down?

Raiffa supposes that each of these questions should be answered in the negative.   But, by inspection, those who do
answer these questions in the negative will either rank A
over B and C over D, or B over A and D over C, or, finally,
both A and B indifferent to one another and C and D indifferent to one another: that is, they will never rank B over
A and C over D.
     Raiffa does not say why these questions should all be
answered in the negative.   What he supposes, apparently, is
that the disposition of most persons to so answer them is
evidence of a commitment on their part to the commutivity
principle.   On this view, Raiffa's task reduces to putting
persons in mind of what they already (if only implicitly)
accept, and getting them to revise their preferences to
bring them into line with this commitment. The problem with
this line of reasoning, however, is that it works only up to
the point where we encounter someone who does not answer all

the questions in the negative, and even Raiffa is prepared
to admit that there are such persons. What argument can be
offered to the holdouts?   How are we to convince them that
their preferences are irrational?

One argument for a negative answer to the question in
(1) above is to be found in the following remark of Arrow's
(offered by him as a gloss on what he terms the Principle of
Conditional Preference):

> ...what might have happened under conditions that we
> know won't prevail should have no influence on our
> choice of actions.   Suppose, that is, we are given in-
> formation that certain states of nature are impossible.
> We reform our beliefs about the remaining states of
> nature, and on the basis of these new beliefs we form a
> new ordering of the actions.   The Principle of Condi-
> tional Preference...asserts that the ordering will de-
> pend only on the consequences of the actions for those
> states of the world not ruled out by the information.[14]

What about the questions posed in (2)?   One is requested to "announce" at 8:55 which alternative one will choose,
in the event a white ball is drawn from the urn.   The request is ambiguous.   It could be taken as a request to predict at 8:55 how one will choose at 9:05, i.e., to state in
advance what one intends to do at 9:05.   Alternatively, it
could be a request to indicate what one's choice would be if
it had to be made right then, at 8:55, prior to finding out
whether a white or a red ball is drawn from the urn.   The
second part of the question posed in (2) above reinforces
the first of these interpretations.   The suggestion is that
the choice is "actually" to be made at 9:05 (when the "chips
are down").   Of course, on this interpretation the second
part of the question in (2) begs to be answered in the negative, for it now reads: Would the choice you expect to make
at 9:05 differ from the choice you would actually make at
9:05 when the chips are down? This won't do at all: Commitment to Rubin's Commutivity Principle surely requires more
than simply a negative answer to this question!

We must suppose, then, that what is requested in the
first part of (2) is whether, in the event one must make
the choice between G and H at 8:55, that choice would depend
upon knowing what prize will be awarded at Q.   In short,
(2) is concerned with ex ante choice between G and H, and
not simply prediction of ex post choice.   But how are we to

understand <u>ex ante</u> choice between G and H? Figure 4 above clearly describes the case of <u>ex post</u> choice between G and H. For the <u>ex ante</u> case we would have the following:

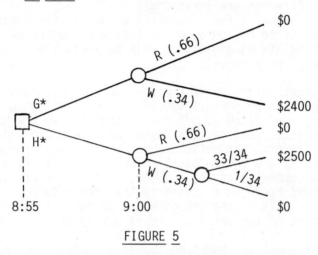

FIGURE 5

Rubin's commutivity principle, then, would require that if G is chosen over H in the problem given in Figure 4,   G* must be chosen over H* in the problem given in Figure 5.

    The ambiguity noted above in the way Raiffa frames his questions, however, leaves us with a pressing problem. How can we be sure any longer that Raiffa's subjects, whom he reports are disposed to answer the questions in the nega-tive, really do have a commitment to Rubin's Commutivity Principle?   The problem, as it turns out, is quite perva-sive.   Markowitz, and also Kahneman and Tversky, have re-ported that subjects who displayed the preference patterns noted at the outset of this paper revised their rankings when presented with a sequential version of the same prob-lem.   But in each case the instructions to the subjects were ambiguous.[15] Machina, who has otherwise presented one of the most interesting reappraisals of the expected utility theory to appear in a long time, seems to fall into a similar trap. After formulating the independence axiom, he suggests that the following case can be made for its plausibility (adap-ting his argument to the notation of the present paper):

    The argument for the "rationality" of this prescription
    [that X $\succsim$ Y <u>iff</u> (X, p; Z, 1-p) $\succsim$ (Y, p; Z, 1-p)] is

straightforward: the choice among the latter pair of
prospects is equivalent in terms of final probabilities
to being presented with a coin which has 1-p chance of
landing tails (in which case you will "win" the lottery
Z) and being asked before the flip whether you would
prefer to win the lottery X or Y in the event of a
head. Now, either the coin will land tails, in which
case your choice won't have mattered, or else it will
land heads, in which case you are in effect back to a
decision between X and Y and you should clearly make
the same choice as you did before.[16]

Machina interprets the problem as one in which the
agent has both an ex ante and an ex post choice to make. If
the agent, upon being requested to make a choice now at
8:55, knows that the choice will, in the event a white ball
is drawn, be presented to him once again at 9:05, then it
would be very odd if he were to make a choice now which was
different from the one planned for later. Such a preference
reversal would be subject to exploitation by others. If
one preferred H* to G* at 8:55, but G to H at 9:05, then
someone else could set up a parallel choice situation in
which one would be permitted to select H* instead of G* only
on payment of a small fee, and then, in the event a white
ball is drawn, permitted to trade back H* for G. One would
then have paid out a fee to end up where one could have been
from the very start, by simply opting at 8:55 to stay with
G*. In this respect, however, ex ante choice which is subject to reconsideration-- what might be termed provisional
choice-- is something quite different from ex ante choice
which is not subject to reconsideration, but rather, is irrevocable. It takes a situation in which the agent has the
opportunity both to choose ex ante, and then reconsider that
choice ex post, for such a preference pattern to be exploited. Rubin's axiom, I suggest, is not about this kind
of situation, but about the relation between irrevocable ex
ante choice and ex post choice.[17]
    If we fix now on the proper interpretation of the com-
mutivity principle, what argument can be offered in favor
of the recommendation that ex ante choice coincide with ex
post choice? Let us refer once again to Figure 5, where ex
ante choice between G and H is represented by G* and H*, and
to Figure 4, where the choice between G and H is ex post.
The choice which the agent confronts at 8:55, in Figure 5,
is not the same choice which he confronts at 9:05 in Figure

4. It is true, of course, that if one focuses on the multi-staged aspect of the choice presented in Figure 5, one can note that the components which differentiate G* and H* at the second stage are what one is to choose between in the problem in Figure 4.   But, as the modern theory of expected utility itself insists, these structural features are to be treated with the greatest caution.   Savage used to insist, when confronted with the fact that even he managed to choose in violation of the independence axiom, that he was grateful to his own theory for setting him straight.[18] The suggestion was that violators of the independence axiom are "taken in" by features of the problem which are irrelevant, from a purely rational point of view.   I must confess that once the confusions I have tried to detail above are cleared up, it seems to me an open question as to who has been taken in by features of the problem which are, if not irrelevant, at least not necessarily relevant from a rational point of view.   I grant that fixing on the components which differentiate G* and H* in Figure 5, asking oneself how one would choose between them, if, counterfactually, one were to be able to choose between them, and then using the answer to this question to determine how one will choose between G* and H*, may be a permissible way to evaluate the choice between G* and H*.   I have been unable to isolate an argument, however, as to why one must evaluate the options in this manner.[19]   I conclude, then, that the case has not been made for the independence axiom as a commutivity principle.

5. THE SURE-THING OR DOMINANCE ARGUMENT

One can discern in the literature a line of argument quite distinct from that just discussed.   It proceeds by way of postulating what has come to be known as the "sure-thing" principle, and then showing that the independence condition follows logically from the "sure-thing" principle when the latter is taken in conjunction with certain other allegedly non-controversial assumptions.   Friedman and Savage introduce the argument in the following manner:

> [The independence] postulate is implied by a principle that we believe practically unique among maxims for wise action in the face of uncertainty, in the strength of its intuitive appeal.   The principle is universally known and recognized....To illustrate the principle before defining it, suppose a physician now knows that

his patient has one of several diseases for each of which the physician would prescribe immediate bed rest. We assert that under this circumstance the physician should and, unless confused, will prescribe immediate bed rest...

Much more abstractly, consider a person constrained to choose between a pair of alternatives a and b, without knowing whether a particular event E does (or will) in fact obtain. Suppose that, depending on his choice and whether E does obtain, he is to receive one of four (not necessarily distinct) gambles, according to the following schedule:

Event

Choice	E	not-E
a	f(a)	g(a)
b	f(b)	g(b)

The principle in sufficient generality for the present purpose asserts: If the person does not prefer f(a) to f(b), and does not prefer g(a) to g(b), then he will not prefer the choice a to b...[20]

If the sure-thing principle can serve to underpin the independence axiom, what can be said in support of the sure-thing principle itself? The argument proceeds along the following lines.[21] The outcome of b is, by hypothesis, at least as good as the outcome of a, regardless of the turn of events (whether E or not-E takes place). So one does at least as well by choosing b as one does by choosing a, regardless of which of a set of mutually exclusive and exhaustive events takes place. But in that case, surely b is at least as good as a. The force of this sort of line of reasoning is perhaps even clearer in connection with the following version of the sure-thing principle. Suppose that every outcome of b is at least as good as the corresponding outcome of a, and at least one outcome of b is strictly preferred to the corresponding outcome of a. Then surely one must prefer b to a. To choose a over b in such a case would be to deliberately bring about an outcome that will be at best no better, and which may well turn out to be worse, than the outcome that one could have brought about had one

chosen b. Such a choice, it can be argued, fails to satisfy
the requirement that one choose so as to maximize one's preferences with respect to outcomes.

On first consideration this seems compelling. But it
needs to be remarked that the principle as formulated is
very strong, for it is framed with respect to outcomes which
are defined in terms of an arbitrarily selected partition of
events. The principle requires that if there exists any partition of events such that the outcomes of the one act are
at least as good as the outcomes of the other act, for each
event in the partition, then the first act is at least as
good as the second. In particular, this means that the
principle is not limited in its application to consequences
or outcomes which can be characterized in non-probabilistic
terms. Consider the example given above: If the doctor
prescribes bed-rest, and the patient turns out to have
disease X, then we need not suppose that the outcome is that
the patient is cured; we need only suppose that the doctor
judges that if the patient has disease X, he or she is more
likely to be cured (or the probability of an earlier cure is
greater), if bed-rest is prescribed than if it is not. The
outcome in this, and the other corresponding cases, is,
then, a lottery over various less proximate outcomes. Similar considerations apply to the decision problem given in
Figure 5. If one chooses H* and a white ball is drawn, then
the outcome is that one confronts a lottery in which one has
33 chances out of 34 of getting $2500 and 1 chance out of 34
of getting $0. The principle as framed by Friedman and
Savage is designed to apply to such probabilistically defined (and hence relatively proximate) outcomes. Thus, for
example, for subjects who report that they prefer $2400 out-
right to receiving the aforementioned lottery, since they
are bound to get $0 in the event a red ball is drawn, re-
gardless of whether they choose H* or G*, the sure-thing
principle requires a choice of G* over H*.

This application of the sure-thing principle to partitions whose outcomes are themselves explicitly defined in
probabilistic terms raises a substantial issue. Consider
the person who prefers $2400 outright to the lottery over
$2500 and $0, but who chooses H* over G*, contra the sure-
thing principle. While there seems no particular bar to
treating the state of affairs which results from choice of
H* and a white ball being drawn from the urn-- having 33 out
of 34 chances of getting $2500 and 1 chance out of 34 of
getting $0-- as an "outcome" of that intersection of a

choice and a chance event, it is not at all clear that this "outcome" is relevant to the "sure-thing" evaluation of G* and H*. Within the framework of the finer partitioning of this very outcome--which finer partitioning is an explicit part of the problem as defined-- it is simply not true that one always does at least as well by choosing G* as by choosing H*, regardless of which events take place. One possible outcome of H* is $2500, and this is, by hypothesis, strictly preferred to any outcome of G*.[22]

I do not mean to suggest that application of the sure-thing principle can be undercut in such cases simply by displaying some (other) partition of events such that the outcomes which it defines fail to satisfy the antecedent conditions of that principle. Nor do I mean to suggest that application of the principle can be undercut by the consideration that the partition to which appeal is made might itself be refined in such a way-- with the specification of even more remote outcomes or consequences-- that the principle would not apply to that refinement. The case upon which I have focussed is one in which the partition to which the principle does not apply is itself an explicit refinement of the partition to which the principle does apply. In such a case, I suggest, the claim that application of the sure-thing principle can be grounded in the notion of the maximization of preferences with respect to consequences, is questionable.

The problem here is, in a sense, parallel to the problem which arises with respect to the commutivity principle. Application of the commutivity principle to the choice situation represented in Figure 5 seems quite plausible if we supress an explitly given feature of that situation, namely, that the only choice to be exercised by the agent is at 8:55, i.e., if we conflate the choice situations in Figures 4 and 5. Similarly, the application of the sure-thing principle seems plausible if we supress the explicit refinement of the outcome associated with H* and the event of a white ball being drawn (W)-- a refinement specified in terms of outcomes which are evaluatively distinct from one another (getting $2500, getting $0)--, and thereby treat the outcome of H* and W as if its internal structure were of no particular relevance.[23]

6. CONCLUSIONS

I do not think that the questions raised above suffice to

show that the sure-thing or independence axiom must be rejected as normative for rational choice.   What they show, I
think, is that the arguments that have been put forward in
support of the principle are less impressive than many have
supposed.   Some will want to argue, no doubt, that since I
have not managed to show that the axiom must be rejected,
and since it has proved so useful and powerful for theory
building in the decision and social sciences, I must lose my
case. If the issue were one concerning the use of the axiom
as part of a descriptive or predictive theory of rational
choice, I think the point would be well taken. But this is
not the issue to which I have addressed myself in this
paper.   My concern has been with the axiom as normative for
rational choice.   With regard to the normative issue, I can
only plead that we enter here into a matter which poses
problems analogous to those which arise with regard to questions of rights and obligations. The issue is one of where
the burden of proof is to lie. I believe that it should lie
with those who would insist that a certain pattern of preference or choice behavior is irrational.   Machina reminds
us that the economist Marschak was so taken with the independence or sure-thing principle that he came close to suggesting that it be taught in curricula along with the principles of arithmetic and logic.[24] This is worrisome. We
reach in our search for norms of rationality for something
which will win the assent of the widest possible group, that
will hopefully transcend ideology; but the reaching is still
for something normative, by means of which we will judge not
only our own choices but the choices of others.   This calls
for great caution.   If the sure-thing or independence axiom
has yet to be linked in any decisive fashion to behavior
which can be taken as paradigmatically rational then we
would be well advised not to judge irrational those patterns
which fail to conform to this principle. Such a presumption
may not ideally serve the ends of theory construction, but
it admirably serves the ideal of tolerance.

Department of Philosophy, Washington University

NOTES

*   The author is greatly indebted to T. Seidenfeld, of
Washington University, for many long discussions (and many

heated debates) on the subject of this paper. He has also benefited greatly from conversations, over the last few years, with I. Levi, of Columbia; F. Schick, of Rutgers; K. Arrow, of Stanford; R.D. Luce, of Harvard; P. Lyon, of Cambridge; M. Machina, of University of California, San Diego; E. Freeman, of The Wharton School; and T. Rader, J. Little, and M. Meyer, all of Washington University.

1. Savage (1972), p. 102.
2. See Kahneman and Tversky (1979), McCrimmon and Larsson (1979), and Schoemaker (1980).
3. For surveys of different versions of the axiom, see McCrimmon and Larsson (1979) and Luce and Suppes (1965).
4. Samuelson (1966), p. 133.
5. The tendency of most of the critics of expected utility theory to focus on the descriptive issue has not helped either to clarify or to resolve the normative issue. M. Allais is a notable exception. He has, from the very outset, been concerned with the theory as normative for choice. It is he who sets in motion what debate there has been. See Econometrie (1953) for the proceedings (in French) of the conference he organized in 1952; and Allais and Hagen (1979) for a translation of one of his early papers, for numerous relevant articles by others, and for a recent statement of his position. Hansson (1975) and Dreyfus and Dreyfus (1978) are also very valuable.
6. This is one of two lines of attack taken by Raiffa. See Raiffa (1970), pp. 83-84; and also Raiffa (1961), pp. 690-694. The other is discussed below in Section 4.
7. Samuelson (1952), p. 672.
8. It would appear that Ellsberg's otherwise powerful attack on Savage's use of the sure-thing principle runs into difficulty precisely because he is unwilling to carry the argument through in this manner. While he is prepared to give up Savage's version of the axiom, he apparently is also inclined to accept the axiom as applied to the case of determinate probabilities--see here Ellsberg (1961), p. 651, footnote 7, in particular, where he seems to concede a great deal to Raiffa, who proceeds in his reply, Raiffa (1961), to catch him out on this point. It is interesting to note that in an earlier article, Ellsberg (1954), he took the position that the strong independence axiom was "indubitab-

ly the most plausible" of the axioms of utility theory. Space considerations preclude my exploring these matters at greater length in this paper. Let me simply note for now that Ellsberg focuses on what are essentially a series of counterexamples to one version of the sure-thing principle. My concern, rather, has been with examining the arguments which others have offered in support of various versions of the principle. For purposes of tracing the debate initiated by Ellsberg, the exchange between Fellner and Brewer in Brewer (1963), Brewer and Fellner (1965), Fellner (1961), and Fellner (1963), is particularly useful.

9. Samuelson (1952), p. 672.
10. Von Neumann and Morgenstern (1953), pp. 17-18; see also Marschak (1951), pp. 502-3.
11. It is very hard to read the results in e.g., Becker, DeGroot, and Marschak (1963), Coombs (1975), and Ellsberg (1961), without taking them as suggesting that subjects behave as if there were certain complementarity-like effects which arise within the context of stochastic goods.
12. Rubin (1949), pp. 1-2.
13. See Raiffa (1970), p. 82.
14. Arrow (1972), p. 23. Chernoff (1949), argues in a similar fashion, but inexplicably treats the point, not as defense of a negative answer to what Raiffa formulates in (1), but as defense of a negative answer to the questions posed in (2). In the final, published version of Chernoff's paper (Chernoff, 1954), a "correction" is effected by virtue of his simply leaving the comment out altogether.
15. See Markowitz (1959), pp. 221-2, and Kahneman and Tversky (1979), pp. 271-2. In each case, the intention seems to have been to ask the subjects how they would choose if the choice had to be made ex ante, in an irrevocable fashion. Yet the accounts which each give of what they said to subjects suggests a double, and conflicting, message. The subjects are first oriented to the problem as a problem in which choice clearly is to be made ex post, and then a redescription is presented; but it is unclear whether the redescription is of a problem in which one is to say now what one will choose later, or a problem in which one is to say now how one will choose now. I am not impressed, then, by the documented results that subjects tend to repeat in regard

to the question about "ex ante" choice what they have already said about ex post choice. Note also that the subjects did have the opportunity to register their choice under a description which was unambiguously of ex ante choice (i.e., when presented with the original, non-sequential version of the problem), and the evidence is that a significant number chose differently when the problem was presented in that fashion. What I conclude from all this is that there isn't any very clear evidence concerning whether persons do, or do not, answer Raiffa's second question (at least as it was presumably intended to be understood) in the negative.

16. See Machina (1981), p. 166-167; for Machina's critique of expected-utility theory, see Machina (1982).

17. For the distinction between irrevocable and reconsiderable ex ante choice, and for very clear examples of the troubles one gets into if this distinction is not preserved, I am indebted to Seidenfeld (1981). See also Levi's reply to Seidenfeld in the same volume.

18. See Savage (1972), pp. 102-103.

19. One way to understand the standard decision tree analysis is that it proceeds as if one problem (a problem in which choice is to be made ex ante) can be resolved by solving another problem (which differs in that there are choices to be made ex post). See, in particular, Schlaifer (1969), pp. 57-58, for a very clear statement of this. The argument of the present paper, simply put, is that this assumption is nowhere subjected to the kind of scrutiny it deserves.

20. Friedman and Savage (1952), pp. 468-69. See also Savage (1951) and (1972) for somewhat similar accounts.

21. For discussions which connect the sure-thing principle and the independence axiom, see Friedman and Savage (1952), p. 468; Savage (1972), p. 22-23 and also Arrow (1972), p. 52ff. It is interesting to note that the Friedman and Savage example of the physician is of a situation in which choice can presumably be exercised now, or deferred until later (after finding out which disease the patient has). This feature plays no role in the formal characterization of the principle, however. There is a gap, then, between the example and the principle the example is supposed to explicate, a gap which needs to be filled in, and which raises,

among other things, just the questions posed in Section
4 above.
22. Savage (1972), p. 99, considers the possibility of re-
     stricting the principle to partitions whose outcomes
     can be characterized in non-probabilistic terms, e.g.,
     cash prizes. By way of rebuttal he argues that "..a
     cash prize is to a large extent a lottery ticket in
     that the uncertainty as to what will become of a person
     if he has a gift of a thousand dollars is not in prin-
     ciple different from the uncertainty about what will
     become of him if he holds a lottery ticket.." (p. 99).
     This is an important point, but space considerations
     preclude my exploring it at the present time. Suffice
     it to say that a view to the effect that there is no
     bedrock level of certainty, that it is risk all the way
     down, would seem to cast more, not less, doubt on the
     attempt to ground the sure-thing principle in the idea
     of maximizing preferences for outcomes.
23. There is perhaps an even deeper connection between the
     two arguments. Both derive their plausibility in part,
     I think, from a presupposition to the effect that there
     could be no complementarity problem in regard to the
     components of disjunctive prospects. I hope to address
     this matter directly in a separate paper.
24. Machina (1981), p. 167. For the original remarks of
     Marschak, see Allais and Hagen (1979), pp. 168-172, and
     also Marschak (1968), p. 49.

REFERENCES

Allais, M. and Hagen, O., eds. (1979). Expected Utility and
     the Allais Paradox, Reidel.
Arrow, K. (1972). "Exposition of the Theory of Choice Under
     Conditions of Uncertainty," in C. B. McGuire and R.
     Radner, eds., Decision and Organization, North-Holland,
     pp. 19-55.
Becker, G.M., DeGroot, M.H., and Marschak, J. (1963). "An
     Experimental Study of Some Stochastic Models for Wa-
     gers," Behavioral Science, 8, pp. 199-202.
Brewer, K.R.W. (1963). "Decisions Under Uncertainty: Com-
     ment," Q.J.Economics, 77, pp. 159-161.
Brewer, K.R.W., and Fellner, W. (1965). "The Slanting of
     Subjective Probabilities--Agreement on Some Essen-
     tials," Q.J.Economics, 79, pp. 657-663.

Chernoff, H. (1949). "Remarks on a Rational Selection of A Decision Function," Cowles Commission Discussion Paper: Statistics: No. 326A, Unpublished.

Chernoff, H. (1954). "Rational Selection of Decision Functions," Econometrica, 22, pp. 422-443.

Coombs, C.H. (1975). "Portfolio Theory and the Measurement of Risk," in M.F. Kaplan and S.Schwartz, eds., Human Judgment and Decision Processes, Academic Press, pp. 63-85.

Dreyfus, H.L., and Dreyfus, S.E. (1978). "Inadequacies in the Decision Analysis Model of Rationality," in C.A.Hooker, J.J.Leach, and E.F.McClennen, eds., Foundations and Applications of Decision Theory, Volume I: Theoretical Foundations, Reidel, pp. 115-124.

Econometrie (XL) (1953). Centre National de la Recherche Scientifique, Paris.

Ellsberg, D. (1954). "Classic and Current Notions of 'Measurable Utility'," The Economic Journal, 64, pp. 528-556.

Ellsberg, D. (1961). "Risk, Ambiguity, and the Savage Axioms," Q.J.Economics, 75, pp. 643-669.

Fellner, W. (1961). "Distortion of Subjective Probabilities as a Reaction to Uncertainty," Q.J.Economics, 75, pp. 670-689.

Fellner, W. (1963). "Slanted Subjective Probabilities and Randomization: Reply to Howard Raiffa and K.R.W. Brewer," Q.J.Economics, 77, pp. 676-690.

Friedman, M., and Savage, L.J. (1952). "The Expected-Utility Hypothesis and the Measurability of Utility," J. Pol. Economy, 60, pp. 463-474.

Hansson, B. (1975). "The Appropriateness of the Expected Utility Model," Erkenntnis, 9, pp. 175-193.

Kahneman, D., and Tversky, A. (1979). "Prospect Theory: An Analysis of Decision Under Risk," Econometrica, 47, pp. 263-291.

Luce, R.D., and Suppes, P. (1965). "Preference Utility, and Subjective Probability," in R.D. Luce, et.al., eds., Handbook of Mathematical Psychology, Vol. III, Wiley, pp. 249-410.

Machina, M. (1981). "'Rational' Decision Making Versus 'Rational' Decision Modelling?" Journal of Mathematical Psychology, 24, pp. 163-175.

Machina, M. (1982). "'Expected Utility' Analysis without the Independence Axiom," Econometrica, 50, pp. 277-323.

Markowitz, H. (1959). Portfolio Selection, Wiley.

Marschak, J. (1951). "Why 'Should' Statisticians and Businessmen Maximize Moral Expectation?" in J. Neyman, ed., Proceedings of the Second Berkeley Symposium on Mathematical Statistics and Probability, University of California Press, pp. 493-506.

Marschak, J. (1968). "Decision Making: Economic Aspects," International Encyclopedia of the Social Sciences, Vol. 4, Macmillan Co. & The Free Press, pp. 42-55.

McCrimmon, K.R., and Larsson, S. (1979). "Utility Theory: Axioms versus 'Paradoxes'," in M. Allais and O. Hagen, eds., Expected Utility and the Allais Paradox, Reidel, pp. 333-409.

Raiffa, H. (1961). "Risk, Ambiguity, and The Savage Axioms: Comment," Q.J. Economics, 75, pp. 690-694.

Raiffa, H. (1970). Decision Analysis, Addison-Wesley.

Rubin, H. (1949). "The Existence of Measurable Utility and Psychological Probability," Cowles Commission Discussion Paper: Statistics: No. 332, Unpublished.

Samuelson, P. (1952). "Probability, Utility, and the Independence Axiom," Econometrica, 20, pp. 670-678.

Samuelson, P. (1966). "Utility, Preference, and Probability," (abstract) in J. Stiglitz (ed.), The Collected Scientific Papers of Paul A. Samuelson, Volume 1, Item No. 13, MIT Press.

Savage, L.J. (1951). "The Theory of Statistical Decision," Am. Stat. Assoc. Journal, 46, pp. 57-67.

Savage, L.J. (1972). The Foundations of Statistics, 2nd Rev. Ed., Dover.

Schlaifer, R. (1969). Analysis of Decisions Under Uncertainty, McGraw-Hill.

Schoemaker, P.J.H. (1980). Experiments on Decision Under Risk, Martinus Nijhoff.

Seidenfeld, T. (1981). "Levi on the Dogma of Randomization in Experiments," in R.J. Bogdan, ed., Henry E. Kyburg, Jr. and Isaac Levi, Reidel, pp. 263-291.

Von Neuman, J., and Morgenstern, O. (1953). Theory of Games and Economic Behavior, 2nd Ed., Wiley.

Robin Pope

THE PRE-OUTCOME PERIOD AND THE UTILITY OF GAMBLING

In order for individuals to experience uncertainty, time must
elapse during which they are aware that they do not know an
aspect of the future. If no such time elapses there is no
uncertainty, i.e., uncertainty is a flow. Risk theorists
have not appreciated this, and hence the fundamental import
of time for uncertainty.

When uncertainty is correctly modelled as a flow it can
be seen that:

(a) The (dis)utility of gambling is the (dis)utility of not
    knowing the outcome.

(b) Expected utility theory is a probability weighted sum of
    the utility of conditional, i.e. certain, outcomes.

Hence (a), which Allais emphasizes, refers to the pre-outcome
period, whereas (b) refers to the subsequent period when the
outcome will be known, i.e.

: Von Neumann and Morgenstern who tried to model (a) and
  (b) as contemporaneous, thereby committed a logical
  error and and as a consequence encountered the problems
  that led them to delete (a) as an interim measure and
  to present (b) as an incomplete model.

: Those who interpret the nonlinear probability weighting
  of certain income theories of Bernard 1974, Blatt 1979,
  Hagen 1979 and Machina 1982, etc. as including (a)
  commit the same logical error of trying to model (a)
  and (b) as contemporaneous.

I thank Ken Arrow, Georges Bernard, and Mark Machina for
discussions; Maurice Allais, John Blatt, Ross Chapman, Jack
Hirshleifer, Jack Meyer, Ed Mishan, and Alex Wearing for
comments on earlier drafts 1979a, 1979b and 1981.

B. P. Stigum and F. Wenstøp (eds.), Foundations of Utility and Risk Theory with Applications,
137–177.
© 1983 *by D. Reidel Publishing Company.*

: Psychological experiments have been prejudiced for they
likewise omit the time dimension and hence have a
crucial vagueness in their experimental design.

Part 1 of this paper presents a discussion of the role
of examples, since the frivolous gambles on which risk
theorists focus obscures the fact that (a) involves weighty
considerations -- hope and fear, planning problems etc. --
and that the pre-outcome period is typically long. In Part
2 a more profitable example is analyzed and a complete
model of risky choice incorporating (a) and (b) is derived.
In Part 3 consistent definitions of uncertainty and risk
aversion are delineated. Part 4 examines the relation
between the complete model and current ones and a range of
misconceptions concerning (a) and (b). Part 5 discusses
current definitions and measures of risk aversion. It is
shown that the set of consistent definitions of risk and
uncertainty aversion includes Allais-style ones, but
excludes the Arrow-Pratt measures.

1. EXAMPLES: 'THE IMPORTANCE OF BEING EARNEST'

Economists and psychologists focus on particular examples
of decision-making under uncertainty and from them distil
their theories of risky choice. There is nothing wrong
with this method of theorising, viz, going beyond the
experimental evidence of the example, introducing concepts
and making generalizations that are not rigorously
justified. On the contrary, as Werner Heisenberg expounded
at the start of his historic lecture series on uncertainty
relations, it is inevitable and advisable to do so, "and
then allow experiment to decide at what points a revision
is necessary", 1930, pp. 1-2.

But not all examples foster equally useful theories.
While some examples inspire powerful theories, other
examples most conspicuously do not. Consider the swings in
the quality of theorising in ethics witnessed in the
English-speaking world. After these philosophers switched
to using trivial moral examples -- such as letter postage --
in the pre- and interwar years, almost nothing more profound
than the logical positivists' "boo/hoorah" theory of ethics
was generated.[1] It was only when philosophers switched back
to examples that involve the major moral issues of life-taking,
military conscription, income distribution and so forth,

that their theorising once again became fruitful, as in
the contributions of Rawls 1958, 1967, 1971.

The trivial moral examples on which these logical
positivists and their linguistic philosophy successors
focussed were chosen chiefly for their triviality. They
were chosen in the belief that trivial examples of moral
choices are somehow simpler, less camouflaged by side
issues, and hence facilitate theorising. Instead, the
triviality of the examples enabled them to remain blind to
the true nature of moral choice.

Consider now the examples on which economists and
psychologists have focussed in their study of risky choice.
Both in constructing and in testing theories the postwar
period has seen a switch to trivial and frivolous instances
of choice -- lotteries and casino gambles -- again, partly
in the belief that trivial examples provide simpler purer
instances of the central problem. Thus in their advocacy
of lotteries Friedman and Savage wrote,

> Lotteries seem to be an extremely fruitful, and
> much neglected, source of information about
> reactions of individuals to risk. They present
> risk in relatively pure form, with little
> admixture of other factors.   (1948, p. 286)

The danger is, therefore, that, as with the logical
positivists, the very triviality of the examples may be
camouflaging the nature of the choices. Accordingly, to
help discern the heart of risky choice, the frivolous and
trivial games of chance are here deserted for a more
crucial decision involving uncertainty, the dilemma of
history's war brides with husbands missing in action.

2. THE PENELOPE MYTH: TO REMARRY OR NOT TO REMARRY

> Penelope, in Homeric legend, the wife of Ulysses
> ...[who] went to the Trojan war. During his long
> wanderings after the fall of Troy he was
> generally regarded as dead, and Penelope was
> vexed by the urgent wooing of many suitors, whom
> she put off on the pretext that she must first
> weave a shroud for Laertes, her aged father-in-
> law. To protract the time she undid by night the

portion of the web which she had woven by day.
When the suitors had discovered this device her
position became more difficult than before; but
fortunately Ulysses returned in time to rescue
his chaste spouse from their distasteful
importunities. Later tradition represents
Penelope in a very different light, asserting
that by Hermes (Mercury), or by all her suitors
together, she became the mother of Pan ...and
that Ulysses on his return, divorced her.
                    (Chambers Encyclopaedia, 1890, p. 26)

Thus, in the first version of the myth, Penelope
decides not to remarry but to wait chastely while Ulysses'
fate is unknown. In the later version she makes the
alternative decision to take a new lover while he is
missing in action. Thereby she shows disloyalty to Ulysses
but contributes creatively to society via Hermes and Pan.
The myth, an exploration of decision making, can be
interpreted as one in which Penelope (i) prefers a resident
to an absentee husband/lover, and (ii) dislikes divorce.
Her dilemma is that preference (i) points to remarrying
while Ulysses is missing, whereas preference (ii) points to
not remarrying/taking lovers until Ulysses' fate is known.
Penelope's decision depends on a number of factors
including the delay before learning Ulysses' fate and how
hope and fear affect her during that delay.

In order to avoid attention being diverted from the
principal uncertainty, Ulysses' fate, it is assumed that
Penelope faces no other uncertainties and knows that:

1. She will die in just over 50 years and one week hence.
2. There is a 50 percent chance that Ulysses will be killed
   in action, a 50 percent chance that he will return alive.
3. She will learn Ulysses' fate in just over N years and
   one week hence, when a vessel will return with Ulysses,
   dead or alive.
4. She has two options, either to never remarry, the "Wait"
   option under which if Ulysses returns alive she and
   Ulysses live together until Penelope's death; or to
   marry Hermes, the "Remarry" option, under which she and
   Hermes live together until Penelope's death.
5. She must choose between these marriage options one week
   hence.

6. Her welfare, which she can cardinally measure, is as follows. The interim week of her marriage decision will be a limbo, yielding no utility. Should she decide on the "Wait" option, hope of Ulysses' return coupled with fear that he is dead would yield 20 utils per annum until she learns his fate. Should she instead decide on the "Remarry" option, present love coupled with fear of divorce would yield 50 utils per annum until she learns his fate. Once Ulysses' fate is known the "Wait" option would yield 90 utils per annum if Ulysses has returned alive, and hope is fulfilled, but none if Ulysses has been returned dead -- all hope gone -- while the "Remarry" option would yield 10 utils per annum if Ulysses has returned alive with shameful divorce in train, 60 utils if Ulysses has been returned dead so that divorce fears are gone.
7. Penelope is indifferent about whether her stream of utils under each option is concentrated in her early or later life, that is Penelope has a zero time preference rate, r_t, between utils received in year t and t + 1.
8. Her decision rule is to maximize her total expected welfare from the point of her marriage decision.

Thus, Penelope distinguishes what may be termed the outcome period of her life when Ulysses' fate will be known to her, from what may be termed the pre-outcome period when she is ignorant of Ulysses' fate but has made her marriage decision and is affected by hopes and fears. Further she distinguishes both these periods from the initial decision week. Table 1 summarizes her three-period analysis.

TABLE 1: PENELOPE'S WELFARE (utils per annum)

Decision Period: one week
- the period up to her marriage decision
a limbo   0

Pre-Outcome Period: N years
- the hope and fear period between her marriage decision and her learning Ulysses' fate

Option	"Wait"	"Remarry"
	20	50

Outcome Period: (50-N) years
- the period in which she knows Ulysses' fate and that lasts up to her death

State/Option	"Wait"	"Remarry"
Ulysses alive	90	10
Ulysses dead	0	60

In reaching her decision, Penelope bypasses the decision period which does not yield her any utility, to focus on the latter two periods of her life, the pre-outcome period covering the span of years between her marriage decision and Ulysses' return, and the outcome period covering the years of Ulysses' return. She selects the marriage option which yields the highest expected welfare summed over these two latter periods. And provided that Penelope has to make her marriage decision before Ulysses' return and hence before she learns his fate, $N > 0$, her welfare under each option is an expected rather than known sum which means that her maximand may be expressed as follows,

$$K(N) = \sum_{t=0}^{N} k_t (1+r_t)^{-t} + \sum_{t>N}^{50} \sum_{j=1}^{2} p_j k_{jt} (1+r_t)^{-t}, \qquad [1]$$

$$\text{total} \qquad\qquad \text{pre-outcome} \qquad\qquad\qquad \text{outcome period}$$

where $K(N)$ is Penelope's total expected welfare under marriage option K, $K = W$ "Wait", R "Remarry"; t is time in years; k_t is welfare per annum under option K during the pre-outcome year t; j is the state of the world, $j = 1$ Ulysses returns alive, 2 Ulysses returned dead; p_j is the probability that state of the world j will occur; k_{jt} is her welfare per annum under option K in state of the world j during the outcome year t.

Penelope's own calculations would be simpler than [1]. First, since Penelope is not impatient ($r_t = 0$ for all t by Assumption 7), the time discount terms can be eliminated. Second, since Penelope's welfare per annum is constant over the N years of the pre-outcome period, and a different constant in each of the (50-N) years of the outcome period ($k_t = k$ and $k_{jt} = k_j$ for all t by Assumption 6), the summation signs for k_t and k_{jt} can be replaced by N and (50-N) respectively. Third, since both states of the world are equally likely to occur (by Assumption 2), p_j can be replaced by 0.5, as in [2] for $N > 0$,

$$K(N) = kN + \sum_{j=1}^{2} 0.5 k_j (50-N). \qquad [2]$$

$$\text{total} \qquad\qquad \text{pre-outcome} \qquad\qquad \text{outcome period}$$

Thus under the "Wait" option, which yields 20 utils per annum for the N pre-outcome years, then for the remaining (50-N) years an expected 0.5(90 utils) + 0.5(0 utils) = 45 utils per annum, her total expected welfare from waiting is

$$\underset{\text{total}}{\text{Wait: W(N)}} = \underset{\text{pre-outcome}}{\text{20N utils}} + \underset{\text{outcome period}}{\text{45(40-N) utils.}} \quad [3]$$

Compared to the "Wait" option, the "Remarry" option yields her more in the N pre-outcome years, 50 utils per annum, and in the subsequent (50-N) outcome years a lesser expected sum, 0.5(10 utils) + 0.5(60 utils) = 35 utils per annum, so that her total expected welfare from remarrying is

$$\underset{\text{total}}{\text{Remarry: R(N)}} = \underset{\text{pre-outcome}}{\text{50N utils}} + \underset{\text{outcome period}}{\text{35(50-N) utils.}} \quad [4]$$

Whether $W(N) \gtrless R(N)$ depends importantly on the first term in [3] and [4], i.e. on the term kN which denotes Penelope's welfare during the pre-outcome period. Just how critical kN is, is explored further in Appendix A. If theorists were to seriously mis-specify or entirely omit kN, their models would lack explanatory and predictive power.

3. PENELOPE: CAUTIOUS OR BRAVE?

Is the Penelope of equations [3] and [4] cautious and uncertainty averse, or brave and uncertainty loving? To say that Penelope is uncertainty averse is to say that Penelope prefers a situation F which has less uncertainty to another situation G which has a reference amount of uncertainty. Thus, Penelope is uncertainty averse, if

$$F \; \rho \; G, \quad [5]$$
and
$$\beta^F < \beta^G, \quad [6]$$

where ρ is the preferred to relation; and β^h, h = F,G is the total amount of uncertainty that Penelope would face if she were about to embark on a situation h, i.e., if h can be chosen, at the point of embarking on option h.

To complete the definition of uncertainty averse it is necessary to detail how the uncertainties β^F and β^G are measured and hence compared. Uncertainty, being a flow, depends on level and duration.

$$\beta^h \quad = \quad \overset{50}{\underset{t=0}{\Sigma}} \quad w_t \; \lambda^h_{t'} \tag{7}$$

total   duration   level

where, w_t is the weight for year t which can incorporate elements such as Penelope's time preference or impatience rate; λ^h_t is Penelope's level of uncertainty under option h in year t; and λ^h_t is obtained by applying a dispersion measure (i.e. an uncertainty measure) to Penelope's possible states -- after these states have been expressed in units appropriate to the perspective from which Penelope's uncertainty is to be judged.

Penelope's uncertainty may be judged with respect to her knowledge of the outcome, Ulysses' fate, or with respect to her knowledge of her own welfare. The latter perspective is the one used by Penelope in calculating her welfare under each option. It is also the derivative perspective, for Penelope's knowledge of her own welfare derives from her knowledge of Ulysses' fate. It is important to carefully distinguish between these two perspectives as they have precisely opposite implications for whether Penelope's uncertainty is located in the pre-outcome or the outcome period and, therefore, for which options are certain, which uncertain.

If uncertainty is judged with respect to Penelope's knowledge of the outcome, then the pre-outcome period when Penelope is ignorant of Ulysses' fate is uncertain, whereas the outcome period, when Penelope knows his fate, contains no uncertainty,

$$\beta^h(N) \quad = \quad \overset{N}{\underset{t=0}{\Sigma}} \quad w_t \; \lambda^h_t \qquad + \qquad 0. \tag{8}$$

total   pre-outcome   outcome period

Ceteris paribus, the uncertainty of an option dimishes as N decreases, and options where N = 0 are certain options. Thus the option of consulting the oracle and thereby selecting N = 0, option C, is a certain option,

$$\beta^C_{total}(0) \quad = \quad \underset{\text{outcome period}}{0,} \qquad\qquad [9]$$

the option of remarrying and setting N = 50, R(50), an uncertain one,

$$\beta^R_{total}(50) \quad = \quad \underset{\text{pre-outcome period}}{\sum_{t=0}^{50} w_t \lambda^R_t(50)} \quad > \quad 0. \qquad [10]$$

But if instead uncertainty is judged with respect to Penelope's knowledge of her own welfare, then the pre-outcome period, for which Penelope knows what her welfare will be, is certain. It is the outcome period, during which Penelope's welfare will depend on the unknown outcome, that is uncertain,

$$\beta^h_{total}(N) \quad = \quad \underset{\text{pre-outcome}}{0} \quad + \quad \underset{\text{outcome period}}{\sum_{t=N}^{50} w_t \lambda^h_t} \qquad [11]$$

Ceteris paribus, uncertainty diminishes as N increases and options where N reaches 50 are certain options. Thus the option R(50) is a certain option,

$$\beta^R_{total}(50) \quad = \quad \underset{\text{pre-outcome period}}{0,} \qquad\qquad [12]$$

the option C an uncertain one,

$$\beta^C_{total}(0) \quad = \quad \underset{\text{outcome period}}{\sum_{t=0}^{50} w_t \lambda^C_t} \quad > \quad 0. \qquad [13]$$

Were Penelope offered the choice between C and R(50), as shown in Appendix A, she would choose C, thereby revealing, C ρ R(50). Let $\beta^R(50)$ be the reference amount of uncertainty. Then if uncertainty is judged with respect to Penelope's knowledge of the outcome, from [9] and [10], $\beta^C(0) < \beta^R(50)$, and Penelope is uncertainty averse. But, if uncertainty is judged with respect to Penelope's

knowledge of her own welfare, from [12] and [13],
$\beta^C(0) > \beta^R(50)$, and Penelope is not uncertainty averse.

The conclusion reached on whether Penelope is
uncertainty averse would depend in general not only on the
perspective used to judge uncertainty. It would depend
also on the particular reference amount of uncerainty used,
the particular dispersion measure used, the particular
units used to express the possible states in common units,
and the particular weighting system used for different
years in Penelope's life, the w_t.. Each particular instance
of applying the procedure set down in the paragraph
beginning this part of the paper provides a conclusion on
whether Penelope is uncertainty averse. And since this
procedure simply spells out the general meaning of the
words "uncertainty averse," each particular instance is a
definition of "uncertainty averse." <u>The set of particular
instances of applying this procedure constitutes the set of
definitions of uncertainty averse and delineates the range
of meaning of this term.</u>

A somewhat different procedure may be required to
determine whether Penelope were risk averse in that in many
languages, risk as exposure to peril is distinguished from
uncertainty as a more neutral condition of not knowing.[2]
For instance, according to <u>Webster's Third New International
Dictionary</u>, an uncertain option involves ignorance.

> <u>Uncertainty</u>: Lack of certitude ranging from a
> small falling short of definite knowledge to an
> almost complete lack of it or even any conviction
> especially about at outcome or result. (1964, p. 2484)

By contrast the hallmark of a risky option is danger:

> <u>Risk</u>: The possibility of loss, injury,
> disadvantage or destruction; the degree or
> probability of loss.   (1964, 1961)

Thus, whereas in measuring uncertainty, both good
and bad possible states are relevant, in measuring risk
only the dangers, the bad possible states, matter. A like
procedure is required to calculate risk and to specify the
set of definitions of risk averse to that discussed above
for uncertainty, except that an injury measure replaces the

dispersion measure and the injury measure is applied only to the subset of bad states.

How then do current decision making procedures compare with Penelope's? And how do current risk aversion measures compare with the set delineated here?

4. CURRENT DECISION MAKING MODELS

Consider first expected utility theory. The differences between this procedure and Penelope's do not concern the goal pursued: in both decision makers maximize their expected utils. The differences concern the way in which utils are assigned, expected utility theory imposing three additional constraints, two concerning the method of deriving the utility index, and one concerning the time period for which such indices should be constructed. Since only the two former have been at all widely recognized, and even there are matters of continuing confusion, the immediate tasks are to identify the three constraints, and then discuss the confusion.

4.1. The constraints

Penelope's utils are expressed solely as functions of her situation under each option, whereas in expected utility theory, utils must be derivable from a series of separable components as follows. The "value" of each possible situation under an option K for the decision maker is first expressed in terms of Y_i^K, a uni-dimensional objective quantity, for the sake of exposition, one frequently chosen, money income -- the arguments that follow do not depend on the particular "objective" quantity used. Y_i^K is then transformed via the decision maker's utility function, U. The requirement that the utils be derived (in a two-stage process) from uni-dimensional objective quantities may be termed constraint (a).

If for the option K there are two possible mutually exclusive outcomes, i = 1,2, then U takes the form,

$$U(K) \quad = \quad U(p_1, Y_1^K, p_2, Y_2^K), \qquad\qquad [14]$$

and

$$U(p_1, Y_1^K, p_2, Y_2^K) \quad = \quad p_1 U(Y_1^K) + p_2 U(Y_2^K). \qquad [15]$$

For $0 > p_1 > 1$, [14] and [15] together imply that there is
a unique separation of the utility derived from the
uncertain option K into probabilities and conditional, that
is to say, certain, money income: in other words expected
utility theory assumes that

> In choosing among alternatives ...whether or not
> these alternatives involve risk, a consumer
> ...behaves as if (his or her) ...preferences
> could be completely described by a function
> attaching a numerical value -- to be designated
> "utility" -- to alternatives each of which is
> regarded as <u>certain</u> ...
>   (Friedman and Savage, 1948, p. 282, emphasis added)

The requirement that U(Y) is a mapping from <u>certain</u> money
incomes may be termed constraint (b).

The third major constraint on how utils are assigned
in expected utility theory derives from the fact that
formal models from axiomatic bases do not differentiate
between the decision period, and pre-outcome period and the
outcome period.[3] As a consequence they do not delineate the
flow of uncertainty. In interpreting these models, the
decision period and the pre-outcome period are largely
ignored, the typical examples of Y's being lottery wins
that accrue in the outcome period. Thus the expected
utility model is de facto interpreted as a model of the
outcome period: it omits consideration of Penelope's
welfare before Ulysses returns, and hence omits row 2 of
Table 1 and the first term of equations [1] to [4]. In
omitting the pre-outcome period, expected utility theory
may be described as omitting the uncertain period, for from
the perspective of the decision maker's knowledge of the
outcome, it is the pre-outcome period that is uncertain.[4]

The irony of omitting the uncertain period from an
uncertainty model is largely due to a lack of appreciation
of the inalienable link between time and the experience of
uncertainty. Time has tended to be regarded as an optional
complication of uncertainty models, the optional, albeit
important, complications of sequential choice problems or
of a non-zero time preference rate.[5] The more basic role
of time has been overlooked, namely that unless there is a
period <u>before</u> the outcome is known, there is no uncertainty.

In modifying expected utility theory to include
the pre-outcome period, would it be appropriate to retain
the U(Y) mapping? This would mean retaining constraint, (b),
that the Y's be certain magnitudes.[6] For the outcome
period, this is uncontroversial, since by then decision
makers know their entire future. But for the pre-outcome
period since this is a period when decision makers do not
yet know their entire future, U(Y) would only apply to a few
rare souls whose well-being depends solely on their current
(certain money income) situation and who are unaffected by
the fact that they face an unknown future. It would not apply
to Penelope: by Assumption 6, her welfare per annum during
the pre-outcome period depends partly on hope and fear of
what the unknown future outcome period will bring.[7]
Accordingly, for the pre-outcome period expected utility
theory's U(Y) mapping is inappropriate. It precludes
considerations of hope and fear, considerations that affect
virtually all the human race. It precludes considerations of
whether individuals rejoice or shrink as life's vagaries are
thrust upon them. It ignores the taste for uncertainty and
risk.

4.2. Confusions

This section canvasses confusions about how to model the
taste for risk and uncertainty; how to interpret the
independence principle; how to interpret the Arrow-Pratt
indices; and how classical utility relates to U(Y).

4.2.1. Modelling the taste for risk and uncertainty

Von Neumann and Morgenstern could not incorporate this
taste, which they termed the "definite utility or
disutility of gambling"[8], due to axiomatic difficulties:

> It constitutes a much deeper problem to formulate
> a system in which gambling has under all
> conditions a definite utility or disutility,
> where numerical utilities fufilling the calculus
> of mathematical expectations cannot be defined by
> any process, direct or indirect.   (1947, p. 629)

The "utility" or "pleasure of gambling" does not mean the
taste for watching a roulette wheel etc, since including
such non-monetary aspects of income does not create any
problems.[9] As Allais put it

"pleasure of gambling" ...doit être
soigneusement distingué du plaisir attaché à
l'opération matérielle du jeu "pleasure of the
game".

"pleasure of gambling." ...must be carefully
distinguished from the physical process of
gambling, "pleasure of the game,."
                                    (1953a, p. 510, footnote 8)

Borch 1969 encounters the same axiomatic difficulties in
the mean-variance approach to asset prices, asserting that
there are inconsistencies in Tobin's model "in which
gambling has under all conditions a definite disutility"
(the negative coefficient attached to the variance of net
returns on an asset), while also giving "numerical
utilities fulfilling the calculus of mathematical
expectations" (attaching a positive coefficient to the mean
net return on an asset).[10]

Once the flow dimension of uncertainty is recognized
these axiomatic difficulties vanish: the definite
(dis)utility of gambling, of not knowing the outcome, must
be modelled for the pre-outcome period, whereas expected
utility theory models the subsequent period. In short, the
axiomatic inconsistencies arose from erroneously trying to
force the (dis)utility of not knowing the outcome to be
simultaneous with the utility that will be derived after
the outcome is known and hence when income is certain.

Consider for example von Neumann and Morgenstern's
struggle over complementarity considerations:

We have for utilities u, v the "natural" relation
u → v (read: u is preferable to v), and the
"natural" operation $\alpha u + (1 - \alpha)v$, $(0 > \alpha > 1)$,
(read: ...combination of u, v with the
alternative probabilities α, $(1 - \alpha)$ ...

(3:1:a) u → v   implies $V(u) > V(v)$
(3:1:b) $V(\alpha u) + (1 - \alpha)v) = \alpha V(u) + (1 - \alpha)V(v)$ ...

> Simply additive formulae, like (3:1:b),
> would seem to indicate that we are assuming the
> absence of any form of complementarity between
> the things the utilities of which we are
> combining. It is important to realize, that we
> are doing this solely in a situation where there
> can indeed be no complementarity. ...our u, v
> are the utilities not of definite -- and possibly
> coexistent -- goods or services, but of imagined
> events. The u, v of (3:1:b) in particular refer
> to alternatively conceived events u, v, of which
> only one can and will become real. I.e. (3:1:b)
> deals with either having u (with the probability
> α) or v (with the remaining probability 1 - α) --
> but since the two are in no case conceived as
> taking place together, they can never complement
> each other.   (1947, pp. 24 and 628, emphasis added)

Such complementarity considerations are of course out of
the question for the outcome period, when one of the
previously possible outcomes has occurred, excluding the
other. By contrast such complementarity questions are of
the essence of the (dis)utility of not knowing the outcome,
i.e., of the essence of utility during the pre-outcome
period during which possible future outcomes can complement
each other.

One serious consequence of subsequent theorists
adhering to the ban on complementarity considerations has
been the application of expected utility state preference
models to firm behaviour, share prices and the scope for
government sponsorhip to alleviate risk disutility. As
analyzed elsewhere, Pope 1982a, this has resulted in a
taboo on risk pooling considerations in the pure risk
literature and the widespread use of models of competitive
equilibrium in which risk pooling cannot enhance a firm's
present worth -- contrary to the marketplace where
competition for funds ensures that only firms that give due
weight to risk pooling are financed, i.e., survive.

4.2.2. Interpreting the independence principle

Within expected utility theory the independence principle
plays a major role in precluding complementarity
considerations, and hence the taste for uncertainty and

risk.[11] Von Neumann and Morgenstern therefore attempted to
relax it. Many later writers, however, have felt no such
pressure and hence it might be expected that their grounds
for ignoring the taste for uncertainty and risk, and
thereby such crucial considerations as fear and hope, would
be extensively argued. Instead, expositions in its favour
are in essence limited to exclamations that surely anyone
would believe in it. Friedman and Savage's explication of
the principle is representative. They introduce it with
the panegyric that it is

> practically unique among maxims for wise action
> in the face of uncertainty, in the strength of
> its intuitive appeal. The principle is
> universally known and recognized; and the Greeks
> must surely have had a name for it, though
> current English seems not to.   (1952, p. 468)

Next they claim to "illustrate the principle," but in fact
describe a prejudged situation that therefore cannot
illustrate how choices are made,[12]

> suppose a physician now knows that his patient
> has one of several diseases for each of which the
> physician would prescribe immediate bed rest. We
> assert that ...the physician should ...prescribe
> immediate bed rest whether he is now, later, or
> never, able to make an exact diagnosis. (1952, p. 468)

This unsupported assertion that the "right" prescription
can be known independently of the probability of the
patient having that disease, independently of his
probability of recovery under alternative prescriptions,
independently of every aspect of his speed of recovery
under alternative prescriptions and so forth, is of course
nonsense (unless all these diseases are identical with
respect to all these probabilities, in which case the
"several" diseases are indistinguishable). This can be
seen by considering just three possible criteria for
selecting the "right" prescription for minimizing the fears
of the patient or his family in the absence of the more
comprehensive welfare information supplied for Penelope in
Table 1, viz minimizing, (i) the length of the pre-outcome
period, or, (ii) the risk of an unfavourable outcome: or,
(iii) the disparity between outcomes. In general which

prescription meets (i), (ii) or (iii) is something that cannot be ascertained by reference to the independence principle -- self-evidently these fear criteria require prior or simultaneous consideration of the probabilities with the outcomes.

The readiness of Friedman and Savage and others to accept the independence principle does not in fact stem from a deliberate policy of excluding hope and fear. Rather it arises from the trivial gambling examples used to evaluate the independence principle. From these examples the frivolous appelative "love of gambling" was chosen to explain the significance of the principle making it appear that a very minor aspect of decision theory has been omitted from the model. As one notable exponent of expected utility theory put it in correspondence to me, "individuals with such tastes can be exploited as a money pump, ...which severely limits how far they can go in this direction and survive." Not only is concern about risk frivolous in the gambling examples, it is of very short duration, since implicitly in these examples the pre-outcome period is extremely brief, and hence easy to overlook.

4.2.3. The Arrow-Pratt measures

Arrow suggested that for decision makers who conform to expected utility theory

$$R_a(Y) = -U''(Y)/U'(Y) \equiv \text{absolute risk aversion, } [16]$$

and

$$R_r(Y) = -YU''(Y)/U'(Y) \equiv \text{relative risk aversion, } [17]$$

where U' and U'' denote respectively the first and second derivatives with respect to Y of the expected utility mapping $U(Y)$.[13] It follows that [16] and [17] relate exclusively to certain income and have no bearing on whether individuals derive a definite utility or disutility from gambling, from not knowing the outcome: they exclude the direct dependence of utility on dispersion that Penelope exhibits in the pre-outcome period. Instead [16] and [17] measure the indirect dependence of utility on dispersion in the outcome period that arises when the utility of certain income curve is nonlinear.

Arrow and Pratt's use of the words "risk aversion" for
[16] and/or [17] has led to confusion for the words "risk
aversion" are widely interpreted as the definite disutility
of gambling. A casual check amongst economists and
psychologists will confirm that a disconcertingly large
number of the theorists and applied researchers who employ
expected utility models erroneously believe that the Arrow-
Pratt measures prove that expected utility theory includes
the definite (dis)utility of gambling.

4.2.3. Classical utility and U(Y)

In a very recent review, Schoemaker states that

> NM utility should not be interpreted as measuring
> the strength of preference under certainty, being
> quite different in this regard from neoclassical
> cardinal utility ...One reason is that
> preferences among lotteries are determined by at
> least two separate factors; namely (1) strength
> of preference for the consequences under certainty,
> and (2) attitude toward risk. The NM utility
> function is a compound mixture of these two.
>
> (1982, p. 533)

In Schoemaker's terminology U(Y) is NM utility and (2) is
the definite (dis)utility of gambling. Schoemaker's
contrast, therefore, is erroneous: NM utility is not a
compound mixture of (1) and (2), but excludes (2) by
assumption.

Schoemaker's error, however, is not a product of
confusing the meaning of the Arrow-Pratt indices. It is
shared by others,[14] and springs from logical positivists'
desire to remove from the expected utility theory's U(Y)
the disreputable tag of cardinality and its associated
metaphysical connotations of psychological satisfaction by
invoking a distinction between (neo)classical utility as
introspective and U(Y) as operational.[15] The process of
reaching this distinction has led some into the error of
thinking that U(Y) operates by definition.

Consider, for instance, the line of reasoning in
Ellsberg 1954, which Schoemaker praises as "lucid".
Ellsberg claims that von Neumann and Morgenstern
"mistakenly" describe U(Y) as a cardinal measure of (1) and
inferences about (1) from their axioms as refutable

hypotheses, "mere estimates", and that evidence on (2) has
no bearing on whether expected utility theory is applicable
-- in striking contrast to the von Neumann and Morgenstern,
1947, p. 18-20 and 630, Robertson, 1952, p. 28, and Allais,
1953b, p. 517 understanding that the more important this
omitted element, the worse the estimates of (1) derived
from expected utility. Ellsberg reaches this astonishing
position by explaining that von Neumann and Morgenstern,
unknown to themselves, "define" the observational evidence
as (1) "and in a matter of definition there can be no
question of truth or falsity", p. 553. In a matter of
definition, no. But this is not the issue. The issue is
the inferential one of how well the components of the
definitions, and the deductions therefrom, relate to
empirical observations. Ellsberg has confused the
definitional deductive process of deriving hypotheses with
that of testing them, whereas von Neumann and Morgenstern
showed a correct grasp of the hypothetico-deductive method.
And instead of testing whether (2) matters, contradicting
U(Y), experiments revealing (2) are sometimes described by
those who share Ellsberg's confusion as revealing the extra
feature of U(Y) over and above (neo)classical utility!

   The error in Ellsberg's view can also be shown by
reductio ad absurdum. His view that U(Y) includes (2)
involves denying constraint (b), p. 12 above, i.e.
Ellsberg denies that expected utility theory imposes the
constraint that Y is certain money income. Suppose that
Ellsberg were correct in this regard and that Y can refer,
to uncertain money income. Expected utility theory
includes certain options, hence Y must also refer to
certain money income. Further Y is uni-dimensional, there
being only one Y symbol -- hence Y must refer to certain
and uncertain money income indiscriminately. But this
assumes that [14] and [15], p. 11 above, simultaneously
hold and do not hold, for there is not a unique separation
of the uncertain situation into probabilities and Y's. It
follows that constraint (b) is necessary to ensure the
consistency of expected utility theory's axioms, and that
von Neumann, Morgenstern, Friedman, Savage, etc. did not
misconstrue these axioms as Ellsberg claims: U(Y) does
omit (2), the definite (dis)utility of gambling and thereby
precludes considerations of hope and fear.

4.3. Expected utility theory as an approximation

Omitting (2) and hence considerations such as hope and
fear, U(Y) might be acceptable if the pre-outcome period,
N, were zero in the typical situation since then (2) would
be limited to the decision period. But this is not the
case. The principal classes of decisions of interest to
economists and psychologists are

(i) decisions to embark on long term investments, as in
career, marriage, physical capital, and

(ii) decisions to engage in short term repeat investments
over long periods of time, as in weekly purchases of
lottery tickets, quarterly purchases of insurance.

For both classes of decision N, the length of the pre-
outcome period, is typically sizable. After deciding to
enroll, a student often waits three to ten years before
learning whether he has become a successful psychologist;
after deciding on a new social welfare programme, a
government often does not know for over a decade whether
these policies have improved society; after deciding on a
mining project, the company must survive several years
before learning whether that particular mine returns a net
profit; after deciding to devote a fraction of the
housekeeping funds to a weekly lottery ticket, housekeepers
can dream from age nineteen to ninety-nine that they will
become millionaires at the next drawing.

     For many decision makers N is sizable because
eliminating it is either physically impossible or buying
the relevant information is prohibitively expensive --
Penelope's scope p.167 below to costlessly eliminate it by consulting the oracle is unusual. Other decision makers, such as the
repeat purchasers of lottery tickets, would not wish to
eliminate N. Thus hope and fear do play a major role in
choices. With regard to a given set of options, those who
enjoy uncertainty, buoyed up by the hope of an eventual
favourable outcome, for whom in R. L. Stevenson's words,
"to travel is better than to arrive" select, ceteris
paribus options that involve large N's. Those who are
overwhelmed by anxiety, for whom "the devil we know is
better than the devil we don't know", select, ceteris
paribus, options that involve small N's.

In omitting (2) and hence the significant influence of considerations such as hope and fear, expected utility theory is unsatisfactory for positive models. It does play a normative role if it is ignoring immoral or irrational elements in behaviour, and thereby presenting the procedure for ideal decision making.

4.4. Is expected utility theory morally superior?

In asking about moral choice only comparatively modern writings can be appealed to: the Penelope myth, as an analysis of appropriate behaviour in the face of uncertainty belongs to one of the earliest bodies of literature discussing this question. The concepts of time, and hence of uncertainty, a period of time when individuals are aware that they do not know an aspect of the future, are apparently comparatively modern. Thus in middle eastern cultures it was only with the Assyrians, between 1300 and 800 BC that time starts to become a concept that people use in their writings and understanding of the world. It is less well-known that writings containing the concept of uncertainty are also comparatively modern. Yet, as for instance Jaynes observed when investigating his controversial consciousness hypothesis, "It is a help here to realize that there was no concept of chance whatever until very recent times", 1977, p. 240. And the period when the notion of chance emerged broadly coincides with the emergence of the concept of time. For while man was unaware of the passage of time he could not be in a state of uncertainty. Awareness of time is a sine qua non of awareness that the world is uncertain. Man by adding the fourth dimension of time to his picture of the world, has been enabled to 'self-consciously' choose among uncertain alternatives. Jaynes himself, however, does not link the emergence of the concepts of time and uncertainty -- it is not relevant to his hypothesis. He does not go beyond recording the emergence of the two concepts in different sections of his study[16], thereby remaining in this sense in the mainstream of economic and psychological theory which misses the integral role of time in the experience of uncertainty.

Modern writings, from the myth of Penelope on, abound in advice against being cowardly and foolhardly, that is against being influenced by certain fears and hopes. Perhaps

the most famous quotation in this regard is from Jewish
literature in the form of Christ's injunction, 'Take no
thought for the morrow'. Epictetus' essay on <u>Courage and
Caution</u>, presenting a similar message from the Stoic
tradition, is also widely cited. However, modern writings
also abound in praise of those who let certain other fears
and hopes influence the decisions. To give but one
example, the Psalms of the Jewish tradition extoll fear of
God and hope in his goodness. Hence in order to establish
that the expected utility procedure of ignoring hopes and
fears corresponds to moral behaviour, it is necesary to
establish that the psalmists, and the numerous other
writers who have praised certain fears and hopes, are
misguided. It is not enough merely to establish that being
swayed by some experiences of hopes and fears constitutes
non-ideal behaviour.

Nor is it correct to suggest that considerations of
hope and fear, while appropriate for an individual making
choices for him or herself, are inappropriate when making
choices on behalf of others.[17] Of course, it is
inappropriate for such agents, managers, politicians, and
the like, to give undue weight to their own hopes and
fears. But it is likewise in general inappropriate for
them to ignore the hopes and fears that will be engendered[18]
in their constituents by decisions taken on their behalf.

A moral role for expected utility theory appears even
more remote when it is realized that hope and fear are
examples -- not the full set -- of crucial considerations
omitted when expected utility theory omits the pre-outcome
period and the taste for uncertainty and risk. Hope and
fear were selected for focus in this paper, but during the
pre-outcome period uncertainty would also in general alter
Penelope's material resources and pecuniary status. Thus
although during the pre-outcome period Penelope's utility
in each possible situation is described in assumption 6 as
depending on emotional dimensions, an alternative scenario
(that would not otherwise alter the conclusions reached in
this paper) would have been one in which her low level of
utility during the pre-outcome period under the "Wait"
option stemmed partly from her ineligibility for a
window's pension. Appendix B deals with planning problems
which provide further evidence of the tangible costs of
uncertainty.

4.5. <u>Are departures from expected utility theory irrational?</u>

The most celebrated instances of behaviour inconsistent
with expected utility theory are Allais-style preferences.
And Ramsey's proof, 1926, revived in Savage 1954, that these
preferences are inconsistent is the principal source of the
view that all departures from expected utility theory are
due to errors of reasoning or perception. This influential
proof involves introducing a sequence of time separable
gambles into Allais' simple one period gamble and then
maintaining that the new time sequenced gamble, C', is
equivalent to C.[19] In turn this means that Ramsey and
Savage go beyond purely deductive reasoning to reach their
conclusion that Allais-style preferences are inconsistent.
Using logic alone, time sequenced gambles cannot be deduced
from one period gambles. Their demonstration of
inconsistency hinges on their <u>empirical</u> hypothesis that
decision makers are indifferent between a one period and a
time sequenced gamble, provided only that for both gambles
each possible lump sum received has the same probability.

The implausibility of this hypothesis concerning C'
and C is more readily seen when an example of it is
presented in the terminology of Part 2. Assume for this
scenario that Penelope knows that:

1. She will die in just over 50 years and one week hence.
2. There is an 11 per cent chance of states of the world
   a and c whereby under Gambles C' and C respectively she
   secures $1,000,000. There is an 89 per cent chance of
   states of the world b and d whereby under Gambles C'
   and C respectively she receives $0.
3. She will learn the outcome of the first spin of the
   wheel in just over N years and one week hence, when
   she will also obtain the receipts of Gamble C'. She
   will learn the outcome of the second spin of the wheel
   in just over (N+N') years and one week hence, when she
   will also obtain the receipts of Gamble C.
4. She has two options, Gambles C' and C.
5. She must choose between these gambling options one
   week hence.
6. Her welfare, which she can cardinally measure, is as
   follows: Prior to being forced to choose between the
   gambles, Penelope enjoyed her normal level of utility,
   30 utils per annum. The week of making her gambling

decision deprives her of all utility, due to her fear
of making the wrong choice and whichever gamble she
chooses, fear of a zero receipt from it deprives her
of all utility until its outcome is known. When the
outcome is known, Penelope reverts to her normal level
of 30 utils if she received $0. If instead she has
received $1,000,000, this would yield her 100 utils
per annum that year, thereafter she would revert to the
normal level of 30 utils per annum.

7. Penelope is indifferent about whether her stream of
utils under each option is concentrated in her early
or later life, that is Penelope has a zero time
preference rate between utils received in year t and
year t + 1.

8. Her decision rule is to maximize her total expected
welfare from the point of her gambling decision.

Table 2 summarizes Penelope's receipts under gambles C' and
C, highlighting the longer delay that Penelope would face
in learning the outcome if she were to choose C, and hence
the greater duration of her fear.

TABLE 2: PENELOPE'S RECEIPTS ($m per annum)

1 Decision Period: one week
- the period up to her gambling decision
                    a limbo   0
2 Pre-Outcome Period: N years
- the period between her gambling decision and her learning
  where the wheel has made its first stop

	Gamble C		Gamble C'	
Receipts	0		0	

3 Outcome Period of Wheel's Fist Stop: (50-N) Years
- the period in which she knows where the wheel has made its
  final stop that lasts up to her death

Receipts/State	Gamble C		Gamble C'	
	a	b	a	b
Years N+1	0	0	1	0
Years N+2, +3...	0	0	0	0

4 Outcome Period of Wheel's Second Stop: (50-N-N') Years
- the period in which she would know where the wheel has
  has made its second stop that lasts until her death

Receipts/State	Gamble C		Gamble C'	
	c	d	c	d
Year N+N'+1	1	0	0	0
Years N+N'+2, +3..	0	0	0	0

Self evidently Penelope would choose option C', and would reap an expected welfare of 0.11(100 utils) + 0.89(0 utils) = 11 utils per annum in the $(N + 1)^{th}$ year, 30 utils per annum for the remaining (50 - N - 1) years, in all, a total expected welfare, C'(N) = 11 utils + 30(50 - N - 1) utils. This exceeds her total expected welfare, C(N), under gamble C, for C(N) = 11 utils + 30(50 - N - N' - 1) utils. Penelope is therefore not indifferent between gambles C' and C. Although for both gambles each possible lump sum received has the same probability, considerations of fear drive a wedge between the utility that Penelope derives from each of them. The Ramsey-Savage hypothesis that Penelope would be indifferent is incorrect.

Expected utility theory adherents might be tempted to make two rejoinders. First, they might wish to contend that the example does not illustrate the Ramsey-Savage hypothesis because the lump sums received differ as regards timing. This objection is invalid. Penelope has by assumption 7. a zero time preference. In any case, the Ramsey-Savage hypothesis cannot be interpreted as imposing the condition that in the pair of gambles C' and C, all outcomes occur at the same time. The consequence of decomposing Allais' one period gamble C' into C, is that the two outcomes of C cannot coincide with each other and hence cannot both coincide with those of C'.

This begs the second rejoinder, that the outcome of C' and C can occur simultaneously because the example carries the implied assumption that no time elapses between the choice of an option and the outcome. This second rejoinder is therefore an example of not appreciating the flow dimension of uncertainty -- that there is no gamble if the decision maker knows the outcome at the point of placing his bet -- the example of Penelope being able to set N = 0 by consulting the oracle and thus knowing Ulysses' fate before placing her bet, p. 167 below.

Adherents of expected utility theory who believe that decision makers should be indifferent to fear and hope may believe a fortiori that decision makers should be indifferent to very brief experiences of fear and hope. It may very well be the case that influence on choices of fear and hope declines as the pre-outcome period declines. But it cannot be asserted that any individual affected by a

brief period of fear or hope is thereby displaying logical
inconsistency.

The germ of truth in the Ramsey-Savage analysis is
that individuals may find the temporal implications of
sequenced outcomes so absorbing that they fail to
adequately discount these time considerations when the
sequences take place rapidly.[20] Among the experimental
subjects used in Markowitz 1970 and Kahneman and Tversky 1979 to
evaluate the Ramsey-Savage conclusion, this is almost to be
expected, since these researchers fail to mention time
scales to their subjects. It is left to their subjects to
imagine (consciously or unconsciously) the time span
intended by the experimenter. And since there is a like
vagueness in most other risk experiments, and since a
rational man can be expected to give different answers
depending on the time involved in each stage of the
sequence, it is not feasible at present to discriminate
between deliberate departures from the expected utility
hypothesis and inadvertant departures, in the way some
researchers claim to have done this. Thus, for instance,
the temporal ambiguities in the experiments used by
Kahneman and Tversky do not warrant their conclusion that
Allais-style preferences arise from erroneous judgments
thwarting the decision maker's attempt to maximize his
expected utility.

Further, the practice adopted by many of "explaining"
to subjects where they have been inconsistent leaves much
to be desired. Given the incontrovertible evidence on the
suggestibility of subjects on more neutral issues, it can
be taken for granted that on the sensitive issue of being
accused of inconsistent behaviour, many subjects are unduly
swayed by the researcher's case and that inadequate
allowance is typically made for this.

4.5. Other Goals

Some have advocated a generalization of the expected utility
maximand in which the probability weights need not be
linear in the probabilities. Others have examined procedures
where the goal is not a maximand at all. Rather it is to
"satisfice" or to minimize the risk of dire consequences.

4.5.1. Nonlinear probability weights

These models replace [15] with

$$U(p_1, Y_1^K, p_2, Y_2^K) = f(p_1)U(Y_1^K) + f(p_2)U(Y_1^K), \qquad [18]$$

where f need not be a scalar, e.g. Edwards 1953, Bernard
1974, Blatt 1979, Hagen 1979, Kahneman and Tversky 1979,
Chew and MacCrimmon 1979, Fishburn 1981, and Machina 1982.
While these writers differ on whether the discrepancy
between [15] and [18] is due to "illusion", they all retain
[14]; hence the utility mapping U(Y) is still a mapping of
utility into <u>certain</u> income. It follows that all the
criticisms of expected utility made above apply to them
with equal force, and that such nonlinearities cannot
capture the (dis)utility of gambling.

Some have incorrectly asserted that the independence
principle is equivalent to the maximand being linear in the
probabilities, Machina 1981, p. 166, and Bernard 1981, p.
109. They are not: Penelope's maximand is linear in the
probabilities, she maximizes her expected welfare measured
in utils, and yet violates the independence principle. It is
her method of assigning utils, the weight she places on her
welfare during the pre-outcome period when she has a
definite taste for risk and uncertainty, that causes her to
violate the independence principle. But without the flow
dimension of uncertainty neither Machina nor Bernard were
able to distinguish between nonlinearities in the
probabilities and different ways of assigning utils. It
follows that much experimental data attributed to
nonlinearities in the probabilities could well be due
instead to the individual's definite (dis)utility of
gambling. Only when the time dimension is satisfactorily
and explicitly introduced into experiments and into the
interpretations of market observations, will there by scope
to try to untangle these two factors.

4.5.2. Satisficing and Minimising Models

There are grounds for developing normative as well as
positive models along these lines. For instance,
experimental subjects who sought to minimize disasters were
typically more successful than those whose goal was a
maximand, Hey 1982 and MacKinnon and Wearing 1982. The
"real world" biological observations of Hirshleifer 1977,
and market observations of Charnes and Cooper 1962 and
Charnes and Stedry 1966 lend further strong support to such
a development.

Such findings also indicate the value of introducing the layman's distinction between risk and uncertainty into the literature, and of devising measures of the taste for risk meaning peril, as distinct from the taste for uncertainty in general, as per pp. 10-11 above. At present the literature uses "risk" for what the layman would term "uncertainty". In other ways too the present terminology is unsatisfactory, as shown below.

5. CURRENT MEASURES OF RISK AVERSION: ALLAIS AND ARROW-PRATT

Allais suggests the following:[21]

$$U = U(A,E(B),\sigma), \quad U_1 > 0, \quad U_2 > 0, \quad\quad\quad [19]$$

where U is utility; A is the quantity of the certain commodity; B is the quantity of the uncertain commodity; E is the expectations operator; σ is the standard deviation of B; $U_3 > 0$ is risk loving; and $U_3 < 0$ is safety loving. Thus Allais in effect here suggests the standard deviation of the outcomes as the dispersion measure, i.e., as the index of the level of uncertainty,[22] with $\sigma = 0$ as the reference amount of uncertainty. In the notation of Part 3, $\lambda = \sigma$, $\beta^G = 0$, and

$$U_3 > 0 \quad \Rightarrow \quad \beta^F > \beta^G \equiv \text{ risk lover.} \quad\quad\quad [20]$$

Definition [20] clearly falls within the set of consistent definitions of uncertainty aversion.

By contrast the Arrow and Pratt measures, [16] and [17], p. 17 above, use functions of Y as dispersion measures, i.e. as indices of the level of uncertainty. Since Y refers to <u>certain</u> money income, see pp. 12, 17-19 above, these are straightforwardly incompatible with the concepts of risk and uncertainty, and therefore inadmissible, as are the Rothschild and Stiglitz 1970 and the Rothschild 1971 "equivalences".

Is it pedantic to point out the inadmissibility of [16] and [17]? Should not economists be free to redefine the words risk and uncertainty in any way they please? The obvious problem in their so doing is that it creates confusion: the words uncertainty and risk are being used, regularly in the same sentence, in not merely different, but incompatible ways and only a limited number of writers avoid thereby confusing themselves. As already noted pp.

17-18 above, a consequence of this confusion is that <u>many mistakenly believe that expected utility theory already includes the taste for risk and uncertainty -- a misconception that has unquestionably slowed the process of incorporating it.</u>

The less obvious, but perhaps equally serious problem is that reserving "risk aversion" for [16] and [17] means that <u>another neutral phrase needs to be found for the taste for risk (and uncertainty).</u>[23]   The difficulty of finding another neutral phrase helps perpetuate the use of phrases with pejorative lottery connotations, e.g. von Neumann and Morgenstern's (dis)utility of gambling. In turn this helps to perpetuate the view that the omitted taste is frivolous and of little consequence, and so slows the process of incorporating it.

<u>Had decision making been investigated using serious examples described in neutral language, it is unlikely that the time dimension of uncertainty would have been overlooked for so long.</u>

APPENDIX A: PENELOPE'S PRE-OUTCOME WELFARE

The crucial role of kN, Penelope's total welfare during the delay that she faces <u>after</u> making her marriage decision <u>before</u> learning Ulysses' fate, that is, her total welfare during the pre-outcome period, can be explored by the procedure of varying either k, her welfare per annum during the pre-outcome, or N, the length of the pre-outcome period. Consider variations in N. As N increases, the pre-outcome period lengthens and the outcome period shortens. And since Penelope's per annum welfare differs in the two periods, lengthening the pre-outcome period, increasing N, alters her welfare. Under the "Wait" option, for $0 > N \geqslant 50$, from Equation [3], $\partial W(N)/\partial N = 20$ utils $- 45$ utils < 0, that is Penelope's total welfare declines as the pre-outcome period lengthens. By contrast, under the "Remarry" option, for $0 > N \geq 50$, from Equation [4], $\partial R(N)/\partial N = 50$ utils $- 35$ utils > 0, that is Penelope's total welfare rises as the pre-outcome period lengthens.

Consider next the effect on Penelope's marriage decision of the length of this pre-outcome period N. Since in this period the relative value of the "Remarry" option is reversed in the subsequent outcome period during which the "Wait" option has the higher expected welfare, neither option is uniformly superior for all values of N within the range $0 > N \geqslant 50$. Hence the length of the delay before Penelope learns Ulysses' fate not only affects Penelope's total welfare, it also affects her very choice: a sufficiently short delay and Penelope will choose the "Wait" option, a sufficiently long delay and Penelope will choose the "Remarry" option. In particular, if the period of uncertainty were to exceed the switch over period N_s,

$$W(N_s) = R(N_s), \qquad\qquad\qquad [21]$$

Penelope would switch her decision from "Wait" to "Remarry." Substituting Equations [3] and [4] into [21], and simplifying, $N_s = 500/40 = 20$. Penelope, therefore, prefers the "Wait" option if the delay between making her decision and learning Ulysses' fate is less than 20 years, prefers the "Remarry" option if this delay exceeds 20 years, and is indifferent between the two options if this delay is 20 years precisely.

Suppose now that Penelope's options are expanded and that she can control the public purse which in turn controls the return speed of the fleet that brings knowledge of Ulysses' fate. Suppose that by the public spending programme, which she selects one week hence, she can vary the return date of the fleet from just over a week hence until her death. In other words she has the additional option one week hence of choosing the uncertain period N in the range $0 > N \geq 50$. Under the "Wait" option, since her total expected utility is a declining function of N, Penelope attains her maximum total welfare from waiting if she chooses the minimal delay, $N > 0$, that is, from Equation [3]. $W(max) = W(N \to 0) \to 2,250$ utils, $0 > N \geq 50$. Under the "Remarry" option since her total expected utility is an increasing function of N, Penelope attains her maximum total welfare from remarrying if she chooses the maximum delay, $N = 50$, that is, from Equation [4], for $N > 0$,

$$R(max) = 2,500 \text{ utils}, \qquad\qquad\qquad [22]$$

and since for N > 0,

$$R(\text{max}) \quad = \quad R(50) \quad > \quad W(\text{max}) \quad = \quad W(N \to 0), \qquad [23]$$

Penelope chooses the "Remarry" option and chooses to never learn Ulysses' fate.[24]

Suppose next that Penelope's options are further expanded. Suppose that she also has the option of deciding whether to consult the Delphic oracle within the first week, and that if she does so decide, the consultation enables her to learn Ulysses' fate by the time she has to choose between the "Wait" and the "Remarry" options. This further option means that Penelope must now choose the duration of her pre-outcome period, N, for N = 0, as well as for $0 > N \geqslant 50$. For N in the latter range, Equations [22] and [23] show that Penelope's best option, to remarry and never learn Ulysses' fate, yields her a total welfare of 2,500 utils. Penelope therefore will only choose N = 0 if thereby her total welfare exceeds 2,500 utils.

Since N = 0 means that Penelope chooses between the "Wait" and "Remarry" options knowing Ulysses' fate, her welfare under each option is conditional on this. If the Oracle divulges that Ulysses is returned alive, Penelope would take the "Wait" option since remarrying is less attractive: it would only yield 10 utils per annum for 50 years, whereas the "Wait" option Penelope reaps 90 utils per annum for 50 years so that her total welfare is

$$\text{Wait: } W(0) \Big|_{\substack{\text{Ulysses} \\ \text{alive}}} = 90 \cdot 50 \text{ utils} = 4,500 \text{ utils.} \qquad [24]$$

If the oracle divulges that Ulysses is returned dead, Penelope would take the "Remarry" option since waiting is less attractive; it would not yield Penelope any utils per annum whereas under the "Remarry" option she reaps 60 utils per annum for 50 years so that her expected welfare is

$$\text{Remarry: } R(0) \Big|_{\substack{\text{Ulysses} \\ \text{dead}}} = 60 \cdot 50 \text{ utils} = 3,000 \text{ utils.} \qquad [25]$$

As the oracle is equally likely to divulge that Ulysses is

returned alive or dead, her total expected welfare from
consulting the oracle, C, is the average of Equations [24]
and [25], Consult: C = 0.5(4,500 utils) + 0.5(3,000 utils)
= 3,750 utils, and since this exceeds the 2,500 utils
attainable from choosing N > 0 and not consulting the
oracle, Penelope selects N = 0 and consults the oracle.

Thus as Penelope's options concerning N changed so did
Penelope's welfare change, whether she decided to remarry or
wait, and whether she selected a "certain" or an "uncertain"
option. Recalling that Penelope's total pre-outcome welfare
is the product of N and her pre-outcome per annum welfare,
k, it follows immediately that in modelling Penelope's choice
procedures, if either N or k were omitted or seriously
mis-specified this would ruin the model's explanatory and
predicative power.

APPENDIX B: PLANNING AND THE PRE-OUTCOME PERIOD

To see how expected utility theory precludes the tangible
costs of not being able to plan optimally due to
uncertainty, suppose that Penelope has a monopoly in
foreign currency dealings and faces a perfectly competitive
credit market in borrowing for currency "speculation".
Suppose further that she knows that there will be a 50 per
cent revaluation of Greek currency against Persian currency
if Ulysses returns alive, a 50 per cent devaluation of
Greek currency if Ulysses is returned dead. This means
that by consulting the oracle, she can make substantial
certain profits on the exchange rate change. If instead
she only knows that there is a 50 percent chance of Ulysses
returning alive, then all she knows is that there is an
even chance of revaluation or devaluation, and hence she
can only make smaller (or zero) profits on the exchange
rate change.[25] Under these circumstances (i) Penelope would
be indifferent between a certain revaluation and a certain
devaluation of the Greek currency of 50 per cent, and (ii)
would prefer both to any uncertainty about whether a
pending 50 per cent overnight change is to be a revaluation
or a devaluation. In other words, Penelope her would
prefer to consult the oracle: she has a definite
(dis)utility of a gambling.

In the notation of p. 14 above, expected utility
theory would on the basis of (i) to assign a number V(u) to

the utility, u, of an overnight devaluation of 50 per cent
in the Greek currency, and an equal number V(v) to the
utility, v, of an overnight revaluation of 50 per cent in
the Greek currency. But then (3:1:b) would hold only
for α = 0 and α = 1, <u>i.e.</u>, holds only for certainty
situations: it holds only for the outcome period, not for
the pre-outcome period. No amount of redefining the
outcomes within the expected utility framework can alter
this: Penelope's preferences violate the axioms of
expected utility theory.

    Again, to relate these examples to the historic ones
proffered by Manne 1952 and Wold 1952, suppose that whether
Ulysses returns dead or alive affects the availability of
wine and milk for Penelope. This need not create planning
complications due to uncertainty, not knowing next period's
outcome. There were none for instance in Wold's 1952
scenario with the individual's indifferences curves as
in Figure 1, the possible outcomes A, B, or C, and a choice

Figure 1

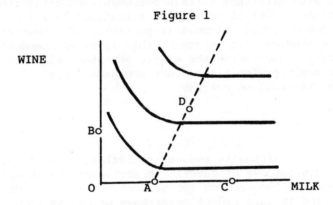

between lottery 1:   (A or C), p_a = 1/12, p_c = 11/12,
or lottery 2: (B or C), p_b = 1/12, p_c = 11/12. Under the
circumstances, the individual chooses lottery 1 in the first
round and faces no planning problems for storage of (C-A) of
milk is costless, should C occur, and no possible outcome in
the second period would warrant storage if A occurs.
Samuelson correctly points out how this and Manne's example
can be recast within expected utility theory, 1952.

    However since such interdependencies lie behind the
definite disutility of gambling, with minor changes, the

examples would have violated the independence principle[26].
Thus in the case of wine-milk substitution, if it were
instead the case that, (i) Penelope has strictly convex
indifference curves everywhere, and (ii) all possible
outcomes lie inside the x-y axes in all periods, then
complementarity issues arise during each pre-outcome
period. It follows that if Penelope does not know whether
Ulysses will return alive or dead and hence which product
will be in relatively scarce supply next period, she
cannot, except by chance, choose the optimal combination of
consuming and storing her current receipts of milk and
wine. In other words, uncertainty would create planning
problems and complementarity considerations that ensure
that Penelope would have a definite disutility of gambling.

A more detailed analysis of these complementarity
issues is left to another paper since it is complicated:
in addition to the obvious assumption changes, it involves
specifying identifiably different common levels of utility
associated with different certain outcomes, and attaching a
lower or higher level of utility to situations in which
more than one of those outcomes is possible. Extended to
unequally ranked certain outcomes, this involves abandoning
for the pre-outcome period the widely accepted principle
that individuals prefer first order stochastically
dominating distribution options.

NOTES

1.   This theory virtually reduces ethical statements such
     as "I dis/approve of murder" to emotional statements
     of the form "boo/hoorah for murder". The errors of
     reasoning in such reductionism have of course long
     since been exposed. See, e.g., Coady, 1980.
2.   Thus individuals are subjected to the risk of
     bankruptcy and are uncertain about the meaning of a
     phrase. See, e.g. Shorter Oxford Dictionary, 1978,
     and Harrap's Shorter English and French Dictionary,
     1958, for the distinction beteen risque and
     incertitude and Langendenscheidt's Universal-
     Worterbuch Englisch, 1976, for the distinction between
     riskieren and ungewib.
3.   See e.g. Ramsey, 1926, von Neumann and Morgenstern,
     1947, Samuelson, 1952, Fishburn 1970, Baumol, 1972.

4. This, the causally prior of the two possible perspectives, is the relevant one when characterizing the basic nature of the model. See pp. 142–143 above.
5. See e.g. Kreps and Porteus 1979 on sequential choice and Arrow 1982 on positive time preference.
6. Since constraint (a) raises complex issues, see p. 170 above, discussion of it is reserved for another paper.
7. If Penelope chooses the "Remarry" option, during the pre-outcome period, her welfare per annum of 50 utils is diminished by fear of a shameful divorce below her current situation of living with Hermes: her welfare per annum from living with Hermes will jump to 60 utils in the outcome period if fear of divorce is gone. Again, if Penelope chooses the "Wait" option during the pre-outcome period, her welfare per annum of 20 utils springs entirely from hope of Ulysses' return: her welfare per annum from the current consequences of living alone will plummet to zero in the outcome period in hope of Ulyses' return is gone.
8. They at times substitute the adjective "specific" for "definite".
9. Samuelson 1952, p. 136 is thus correct as regards those attributes of gambling which Allais terms "secondary".
10. See also Feldstein 1969, and Sharpe's criticism, 1964, p. 428, footnote 10, of Farrar.
11. See Samuelson 1952 and Malinvaud 1952 on where this principle enters their axiomatics.
12. In the context of a physician's prescriptions, the independence principle is a postulate about how the physican reaches his judgment on what he would prescribe. But in Friedman and Savage's illustration, that judgment has already been made, and is merely reported in the first sentence of the illustration before they apply the independence principle to the situation.
13. These are reproduced in Arrow 1974. Pratt for similar reasons suggests [17] as a measure of local risk aversion, 1964, p. 122.
14. Dyer and Sarin make the identical erroeneous claim: 'A von Neumann-Morgenstern utility function "confounds an individual's risk attitude with the strength of preference he feels for the outcome", 1982, p. 877, as do Fischer 1979, p. 455, Bell 1980, p. 2, Krystofowicz

1982, pp. 2-4, and Bernard 1982, p. 1. See also
Camacho, 1979, p. 124.

15. See e.g. Baumol 1958 and Pope 1982b.

16. See Jaynes' chapter, "A Change of Mind in
     Mesopotamia', pp. 223-254, especially the sections on
     'Sortilege', pp. 239-242 and 'The Spatialisation of
     Time', pp. 250-251.

17. See Samuelson 1952, p. 144, and Harsanyi 1982.

18. This is not of course to deny that in their
     paternalistic/maternalistic role such decision makers
     may on occasion be justified in giving a different
     weighting to the various aspects of an option,
     including hope and fear, than would their
     constituents.

19. See. e.g. Markowitz 1970, pp. 220-221, and Kahneman
     and Tversky 1979, pp. 263, 271-273 and 277.

20. This might be inferred as Samuelson's position.

> It is desirable ...that opponents of the
> Bernoulli theory should make a direct attack
> upon the independence axiom. Thus, in
> dealing with compound lotteries ...you might
> explicitly introduce some time interval
> between drawings, so that suspense elements
> might enter to contaminate the choices, etc.
> Reasons like this impress me as valid causes
> of deviation from any simply expressed
> independence postulate. But in the absence
> of such complications, I don't see why a
> "reasonable" man should not be willing ...to
> repeat firmly over and over again that the
> events faced are mutually exclusive.
>
>   (1952, pp. 144-145)

But "such complications" can never be entirely absent,
i.e., there is always a pre-outcome period for lottery
options, and hence always scope for complementarity
issues to arise.

21. Allais 1953b, equations (3) - (11), pp. 271-275.

22. This is an objective measure compatible with judging
     uncertainty from the perspective of the decision
     maker's knowledge of the outcome.

23. Allais' more neutral, if somewhat lengthy, suggestion
     in this regard, the "pleasure (or displeasure) inherent
     in risk itself", 1953a, p. 510, might have had wider

currency and forestalled the problem, had his
contributions been translated into English sooner.

24. To make sense of Assumption 6 in this boundary
position, whereby the "Remarry" option still yields her
50 utils per annum, Penelope's fear of divorce extends
to being divorced in her "after" life.

25. Financial intermediaries would lend only at higher
interest rates.

26. With minor changes, it in fact constitutes an example
of the sequential investment-consumption choice problem
that Markowitz 1970, and subsequent writers, e.g. Kreps
and Porteus 1979, have realized violate this principle.

REFERENCES

Allais, M.: 1953a, 'L' Extension des Théories de l'Equilibre
Economique Générale et du Rendement Social du Risque',
Econometrica, 21, 268-288.

Allais, M.: 1953b, 'Le Comportement de l'Homme Rationnel
devant le risque: critique des postulats et axiomes de
l'école américaine', Econometrica, 21, 503-546.

Arrow, K.: 1974, Essays in the Theory of Risk Bearing,
Markham, Chicago.

Arrow, K.: 1982, 'Risk Perception of Psychology and
Economics,' Economic Inquiry, 20, 1-9.

Baumol, W.: 1958, 'The Cardinal Utility Which Is Ordinal',
Economic Journal, 68, 665-672.

Baumol, W.: 1972, Economic Theory and Operations Analysis,
Prentice Hall, New Jersey.

Bell, D.: 1980, 'Components of Risk Aversion', mimeo, Harvard.

Bernard, G.: 1974, 'On Utility Functions', Theory and Decision,
5, 205-242.

Bernard, G.: 1981, 'Allais, Maurice and Hagen, Ole (eds):
Expected Utility Hypotheses and the Allais Paradox:
Review Article', Kyklos, 34, 106-109.

Bernard, G.: 1982, 'On Utility Functions Present State',
mimeo, Paris.

Blatt, J.: 1979, 'The Utility of Being Hanged on the Gallows',
Journal of Post Keynesian Economics, 4, 322-329.

Borch, K.: 1969, 'A Note on Uncertainty and Indifference
Curves', Review of Economic Studies, 36, 1-4.

Charnes, A. and W. Cooper: 1962, Deterministic Equivalents
for Optimizing and Satisficing Under Chance Constraints,

Northwestern University Technological Institute and Carnegie Institute of Technology.

Charnes, A. and A. Stedry: 1966, 'The Attainment of Organizational Goals through Appropriate Selection of Subunit Goals, in Operational Research and the Social Sciences, J. Lawrence (ed.), Tavistock, London, 147-164.

Camacho, A.: 1979, 'Maximizing Expected Utility and the Rule of Long Run Success', in M. Allais and O. Hagen (eds.), Expected Utility Hypotheses and the Allais Paradox, Reidel, Dordrecht, 203-222.

Chew, S. and K. MacCrimmon: 1979, 'Alpha-Nu Choice Theory: A Generalization of Expected Utility Theory', Working Paper 669, University of British Columbia, Vancouver.

Coady, T.: 1980, 'Logical Positivism', mimeo, Melbourne University, Melbourne.

Dyer, J. and R. Sarin: 1982, 'Relative Risk Aversion', Management Science, 28, 875-886.

Edwards, W.: 1953, 'Probability Preferences in Gambling', American Journal of Psychology, 66, 349-364.

Ellsberg, D.: 1954, 'Classic and Current Notions of Measurable Utility', Economic Journal, 64, 528-556.

Feldstein, M.: 1969, 'Mean-Variance Analysis in the theory of Liquidity Preference and Portfolio Selection', Review of Economic Studies, 36, 5-11.

Fischer, G.: 1979, 'Utility Models for Multiple Objective Decisions: Do They Accurately Represent Human Preferences?', Decision Sciences, 10, 451-477.

Fishburn, P.: 1970, Utility Theory for Decision Making, Wiley, New York.

Fishburn, P.: 1981, 'Non-transitive Measurable Utility', Bell Laboratories Economics Discussion Paper, No. 209, Bell Laboratories, New Jersey.

Friedman, M. and L. Savage: 1948, 'Utility Analysis of Choices Involving Risk', Journal of Political Economy, 56, 279-304.

Hagen, O.: 1979, 'Towards a Positive Theory of Preferences under Risk', in Allais, M. and Hagen, O.(eds.),Expected Utility Hypotheses and the Allais Paradox, Reidel, Dordrecht, 271-302.

Harsanyi, J.: 1982, 'Comments -- Panel Discussion', presented to First International Conference on the Foundations of Utility and Risk Theory, Olso.

Heisenberg, W.: 1930, Physical Principles of the Quantum Theory, Dover Publications, New York.

Hirshleifer, J.: 1977, 'Economics from a Biological

Viewpoint', Journal of Law and Economics, 20, 1-5.
Hey, J.: 1982, 'Sample Results of Dynamic Decision-Making', First International Conference on the Foundations of Utility and Risk Theory, Oslo.
Jaynes, J.: 1977, The Origins of Consciousness in the Breakdown of the Bicameral Mind, Houghton, Boston.
Kahneman, D. and A. Tversky: 1979, 'Prospect Theory: An Analysis of Decision-Making Under Uncertainty', Econometrica, 47, 263-291.
Kreps, D. and E. Porteus: 1979, 'Temporal von Neumann-Morgenstern Induced Preferences', Journal of Economic Theory, 20, 81-109.
Krysztofowicz, R.: 1982, 'Risk Attitude Hypotheses of Utility Theory', paper presented to First International Conference on the Foundations of Utility and Risk Theory, Oslo.
Machina, M.: 1981, '"Rational" Decision-Making versus "Rational" Decision Modelling?' A Review of Expected Utility Hypotheses and the Allais Paradox, Journal of Mathematical Psychology, 24, 163-175.
Machina, M.: 1982, 'Expected Utility Analysis Without the Independence Axiom', Econometrica, 50, 277-323.
Mackinnon, A. and Wearing, A.: 1982, 'Decision Making in a Dynamic Environment', presentation to First International Conference on the Foundations of Utility and Risk Theory, Oslo.
Malinvaud, E.: 1952, 'A Note on von Neumann-Morgenstern's Strong Independence Axiom', Econometrica, 20, 679.
Manne, A.: 1952, 'The Strong Independence Assumptions-Gasoline Blend and Probability Mixtures', Econometrica, 20, 665-668.
Markowitz, H.: 1970, Portfolio Selection: Efficient Diversification of Investment, Wiley, New York.
Pope, R.: 1979a, 'Starting to Bury the Expected Utility Hypothesis', mimeo, Duke University, Durham.
Pope, R.: 1979b, 'Revisiting Allais' Alternative to Expected Utility Theory', Eighth Conference on Economists, La Trobe University, Melbourne.
Pope, R.: 1981, 'Time and Uncertainty', mimeo, University of South Wales, Sydney.
Pope, R.: 1982a, "Risk Pooling, Firm Strategy and the Government', Working Paper 82/83-3-4, Department of Finance, University of Texas, Austin.
Pope, R.: 1982b, 'Expected Utility Theory Minus Classical Cardinality: A Theory Minus a Rationale', mimeo,

Viewpoint', Journal of Law and Economics, 20, 1-5.

Hey, J.: 1982, 'Sample Results of Dynamic Decision-Making', First International Conference on the Foundations of Risk and Uncertainty, Oslo.

Jaynes, J.: 1977, The Origins of Consciousness in the Breakdown of the Bicameral Mind, Houghton, Boston.

Kahneman, D. and A. Tversky: 1979, 'Prospect Theory: An Analysis of Decision-Making Under Uncertainty', Econometrica, 47, 263-291.

Kreps, D. and E. Porteus: 1979, 'Temporal von Neumann-Morgenstern Induced Preferences', Journal of Economic Theory, 20-81-109.

Krysztofowicz, R.: 1982, 'Risk Attitude Hypotheses of Utility Theory', paper presented to First International Conference on the Foundations of Utility and Risk Theory, Oslo.

Machina, M.: 1981, '"Rational" Decision-Making versus "Rational" Decision Modelling?' A Review of Expected Utility Hypotheses and the Allais Paradox, Journal of Mathematical Psychology, 24, 163-175.

Machina, M.: 1982, 'Expected Utility Analysis Without the Independence Axiom', Econometrica, 50, 277-323.

Mackinnon, A. and Wearing, A.: 1982, 'Decision Making in a Dynamic Environment', paper presented to First International Conference on the Foundations of Utility and Risk Theory, Oslo.

Malinvaud, E.: 1952, 'A Note on von Neumann-Morgenstern's Strong Independence Axiom', Econometrica, 20, 679.

Manne, A.: 1952, 'The Strong Independence Assumptions-Gasoline Blend and Probability Mixtures', Econometrica, 20, 665-668.

Markowitz, H.: 1970, Portfolio Selection: Efficient Diversification of Investment, Wiley, New York.

Pope, R.: 1979a, 'Starting to Bury the Expected Utility Hypothesis', mimeo, Duke University, Durham.

Pope, R.: 1979b, 'Revisiting Allais' Alternative to Expected Utility Theory', Eighth Conference on Economists, La Trobe University, Melbourne.

Pope, R.: 1981, 'Time and Uncertainty', mimeo, University of South Wales, Sydney.

Pope, R.: 1982a, "Risk Pooling, Firm Strategy and the Government', Working Paper 82/82-3-4, Department of Finance, University of Texas, Austin.

Pope, R.: 1982b, 'Expected Utility Theory Minus Classical Cardinality: A Theory Minus a Rationale', mimeo,

University of Wisconsin, Madison.

Pratt, J.: 1964, 'Risk Aversion in the Small and in the Large', Econometrica, 32, 122-136.

Ramsey, F.: 1926, 'Truth and Probability', reproduced in The Foundations of Mathematics and Other Logical Essays, R. Braithwaite (ed.), 1950, Humanities Press, New York.

Rawls, J.: 1958, 'Fairness as Justice', The Philosophical Review, 67, 164-194.

Rawls, J.: 1969, 'Distributive Justice: Some Addenda', Natural Law Forum.

Rawls, J.: 1971, 'A Theory of Justice', Belknap Press, Cambridge.

Rothschild, M. and J. Stiglitz: 1970, 'Increasing Risk: 1. A Definition', Journal of Economic Theory, 2, 225-243.

Rothschild, M.: 1971' Increasing Risk II: Its Economic Consequences', Journal of Economic Theory, 3, 66-84.

Samuelson, P.: 1952, 'Probability, Utility and the Independence Axiom', Econometrica, 20, 670-678.

Samuelson, P.: 1966, 'Utility, Preference and Probability', in The Collected Scientific Papers on Paul A. Samuelson, 1, J. Stiglitz, (ed.), Massachusetts Institute of Technology Press, Cambridge.

Savage, L.: 1954, The Foundations of Statistics, Wiley, New York.

Sharpe, W.: 1964, 'Capital Asset Prices: A Theory of Market Equilibrium under Conditions of Risk', Journal of Finance, 19, 425-442.

Schoemaker, P.: 1982, 'The Expected Utility Model: Its Variants Purpose, Evidence and Limitations', Journal of Economic Literature, 20, 529-563.

Wold, H.: 1952, 'Ordinal Preferences or Cardinal Utility', Econometrica, 20, 661-665.

Von Neumann, J. and O. Morgenstern: 1947, Theory of Games and Economic Behavior, Princeton University Press, New Jersey.

University of New South Wales

PART IV

PROBABILITY AND UTILITY IN REALITY

Mark McCord and Richard de Neufville

EMPIRICAL DEMONSTRATION THAT EXPECTED UTILITY
DECISION ANALYSIS IS NOT OPERATIONAL

1. INTRODUCTION

Decision analysis can be thought of as a discipline whose
objective is to help an individual who must choose one, or
a few, alternatives from a set of possible actions. One of
the most commonly practiced techniques used in decision
analysis where future consequences of each action are not
known with certainty is based upon the axiomatic theory
proposed by von Neumann and Morgenstern (vNM) in 1947. The
presentation of the original vNM axioms has been modified
several times in order to render them more intuitively, and
thus normatively, appealing (see, for example, the review
by MacCrimmon and Larsson, 1979), but the essence remains
the same. Any of these sets of the axioms implies that:
(1) an interval-scaled utility function for outcomes,
dependent only on the outcome levels, exists; and (2)
actions with specified probability distributions can be
ranked by the expectations of the associated vNM utilities.
Thus, the theory is also known as expected utility theory,
and one can speak of the expected utility decision analysis
(EUDA).
     The popularity of EUDA over the past twenty years is
partly due to the normative appeal and mathematical
implications of the underlying axioms, but only partly.
Many practicing decision analysts remember only dimly its
axiomatic foundation. Moreover, the axioms themselves are
quite controversial on theoretical and practical grounds.
The more likely reason for the dominant use of EUDA for
analyzing decision problems under uncertainty is that the
associated methodology now consists of simple, routine, and
apparently reliable procedures that make it easy to apply.
In short, the prevalence of EUDA is due more to its pragmatic appeal than to its contested theoretical underpinnings.
     We wished to investigate the basis for this pragmatic
appeal by identifying and testing aspects critical to the
application of EUDA. The results of our tests, which we

B. P. Stigum and F. Wenstøp (eds.), Foundations of Utility and Risk Theory with Applications,
181–199.
© 1983 *by D. Reidel Publishing Company.*

performed with extreme care and believe to be easily
replicable, indicate serious limitations to the appropriateness of EUDA as currently practiced. To what extent these
limitations stem from deficiencies in the operational
methods of analysis or from insufficient theory is debatable.
The conclusion is the same however: the ability to use
EUDA for prescribing decisions is beyond state-of-the-art.

The organization of the paper is as follows. We
indicate briefly some of the previous literature on the
appropriateness of expected utility theory and then show how
our work has a different twist, being concerned with the
practice of decision analysis. Next, the research strategy,
the assessment methods, and the protocol of the experiments
are presented. We then give the empirical results and
discuss their implications.

2. PREVIOUS OBJECTIONS

Objections to the underlying theory deal mostly with the
normative appeal of the axioms. Once the axioms are
accepted, no one questions the implications. The axioms
are questioned both by presenting reasons why one might
not want to adhere to them (Machina, 1981; Roy and Hugonnard,
1982; Allais, 1953) and by presenting evidence that seemingly
rational individuals act in voluntary contradiction to their
results (Allais, 1954, 1979; Hagen, 1979; MacCrimmon and
Larsson, 1979; Kahneman and Tversky, 1979).

Some of the previous empirical studies (Karmarkar,
1974; and Allais, 1979) hint at operational implications for
EUDA. The results are limited, however. Moreover the
authors framed their experiments and interpreted the
evidence from descriptive and normative, rather than
prescriptive viewpoints.

Whereas the debate as to whether or not the axioms
should be accepted as dictating rational choice under
uncertainty is abstract, both defenders and critics of EUDA
agree that there are concrete empirical violations to
expected utility theory. But while the critics see these
violations as evidence of fundamental flaws in the theory,
the defenders claim that the violations only emphasize the
need for their methods. They argue that it is precisely
because individuals make mistakes that decision analysis is
useful, and they define (implicitly or explicitly) mistakes
as deviations from their set of normative axioms. By
defining a priori their axioms as being normative, and

thereby rejecting any <u>ex post</u> validation of their desirability
with descriptive evidence, they manage to side-step a whole
body of critical arguments. They essentially cloak themselves
in a "normative immunity" to the empirical evidence.

3. THE ESSENCE OF THE EXPERIMENT

The debate as to the applicability of EUDA has centered
almost entirely about the issue of whether the set of axioms
are desirable to act as norms for individual behavior. But
if the interest is in the practical aspect (i.e. the use
of vNM utility theory for decision analysis), the question
can no longer be limited to, "Should it work?", but must
include the equally important, "Does it work?".

In theory, the vNM axioms imply the ordering of the
probability distributions associated with the possible
decisions. But, in practice, this ordering is determined
via a vNM utility function which <u>describes</u> the individual
attitudes of the decision maker. The axioms imply that,
for an individual, this utility function exists, is unique
up to a positive linear transformation, and is independent
of the probabilistic situation used to elicit it. This
feature is crucial to the application of EUDA. It forms
the bridge between an abstract theory and a practical
methodology by allowing the analyst to obtain a utility
function in one probabilistic setting which can then be used
in all others, rather than demanding a different function
for every possible setting.

If the assessed utility function depends on the
probabilistic situation used in elicitation, one is confronted
with a dilemma where both choices lead to the same unfortunate
result. Either the axioms, and thus the whole theory of
EUDA, must be rejected, or the axioms are still adhered to,
and the ability to obtain a unique utility function, and
thereby conduct the analysis with existing tools, must be
rejected. Either way, an empirical dependence between the
utility function and the probabilistic setting invalidates
the practical application of EUDA.

The practicing decision analyst must be concerned about
the descriptive ability of his methods, even though he may
propose that his is a prescriptive discipline. Normative
immunity is irrelevant. The practice of EUDA as we know it
today is critically vulnerable to this issue.

4. RESEARCH DESIGN

The central objective of the experiments was to test if
vNM utility functions depend significantly on the probabilistic situation in which they are assessed. This involved
three basic elements:

> (1) Assessment of the utility functions by methods
>   currently used in practice with different proba-
>   bility distributions which ought, theoretically,
>   to give the same results;
> (2) Analysis of the evidence to determine if the
>   differences observed were significant; and
> (3) Extreme care in executing the study to ensure
>   replicability and to avoid the attribution of any
>   differences to extraneous factors.

The vNM utility functions were assessed using standard
lotteries in the usual way. As described in the next section,
we investigated different probabilistic situations by using
the fractile method, with different pairs of complementary
probabilities, and the varying probability method, in which
the outcomes of the lottery remain fixed but the probability
of obtaining them changes. Additionally, we assessed the
deterministic value function which is used for analysis
under certainty.

Since there are no standard statistical methods to
investigate differences in curves such as utility functions,
we developed indices to measure the relative accuracy of
the procedures. We also looked at the distribution of the
differences to see if they could be attributed to random
errors, or if they showed directional bias.

Extreme care was taken at three levels. First the
analysts were skilled and experienced. We were, in fact,
associated with one of the major demonstrations of the
applicability of decision analysis, the case of the Airport
for Mexico City (de Neufville and Keeney, 1973), and have
taught and practiced the techniques for many years. Second,
we worked with technically competent subjects familiar with
probabilistic concepts. Third, we paid special attention to
the details of the measurements, using the best available
psychometric procedures.

5.   ASSESSMENT METHODS

The functions were obtained through personal interviews
between the analyst and the decision maker, as is common
in decision analysis.

5.1 vNM Utility Functions

The assessment of the vNM utility function, $U(X)$, proceeds
from two ideas:

(1)   Since vNM utility is constant up to a positive
      linear transformation, two points of the function
      can be assumed arbitrarily;

(2)   The utility of a probabilistic situation is,
      according to the axioms, equal to the expectation
      of the utility of the possible outcomes.

The analyst thus works with the client to determine
for what amount the client is indifferent between having
some amount for sure (thus, the name certainty equivalent)
and possession of a lottery which has two possible outcomes
whose probabilities must be complementary. Specifically,
if the client states indifference between X_1 and the lottery
involving the upper and lower bounds of the range of the
attribute, X^* and X_*, whose probabilities of occurrence are
p and $(1-p)$, respectively, we have:

$$U(X_1) = U(\text{lottery}) = pU(X^*) + (1-p)U(X_*). \quad (1)$$

Assuming the utility for the two points X^* and X_* (e.g.
$U(X^*) = 1.0$ and $U(X_*) = 0.0$, Eq. (1) gives the utility of
the third point X_1 ($U(X_1) = p$ here).
   The most common form of interview technique uses the
"fractile method", so named because the probabilities used
in the two lotteries are fixed, and thus the differences in
the utilities of the outcomes of the lotteries are split
into constant fractions. The procedure starts with Eq. (1)
and then sets up a second lottery, identical to the first
except that X_1 replaces X^*. A second certainty equivalent,
X_2, is obtained, such that $U(X_2) = p^2$. And so on. Points
in the upper portion of the curve are similarly determined
by replacing the less desirable outcome by the certainty
equivalent of the preceding lottery.
   In the fractile method, the most frequently used

probability is 0.5, resulting in "50-50" lotteries. There
is no theoretical reason why p should equal 0.5. Indeed,
it follows from the axioms that the utility functions
obtained by the fractile method using different values of p,
say p' and p", should be equal.

The "varying probability" method of assessment differs
from the fractile method in that the probability used in the
sequence of lotteries varies, while the outcomes remain
fixed at X* and X*. Again, the axioms indicate that the
utility function encoded using the variable probability
method, U_{pv}, should equal (up to a positive linear transformation) the utility functions obtained by the fractile
method. That is:

$$U_{pv}(X) = U_{p'}(X) = U_{p''}(X) \qquad\qquad (2)$$

We tested these equalities empirically.

5.2 Deterministic Value Functions

A special case of the dependence of the vNM utility on the
probability distribution is that in which one outcome
occurs with certainty. Some believe that the vNM utility
of a certain outcome is equivalent to the subjective value
of this outcome determined by methods in which no uncertainty
is present (Halter and Dean, 1971; Allais, 1979a). This
equivalence is disputed, however.

We were not concerned with the question of theoretical
equivalence. We were interested in the value function,
$V(X)$, for two reasons:

(1) For those who claim $V(X)$ and $U(X)$ are identical
     in theory, we wanted to see if they could be
     assumed to be in practice.
(2) For those who claim they are different, the
     difference between $V(X)$ and $U(X)$ would serve
     as a benchmark to indicate roughly the size of
     difference one could expect from two functions
     that are "really different". The differences
     between vNM functions could then be put in
     perspective to see if they differed fundamentally
     or if the differences could be attributed to
     measurement and experimental error.

Single-attribute value functions can be determined in

several ways (see, for example, Fishburn, 1967; Keeney and
Raiffa, 1976; Sarin et al., 1980; Huber et al., 1971;
Allais, 1979; Krzysztofowicz, 1982). We used the concept
of equal value differences since it seemed both most
effective and most prevalent. The basic idea is that, if the
degree of satisfaction obtained from a change in the level
of an attribute X_i to X_j is considered equivalent to that
associated with a change from X_r to X_s, then the differences
in the respective subjective values are equal. Notationally:

$$X_i \rightarrow X_j \sim X_r \rightarrow X_s \Rightarrow V(X_j) - V(X_i) = V(X_s) - V(X_r) \quad (3)$$

where $X_i \rightarrow X_j$ indicates the change from X_i to X_j, $\sim$ indicates
indifference and $V(X)$ is the deterministic value of the
level X.

We developed $V(X)$ by a procedure similar to the fractile
method using 50-50 lotteries. Starting with the extremes
of the attribute range, X^* and X_*, we determined X_1 as the
point which divided that range into two ranges of equal
value difference. Scaling the end points of the value
function as $V(X^*) = 1.0$ and $V(X_*) = 0.0$, as we did for the
vNM utility, we obtained $V(X_1) = 0.5$. By further subdivision
of the ranges X_* to X_1 and X_1 to X^*, we obtained quarter
and eighth points.

6. PROTOCOL OF THE EXPERIMENT

Utility functions using the varying probability method and
two or more fractile methods were assessed for twenty-three
subjects, and deterministic value functions were obtained
for twenty-two. Most subjects were technically trained,
being MIT professors, graduate students, and undergraduates
in engineering or sciences. There were two non-science
college graduates.

The interviews were designed, supervised, and carried
out by persons with extensive theoretical and field
experience in such matters. Extreme care was taken to
facilitate responses, eliminate boredom and ensure unbiased
and replicable results. Consistency for individual subjects
and some follow-up questions indicated that the answers
given were representative of the subjects' attitudes. The
utility value functions were assessed for a single
attribute, dollars gained. The range was between $0 and
$10,000.

6.1 vNM Utility Functions

We attempted to encode at least three, and sometimes four, utility functions for each subject. For most subjects, we first obtained the varying probability utility function, $U_{pv}(X)$, with the following probabilities: $p = 0.500$; one of either $p = 0.250$ or $p = 0.625$; and a few points for either $p = 0.125$ or $p = 0.750$. The order in which the fractile methods were presented was equally distributed among subjects to curtail bias due to the order of presentation.

Scenarios were described at the beginning of the assessment to define a realistic context. Students were confronted with scenarios involving fellowships, professors with research grants, and others with one-time cash bonuses. Probabilities were defined in the context of the scenario, but were highlighted by the use of playing cards in order to limit any difference in perception of stated probabilities. For a more detailed description of the protocol, see McCord and de Neufville, (1982).

6.2 Value Functions

The essential methodological issue here centers on the fact that direct comparison to the psychological value of changes in asset positions may be difficult. To circumvent this problem we introduced a surrogate measure of this psychological value. The approach was inspired by the procedures described by Keeney and Raiffa (1976) and Sarin et al. (1980).

The surrogate measure of the value of changing from one asset position to another was the maximum amount of time, outside of current working hours, that the subject would engage in a job of no personal value other than the monetary remuneration represented by the change in asset position. For this procedure to be valid, working hours and dollars gained must be value additive. But because of the way in which the assessment proceeded, this assumption was necessary only over a small range of working hours. Furthermore, it was felt that this assumption is more innocuous than others needed for assessment.

7. RESULTS

The experimental data lead to two immediate conclusions:

(1) Large descriptive differences exist between the

functions resulting from the various methods
of assessment.
(2) Individuals preferred to deviate in a fairly
consistent fashion from the behavior presumed
by the axioms.

The consistent deviations are qualitatively apparent
when looking at free-hand curves traced through the data
and are even more striking when the sample is divided into
two traditional groups, those of risk seekers and risk
averters. For this reason, the two populations should not
generally be pooled in analyzing the data.

7.1 Measure of Differences Between Functions

To summarize the deviations, portray their order of magnitude, and facilitate discussion, we had to develop special
indices. Statistical tests were considered but rejected as
impractical, if not useless, for this study. We sought
illustrative measures with a clear operational meaning,
which would be sufficiently general to allow repeatable
analyses, and which would permit comparison both between
functions and pairs of functions.

The index we developed for this analysis relates the
difference between two purportedly equivalent levels of
value to a normalizing standard. The measure is thus one of
"relative difference" between two functions, $f(X)$ and $g(X)$,
associated with a specific ordinate, A. The differences
themselves are taken along the abscissa and are normalized
with reference to a standard function, $h(X)$, also associated
with A. Notationally:

$$w(a)f,g = [f^{-1}(A) - g^{-1}(A)]/h^{-1}(A) \qquad (4)$$

In practice $h(X)$ may be chosen as any reference function,
including $f(X)$ or $g(X)$. Figure 1 illustrates the definition
of the measure.

To portray the size of the discrepancies between two
functions for a set of N individuals, we resorted to the
concept of average absolute differences:

$$\overline{|w(A)_{f,g}|} = \frac{1}{N} \Sigma_i \; |w_i(A)_{f,g}| \qquad (5)$$

Likewise, we can speak of average differences when taking

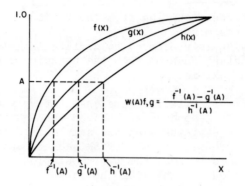

Figure 1. Illustration of Definition of Measure of
Relative Difference between Functions.

signs into account. We can also apply either formula to
specific subsets of the sample, such as the risk averters
or the risk seekers.

7.2 General Considerations

To pursue the idea that the differences between functions
depended systematically on whether a person was risk
averse or risk seeking, we had to classify all subjects
into these groups. This we did on the basis of the certainty
equivalent furnished for the 50-50 lottery over the extreme
range of outcomes, $0 and $10,000. There were seventeen
risk averters, five risk seekers, and one risk neutral
individual. Risk attitudes can -- and did -- change for
an individual over the range of the attribute; so this
classification scheme is not absolute. Alternative schemes
might alter slightly the partition, but we believe the
evidence is striking enough to be insensitive to marginally
different classifications.

7.3 Comparison of vNM Utility Functions

We made binary comparisons between: (1) utility functions
elicited with the varying probability method and the 50-50
fractile method; and (2) between utility functions elicited
with fractile methods of different probabilities. In both
cases, the normalizing standard, h(X), was taken as the
utility obtained with the 50-50 fractile method since it is
the most commonly used vNM utility function. When comparing

the varying probability and 50-50 fractile methods, $f(X)$ was $U_{pv}(X)$. When comparing two fractile methods, it was the fractile curve whose probability of gaining the more valuable prize was greater. Comparisons between the functions were made at levels of utility of $A = 0.25$, 0.50, 0.75.

The discrepancies between these utility functions, which should be equivalent axiomatically, were very large. As shown in Table 1, the average differences in certainty equivalents range from 30% to 100%.

TABLE 1

AVERAGE ABSOLUTE PERCENT RELATIVE DIFFERENCES,

$|\overline{w}(X)|$, BETWEEN vNM UTILITY FUNCTIONS

FUNCTIONS COMPARED		DIFFERENCES IN CERTAINTY EQUIVALENTS (%) AT UTILITY LEVEL		
Theoretically Equivalent?	Type	0.25	0.50	0.75
Yes	$U_{p'}(X)$, $U_{p''}(X)$ p', p'' vary	99	86	49
	$U_{pv}(X)$ and $U_p(X)$, p= 0.50	54	--	31
No	$V(X)$ and $U_p(X)$, p = 0.50	56	34	21

The effects are visually striking. Figure 2 is illustrative of the directional tendency seen when comparing fractile methods of different probabilities. As shown for this subject, the utility function obtained using the higher probability of getting the more valuable outcome of the lottery tended to lie above the utility function obtained using a lower probability.

To investigate the trends in the discrepancies, we plotted their distribution (Figures 3 and 4). They are clearly biased for both the risk averters and the risk seekers. To quantify this effect, we calculated $\overline{w}$, the average relative difference -- taking sign into account -- for each set of observations. If the discrepancies were random, the values of $\overline{w}$ would be randomly distributed around zero. Instead, as shown in the figures, the discrepancies have a consistent bias.

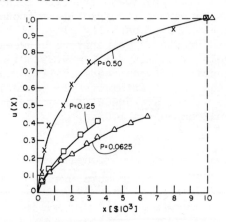

Figure 2. Different vNM Utility Functions obtained by various Fractile Sequences (Subject 34)

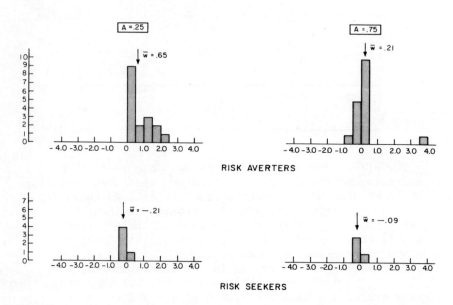

Figure 3. Frequency Diagram of Relative Differences between Utility Functions obtained by the Varying Probability and 50:50 Fractile Methods.

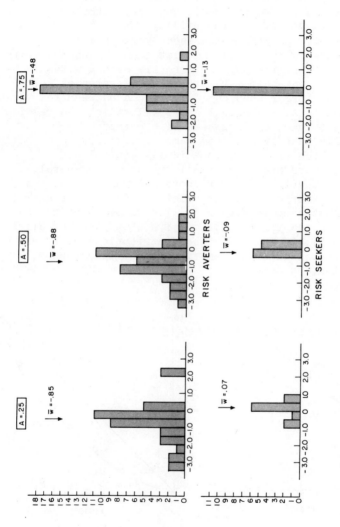

Figure 4. Frequency Diagram of Relative Differences between Utility
Functions obtained using Fractile Methods with Different Probabilities

7.4   Comparison of Value and Utility Functions

In comparing the graphs, it was readily apparent that the
deterministic value function did not replicate, even
approximately, any of the vNM utility functions. To limit
the discussion, analytic comparisons were only made between
the preference function and the most commonly used utility
function, that obtained by the fractile method with
probability of one-half. The relative differences were
large, but no larger than the differences between the various
utility functions, as Table 1 shows. That is, the results
indicate that functions assessed with methods which
theoretically must produce the same curves perform as badly
as methods which are not axiomatically equivalent.
     Again, there are directional trends. In general,
the utility functions lie far above the value functions
for the risk averters and far below for the risk seekers.
This is illustrated in Figure 5. The value function was
used for both the first function, $f(X)$, and the normalizing
function, $h(X)$, in Eq. (4). The distributions of Figure 6
reinforce the claim of systematic, rather than random,
discrepancies.

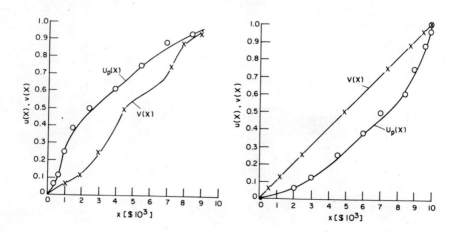

Figure 5. Examples of Utility Function obtained by 50:50
Fractile Sequence and Deterministic Value Functions for
Two Subjects.

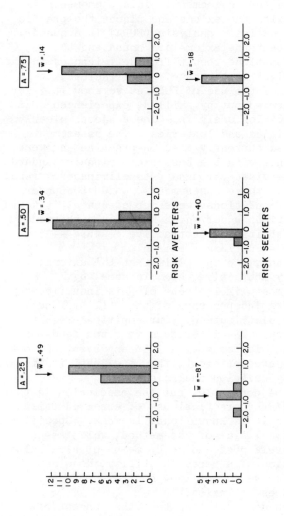

Figure 6. Frequency Diagram of Relative Differences between Value
Functions and Utility Functions obtained by the 50:50 Fractile
Method

8. DISCUSSION AND CONCLUSIONS

In summary, the empirical result is that very different
utility functions are obtained depending on the probability
distribution used in the assessment. This phenomenon is
quite incompatible with the axioms and places the practice
of expected utility decision analysis (EUDA) in a quandry.

One may claim that the axioms are sound and the
different utility functions result from deficiencies in the
assessment. This might be the case. Nevertheless, it
implies a rejection of the use of EUDA as we know it. Our
assessments were carried out by skilled, experienced
practitioners of decision analysis. The subjects clearly
understood probabilities and lotteries. The assessment
procedures were those currently used in practice and were
executed in accordance with the best professional standards.
Extreme care was exercised throughout to eliminate extraneous
sources of error. If these assessments, conducted under
extremely favorable conditions, were not adequate, it would
seem that the conditions under which EUDA could be used
would be so rare that its most attractive feature -- its
operational ability -- no longer exists.

On the other hand, one may claim that the axioms,
though superficially attractive, are, in some way,
insufficient. The most likely locus of this insufficiency
is the axiom claiming independence of the utility function
and the probability distribution. Our empirical results
indicate a dependency. The literature we cited tends to
point the finger at this assumption. In any event, if one
believes the axioms are deficient, then the justification
for expected utility decision analysis fails.

The cause may be debatable, but the conclusion is that
the justification of the practical use of expected utility
decision analysis as it is known today is weak. Specifically,
the whole computational side of the method, which seeks to
prescribe a normatively best choice by means of a calculus
based on a description of a person's utility, does not
appear valid. Either we do not know how to encode this
vNM utility or it does not exist.

This conclusion does not mean that the concept of
decision analysis is worthless. Professional experience
confirms that there is much value in helping people
structure their choices, think about the uncertain nature
of the outcomes and recognize that their preferences are a
non-linear response to risk and quantity. Even this limited

exercise is often instrumental in helping decision makers
understand their problem and arrive at more enlightened
decisions.

The results also imply a heavy agenda for further work.
Confirmation and replication of our findings is one major
task. Understanding the systematic nature of the discrepancies and reconciling it with the existing or alternative
axiomatic frameworks is another. Discovering what can be
salvaged from the present methodology, what must be fore-
saken, and what must be developed for use in practice is a
third.

9. ACKNOWLEDGMENTS

Roman Krzycztofowicz and Héctor Múnera particularly helped
us formulate this investigation. We also thank Maurice
Allais, Gregory Baecher, David Bell, Simon French,
Jean-Yves Jaffray, Ralph Keeney, Howard Raiffa, Bernard Roy,
J. Edward Russo, Paul Schoemaker, Mark Thompson, and
D.J. White for their advice and comments. The MIT Technology
and Policy Program and the French Government helped finance
the work.

Mark McCord is a Doctoral Candidate, Massachusetts
Institute of Technology, Cambridge, MA. Richard de
Neufville is Professor and Chairman of the Technology
and Policy Program, Massachusetts Institute of Technology,
Cambridge, MA

LIST OF SYMBOLS

X = levels of an attribute

X_*, X^* = lower and upper bounds of X

X_i, $i = 1, 2,$ = certainty equivalents to lotteries;
or endpoints of equal value difference
statement

p = probability in a lottery

p', p'' = specific values of p

$U(X)$ = vNM utility of X

$U_{pv}(X)$ = U(X) assessed using variable
                        probability method

$U_p(X)$ = U(X) assessed by fractile method
                        using probability p

$V(X)$ = deterministic value function

$f(X),g(X),h(X)$ = generic two-dimensional functions,
                        h(x) being the normalizing
                        standard

$W_{f,g}(A)$ = relative difference between f(X)
                        and g(X), normalized by h(X),
                        taken at U(X) or V(X) = A

$\bar{W}$ = average relative difference

N = number of individuals in a set

REFERENCES

Allais, M.: 1953, 'Le Comportement de l'Homme Rationnel
    devant le Risque: Critique des Postulats et Axiomes de
    l'Ecole Americaine', Econometrica 21, 503-46.
Allais, M.: 1979, 'The Foundations of a Positive Theory
    of Choice Involving Risk and a Criticism of the
    Postulates and Axioms of the American School', in
    M. Allais and O. Hagen, (eds.), Expected Utility
    Hypotheses and the Allais Paradox, D. Reidel, Dordrecht,
    Holland, 27-148.
Allais, M.: 1979, 'The So-Called Allais Paradox and
    Rational Decisions Under Certainty', in M. Allais
    and O. Hagen, (eds.), Expected Utility Hypotheses
    and the Allais Paradox, D. Reidel, Dordrecht, Holland,
    437-682.
de Neufville, R. and R. Keeney: 1973, 'Multiattribute
    Preference Analysis for Transportation Systems
    Evaluation', Transportation Research 7:2, 1-16.
Fishburn, P.C.: 1967, 'Methods of Estimating Additive
    Utilities', Management Sciences 13:7, 435-53.

Hagen, O.: 1979, 'Toward a Positive Theory of Preferences Under Risk', in M. Allais and O. Hagen (eds.), Expected Utility Hypotheses and the Allais Paradox, D. Reidel, Dordrecht, Holland, 271-302.

Halter, A.N. and G.W. Dean: 1979, Decisions Under Uncertainty, Southwestern Publishing, Cincinnati, OH.

Huber, G.P., R. Daneshyar, and D.L. Ford: 1971, 'An Empirical Comparison of Five Utility Models for Predicting Job Performances', Organizational Behavior and Human Performance 6, 267-82.

Kahneman, D. and A. Tversky: 1979, 'Prospect Theory: An Analysis of Decision Under Risk', Econometrica 47:2, 263-91.

Karmarkar, U.S.: 1974, 'The Effect of Probabilities on the Subjective Evaluation of Lotteries', MIT Working Paper No. 698-74, Sloan School of Management, MIT, Cambridge, MA.

Keeney, R.L. and H. Raiffa: 1978, Decisions With Multiple Objectives: Preferences and Value Tradeoffs, John Wiley and Sons, New York.

Krzysztofowicz, R.: 1982, 'Strength of Preference and Risk Attitude in Utility Measurement', Organizational Behavior and Human Performance, forthcoming.

MacCrimmon, K.R. and S. Larsson: 1979, 'Utility Theory: Axioms Versus "Paradoxes"', in M. Allais and O. Hagen (eds.), Expected Utility Hypotheses and the Allais Paradox, D. Reidel, Dordrecht, Holland, 333-410.

Machina, M.J.: 1981, '"Rational" Decision Making Versus "Rational" Decision Modelling?', Journal of Mathematical Psychology 24:2, 163-75.

McCord, M. and R. de Neufville: 1982, 'Fundamental Deficiency of Expected Utility Decision Analysis', paper presented at Multiobjective Conference, Manchester, England.

Roy, B. and J.C. Hugonnard: 1982, 'Ranking of Suburban Line Extension Projects on the Paris Metro System by a Multi-criteria Method', Transportation Research 16A:4, 301-312.

Sarin, R.K., J.S. Dyer, and K. Nair: 1980, 'A Comparative Evaluation of Three Approaches for Preference Function Assessment', paper presented at the Joint National Meeting, TIMS/OSRA, Washington, D.C., May 4-7.

von Neumann, J. and O. Morgenstern: 1947, Theory of Games and Economic Behavior, 2nd ed., Princeton University Press, Princeton, NJ.

Roman Krzysztofowicz

RISK ATTITUDE HYPOTHESES OF UTILITY THEORY[1]

Two behavioral concepts have recently emerged as a result of
an interpretation of the expected utility theory: relative
(with respect to the strength of preference) risk attitude
and intrinsic (or invariant between decisions and attributes)
risk attitude. They lead us to formulate several behavioral
hypotheses which next have been tested experimentally. We
present the results and ponder their implications.

1. INTRODUCTION

This article investigates several hypotheses about risk
attitude. The framework of this investigation is a theoretical and empirical relationship between a value function,
v, compatible with the theory of ordered value differences
(Frisch, 1926; Pareto, 1927) and a utility function, u,
compatible with the expected utility theory (von Neumann and
Morgenstern, 1947). Both functions map an attribute set X
into real numbers and are unique up to a positive linear
transformation (interval scale), but v results from an axiomatization of riskless decision making while u holds under
an axiomatization of risky decision making. Recent enquiries
into the theory and psychology of preference assessment
(e.g., Bell and Raiffa, 1979, 1980; Sarin et al., 1980;
Dyer and Sarin, 1981) suggest a behavioral interpretation
according to which v encodes the strength of preference
while u encodes the strength of preference and risk attitude.
A similar interpretation also transpires from the works of
Fischer (1977, 1979), Hagen (in Allais and Hagen, 1979,
p.22), and Hershey and Schoemaker (1980).

The theoretical framework of our investigation is
established by a mapping w such that

$$u(x) = w(v(x)) \quad , \quad x \in X .\tag{1}$$

As a testable hypothesis concerning the form of w, we
employ a specialized version of the theorem due to

B. P. Stigum and F. Wenstøp (eds.), Foundations of Utility and Risk Theory with Applications,
201–216.
© Roman Krzysztofowicz

Pratt (1964). It states that a certain unique (exponential or linear) transformation w holds if and only if the decision maker's relative risk attitude is constant. We test this hypothesis first, and then, upon accepting it, we use the model of w for inference concerning other hypotheses about risk attitude.

2. THEORETICAL BACKGROUND

2.1. Expected utility

Let $X = \{x\}$ be the set of outcomes and $\succsim$ be a binary preference-indifference relation on a set of gambles over X. Under von Neumann-Morgenstern (1947) axioms, there exists a utility function $u : X \to Re$, unique up to a positive linear transformation, and such that the relation

$$\hat{x} \sim \langle x_1, p, x_2 \rangle , \qquad (2)$$

wherein receiving an outcome $\hat{x}$ is viewed as indifferent to a gamble that yields outcome x_1 with probability p and outcome x_2 with probability $1 - p$, implies

$$u(\hat{x}) = p\, u(x_1) + (1 - p)\, u(x_2) . \qquad (3)$$

Relations (2) and (3) provide the basis for assessment of u. In a standard method, one sets $u(x^o) = 0$, $u(x^*) = 1$, and elicits a certainty equivalent x_1 to an even-chance $(p = .5)$ gamble $\langle x^o, x^* \rangle$ so that from (3), $u(x_1) = .5$, etc.

According to the behavioral interpretation hypothesized herein, u encodes the decision maker's strength of preference and risk attitude. The classical interpretation attributes the shape of u (concave, convex, linear) entirely to risk attitude[2]. Risk attitude is inferred from the shape of u via Pratt's (1964) measure:

$$c(x) = -\frac{u''(x)}{u'(x)} \begin{cases} > 0 & \Rightarrow \text{risk averse} \quad (\text{RA}) \text{ attitude,} \\ < 0 & \Rightarrow \text{risk seeking} \ (\text{RS}) \text{ attitude,} \\ = 0 & \Rightarrow \text{risk neutral} \ (\text{RN}) \text{ attitude.} \end{cases}$$

$$(4)$$

2.2. Ordered value differences

With X the set of outcomes, a binary preference-indifference relation $\succsim$ is now assumed on X $\times$ X. The comparisons involve ordered pairs of outcomes. An axiomatization of the notion of the directed difference in preference (e.g., Scott and Suppes, 1958; Debreu, 1960; Suppes and Zinnes, 1963; Krantz et al., 1971) implies the existence of a value function $v : X \to Re$, unique up to a positive linear transformation, and such that

$$(x_1, x_2) \sim (x_2, x_3) , \tag{5}$$

wherein the difference in preference from x_1 to x_2 is equal to the difference in preference from x_2 to x_3, implies

$$v(x_2) - v(x_1) = v(x_3) - v(x_2) . \tag{6}$$

The relations (5) and (6) serve for construction of an assessment method. We discuss here the exchange method (Dyer and Sarin, 1979). Set $v(x^0) = 0$, $v(x^*) = 1$, and elicit an equal difference point x_1 such that the decision maker is indifferent between exchanging x^0 for x_1 (if his initial position were x^0) and exchanging x_1 for x^* (if his initial position were x_1). Applying (6) gives $v(x_1) = .5$, etc.

The value function v encodes the decision maker's strength of preference over X, and the shape of v (concave, convex, linear) implies monotonicity of the marginal value function. In analogy to $c(x)$, we can define

$$m(x) = - \frac{v''(x)}{v'(x)} \begin{cases} > 0 & \Rightarrow \text{decreasing marginal value,} \\ < 0 & \Rightarrow \text{increasing marginal value,} \\ = 0 & \Rightarrow \text{constant marginal value.} \end{cases} \tag{7}$$

2.3. Relative risk attitude

Inasmuch as v encodes the strength of preference over the set X of sure (riskless) outcomes while u encodes the strength of preference over outcomes in X and risk attitude towards gambles on X, one is tempted to separate the notion of risk attitude from the notion of strength of preference.

We adopt the following definition:

$$
c(x) \begin{cases} > \\ < \\ = \end{cases} m(x) \begin{array}{l} \Rightarrow \text{ relatively risk averse } \text{(RRA) attitude,} \\ \Rightarrow \text{ relatively risk seeking (RRS) attitude,} \\ \Rightarrow \text{ relatively risk neutral (RRN) attitude.} \end{array} \tag{8}
$$

The type of relative risk attitude can be related to the analytic properties of the transformation w (Equation 1). Since w can be viewed as a utility function defined on the set of values v(X), all properties of the von Neumann-Morgenstern functions apply to w. The result most relevant to our study is summarized in the following theorem.

Theorem 1. Let u and v be strictly increasing on X. Define $n(x) = -w''(x)/w'(x)$. The transformation w takes the form:

$$
u(x) = \frac{1 - e^{-bv(x)}}{1 - e^{-b}} \quad \Longleftrightarrow \quad n(x) \equiv b > 0 \quad \Longleftrightarrow \quad \text{RRA,} \tag{9.1}
$$

$$
u(x) = \frac{e^{-bv(x)} - 1}{e^{-b} - 1} \quad \Longleftrightarrow \quad n(x) \equiv b < 0 \quad \Longleftrightarrow \quad \text{RRS,} \tag{9.2}
$$

$$
u(x) = v(x) \quad \Longleftrightarrow \quad n(x) \equiv b = 0 \quad \Longleftrightarrow \quad \text{RRN.} \tag{9.3}
$$

The theorem asserts that u (which according to our hypothesis encodes the strength of preference and risk attitude) is related to v (which encodes the strength of preference only) by a unique transformation if and only if the decision maker's relative risk attitude is constant.

3. EXPERIMENTAL DESIGN

3.1. Hypotheses

In this experimental study we employ Theorem 1 as a hypothesis concerning the superposition of the relative risk attitude on the strength of preference. The data used for the inference are the assessed value functions v and utility functions u. Two kinds of data analysis are performed.

The descriptive model. A value function v and a utility function u having been assessed for a subject, the best estimate of the parameter b in (9) is determined as the minimizer of the norm

$$\rho = \int |u'(x) - u(x)| dx \Big/ \int |v(x) - u(x)| dx , \qquad (10)$$

where u' denotes the utility function computed from (9). By definition $0 < \rho$, while (9.3) implies min $\rho \leq 1.0$. The values of ρ obtained for a number of subjects provide a sample for statistical testing of the hypothesis concerning the validity of (9) as a descriptive model. The acceptance of the model (9) for the transformation w implies, via Theorem 1, the acceptance of the constant relative risk attitude hypothesis. If this is the case, the sample of b values will be used for inference concerning other behavioral hypotheses.

The predictive model. From the viewpoint of the decision analysis, the most significant is the prediction problem. That is, having assessed v, one wants to obtain u by a superposition of the relative risk attitude on v rather than by the direct assessment of u. (Decision problems calling for such an approach are discussed, for instance, by Dyer and Sarin (1981) and Krzysztofowicz and Jagannathan (1981).) The model (9) allows one to accomplish such a superposition by assessing just one parameter – the certainty equivalent $\hat{x}$ of the gamble $\langle x^o, x^* \rangle$. The resulting utility function u' is actually a prediction of u based on v and this certainty equivalent $\hat{x}$. The accuracy of this prediction is measured by ρ $(0 \leq \rho)$. Again, a sample of ρ values is used for testing the hypothesis about the validity of (9) as a predictive model.

3.2. Experiments

The above hypotheses have been tested on four sets of data. (1) Data from Experiment I in which the subjects were experts and the decision problem was a real one (12 cases). (2) Data from Experiment II in which the subjects were graduate and undergraduate students and the decision problem was hypothetical (12 cases). (3) Data reported by

Allais (1979) (4 cases). (4) Data reported by Sarin et al.
(1980) (6 cases).

Experiment I had an additional feature: two utility
functions were assessed for each of the six subjects. These
functions, u_o and u_*, correspond to distinct decision
scenarios. In the first scenario, the random outcome
$x \in [x^o,x^*]$ was framed as an opportunity gain $(x-x^o)$, i.e.,
it was to be realized after the decision maker had to make
an extremely pessimistic decision and expected the outcome
x^o (the least preferred outcome). In the second scenario,
the random outcome $x \in [x^o,x^*]$ was framed as an opportunity
loss $(x-x^*)$, i.e., it was to be obtained after the decision
maker had made an extremely optimistic decision from which
he expected the outcome x^* (the most preferred outcome). In
essence, u_o and u_* are the conditional utility functions,
the conditioning variable being the decision or the prior
expectation about the outcome.

3.3. Results

A sample of results of the prediction is displayed in
Figures 1, 2 and 3$3/$. In Figure 1 (Experiment I), there are
two displays for each subject. Display A shows the assessed
value function v, the assessed utility function u_o, and the
computed utility function $u_o' = w(v)$. Display B shows again
v, the assessed utility function u_*, and the computed
utility function $u_*' = w(v)$.

The utility functions u_o of Subject 5 and u_* of
Subject 6 exemplify the distinction between the classical
definition of risk attitude (Equation 4), and the notion of
relative risk attitude (Equation 8). We see this in Display
6B. According to the classical definition, a concave (in
the large) utility function u_* implies RA attitude. But
with respect to the value function v, u_* implies RRS attitude since $b < 0$ and the transformation w is convex (in the
large).

Taken together, the results of our experiments and the
data reported in the literature form a sample of 34 fairly
independent and diversified (with respect to the types of
decision problems) observations. We assume this sample is
random.

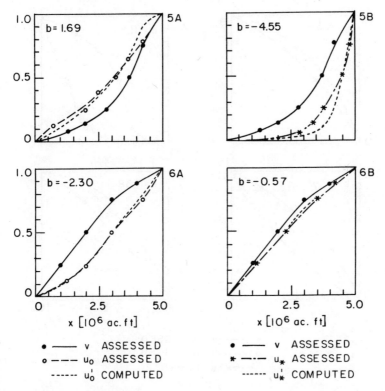

Figure 1. Transformation of v to u_0 and u_* under assumption of constant relative risk attitude (Experiment I, predictive model).

4. CONSTANT RELATIVE RISK ATTITUDE

4.1. Is relative risk attitude constant?

The sample statistics of the error ρ (Equation 10) are given in Table 1. As expected, the predictive model is out-performed by the descriptive model, but the difference is very small. Based on the likelihood ratio test, (9) cannot be rejected as a descriptive model with the expected error $E[\rho]$ less than 13% at the significance level 5%. By virtue of Theorem 1, the constant relative risk attitude hypothesis cannot be rejected at the same levels of the expected error and significance. Furthermore, (9) cannot be

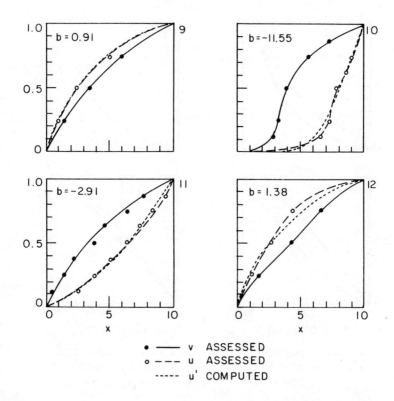

Figure 2. Transformation of v to u under assumption of
         constant relative risk attitude (Experiment II,
         predictive model).

rejected as a predictive model with the expected error $E[\rho]$
less than 17% at the significance level 5%.

    Having verified the hypothesis of constant relative
risk attitude, we proceed now to investigate several
hypotheses using the descriptive model (9) for inference.

4.2. Can identity relationship u = v be assumed?

The first question is whether the departure of the utility
function u from the value function v is significant to
warrant the concept of relative risk attitude. The identity
relationship u = v cannot be dismissed if the hypothesis

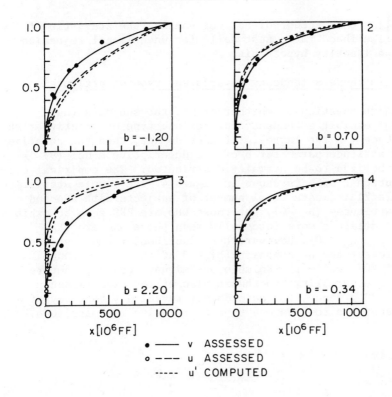

Figure 3. Transformation of v to u under assumption of
constant relative risk attitude (Allais' data,
predictive model).

Table 1. Sample statistics of the error ρ.

Statistic	Descriptive Model	Predictive Model
Sample Size, n	34	34
Mean, $\bar{\rho}$	.186	.239
Median, $\bar{\bar{\rho}}$	.076	.142
Standard Deviation, S_ρ	.277	.298
Coefficient of Skewness, g_ρ	2.164	1.937

$E[|b|] = 0$ is accepted. For our sample, the statistic of the likelihood ratio test calls for unequivocal rejection of the identity hypothesis.

4.3. Is there a tendency towards one type of attitude?

The next question is whether or not the subjects (as a group) exhibit a tendency towards one type of relative risk attitude (in the large). If they do not, then the relative risk attitude parameter b of the descriptive model (9) is hypothesized to be normally distributed. The empirical distribution F of b is shown in Figure 4. The sample statistics (Table 2) indicate equal number of subjects with RRA and RRS attitudes ($\bar{b} = 0$), but those who are RRS seem to exhibit their attitude more forcefully than those who are RRA ($\bar{b} < 0$, $g_b < 0$). However, the likelihood ratio test does not reject the hypothesis $E[b] = 0$ at the significance level 20%, while the Kolmogorov-Smirnov test does not reject the normality hypothesis also at the significance level 20%. Hence, the data do not reveal any tendency of the subjects towards one type of relative risk attitude.

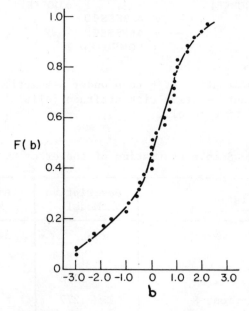

Figure 4. Empirical distribution F of the relative risk attitude parameter b (descriptive model).

Table 2. Sample statistics of the relative
risk attitude parameter b.

Statistic	Descriptive Model	Predictive Model
Sample Size, n	34	34
Mean, $\bar{b}$	-.38	-.47
Median, $\bar{\bar{b}}$	.00	.00
Standard Deviation, S_b	2.34	2.44
Coefficient of Skewness, g_b	-3.12	-2.83

5. INTRINSIC RISK ATTITUDE

5.1. Is relative risk attitude invariant?

Experiment I supplied two utility functions u_o' and u_*' for
the same subject, attribute, and decision context, but for
two different decisions (pessimistic and optimistic). These
data allow us to test the hypothesis that relative risk
attitude is invariant between decisions, or, in other words,
that an individual possesses intrinsic risk attitude which
he exhibits in every choice among gambles. This hypothesis
must be accepted if $b_o = b_*$ for each subject. For the test,
we employ the best estimates of b_o and b_* (Table 3).

First, we note that only three subjects (2,3,6) have
the same relative risk attitude (in the large) for both
decisions. The remaining subjects change their relative
risk attitude from RRS to RRA or vice versa. With
$d = |b_o - b_*|$, we test the hypothesis $E[d] = 0$. For the
sample at hand, the statistic of the likelihood ratio test
calls for the rejection of this hypothesis at the significance level 5%.

This result calls for a cautious examination of the
domain of validity of the notion of "intrinsic risk
attitude" which was suggested in the literature (e.g.,
Bell and Raiffa, 1979; Dyer and Sarin, 1981). A hypothesis
was raised that within a specific decision context, the
individual's relative risk attitude parameter b is

Table 3. Relative risk attitude parameters from
Experiment I (descriptive model).

Subject	Pessimistic Decision b_o	Optimistic Decision b_*	Total Sample
1	-2.45	.75	
2	.90	1.00	
3	-1.60	-1.90	
4	-.90	1.40	
5	1.70	-3.00	
6	-2.30	-.60	
Mean, $\bar{b}$	-.78	-.39	-.59
Std. Deviation, S_b	1.57	1.61	1.60

independent of the particular attribute over which the
utility function is assessed. This hypothesis is stronger
than the one tested herein, and, therefore, is not supported by the data.

5.2. Is framing effect present?

The data in Table 3 indicate the subjects exhibit, on the
average, RRS attitude ($\bar{b}$ = -.59), which is more pronounced
for the pessimistic decision ($\bar{b}_o$ = -.78) than for the optimistic decision ($\bar{b}_*$ = -.39). Kahneman and Tversky (1979)
observed that people generally are risk seeking in the
domain of losses and risk averse in the domain of gains.
Without knowing the value functions of their subjects, it
is not possible to transform this observation into an
equivalent statement in terms of relative risk attitude.
However, this observation does imply that if relative risk
attitude is constant, then the value of b is smaller for
attributes representing losses than for attributes representing gains. In the present case, the domain X of the
attribute x was restricted to positive values, but an
effect of perceived losses or gains was introduced indirectly via the decision scenarios (extremely pessimistic

and extremely optimistic). In light of this, the finding $\bar{b}_0 < \bar{b}_*$ suggests a generalization of the Kahneman and Tversky's observation. Namely, people's tendency towards RRS attitude is stronger when the outcomes are losses or opportunity gains than when the outcomes are gains or opportunity losses.

In their study on the effects of framing, Slovic et al. (1982) report that if an outcome representing a monetary loss is framed as an "insurance premium" rather than a "sure loss," then a reversal in risk attitude (typically from RS to RA) is commonly observed. The two scenarios (pessimistic and optimistic) analyzed in Experiment I constitute two framings of the same outcome space. Thus, the finding $\bar{b}_0 \neq \bar{b}_*$ can be interpreted as an effect of framing of outcomes on relative risk attitude. Apparently, the framing effect is likely to be also observed in decision contexts other than insurance purchasing.

6. CONCLUSIONS

1. The results of our experiments reinforce earlier opinions and experimental findings that a value function (compatible with the theory of ordered value differences) and a utility function (compatible with the expected utility theory) are distinct constructs not only theoretically but also behaviorally. A behavioral hypothesis explaining the difference is that a value function encodes the strength of preference while a utility function encodes the strength of preference and risk attitude.

2. In light of this, the classical interpretation of a von Neumann-Morgenstern utility function must be re-examined. What has been traditionally termed "risk attitude" is a joint effect of the strength of preference and risk attitude, and what has been labelled herein "relative risk attitude" is, from a behavioral standpoint, risk attitude in the absolute sense.

3. Within a specific decision scenario the individual's relative risk attitude is likely to be constant.

4. People (as a group) do not have any tendency toward one type of relative risk attitude (averse or seeking).

5. The hypothesis that the individual's relative risk attitude is invariant between decisions and attributes, or constitutes an intrinsic behavioral characteristic of an individual, is not supported by the data.

6. The effect of framing of outcomes on relative risk attitude is vividly present, and it suggests a generalization of the Kahneman and Tversky's observation as follows. People's tendency towards relatively risk seeking attitude is stronger when the outcomes are losses or opportunity gains than when the outcomes are gains or opportunity losses.

Massachusetts Institute of Technology

NOTES

1. This material is based upon work supported by the National Science Foundation, under Grant No. CEE-8107204. It is an abbreviated version of the article "Strength of Preference and Risk Attitude in Utility Measurement," Organizational Behavior and Human Performance, 30, 1982.
2. For the sake of simplicity, we limit our discussion to risk attitude in the large; i.e., we assume that u is either concave, convex, or linear on the entire domain. This assumption, however, has no bearing on the design of the experiments.
3. We display the predicted functions rather than the best fit functions since the former are indicative of the latter (to the extent that the error of the best fit is not greater than the error of the prediction) and should be of more interest to decision analysts.

REFERENCES

Allais, M.: 1979, 'The So-Called Allais Paradox and Rational Decisions Under Uncertainty'. In Allais, M. and O. Hagen (Eds.), Expected Utility Hypotheses and the Allais Paradox, D. Reidel Publishing Co., London, pp. 437-681.
Allais, M. and O. Hagen (Eds.): 1979, Expected Utility Hypotheses and the Allais Paradox, D. Reidel Publishing Co., Dordrecht, Holland.
Bell, D.E. and H. Raiffa: 1979, 'Marginal Value and Intrinsic Risk Aversion', Working Paper, HBS 79-65, Harvard

Business School, Harvard University, Cambridge,
   Massachusetts.
Bell, D.E. and H. Raiffa: 1980, 'Decision Regret: A Compo-
   nent of Risk Aversion?', Working Paper, HBS 80-56,
   Harvard Business School, Harvard University, Cambridge,
   Massachusetts.
Debreu, G.: 1960, 'Topological Methods in Cardinal Utility
   Theory'. In Arrow, K.J., Karlin, S. and P. Suppes (Eds.),
   Mathematical Methods in the Social Sciences, 1959,
   Stanford University Press, Stanford, California, pp. 16-26.
Dyer, J.S. and R.K. Sarin: 1979, 'Measurable Multiattribute
   Value Functions', Operations Research, 27(4), 810-822.
Dyer, J.S. and R.K. Sarin: 1981, 'Relative Risk Aversion',
   Working Paper No. 310, Western Management Science Insti-
   tute, Graduate School of Management, University of Cali-
   fornia, Los Angeles, California.
Fischer, G.W.: 1977, 'Convergent Validation of Decomposed
   Multi-Attribute Utility Assessment Procedures for Risky
   and Riskless Decisions', Organizational Behavior and
   Human Performance, 18, 295-315.
Fischer, G.W.: 1979, 'Utility Models for Multiple Objective
   Decisions: Do They Accurately Represent Human Prefer-
   ences?', Decision Sciences, 10(3), 451-479.
Frisch, R.: 1926, 'Sur un Problème d'Économie Pure', Norsk
   Matematisk Forenings Skrifter, 1(16), 1-40.
Hershey, J.C. and P.J.H. Schoemaker: 1980, 'Risk Taking and
   Problem Context in the Domain of Losses: An Expected
   Utility Analysis', The Journal of Risk and Insurance,
   46(1), 111-132.
Kahneman, D. and A. Tversky: 1979, 'Prospect Theory: An
   Analysis of Decision Under Risk', Econometrica, 47(2),
   263-291.
Krantz, D.H., Luce, R.D., Suppes, P. and A. Tversky: 1971,
   Foundations of Measurement, Vol. I, Academic Press, New
   York.
Krzysztofowicz, R. and E.V. Jagannathan: 1981, 'Stochastic
   Reservoir Control with Multiattribute Utility Criterion',
   Proceedings, International Symposium on Real-Time Opera-
   tion of Hydrosystems, University of Waterloo, Waterloo,
   Ontario, Canada, 145-159.
Pareto, V.: 1927, Manuel d'Économie Politique, 2nd Ed.,
   Marcel Giard, Paris.
Pratt, J.W.: 1964, 'Risk Aversion in the Small and in the
   Large', Econometrica, 32(1-2), 122-136.
Sarin, R.K., Dyer, J.S. and K. Nair: 1980, 'A Comparative

Evaluation of Three Approaches for Preference Function
Assessment', Presented at the Joint National Meeting
TIMS/ORSA, Washington, D.C., May 4-7.

Scott, D. and P. Suppes: 1958, 'Foundational Aspects of
Theories of Measurement', Journal of Symbolic Logic, 23,
113-128.

Slovic, P., Fischhoff, B. and S. Lichtenstein: 1982,
'Response Mode, Framing, and Information Processing
Effects in Risk Assessment'. In Hogarth, R.M. (Ed.),
New Directions for Methodology of Social and Behavioral
Science: The Framing of Questions and the Consistency of
Response, Jossey-Bass, San Francisco, California, in
press.

Suppes, P. and J.L. Zinnes: 1963, 'Basic Measurement Theory'.
In Luce, R.D., Bush, R.R. and E. Galanter (Eds.), Handbook
of Mathematical Psychology, Vol. 1, Wiley, New York, pp.
1-76.

von Neumann, J. and O. Morgenstern: 1947, Theory of Games
and Economic Behavior, 2nd ed., Princeton University
Press, Princeton, N.J.

George Wright

PROBABILISTIC FORECASTS: Some results
and speculations

Abstract

This paper introduces the concept of calibration
which refers to the external correspondence
between assessed subjective probabilities and
hit-rate. Evidence is presented that the
psychological processes involved in forecasting
future events are different from those involved in
evaluating the truth of one's own knowledge. The
implication is that the results of research that
has investigated the calibration of probability
assessments given to general knowledge questions
will not generalize to the real world where
uncertainty is located in the future. Finally,
future directions for research on probabilistic
forecasting are sketched out. This research should
lead to effective evaluation of probabilistic
forecasts and selection of probabilistic
forecasters.

1. INTRODUCTION

In the 1950s subjective probability estimates
replaced objective or relative-frequency based
probability as input to decision theory (see
Edwards, 1954). Under this approach, the
probability of an outcome, given an act by a
decision maker, and the attractiveness or utility
of that outcome determines optimal art choice (see
Lindley, 1971; Wright, 1983, for outlines of
behavioural decision theory and Brown et al, 1974,
for the related technology, decision analysis). A
'probability' entered into a decision analysis is
usually a subjective 'degree of confidence'

B. P. Stigum and F. Wenstøp (eds.), Foundations of Utility and Risk Theory with Applications,
217–232.
© 1983 *by D. Reidel Publishing Company.*

(Bernoulli, 1713). Even though people may differ
in their probability assessments, each is equally
'correct' provided the probabilities so assessed
conform to the axioms of probability theory (De
Finetti, 1937; Savage, 1954).

However, probability assessors can be
examined for their accuracy given hindsight, that
is, in the light of subsequent events. Winkler and
Murphy (1968) thus identified two measures of a
probability assessor's adequacy; normative
goodness, which reflects the degree to which the
assessments conform to the axioms of probability,
and substantive goodness, which reflects the
amount of knowledge of the topic area contained in
the assessments. Lichtenstein, Fischhoff, and
Phillips (1977) delineated a further aspect of a
probability assessor's adequacy, "calibration". A
probability assessor is "well-calibrated" if, over
the long run, for all propositions assigned the
same probability, the proportion that is true is
equal to the probability assigned.

Most studies of calibration have used general
knowledge items in the form of dichotomous
questions such as "which canal is longer? (a) Suez
Canal (b) Panama Canal". Subjects are required to
indicate the answer they think correct and then to
assess a probability between .5 and 1 indicating
their degree of belief in its correctness. General
knowledge questions have been used because
subjects' answers can be immediately and
conveniently evaluated by the experimenter.

Research on the calibration of subjective
probabilities has documented the generality of
'over-confidence' in these assessments. Generally
for all propositions assessed as having a .XX
probability of being true, less than XX% actually
are true. Lichtenstein et al. (1977) concluded
that the most pervasive finding in recent research
is that people are overconfident with general
knowledge items of moderate or extreme difficulty.
Difficulty is measured as the proportion of
responses where the highest probability was
assigned to what turned out to be the correct
answer. Lichtenstein and Fischhoff (1977)
investigated the calibration/difficulty

relationship in more detail, they concluded that
"with increasing knowledge comes decreasing
over-confidence until, for those whose percentage
correct exceeded 80%, we found a moderate
underconfidence. This relationship resulted in a
non-monotonic relationship between knowledge and
calibration, with the best calibration found at
approximately 80% correct". These conclusions were
essentially confirmed by Lichtenstein, Fischhoff
and Phillips (1981).

      Is it important for probability assessors to
be well-calibrated? Imagine a simple
two-alternative decision problem where a business
man has to decide whether to re-tool to
manufacture product A or whether to re-tool to
manufacture product B. Each of the two products
requires a different type of production and plant
and because re-tooling is extremely expensive the
businessman can only produce one type of product.
Suppose that the utilities attached to the
outcomes are such that the production of A is more
attractive if the probability of making a
"reasonable" return is >.7, otherwise it is better
to manufacture product B. If the businessman
assesses the probability of a reasonable return on
product A is .8, but is poorly calibrated; so the
appropriate probability is .6, then the
businessman would not maximise expected utility by
re-tooling for product A. Furthermore, when the
decision problem is complicated by an extensive
set of act and event sequences and large potential
payoffs, compounded miscalibration can mean a
large expected loss.

      In an attempt to improve individuals'
calibration and thus, by implication, decision
making, Lichtenstein and Fishhoff (1980) trained
subjects by giving them extensive individual
calibration feedback after they had completed
several sets of two alternative general knowledge
questions. They found considerable improvement in
calibration, all of which occurred between the
first and second session but only modest
generalisation for tasks with different difficulty
levels, content and response mode (four rather
than two alternatives).

In another approach to improving calibration, Koriat et al. (1980) attempted to aid the probability assessors to restructure the task in a way that they hoped would discourage over-confidence. In this study subjects were required to respond to two alternative general-knowledge questions in the usual way and were then given additional items. For the additional items subjects were asked first to choose a preferred answer and then to provide either (a) one reason supporting their chosen answer or (b) one reason contradicting their chosen answer or (c) two reasons, one supporting and one contradicting. The subjects then assessed the probability that their chosen answer was correct. Only the group of subjects asked to write contradicting answers showed improved calibration, indicating that one reason for over-confidence is a failure to generate negative evidence.

In contrast to the research outlined above, the research findings underpinning the arguments to be developed in this paper question the implicit generalisation of the result of research that has used general knowledge questions to the real world where uncertainty is located in the future

2. PROBABILISTIC FORECASTING

2.1. Calibration for questions concerning future events

Wright and Wisudha (1982), in their calibration study, used two types of questions. The first set consisted of general knowledge items whilst the second set consisted of then-future event items, where the answer was not at that time known to the experimenter. For example, "will Rudolf Hess die in Spandau jail in the next thirty days? (a) yes, (b) no". Respondents were required to indicate their degree of belief in the answer they indicated to be correct one in a similar way to both sets of questions. The two questions sets were intermixed in a standard random manner.

Wright and Wisudha found that subjects were less likely to use certainty assessments in response to the then-future questions even though the then-future questions were, overall, less difficult than the general-knowledge questions. The proportion of certainty responses used by Wright and Wisudha's subject differed in a direction opposite to that which had previously been found for a comparable change in difficulty (Lichtenstein and Fischhoff, 1977). Wright and Wisudha suggested that one account for this finding might be that there is a positive social utility attached to expressing certainty in a situation where there is known to be an answer, whereas only a fool or a clairvoyant tries to predict the future with total confidence. They also suggested the possibility that calibration may vary as a function of question type as well as a function of task difficulty but they were unable to test this assertion due to the different difficulty of their two question sets.

Wright (in press) investigated calibration for past and future events. His questionnaire presented 140 questions such as "will at least one member of the British Parliament die within the next fourteen days? (a) yes (b) no", (then-future event question), or "has at least one member of the British Parliament died within the last fourteen days? (a) no (b) yes" (past event question). Wright found that with task difficulty held constant at roughly .80, calibration and over-confidence[1] differed between sets of past and future event items. The less-than-perfect calibration for probability assessments given to past events was associated with over-confidence whilst the poor calibration for then-future events was associated with under-confidence. Probability assessments for future events tended to be less certain than probability assessments for past event and general knowledge questions. This result contradicts that of Fischhoff (1976) who found no consistent differences in either the central tendency or the dispersion of subjects' probability estimates regarding past and future events which differed solely in their temporal

setting. However, Fischhoff used event
descriptions in the form of stories where the
tense was changed for past and future events. As
subjects were asked to evaluate the likelihood of
a series of imaginary outcomes it may be that the
tasks were seen by the subjects as artificial, and
so responses were not influenced by the positive
social utility of expressing certainty in a
situation where there is known to be an answer.

In their extensive study of calibration with
general knowledge items, Lichtenstein and
Fischhoff (1977) have argued that it may be
possible to externally recalibrate a person's
assessed probabilities given an indication of task
difficulty. They suggested that mean response may
be taken as an index of task difficulty in a
situation where true outcomes are not known (they
found a high correlation between the two measures,
based on grouped data). However, it is clear from
the present research that, for such an exercise to
be of use in real-world decision making, the
relationship between mean response and task
difficulty must be mapped out separately for
future event item sets.

What factors may have caused the obtained
difference in the calibration and distribution of
probability assessment given to remembered as
opposed to then-future events? Wright (in press)
has argued that in real-life people do not
naturally put a probability to the veracity of
their memories whereas judgements about the
likelihoods of future events contain explicit
uncertainty because the correct answer is unknown
to both subject and experimenter. An initial
response "anchor" for past event or general
knowledge items may be a feeling of certainty
which has such a profound influence that any
adjustment from it to accommodate subsequently
recognised uncertainty may be insufficient; hence
assessed probabilities are too high, yielding
over-confidence. Conversely, with future event
questions the initial response anchor may be a
'don't know', .5 probability response, which
indicates immediate recognition of uncertainty.
Insufficient adjustment from this anchor would

result in the under-confidence shown for the
future event questions.

These findings of differences in the
distribution and calibration of subjective
probabilities given to general knowledge and past
event questions compared to future event questions
raise problems in the interpretation of previous
calibration research, for most real-life decisions
involve uncertainty which is located in the
future. The next section of this chapter sketches
out areas of future research that would now seem
important for evaluation of probabilistic
forecasts and for the selection of probabilistic
forecasters.

3. DIRECTIONS FOR RESEARCH

3.1. Relative desirability of future events

Slovic (1966) explored the manner in which the
desirability of an event influences its judged
probability. Desirability was found to bias
probability estimates in a complex manner and
individual differences were found to be an
important source of variance. Some of his subjects
were consistently optimistic and some were
consistently pessimistic. Zakay (unpublished)
asked subjects to estimate the subjective
probabilities of desirable events (e.g. success in
marriage) and for undesirable events (e.g. hurt in
a road accident) for themselves (individually) and
for a random single member of their peer group. He
found that his subjects felt that desirable events
were more likely to happen to themselves than to
other people, whereas the converse held true for
undesirable events.

In real-life probability assessment it seems
intuitively reasonable that future events have
differential utilities. We could investigate the
relative influence of the rated desirability of an
event upon the calibration of the subjective
probability of its occurrence. Rated desirability
may have an effect on calibration independent from
task difficulty.

3.2. Question format

A basic probability axiom is that the
probabilities of a set of mutually exclusive and
exhaustive events should sum to one. In many
calibration studies it has been assumed that this
axiom is satisfied, point probability estimates
for the occurrence of an event or the truth of a
proposition are elicited but not the probabilities
of the complementary events or the falsehood of
the proposition. Wright and Whalley (this volume)
have shown that the subjective probabilities given
by untrained assessors (the type who are typically
used in calibration studies) tend to sum more than
one. This finding may account to some degree for
the 'over-confidence' typically found in
calibration studies. We should explore this
possibility by requiring subjects to obey the
additivity axiom using a set of general knowledge
questions. We could then compare resulting
calibration scores with previous findings.
       Finally, we should investigate the
possibility that the question format which has
been extensively used in calibration studies has
influenced research findings. In all studies so
far undertaken in the general knowledge
calibration literature, subjects have known that
one of the alternative answers is, in fact,
correct. As noted earlier it may be that the
tendency of people to be over-confident reflects
the heuristic called "anchoring and adjustment".
When asked to give a probability judgement, people
'anchor' on what they believe is the correct
answer and then adjust their confidence downward.
However, the anchor may have such a dominating
influence that adjustment is insufficient, hence
over-confidence. We could introduce a simple
variation into the general knowledge calibration
task by (1) instructing subjects that neither of
the alternative answers may be correct, or (2)
introducing another alternative answer, "neither
of the other answers". It seems intuitively
reasonable that this manipulation will render the
general knowledge calibration task nearer to real
life decision making where none of a set of

alternative events (excluding the non-occurrence
of an event) may occur. It may be that this
manipulation may reduce subjects' confidence in
their choice of alternative answers and so reduce
over-confidence.

3.3. Calibration and Difficulty

Wright (1982) investigated the relationship
between Lichtenstein et al.'s (1977) measure of
task difficulty (overall proportion correct) and a
subjective measure of task difficulty using
general knowledge calibration questions (in the
context of a study investigating the relationship
between probability assessment and decision time).
After answering each question the respondent was
required to indicate how difficult he or she found
the question on a seven-point scale with two end
points marked extremely easy and extremely
difficult, respectively. Wright obtained a
near-zero intercorrelation between subjective task
difficulty and overall proportion correct. On the
basis of between-subject analysis, increased
subjectively perceived task difficulty is
associated with less use of certainty responses
and a lower mean probability assessment. Also, on
the basis of grouped data, increased subjectively
perceived task difficulty is related to increased
decision time. These results are intuitively
reasonable whereas the absence of a similar
pattern of inter-relationships between overall
proportion correct and the response distribution
and decision time measures seems unreasonable.
These findings question the nature of Lichtenstein
et al.'s task difficulty measure.
    It would seem important to extend
investigation of the relationship between
subjective difficulty and overall proportion
correct with future event calibration questions.
If the same relationships hold as those shown by
Wright (1982) we should investigate the
relationship between calibration and future event
item sets varying in subjective difficulty in the
hope of obtaining an a priori index of the type
and degree of recalibration that may by needed by

a probability assessor. This investigation may
resolve Lichtenstein and Fischhoff's dilemma:

> "If we know how difficult an item is, then we
> can make a much more accurate (calibration)
> correction. In practice, however, such
> situations will be rare. To know how
> difficult an item is, we must know the
> correct answer. But as we know the correct
> answer, we will not have any practical need
> for the judge's assessment." (Lichtenstein
> and Fischhoff, 1977: 181).

3.4. Individual differences in probabilistic
     forecasting

Wright and Phillips (1979, 1981) have studied the
relationship between personality measures of
authoritarianism, dogmatism and intolerance of
ambiguity and probabilistic thinking, where
probabilistic thinking was defined as the tendency
to adopt a probabilistic set, discrimination of
uncertainty and the ability to express that
uncertainty meaningfully either verbally or as a
numerical probability. However, the strong
anticipated relationships between the two sets of
variates were not confirmed. In addition, Wright
and Phillips (in press) concluded that
probabilistic thinking, itself, may be a
multi-factored ability, largely situation
specific.
     However, Wright (in press), using two
calibration tasks, found evidence that the degrees
to which the two sets of questions were seen in
terms of certainty or total uncertainty may be
stable individual differences. This finding
parallels that of Wright and Phillips' (1980)
cross-cultural study which identified two
alternative ways of dealing with uncertainty, one
of which did not involve the notion of
probability.
     Clearly, someone who does not naturally see
the world in probabilistic terms but in terms of
certainty or total uncertainty may be at a
disadvantage in the typical calibration task,

where instructions emphasise the need to assess degrees of belief. One study pointing to this possibility was undertaken by Martin and Gettys (1969) in the context of a probability revision task. Their subjects were required to choose which of three possible data generators was generating data.

Subjects chose what they thought was the more likely data generator, given the data, in one of two forms: (1) deterministic, where a subject was required to make a nominal selection. (2) probabilistic where a subject was required to estimate the likelihood that each of the three generators generated the data. This probability response was then translated to a nominal response on the basis of the highest probability attached to a data generator. The results of their experiment surprised Martin and Gettys:

> "Originally it was thought that the use of a probability response mode would cause S's to exhibit a more exacting type of inference and thereby improve their inferred nominal response performance. The results indicate that the opposite was true ... A possible explanation ... would be that probability responses require different information processing behaviour than nominal responses require. When nominal responses are made, for example, perhaps only the few hypotheses judged to be most likely need to be considered since S's task is simply to choose the most likely hypothesis. If S's response is a probability, he should be concerned with the likelihood of all the hypotheses." (Martin and Getty, 1969: 416).

However, Lichtenstein and Fischhoff (1977) would argue that Martin and Getty's result is simply a result of a difference in overall proportion correct between the deterministic and probabilistic response modes. The subjects who performed under the deterministic response mode found the task easier (i.e. achieved a higher proportion correct) than those subjects performing under the probabilistic response mode.

We could attempt to evaluate the validity of these two competing explanations of Martin and Getty's findings by requiring selected subjects to give deterministic or probabilistic responses to future event questions. Selection would be based upon strong probabilistic or non-probabilistic (deterministic) set in the View of Uncertainty Questionnaire which poses questions like "Will you catch a head cold in the next three months?" and "Will you ever own a television receiver so flat it can be hung on the wall?" Subjects are asked to write an "appropriate response" to each question. The main categories into which responses are coded include the number of Yes or No responses, the number of Don't Know responses and the number of probability words or phrases. Many Yes or No responses indicate a non-probabilistic set, while many probability words or phrases indicate a probabilistic set. This questionnaire was first used in a study reported by Phillips and Wright (1977). Non-probabilistic thinkers should perform better with a deterministic response mode than with a probabilistic response mode. The converse may hold for probabilistic thinkers.

Research, to date, has frequently presented calibration analyses at the group level because many responses are needed in order to get a stable measure of calibration. However, individual difference research should not be neglected for a well-calibrated individual will naturally provide better inputs for a decision analysis and also may well be a better "intuitive" decision-maker.

4. CONCLUSIONS

This discussion of the calibration of subjective probabilities has presented evidence that the psychological process involved in forecasting future events are different from those involved in placing probabilities on the veracity of one's own knowledge. Since most real-life decisions involve forecasts of future events it would seem important to explore further probabilistic forecasting with the aim of improving evaluation of forecasts and the selection of forecasters.

Explorations of the future direction for research sketched out in this paper should make a further contribution to the cognitive psychology of how people develop and express feelings of uncertainty. Current research on calibration has documented the empirical relationship between calibration and overall percentage correct using general knowledge items and has also suggested some methods for improving calibration. However, psychological theory is often absent, either as motivation for the research or as explanation of the results. At the moment we are unable to account, psychologically, in any measure for task and individual influences on calibration.

Research of the type indicated in this paper also has important implications for the application of decision analysis. Most real life decisions involve uncertainty that is located in the future but calibration research has concentrated on subjects' uncertainty about their general knowledge. Furthermore, the desirability of a future event prediction may influence the assessment of its likelihood, as may the method of likelihood assessment. Our results suggest that current calibration research based on responses to general knowledge questions in restricted formats cannot be generalised to future event probability assessment. If good calibration leads to improved decision making (as acceptance of the normative status of subjective expected utility theory would imply) then it is of prime importance to investigate individual differences in calibration with a view to improving the selection of decision makers in future.

NOTES

1. Mathematical measures of individual and group aggregated calibration and over-confidence, for the whole range of assessed probabilities, are detailed in Wright (in press).

REFERENCES

Bernoulli, J.: 1713, Basel.

Brown, R.V., Kahr, A.S. and Peterson, C.R.: 1974,
Decision Analysis: an overview, London:
Holt-Blond.

De Finetti, B.: 1964, 'La prevision: des logiques,
ses sources subjectives', Annals de l'Institut
Henri Poincare, 7, 1-68. (English translation in
M.E. Kyborg Jr. and H.E. Smokler (eds.), Studies
in Subjective Probability, New York: Wiley.

Edwards, W.: 1954, 'The theory of decision
making', Psychological Bulletin, 51, 380-417.

Fischhoff, B: 1976, 'The effect of temporal
setting on likelihood estimates', Organizational
Behavior and Human Performance, 15, 180-194.

Koriat, A., Lichtenstein, S. and Fischoff, B.:
1980, 'Reasons for confidence', Journal of
Experimental Psychology: Human Learning and
Memory, 6, 107-118.

Lindley, D.V.: 1971, Making Decisions, New York:
Wiley.

Lichtenstein, S. and Fischhoff, B.: 1977, 'Do
those who know more also know more about how
much they know', Organizational Behavior and
Human Performance, 20, 159-183.

Lichtenstein, S. and Fischhoff, B. and Phillips,
L.D.: 1977, 'Calibration of probabilities the
state of the art' in H. Jungermann and G. de
Zeeuw (eds.) Decision making and change in human
affairs, D. Reidel Publ. Co., Dordrecht, Holland.

Lichtenstein, S. and Fischhoff, B.: 1980,
'Training for calibration', Organizational
Behavior and Human Performance, 26, 149-171.

Lichtenstein, S., Fischhoff, B. and Phillips,

L.D.: 1981, 'Calibration of probabilities: the
state of the art to 1980', in D. Kahneman, P.
Slovic and A. Tversky (eds.), Judgement under
uncertainty: Heuristics and Biases, New York:
Cambridge.

Martin, D.W. and Gettys, C.F.: 1969, 'Feedback and
response mode in performing a Bayesian decision
task', Journal of Applied Psychology, 53,
413-418.

Phillips, L.D. and Wright, G.N.: 1977, 'Cultural
differences in viewing uncertainty and assessing
probabilities', in H. Jungermann and G. de Zeeuw
(eds.), Decision making and change in human
affairs, D. Reidel Publ. Co., Dordrecht, Holland.

Savage, L.J.: 1954, The foundations of statistics,
New York: Wiley.

Slovic, P.: 1966, 'Value as a determiner of
subjective probability', IEEE Transactions on
Human Factors in Electronics?, 22-28.

Winkler, R.L. and Murphy, A.H.: 1968, '"Good"
probability assessors', Journal of Applied
Meteorology, 1, 751-758.

Wright, G.N.: 1982, 'Subjective probability,
decision time and task difficulty', Technical
Report 82-2, Department of Psychology, City of
London Polytechnic.

Wright, G.N.: 1983, Behavioural decision theory:
an introduction, Harmondsworth: Penguin.

Wright, G.N.: (in press) 'Changes in the realism
and distribution of probability assessments as a
function of question type', Acta Psychologica.

Wright, G.N. and Phillips, L.D.: 1979,
'Personality and probabilistic thinking',
British Journal of Psychology, 70, 295-303.

Wright, G.N. and Phillips, L.D.: 1980, 'Cultural

variation in probabilistic thinking: Alternative
ways of dealing with uncertainty', International
Journal of Psychology, 15, 239-257.

Wright, G.N. and Phillips, L.D.: 1981, 'Individual
differences in probabilistic thinking', in L.
Sjoberg, T. Tyska and J. A. Wise (eds),
Extrapolation of decision theory to the
individual and the group, Lund: Doxa.

Wright, G.N. and Phillips, L.D.: (in press)
'Decision-making: cognitive style or task
specific behaviour?', in H. Bonarius, G. van
Heck and N. Smid (eds), Personality psychology
in Europe, London: Lawrence Erlbaum Associates.

Wright, G.N. and Whalley, P.C. 'The
supra-additivity of subjective probability',
pp. 233-244 (this volume).

Wright, G.N. and Wisudha, A.: 1982, 'Distribution
of probability assessments for almanac and
future events questions', Scandinavian Journal
of Psychology, 23, 219-224.

George Wright and Peter Whalley

THE SUPRA-ADDITIVITY OF SUBJECTIVE
PROBABILITY

Abstract

This study investigates the descriptive relevance
of the additivity axiom for untrained probability
assessors. Most subjects followed the axiom in
simple two-outcome assessments but as the number
of events in a set increased more of them, and to
a greater degree, became 'supra-additive'. With
the number of events in a set held constant more
.subjects were supra-additive, and supra-additive
to a greater degree, in the assessment of
probabilities for an event set containing
individuating information. A major implication of
the present study is that the subjective
probability for the occurrence of an event should
not be assessed in isolation from the other events
in its set. The implications of axiom tests for
the normative status of subjective expected
utility theory are discussed.

1. INTRODUCTION

A basic axiom of probability theory is that the
probabilities assigned to a set of mutually
exclusive and exhaustive events should sum to one.
In many studies of subjective probability
estimation this additivity axiom has not been
tested because the response mode ensured that it
was satisfied. Other studies assume that the axiom
is satisfied by eliciting point probability
estimates for the occurrence of an event or the
truth of a proposition and failing to elicit the
probability of the complementary event or the
falsehood of the proposition.

B. P. Stigum and F. Wenstøp (eds.), Foundations of Utility and Risk Theory with Applications,
233–244.
© 1983 by D. Reidel Publishing Company.

Research on descriptive validity of the axiom has been meagre and contradictory. Phillips et al. (1966), in a probability revision task, found four out of their five subjects assessed probabilities that were greater than unity. These four subjects increased their probability estimates for likely hypotheses but failed to decrease probabilities attached to unlikely hypotheses. In another probability revision study, Marks and Clarkson (1972) found that 49 out of their 62 subjects gave probability estimates for complementary events that summed to more than unity. Conversely a study by Alberoni (1962), which asked subjects to estimate sampling distributions from binomial populations on the basis of small samples, found that in most cases subjective probabilities summed to less than unity. If the additivity axiom is not satisfied the implications for subjective expected utility theory (SEU) are far-reaching. Edwards (1962) has argued that one consequence would be that both subjective probability and utility must be measured on a ration scale.

The present study reports an investigation of the descriptive relevance of the additivity axiom for subjects who had no prior training in probability assessment. It is assumed that the study will thus provide insight into the general process of subjective probability estimation.

2. METHOD

Thirty-nine undergraduates at Huddersfield Polytechnic, with no prior training in probability assessment completed a questionnaire containing problems presented on separate pages in the following order. Subjects were told that once they had answered a problem they should proceed to the next problem and not return to preceding problems.

1) assessment of the probability of 'heads' and of !tails' in a single coin toss.

2) assessment of the probability that each of the six sides of a dice would land 'face up' on a

single throw.

3) assessment of the probability of rain tomorrow
   at a specified time and place, together with
   an assessment of the complementary probability
   of no rain.

4) assessment of the probability that at exactly
   6pm next Wednesday you will be doing one of a
   set of 16 mutually exclusive and exhaustive
   acts, e.g.: washing yourself, driving a car,
   buying something in a shop, sitting down
   watching television at home and a catch-all of
   neither of these acts.

6) assessment of the probability that each of
   five horses will win a race that is about to
   start in five minutes. Each horse has a 'track
   record' of wins, places, and losses. Only one
   horse will win the race.

7) assessments as in 6) but with a sixth horse
   entered for the race at the last-but-one
   minute. The previous set of mutually exclusive
   and exhaustive events is thus expanded.

8) assessments as in 7) but with a seventh horse
   entered at the last minute.

For each problem the number of people who assessed
additive, sub-additive or supra-additive
probabilities was noted. The mean summed
probability for each set of mutually exclusive and
exhaustive events was also computed. Also, in
problems 7 and 8, the mean summed probability for
the original set of five horses, given in problem
6, was calculated.

3. RESULTS

All subjects followed the additivity axiom in
problem 1 whilst in the remaining problems the
proportion of subjects who followed the axiom
varied from 0.15 to 0.95. Most people who did not

follow the additivity axiom on a problem responded
in a supra-additive way - the probabilities
assessed summed to more than unity. Table 1 sets
out these findings in more detail.

	Problem 1	Problem 2	Problem 3	Problem 5	Problem 6	Problem 7	Problem 8
Proportion of additive responses	1.00	0.56	0.95	0.31	0.34	0.15	0.23
Proportion of supra-additive responses	0.00	0.36	0.05	0.67	0.64	0.72	0.64
Proportion of sub-additive responses	0.00	0.08	0.00	0.02	0.02	0.13	0.13

Table 1: Proportion of response types on the
problems

        Restricting analysis to the supra-additive
responses, chi-square analysis of proportions
revealed that the proportions of supra-additive
responses in problems 1 and 3 were similar (p>.05)
whilst these proportions were less than the
proportion of supra-additive responses on all
other problems (p<.05). The proportions of
supra-additive responses on problems 5, 6, 7 and 8
were also similar (p>.05) whilst the proportion of
supra-additive responses in problem 2, apart from
being more than on problems 1 and 3, was less than
on problems 5 and 7. These results indicate that a
person is more likely to be supra-additive on
those problems containing more than two possible
outcomes. Interestingly, on those problems
containing six possible outcomes, problems 2 and
7, more people exhibited supra-additivity on
problem 7, suggesting that the two problems were
viewed differently by subjects.
        Analysis of the mean summed probabilities for
the problems clarifies this issue. Problems 1 and
3 were not included in this analysis because most
responses on these problems were additive. Table 2
sets out the comparisons.

	Problem 2 (6 outcomes)	Problem 5 (16 outcomes)	Problem 6 (5 outcomes)	Problem 7 (6 outcomes)	Problem 8 (7 outcomes)
mean sum of assessed probabilities	1.65	3.04	1.70	2.03	2.13
sd	0.97	2.91	0.78	0.96	1.14

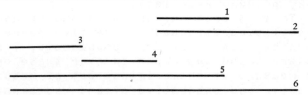

Inference about the differences in means between problems: an underline connecting a pair of problems indicates either (1) that the 95 (or 99%) credible interval of the mean of the difference scores between a pair of problems does not include zero (using the student-t distribution) or (2) that the Wilcoxen test shows a significant difference at the 5% level. No underline between a pair of problems indicates either (1) that the 95% credible interval includes zero or (2) the Wilcoxen test was not significant.

1 $P(-0.56 \leqslant \mu \leqslant -0.10) = .99$
2 $P(-0.68 \leqslant \mu \leqslant -0.17) = .99$
3 $Z = -3.18, p < .05, \text{2-tailed}$
4 $Z = -2.86, p < .05, \text{2-tailed}$
5 $P(-0.76 \leqslant \mu \leqslant -0.007) = .95$
6 $P(-0.92 \leqslant \mu \leqslant -0.043) = .95$

Table 2: Mean comparisons of the sum of probabilities attached to the problems

These comparisons reveal generally that as the number of mutually exclusive and exhaustive events in an event set increased the mean sum of probabilities attached to the event set also increased. With the number of events in a set held constant, problems 2 and 7, more people, and more people to a greater degree, were supra-additive in the assessment of probabilities for an event set

containing individuating information, ie, problem
7. A linear trend test (Meddis, 1975) confirmed
that as the number of possible outcomes increased
over problems 6, 7, 8 and 5 the mean sum of
assessed probabilities attached by subjects to
these problems also increased (F = 11.84, df
1,152, p<.002, 2-tailed).

     Table 3 sets out the mean sum of assessed
probabilities attached to the five horses held in
common between race-horse problems 6, 7 and 8. No
downward trend was observed over these problems on
this measure as the original set of mutually
exclusive and exhaustive events was expanded (F =
0.66, df 1,114, p>.05) In fact, one-way analysis
of variance revealed that the mean sum of
probabilities remained constant (F = 0.54, df
2,114,p>.05). The mean between-subject correlation
obtained for this common measure was .89,
indicating consistency in subjects' responses.

	Problem 6	Problem 7	Problem 8
$\bar{x}$	1.70	1.72	1.55
sd	0.779	0.816	0.835

Table 3: Mean sum of probabilities attached to the
five race horses held in common on problems 6), 7)
and 8)

     The mean subjective probability placed on the
possibility that at exactly 6pm next Wednesday the
respondent would be sitting down watching
television at home (problem 4) was 0.36. This
probability was similar to that placed on the same
possibility in the context of problem 5, where the
mean probability was 0.32 [P = (-0.003≤μ≤0.082) =
.95]. The correlation between the two measures was
.95, again showing consistency in subjects'
responses.

3.1. Association between problems

Using chi-square as a measure of association no
relationship was obtained between the additive,
supra-additive and sub-additive styles of
responding on problems 2 and 5 and type of
response on problems 6, 7 and 8. Between problems
6, 7 and 8 significant associations were obtained
indicating consistent responses (Problems 6 and
7, χ^2 = 30.64, 4df, p<.001; problems 6 and 8, χ^2 =
40.66, 4df, p<.001; problems 7 and 8, χ^2 = 48.54,
4df, p<.001).
    The mean between-subjects correlation for the
mean summed probabilities computed for each of the
race-horse problems was .88, indicating
consistency in degree of supra-additivity.

4. DISCUSSION AND CONCLUSIONS

Most of the untrained probability assessors
followed the additivity axiom in simple
two-outcome assessments. However, as the number of
mutually exclusive and exhaustive events in a set
was increased, more subjects, and to a greater
extent became supra-additive.
    With the number of mutually exclusive and
exhaustive events in a set held constant, more
subjects were supra-additive, and supra-additive
to a greater degree, in the assessment of
probabilities for an event set containing
individuating information. Individuating
information about the likelihood of an event's
occurrence may psychologically dis-associate an
event from its event set. In the present study,
the individuating background information
associated with the possible success of a
racehorse in a race that was about to start
consisted simply of a record of that horse's
previous performances. It seems intuitively
reasonable that most probabilistic predictions are
based, in the main, on one's knowledge and not to
any large extent on abstract notions such as
additivity. Only when one's previous knowledge is
specifically excluded as in problem 2, the dice

problem, does additivity become evident. A similar
phenomenon was noted by Kahneman and Tversky
(1972) who coined the term 'representativeness' to
refer to the dominance of individuating
information in intuitive prediction. One of their
tasks illustrating the phenomenon asked subjects
individually to judge the likelihood that an
individual, Tom W., is a graduate student in a
particular field of specialization. All the
subjects had available was a brief description of
the student in the form of a personality sketch
and the prior probabilities as determined by the
base-rates for the graduate programmes. Kahneman
and Tversky found that subjects had an apparent
inability to integrate the low validity
personality sketch with the base-rate information
in a situation where the base-rate should have
been predominant. Similarly, Dostoevsky observed
that in roulette "... after the red has come up
ten times in a row, hardly anyone will persist in
betting on it." However, the belief that the black
is more likely to come up after a long run of red
is fallacious, the roulette ball has no memory!
     If a person violates the additivity axiom but
accepts its normative status then a major
implication from the present study is that the
subjective probability for the occurrence of an
event should not be assessed in isolation from the
other events in its set. The subjective
probability attached to the non-occurrence of an
event should be decomposed into the probabilities
of occurrence of the other possible events. On the
basis of responses to problems 4 and 5, subsequent
normalisation would have reduced the initially
assessed probability of the alternative outcome
"watching television" by about one-third.
Lichtenstein, Fischhoff and Phillips (1977) have
noted that in a two-alternative calibration
question the assessor is usually required to
select the more likely alternative and then state
the probability that this choice is correct. The
complementary probabilities that the other
alternatives are correct are seldom elicited.
Fortunately, it is clear from the present results
that most subjects satisfy the additivity axiom in

simple two-alternative assessments. But this
finding does not hold true for multi-alternative
assessments.

However normalisation may not be a quick and
easy solution to incoherence. Bartholemew (1979)
in the discussion of a theoretical paper by
Lindley, Tversky and Brown (1979, p168) outlined a
major problem:

> Suppose that I assess the
> probabilities of a set of mutually
> exclusive and exhaustive events to be
>
> 0.001, 0.250, 0.200, 0.100, 0.279 ...
>
> It is then pointed out to me that
> these probabilities sum to 0.830 and
> hence that the assessment is
> incoherent. If we use the
> method...with the probability metric,
> we have to adjust the probabilities by
> adding 0.034 to each (= (1/5)
> (1-0.830)) to give
>
> 0.035, 0.284, 0.234, 0.134, 0.313
>
> The problem is with the first event,
> which I originally regarded as very
> unlikely, has had its probability
> increased by a factor of 35! Though
> still small it is no longer smaller
> than the others by two orders of
> magnitude.

The results from the present study indicate
that the additivity axiom has little descriptive
relevance for the assessment of probability by
untrained assessors. Tests revealing the
descriptive violation of another axiom of SEU, the
independence principle, have been conducted by
Ellsberg (1961). MacCrimmon (1968) has shown that
business executives who violated the independence
principle could be easily led, via discussion, to
accept its normative status. However, Slovic and
Tversky (1975) criticised MacCrimmon's procedure

and argued that the discussion conducted by a
prestigeous decision theorist influenced the
subjects to accept the normative status of the
axiom. They presented subjects with arguments for
and against the independence axiom and found
persistent violations.

Given that individuals violate the axioms of
SEU in their intuitive decision making it is
little wonder that SEU is not descriptive of human
choice behaviour in more complex settings. Here
experience of the real world is more likely to be
one of interdependent rather than mutually
exclusive events. Moreover if subjects
consistently violate the axioms after the
principles have been clarified in such a way as to
maximise their acceptability, then the normative
status of SEU and its related technology of
decision analysis becomes suspect. Many
researchers consider this supra-additivity problem
to one of only trivial mathematical error that can
be resolved by the adoption of a suitable
restrictive response mode. However the work of
Zadeh (1978) and other concerned with the
intrinsic imprecision in natural language,
suggests that it may well be a fundamental
psychological problem.

They have posited a theory of 'possibilistic'
thought as an alternative to conventional
probabilistic ideas. They claim that this is more
appropriate when the individual is concerned with
"meaning of information - rather than with its
measure". Zadeh's contention is that "contrary to
what has become a widely accepted assumption -
much of the information on which human decisions
are based is possibilistic rather than
probabilistic in nature". The implication is that
under certain circumstances it may be better to
obtain possibilistic judgements and then map them
into probabilities rather than to directly elicit
probabilities. It remains to be proven whether
this is indeed a useful analytic framework for
exploring such problems as supra-additivity,
however research of this type is urgently needed,
for decision analysis is becoming a widely-used
decision aid.

NOTES

1. Dostoevsky, F. 'The Gambler', translated by
   A.R. MacAndrew (1964). New York. Bantam Books,
   p47.

REFERENCES

Alberoni, F.: 1962, 'Contribution to the study of
   subjective probability', Journal of General
   Psychology 66, 241-264.

Edwards, W.: 1962, 'Subjective probabilities
   inferred from decisions', Psychological Review
   69, 109-135.

Ellsberg, D.: 1961, 'Risk, ambiguity and the
   Savage axioms', Quarterly Journal of Economics
   75, 643-649.

Kahneman, D. and Tversky, A.: 1972, 'Subjective
   probability: a judgement of representativeness',
   Cognitive Psychology 3, 430-454.

Lichtenstein, S., Fischhoff, B. and Phillips,
   L.D.: 1977, 'Calibration of probabilities: the
   state of the art', in H. Jungerman and G. de
   Zeeuw (eds.) Decision Making and Change in Human
   Affairs, D. Reidel Publ. Co., Dordrecht. Holland.

Lindley, D.V., Tversky, A. and Brown, R.V.: 1979,
   'On the reconciliation of probability
   assessments', Journal of the Royal Statistical
   Society 142, 146-180.

MacCrimmon, K.R.: 1968, 'Descriptive and normative
   implications of the decision theory postulates',
   in K. Borch and J. Mossin (eds.) Risk and
   Uncertainty, New York: St. Martin's.

Marks, D.F. and Clarkson, J.K.: 1972, 'An
   explanation of conservatism in the book
   bag-and-pokerchips situation', Acta Psychologica
   36, 145-160.

Meddis, R.: 1975, <u>Statistical Handbook for
Non-Statisticians</u>, McGraw-Hill: London.

Phillips, L.D., Hayes, W.L. and Edwards, W.: 1966,
'Conservatism in complex probabilistic
inference', <u>IEEE Transactions in Human Factors
in Electronics</u> 7, 7-18.

Slovic, P. and Tversky, A.: 1974, 'Who accepts
Savage's axiom', <u>Behavioural Science</u> 19,
368-373.

Zadeh, L.A.: 1978, 'Fuzzy sets as a basis for a
theory of possibility', <u>Fuzzy Sets and Systems</u>
1, 3-28.

PART V

CHOICE WITHOUD EXPECTED UTILITY

Héctor A. Múnera and Richard de Neufville

A DECISION ANALYSIS MODEL WHEN THE SUBSTITUTION
PRINCIPLE IS NOT ACCEPTABLE

1.   INTRODUCTION

A basic axiom of standard utility theory, the substitution
principle, severely restricts the component of uncertainty
of a choice. As von Neumann and Morgenstern (1944) wrote:
"May there not exist in the individual a (positive or
negative) utility of the mere act of 'taking a chance', of
gambling, which the use of mathematical expectation
obliterates?"
       Practitioners of expected utility decision analysis
have been happy to accept this restriction, on the grounds
that any sensation caused by the uncertainty of a choice
should not be part of the thinking of a "rational" person,
as they conceive him. Some argue with Harsanyi that people
ought to be "result-oriented" and focus on end consequences
only, not on the path or process by which one arrives
there. In principle, this argument is weak as there
evidently are many instances — having children is one —
where the process is important. They must argue that what
happens during the process is irrelevant to rational
thinking. This they generally do either by ridicule,
calling any sensation about uncertainty an irresponsible
"love of gambling", or by smugly ignoring the process,
thus: "The principle result of utility theory for risk is
that a linear utility index can be defined which reflects
completely a person's preferences among risky alternatives."
(Luce and Raiffa, 1958; emphasis not in original)
       Our premise, however, is that in a great many
situations the process or path by which one arrives at the
end consequences cannot be ignored. Most obviously, the
sensation about uncertainty is often a legitimate feeling
held by rational people. Such is the case, for example,
for the abutters of a nuclear power plant, to whom the
sense of "gambling" in which they are forcibly involved is
distinctly hateful. More subtly, different paths and
consequences offer different degrees of flexibility,

B. P. Stigum and F. Wenstøp (eds.), Foundations of Utility and Risk Theory with Applications,
247–262.
© 1983 by D. Reidel Publishing Company.

opportunities to do something else, and are not logically
equivalent. Our starting point, in brief, is that the
substitution principle which has a great deal of immediate
appeal conflicts with more subtle principles, cannot be
supreme, and must, in many situations, give way.

In this paper, we propose a general model of decision
analysis which is consistent with all the axioms normally
required for the "rational" individual: transitivity,
continuity, monotonicity and complete ordering, but does
not incorporate any independence or substitution axioms.
As a special case, it reduces to a linear function similar
to the standard expected utility model. The presentation
begins with a summary of the evidence of situations in
which the substitution principle is not acceptable to
everyone. Following theoretical arguments for a flexibility
principle, we present our model in the form of a general
uncertainty operator which incorporates individual
attitudes towards uncertainty. Finally, we show how the
model is consistent with the full range of responses of
real persons, experimental and otherwise.

2. SUMMARY OF ARGUMENTS AGAINST THE SUPREMACY OF THE SUBSTITUTION PRINCIPLE

These are both empirical and theoretical. We deal with
them in turn. In both cases, we argue that while the
substitution principle is attractive, which it certainly
is, it cannot account for all we wish for rational behavior
and, in general, must give way as a rule which excludes
these other possibilities.

2.1 Empirical

The Allais "paradox" (Allais, 1953) is a most immediate
example of the failure of the substitution principle to
be generally acceptable. Following an accepted procedure
in other sciences, Allais proposed a Gedanken experiment
involving two simple, transparent situations of choice, for
each of which intelligent people can easily make a
decision which by definition is rational. The "paradox" is
made to appear when the two decisions are compared to the
choices required by the expected utility model, which
purports to be the model for rational behavior. As it
happens, many people rationally choose differently, thus
the "paradox". To resolve this conflict, there are two

possibilities, each equally valid logically:
- either the individuals are wrong, the position
  of proponents of the substitution principle;
- or, the substitution principle fails to apply always
  to all rational individuals.

With Allais and others, we subscribe to the second
possibility. In fact, this seems the realistic alternative
since the substitutions proposed in the Gedanken experiment
- by creating uncertainty where there was certainty or vice
versa - fundamentally alter the nature of the choice
problem in a way that is not acceptable to everybody.

The fact that utility functions elicited from
individuals are sensitive to the probability distribution
used is the more fundamental demonstration against the
universality of the substitution principle. Indeed, the
essence of the substitution principle is that the utility
functions should be independent of the probability
distribution. But they clearly are not. Allais shows this
by comparing the utility functions assessed using 50:50
probability fractions, $B_{1/2}$, with those obtained using
varying probabilities for a fixed price, B_{200} (Allais,
1953, 1979). As Figure 1 illustrates, the results are not
even similar. McCord and de Neufville (1982) reaffirm

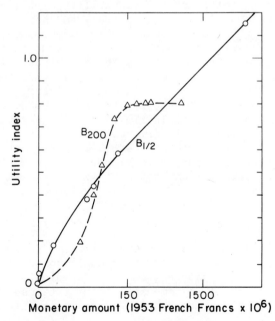

Fig. 1. Allais' Empirical Findings B_{200} and $B_{1/2}$ for de Finetti.

this conclusion with a further empirical analysis.

Related to the above is the issue of whether the utility function is continuous for low probabilities, whether there is a "certainty effect". Formally, the question can be put as to whether, for a binary lottery with outcomes A and B, the latter having a low probability ε, the certainty equivalent $C_e = A$, $\varepsilon \to 0$? The answer given by standard utility theory is positive, since utility is, supposedly, unaffected by the probabilities. But many investigators have found otherwise. In particular, Kahneman and Tversky (1979) concluded, on the basis of extensive experiments, that their weighting functions for outcomes had "sharp drops or apparent discontinuities. . . at the end points." The special importance of this particular evidence against the substitution principle lies in the desire to apply decision analysis to catastrophic events where probabilities are very small, such as earthquakes (de Neufville, 1975) or nuclear meltdowns (Keeney and Nair, 1975). If the premises of conventional expected utility analysis are unacceptable, some revision is necessary so that we can correctly address these problems with low probabilities of high consequences.

Finally, numerous different experiments in psychology suggest that higher moments of the probability distribution are relevant to a person's choice, contrary to what the substitution principle would have us believe. Coombs and his co-workers have presented numerous papers arguing for consideration of the third moments of the distributions; the Oregon group has likewise consistently suggested that considering only first moment expectations is insufficient; and there are also many other studies to this effect. Slovic, Fischoff and Lichtenstein (1977) provide a good guide to this literature. Furthermore, before conventional utility theory became the orthodox model, many theoreticians insisted on the need to incorporate higher moments of the probability distribution in any model of evaluation (e.g. Tintner, 1941, Allais, 1953).

2.2 Theoretical

The expected utility model derives its normative power from a set of axioms that presumably are logically compelling to all individuals. As it happens, in some formulations the axioms either do not have an immediate intuitive meaning that allows the individual to decide on the logical

acceptability of the principle, or are imbedded in a
mathematical space that implies some additional axioms.
Von Neumann and Morgenstern (1944) were quite aware of this
difficulty: "Have we not begged the question? Do not our
postulates introduce, in some oblique way, the hypotheses
which bring in the mathematical expectations?"

In our view, the derivation of the expected utility
model in which the intuitive meanings of the axioms is more
readily evident was proposed by Luce and Raiffa (1958).

Out of Luce and Raiffa's six axioms, the substitution
principle is the weakest and seems unacceptable, as
indicated previously. What theoretical alternative can we
offer? Múnera (1978) presented an argument based on the
flexibility content of the decision process as follows.

Consider the sequential decision-making process shown
in Figure 2a. At time t_o the individual decision-maker
(DM), is asked to choose between the status quo and a free
lottery. Assume that the DM chooses the lottery. At time
t_1, <u>after</u> resolution of the uncertainty and knowing (as far
as possible) what is the state of the environment

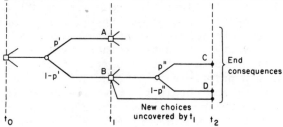

(a) Tree representing more flexible situation , with choices
     actually available by time t_1

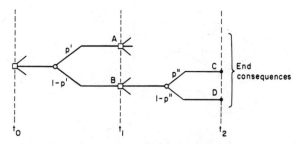

(b) Tree for situation where complete decision
     is to be made at t_o

Fig. 2. Decision Trees should be different depending on whether
choices are to be made before or during unfolding of events.

surrounding the individual, the DM decides again whether to accept or not a new lottery. To analyze the decision, the DM uses all information <u>really available</u> at t_1. In an actual problem, t_1 may be anything from a very short to a very long time period. It is obvious that the decision tree of Figure 2a is the only representation of the decision problem when the DM is actually to receive the tangible consequences of A or B of the first lottery.

We believe that there exists a different problem that some people mistakenly confound with the former. In effect, the DM might have at time t_o some estimate of what to do at time t_1 whether condition A or condition B obtains, for instance, the DM might want to choose in both cases the new lottery, with the information available at t_o. This is the case shown in Figure 2b. There are no particular reasons to believe that this situation must be identical to the previous one, although, of course, some individuals may consider them the same. The fact is, that the first situation has far much more flexibility than the second.

In the derivation of the expected utility model, the probabilities in the tree of Figure 2b are varied until the DM is indifferent between the status quo at t_1, for example B, and the new lottery. No consideration whatsoever is given to other "irrelevant" alternatives that might in fact dominate both the status quo and the lottery. At this point, the substitution principle is brought in to erase the decision nodes at t_1 and obtain the new tree shown in Figure 3. According to the substitution principle the decision tree of Figure 3 is equivalent not only to the tree of Figure 2b, but also to that of Figure 2a which, as mentioned before, represents a completely different

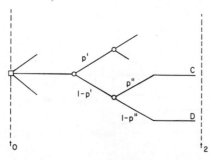

Fig. 3. Decision Tree obtained by elimination of nodes at t_1. According to substitution principle this is equivalent to Fig. 2a. Note, however, that the end consequences are not the same.

problem. Nonetheless, the substitution principle claims that they must be identical for all individuals. We find this claim unjustified.

For further discussion of the matter in terms of the flexibility content of the trees, see Múnera (1978). McClennen (1982) also puts forward a similar argument against the substitution principle, but in terms of the non-commutability of the sure prospects (as in Figure 2a) and the uncertain prospects (as in Figure 3).

3. A GENERALIZED MODEL TO EVALUATE PREFERENCES TOWARDS LOTTERIES

We propose a model that satisfies the axioms of conventional utility theory except for the substitution principle. This we downgrade from being a postulate of behavior to the lower status of a descriptive condition some individuals may fulfill in various circumstances.

As with conventional expected utility decision analysis, the model generates a preference index over lotteries, $H (\cdot)$, such that higher values are associated with preferred lotteries. The index is valid on a bounded segment of the real line. By a lottery we mean the set of pairs (c_j, p_j) in which c_j is any one of the j possible consequences related to a decision, and p_j is the probability (frequential, derived, or subjective) that it may occur. In making a decision, the individual would seek to maximize $H(\cdot)$.

Instead, however, of attempting to define a utility function and probabilities as in expected utility decision analysis, we propose to disentangle the notions of probability and psychological value for states of the system. Specifically, we propose to use a deterministic measure of value over consequences, $h(\cdot)$, and then an uncertainty operator to take into account the probability portion. The operator defines the preference index for any lottery in terms of the deterministic values and the several moments of the probability distribution of the lottery.

The deterministic value function is similar to von Neumann-Morgenstern utility in that it is on an interval scale unique up to a positive linear transformation. It is different in that is is measured without reference to probabilities in any one of several standard ways, as illustrated by Krzysztofowicz (1982) and McCord and de Neufville (1982).

The general uncertainty operator, which maps the lotteries
into their preference index, is a functional that satisfies
a set of axioms weaker than those of the expected utility
model. Specifically, it satisfies axioms of completeness,
reduction of compound lotteries, transitivity, continuity
and monotonicity, but does not satisfy any axiom equivalent
to the substitution principle. As a consequence of meeting
weaker conditions, the model is not unique up to a positive
linear transformation, as is the expected utility model.
Indeed, there is a large class of models which meet our
requirements. Machina (1982) explores such possibilities.

The uncertainty operator we propose is:

$$H(\cdot) = h_o - \Sigma_k \ (-1)^k \ r_k \ M_k^{1/k} \qquad (1)$$

where M_k is the kth moment of the probability distribution
over value functions $h(\cdot)$:

$$M_k = \Sigma_j (h_j - h_o)^k \ p_j \qquad (2)$$

h_o is a reference value of the deterministic value function
and h_j is the value of the jth consequence, occurring with
probability p_j. The r_k are real dimensionless numbers
characterizing an individual's attitudes toward the various
elements of the uncertainty.

The essential feature of the operator lies in its
inclusion of higher moments of the probability distribution.
For the special case where only the first moment is taken
into account, it reduces to an expected utility model, based
on the value function assessed deterministically. The
moment term is taken to the kth root to maintain
dimensionality. The signs of the terms were chosen by the
following reasoning. Even moments are always positive, as
such they can be interpreted as carrying information on the
pleasure or displeasure of being in lotteries. Believing
that people are commonly uncomfortable in the presence of
uncertainty, and wishing to avoid negative r_k for esthetic
reasons, we made the terms with even moments negative. Odd
moments, on the other hand, are negative or positive
depending on whether the lottery is favorable (meaning
that an individual stands to gain, $h_j > h_o$) or not.
Believing that people strive to choose favorable situations,
we made these moments positive.

The model satisfies the required axioms, as Múnera
(1978) demonstrated, with the restriction that the

individual's parameters r_k fall within a feasible set. This is demonstrably large, as he shows.

4. THE DESCRIPTIVE CONTENT OF THE MODEL

The model is paricularly attractive in that its components can each be given a useful behavioral interpretation. This is due in great part to the fact that the model not only separates the individual's feelings about uncertainty from the lottery being considered, but also gives them several dimensions.

A special feature of the moments is that they represent changes in the psychological value relative to a reference state, h_o. This may either be the value function of the state prevailing before making a decision, or of that which might have been if a different decision had been made. In this sense, the model can incorporate feelings of regret or the hopes and fears of expectation. This constant also permits the model to incorporate any reflection and asymmetry effects around the status quo, as have sometimes been observed in practice (e.g. Kahneman and Tversky, 1979).

The parameter of each moment can be given a particular meaning. The first moment term represents the average psychological gain or loss, and thus contains approximately the same information as the expected utility model. The second moment reflects the spread of consequences, the randomness associated with a decision. The coefficient r_2 can therefore be related to a person's willingness to enter into uncertain situations. The third moment is a measure of events with low probability but high consequences. Higher moment terms would accentuate the person's sensitivity to the spread or the skewness of the distribution of the uncertainty, according to whether they are even or odd.

From this analysis, it appears that a model using just the first three moments may be sufficient to capture the main characteristics of the probability distribution, at least as an initial approximation. Hence we propose that attention focus on the simple uncertainty operator:

$$H(L) = h_o + r_1 M_1 - r_2 M_2^{1/2} + r_3 M_3^{1/3} \qquad (3)$$

5. CONSISTENCY OF MODEL WITH OBSERVATIONS

A practical advantage of the model is that it is easily

consistent — even in the simple form of Eq (3) — with the
entire range of observations which are counter to the
expected utility model. This we now show in detail.

5.1 Allais Paradox

The two preferences expressed between the four chance
situations in Allais' Gedanken experiment lead to two
inequalities among the values for the lotteries $h(L)$. Since
our model provides several degrees of freedom in the
selection of the r_k parameters, it is easy to find a class
or r_k n-tuples consistent with the preferences expressed.
Múnera (1978) provided examples for specific distributions
and value functions.

5.2 The Certainty Effect

The certainty effect is almost an inherent consequence of
our model. Because of the higher order terms, the value of
a lottery does not tend toward the value of a consequence
as that consequence becomes certain in the limit. There is
a discontinuity: certainty extinguishes the effect of
higher moments which otherwise maintain their importance
even for low probabilities. However small the uncertainty,
our model factors in the feeling towards it which psychological experiments reveal. It is the case of no certainty
effect which is a special case and entails particular
combinations of the r_k parameter.
     Indeed, the certainty effect should in practice
provide an excellent means to define the parameters. For
example, if a person is pessimistic in that he tends to
believe that an almost certain loss is equivalent to a sure
loss of the same magnitude, but that an almost certain gain
is not equivalent to that sure gain, these preferences
impose the following restrictions on the parameters:

$$\Sigma_k r_k = 1 \qquad\qquad (4)$$

which we refer to as negative normalization. Conversely,
if the person is optimistic in that he accepts the gain
as equivalent but not the loss, we have positive normalization:

$$\Sigma_k (-1)^k r_k = -1 \qquad\qquad (5)$$

The implication of such normalizations, where they are possible, is that we can in the simple model define a person's attitudes toward uncertainty in a planar graph of r_2, the feeling about the spread of uncertainty, and r_3, the feeling about its skewness (see Múnera, 1978, for details).

Furthermore, the extent of the uncertainty effect can be stated in terms of the parameters. Defining the Uncertainty Pleasure Index (UPI) as the difference between the value of the lottery in the limit as the probability tends to zero and the value of the certainty we obtain, when normalization holds:

$$UPI = -2r_2 \qquad\qquad (6)$$

This confirms r_2 as a measure of the dislike of uncertainty.

Figure 4 illustrates the possibilities. The straight diagonal is associated with a person with no certainty effect and is generated in this case by an expected utility maximizer for whom $r_2 = r_3 = 0$. The other family of curves, for $r_2 = 0.25$ and a variety or r_3, shows how the model can fit observations.

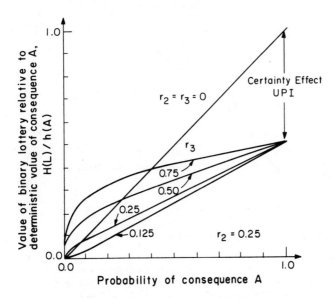

Fig. 4. Example of how the proposed model generates curves consistent with observed possiblities of the certainty effect.

5.3 Dependence of Utility on Probability Distribution

The dependence of utility on the probability distribution
is a natural consequence of our model, because of the
inclusion of higher moments. Appropriate selection of the
parameters allows the model to replicate easily the variations
observed.

A strong independent check on the validity of the
model can, in this way, be obtained from Allais' (1979)
data. Indeed, we first used his results for B_{200} to
estimate the r_k. Then we checked to see if we could
predict the various shapes of the $B_{1/2}$ utility functions
we obtained using 50:50 lotteries. In this, we were
successful (Múnera, 1978), see Figure 5. The result is all
the more remarkable because Allais' respondents displayed
a wide variety of risk adverse and risk positive utility
functions. We regard this as a particularly powerful
initial validation of the model.

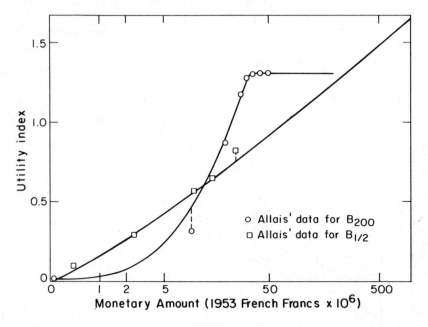

Figure 5. Consistency of model with the dependence of
Utility on Probability (Allais' data for Malinvaud replicated by $r_2=0.15$, $r_3=0.82$, negative normalization).

5.4 Asymmetric Effects

Many studies have reported that utility functions assessed
in practice are asymmetric about the status quo. This is
clearly illustrated by Swalm's (1966) data (Figure 6).
Kahneman and Tversky (1979) observed apparent risk aversion
toward gains and risk-seeking behavior toward losses, which
they labeled a "reflection effect". This phenomenon should
be troublesome to the expected utility model, which has no
explanation for it.

Our model suggests however that asymmetric effects are
normal, indeed fundamental, to an individual's feeling
about uncertainty. The phenomenon is a natural consequence
of the asymmetric contributions of the odd and even moments
to the uncertainty operator in the model.

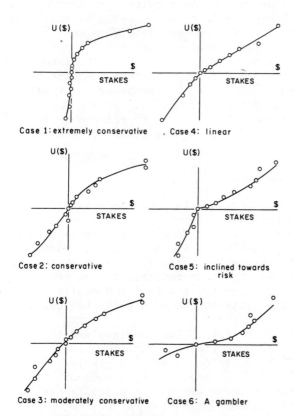

Fig. 6. Examples of Swalm's data on utility assessment,
illustrating this "Scatter".

5.5 Scatter in Utility Assessments

Assessments of utility functions are replete with scatter.
Swalm (1966) for instance, in what still today seems to be
the most extensive publication of utility functions assessed
in the conventional way, found "that in most cases the
points do not lie on a smooth curve". This can be
attributed all to experimental error. But if the utility
functions do depend on the probability distributions and
reference value, h_o, as in our model, perhaps much of this
"experimental" error is actually "model" error.

   Our contention is that the points determined for a
utility function by Swalm or in any other assessment must
be scattered because they represent truly different objects.
Since the probability content and consequences for the
fractile lotteries differ, so do the results.

   We validated this hypothesis by using Swalm's detailed
description of his experimental procedure to show that our
model can provide a consistent explanation of the "scatter".
Our procedure was to assume values of r_2 and r_3 consistent
with his characterization of his subjects, and then use a
small computer program to simulate the responses to Swalm's
original questions (full details in Múnera, 1978). The
results are remarkable in that they both reproduced curves
including the reflection effect, and accounted for much of
the "scatter", Figure 6.

6. PRACTICAL USE OF THE MODEL

The model we have proposed for use in decision analysis
when the substitution principle is not acceptable has the
advantage of being practical. Its functional form is simple
and open to easy interpretation of its parameters, and the
model is applicable to all lotteries independently of the
probability distribution. In other proposals, however,
indeterminate functional forms are involved and explicitly
contain each probability distribution as a parameter (e.g.
Machina, 1982).

   The model is simple to apply. Its use involves three
steps: (1) Assessment of the preference function $h(\cdot)$;
(2) Representation of the decision; and (3) Analysis.

   The preference function is assessed by standard
deterministic techniques. These are not essentially any
more difficult than the lottery methods used for the utility
model. With a little practice they can be used efficiently,

as Krzysztofowicz (1982) and McCord and de Neufville (1982) demonstrate.

The decision problem is represented by an extensive tree, with probability distributions and outcomes indicated. Where the lotteries involve several chance modes with intermediate decisions, these compound lotteries can be reduced to simple ones using the principles of probability. Where the problem entails a sequence of decisions, however, these cannot be simplified — since use of the model implies that the substitution principle is not acceptable for the person or for the situation.

The analysis is straightforward. At each decision node, the preference index is calculated for each possible choice, and the highest value is selected. The certainty equivalents of each optimal choice at a decision node are defined by $h(\cdot) = \max H$ of the decision. Sequential decision problems are thus solved backwards. The methodology is completely similar to that of expected utility decision analysis except in the use of $H(\cdot)$ at each decision node.

7. CONCLUSIONS

The model proposed deserves testing and independent validation. A priori it is theoretically sound, it is experimentally congruent with the essential observations on rational behavior, and it is operationally feasible. Field use is the next order of business.

8. ACKNOWLEDGEMENTS

We are grateful to Professors Maurice Allais and Andreu Mas-Collel for their encouragement, comments and suggestions; to Paul Schoemaker and Mark Thompson for their detailed reviews. We also thank the Norwegian School of Management for the opportunity to participate in the conference.

Héctor A. Múnera is a partner with Tecnicontrol Ltda., A.A. 2986, Bogota, Colombia, and Principle Investigator at Instituto SER de Investigacion, Bogota, Colombia. Richard de Neufville is Professor and Chairman of the Technology and Policy Program, Massachusetts Institute of Technology, Cambridge, MA 02139, U.S.A.

REFERENCES

Allais, M.: 1953, 'Le Comportement de L'Homme Rationnel
  Devant le Risque: Critique des Postulats et Axiomes de
  l'Ecole Americaine', Econometrica 21, 503-46.
Allais, M.: 1979, 'The So-Called Allais Paradox and
  Rational Decisions Under Uncertainty', in M. Allais and
  O. Hagen (eds.) Expected Utility Hypotheses and the Allais
  Paradox, D. Reidel, Dordrecht, Holland, pp. 437-682.
de Neufville, R.: 1976, 'How Should We Establish Public
  Policy of Settling Design Codes?', Proc. National Confer-
  ence on Earthquake Engineering, Ann Arbor, MI.
Kahneman, D., and Tversky, A.: 1979, 'Prospect Theory: An
  Analysis of Decision Under Risk', Econometrica 47:2,
  263-91.
Keeney, R.L., and Nair, K.: 1975, 'Decision Analysis for the
  Siting of Nuclear Power Plants — The Relevance of Multi-
  attribute Utility Theory', Proc. IEEE 63:3, 494-501.
Krzysztofowicz, R.: 1982, 'Strength of Preference and Risk
  Attitude in Utility Measurement', J. Organizational
  Behavior and Human Performance, forthcoming.
Luce, R.D. and Raiffa, H.: 1958, Games and Decisions,
  2nd printing, Chapter 2, John Wiley and Sons, New York.
Múnera, Hector A.: 1978, Modeling of Individual Risk
  Attitudes in Decision-making Under Uncertainty: An
  Application to Nuclear Power, Ph.D. Dissertation,
  Department of Nuclear Engineering, University of
  California, Berkeley, CA.
McClennen, E.: 1982, 'Sure-thing Doubts', published in
  these Proceedings.
McCord, M. and de Neufville, R.: 1982, 'Empirical
  Demonstration that Expected Utility Decision Analysis is
  Not Operational', published in these Proceedings.
Machina, M.J.: 1982 'Generalized Expected Utility Analysis
  and the Nature of Observed Violations of the Independence
  Axiom', published in these Proceedings.
Slovic, P., Fischoff, B. and Lichtenstein, S.: 1977,
  'Behavioral Decision Theory', Annual Review of Psychology.
Swalm, R.O.: 1966, 'Utility Theory, Insights into Risk
  Taking', Harvard Business Review 44 (Nov.-Dec.), 123-36.
Tintner, G.: 1941, 'The Theory of Choice Under Subjective
  Risk and Uncertainty', Econometrica 9, 298-304.
von Neumann, and Morgenstern, O.: 1944, Theory of Games and
  Economic Behavior, Princeton University Press, Princeton,
  (3rd ed. pub. by John Wiley and Sons, New York, 1964).

Mark J. Machina[1]

GENERALIZED EXPECTED UTILITY ANALYSIS AND THE NATURE
OF OBSERVED VIOLATIONS OF THE INDEPENDENCE AXIOM

1. INTRODUCTION

First expressed by Allais in the early fifties, dissatisfaction
with the expected utility model of individual risk taking behavior has mushroomed in recent years, as the number of papers in
this volume, its predecessor (Allais & Hagen(1979)), and elsewhere[2] indicates. The nature of the current debate, i.e. whether to reject a theoretically elegant and heretofore tremen-
dously useful descriptive model in light of accumulating evidence against its underlying assumptions, is a classic one in
science, and the spur to new theoretical and empirical research
which it is offering cannot help but leave economists, psychologists, and others who study this area with a better understanding of individual behavior toward risk.
   In terms of its logical foundations, the expected utility
model may be thought of as following from three assumptions
concerning the individual's ordering of probability distributions over wealth: completeness (i.e. any two distributions can
be compared), transitivity of both strict and weak preference,
and the so-called "independence axiom." This latter axiom,
really the cornerstone of the theory, may be stated as "a risky
prospect A is weakly preferred (i.e. preferred or indifferent)
to a risky prospect B if and only if a $p:(1-p)$ chance of A or C
respectively is weakly preferred to a $p:(1-p)$ chance of B or C,
for arbitrary positive probability p and risky prospects A, B,
and C." While the first two assumptions serve to imply that
the individual's preferences may be represented by a real-valued maximand or "preference functional" defined over probability distributions, it is the independence axiom which gives the
theory its main empirical content by placing a restriction on
the functional form of the preference functional, implying that
it (or some monotonic transformation of it) must be "linear in
the probabilities" and hence representable as the mathematical
expectation of some von Neumann-Morgenstern utility index defined over the set of pure outcomes.
   Although the normative validity of the independence axiom

B. P. Stigum and F. Wenstøp (eds.), Foundations of Utility and Risk Theory with Applications,
263–293.
© 1983 *by D. Reidel Publishing Company.*

has often been questioned in the past (see for example Allais
(1952), Tversky(1975), Wold(1952), and the examples offered in
Dreze(1974) and Machina(1981)), the primary form of attack on
the expected utility hypothesis has been on the empirical validity of the independence axiom. Beginning with the famous
example of Allais (discussed in detail below), the empirical/
experimental research on the independence axiom has uncovered
four types of *systematic* violations of the axiom: the "common
consequence effect," the "common ratio effect" (which includes
the "Bergen Paradox" and "certainty effect" as special cases),
"oversensitivity to changes in small probabilities," and the
"utility evaluation effect" (described below). While defenders of the expected utility model have claimed that such violations, systematic or otherwise, would disappear once the nature of such "errors" had been pointed out to subjects (e.g.
Raiffa(1968,pp.30-86), Savage(1972,pp.102-103)), empirical
tests of this assertion (MacCrimmon(1968,pp.9-11), Slovic &
Tversky(1974)) have fairly convincingly refuted it, and it is
now generally acknowledged that, as a descriptive hypothesis,
the independence axiom is not able to stand up to the data.

Accordingly, the defense of the expected utility model
has shifted to the other two *sine qua non's* of a useful theory,
namely analytic power and the ability to generate refutable
predictions and policy implications in a wide variety of situations.[3] Expected utility supporters have pointed out that
descriptive models are like lifeboats in that "you don't abandon a leaky one until something better comes along," and insist that a mere ability to rationalize "aberrant" observations
is not enough for an alternative model to replace expected
utility- to be acceptable, the alternative must at least approximate the analytic power and versatility of expected utility analysis. On the whole they have been correct in so arguing, as many of the alternatives which have been offered have
had little predictive power, and various ones have been restricted to only pairwise choice, have implied intransitive
behavior, were able to accommodate only discrete probability
distributions, or even possessed the property that the individual can be led into "making book against his/herself!"

The purpose of this chapter is to describe an alternative
to expected utility analysis (in fact, a generalization of it)
which is designed to possess the high analytic power of expected utility as well as to parsimoniously capture the nature of
observed departures from the independence axiom. On the one
hand, this technique, termed "generalized expected utility
analysis," allows us to apply the major concepts, tools, and

results of expected utility theory to the analysis of almost
completely general preferences (specifically, any set of preferences which is complete, transitive, and "smooth" in the
sense described below). On the other hand, however, this technique is capable of simply characterizing any additional behavioral restrictions we might feel are warrented, such as general risk aversion, declining risk aversion, comparative risk
aversion between individuals, and in particular, a simple condition on preferences which serves to generate all four of the
above mentioned systematic violations of the independence axiom. In addition, because of the very weak assumptions required, it turns out that many of the other alternatives and
generalizations of expected utility theory which have been
offered are special cases of the present analysis, which can
therefore be used to derive further results in these special
cases.
      The following section offers a brief overview of those
aspects of expected utility theory which will be relevant for
the present purposes. Section 3 offers a simple graphical and
algebraic description of generalized expected utility analysis,
including extensions of the expected utility concepts of the
"risk averse concave utility function" and the Arrow-Pratt measure of risk aversion to the general case of "smooth" preferences.[4] Section 4 offers a survey of the four known types of
systematic violations of the independence axiom, as well as a
description and discussion of the simple condition on preferences which serves to generate each of these four types of
behavior. Section 5 offers a brief conclusion.

2. THE EXPECTED UTILITY MODEL

In this and the following sections, we adopt the standard
choice-theoretic approach of assuming that the individual has
a complete, transitive preference ordering over the set $D[0,M]$
of all cumulative distribution functions $F(\cdot)$ over the wealth
interval $[0,M]$. As in standard consumer theory (see, for example, Debreu(1959,Ch.4)), completeness and transitivity are
sufficient to imply that we can represent the individual's
ranking by some real-valued preference functional $V(\cdot)$ over
$D[0,M]$, so that the probability distribution $F^*(\cdot)$ is weakly
preferred to $F(\cdot)$ if and only if $V(F^*) \geq V(F)$. (In those cases
when we find it useful to consider the subset $D\{x_1,...,x_n\}$ of
probability distributions over the payoffs $x_1 < ... < x_n$, we
shall represent the typical distribution in $D\{x_1,...,x_n\}$ by
the vector of corresponding probabilities $(p_1,...,p_n)$ and

represent the restriction of $V(\cdot)$ to $D\{x_1,\ldots,x_n\}$ by $V(p_1,\ldots,p_n))$.

Now, if we in addition assume that the individual satisfies the independence axiom, it follows (see, e.g. Herstein & Milnor(1953)) that $V(\cdot)$ or some monotonic transformation of $V(\cdot)$ will possess the functional form $V(F) \equiv \int U(x)dF(x)$ (or in the discrete case, $V(p_1,\ldots,p_n) \equiv \Sigma U(x_i)p_i$), i.e., the mathematical expectation of the von Neumann–Morgenstern utility function $U(\cdot)$ with respect to $F(\cdot)$ (or $(p_1,\ldots,p_n)$). In other words, $V(\cdot)$ can be represented as a linear functional of $F(\cdot)$ (or in the discrete case, as a linear function of $(p_1,\ldots,p_n)$), hence the phrase that the preferences of an expected utility maximizer are "linear in the probabilities." In this case it is also clear that the distribution $F^*(\cdot)$ will be weakly preferred to $F(\cdot)$ if and only if $\int U(x)dF^*(x) \geq \int U(x)dF(x)$, or equivalently, if and only if

$$\int U(x)[dF^*(x)-dF(x)] \geq 0. \tag{1}$$

For purposes of illustration, it is useful to consider the subset $D\{x_1,x_2,x_3\}$ of all probability distributions over the wealth levels $x_1 < x_2 < x_3$ in $[0,M]$, which may be represented by the points in the unit triangle in the (p_1,p_3) plane, as in Figure 1 (with p_2 defined by $p_2 = 1 - p_1 - p_3$). Because of the "linearity" property of expected utility maximizers, such individuals' indifference curves in this space (the solid

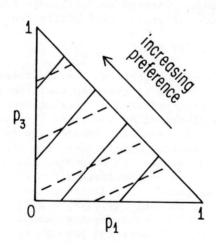

FIGURE 1

lines in Figure 1) will be parallel straight lines, with
preferred indifference curves lying to the northwest.[5] The
dashed lines in the figure are what may be termed "iso-
expected *value* loci," i.e. loci of probability distributions
with the same mean. Northeast movements along such loci,
since they represent changes in the distribution which preserve the mean but increase the probability of the worst and
best outcomes (i.e. increase p_1 and p_3 at the expense of p_2),
are seen to be precisely the set of "mean preserving spreads"
in the sense of Rothschild & Stiglitz(1970). Thus, if the
indifference curves are steeper than these loci, as in Figure
1, mean preserving spreads will always make the individual
worse off, or in other words, the individual is risk averse.
Conversely, if the indifference curves are flatter than the
iso-expected value loci, the individual will be risk loving in
the sense that mean preserving spreads will be preferred.

   In fact, there is even a stronger sense in which the
steepness of the indifference curves provides a measure of
risk aversion. Solving the equation in footnote 5, we obtain
that the slope of these indifference curves is equal to

$$- \frac{(U(x_3)-U(x_2)) - (U(x_2)-U(x_1))}{U(x_3) - U(x_2)} + 1. \qquad (2)$$

Neglecting the addition of the constant 1, this expression
(negative the ratio of a second difference of utility to a
first difference) may be thought of as the discrete analogue
of the Arrow-Pratt measure $-U''(x)/U'(x)$, and indeed, Pratt
(1964,Thm.1) has shown that they are related in that the more
concave the utility function, the greater the value of expression (2) for fixed x_1, x_2, and x_3. Thus, given two expected
utility maximizers, the one with the steeper indifference
curves will be the more risk averse over $D\{x_1,x_2,x_3\}$.

3. GENERALIZED EXPECTED UTILITY ANALYSIS: A BRIEF OVERVIEW

Although there certainly have been studies which have found
individual preferences over uncertain *and* certain prospects
which violate both transitivity and completeness,[6] by far the
largest and most systematic body of empirical results are those
revealing systematic violations of the independence axiom.
Of the three, it is in some sense fortunate that it is independence and not the other two which is most frequently vio-
lated- while dropping either transitivity or completeness

would lead to a fundamental break with the traditional theory
of choice, dropping independence (i.e. linearity of $V(\cdot)$)
amounts to simply changing the functional form of the preference functional, something which is done frequently in economic theory and econometrics.

One of the virtues of generalized expected utility analysis is that it can be developed with extremely weak assumptions on the functional form of the preference functional.
Specifically, we need only assume that $V(\cdot)$ is a differentiable functional of $F(\cdot)$ (i.e. "smooth in the probabilities"),
which is equivalent to assuming that indifference curves in
$D\{x_1,x_2,x_3\}$ (or more generally, indifference hypersurfaces in
$D[0,M]$) are smooth (i.e. are differentiable manifolds). Differentiability or smoothness of preferences is considered to
be an extremely weak assumption in standard choice theory, and
it is sufficiently weak so that many (though not all) of the
functional forms which have been offered to replace expected
utility are special cases of it (see below).

Algebraically, the assumption that the preference functional $V(\cdot)$ is differentiable in $F(\cdot)$ means that we can take
the usual first order Taylor expansion of $V(\cdot)$ about any point
in its domain, i.e. about any distribution $F_0(\cdot)$ in $D[0,M]$, so
that for each $F_0(\cdot)$ in $D[0,M]$ there will exist some linear
functional $\psi(\cdot;F_0)$ (linear in its first argument) such that

$$V(F) - V(F_0) = \psi(F-F_0;F_0) + o(\|F-F_0\|), \qquad (3)$$

where, as in standard calculus, $o(\cdot)$ denotes a function of
higher order than its argument, and $\|\cdot\|$ is the L^1 norm, a
standard measure of the "distance" between two functions.

Because $\psi(F-F_0;F_0)$ is linear in its first argument, it
can be represented as the expectation of some function with
respect to $F(\cdot)-F_0(\cdot)$, so that we may rewrite (3) as

$$V(F) - V(F_0) = \int U(x;F_0)[dF(x)-dF_0(x)] + o(\|F-F_0\|), \qquad (4)$$

where the notation $U(\cdot;F_0)$ is used to denote the dependence of
$\psi(\cdot;F_0)$, and hence its integral representation, upon the function $F_0(\cdot)$, i.e. upon the point in the domain about which we
are taking the Taylor expansion. As in standard calculus, we
know that for differential movements about the domain of $V(\cdot)$,
(i.e. for changes from $F_0(\cdot)$ to some "very close" $F(\cdot)$), the
first order or linear term in (4) will dominate the higher
order term, so that the individual with preference functional
$V(\cdot)$ will rank differential shifts from $F_0(\cdot)$ according to the

sign of the term $\int U(x;F_O)[dF(x)-dF_O(x)]$. Recalling expression
(1), however, we see that this is *precisely* the same ranking
that would be used by an expected utility maximizer with a
utility function $U(\cdot;F_O)$. Of course in some sense this is no
surprise: preferences which are "smooth" (i.e. differentiable)
are locally linear, and we know that in ranking probability
distributions, linearity is equivalent to expected utility
maximization.

Thus, even though an individual with smooth preference
functional $V(\cdot)$ will not necessarily satisfy the independence
axiom and possesses no "global" von Neumann-Morgenstern utility
function, we see that at each distribution $F_O(\cdot)$ in $D[0,M]$
there will exist a "local utility function" $U(\cdot;F_O)$ over $[0,M]$
which represents the individual's preferences at $F_O(\cdot)$. Because
of the analogy between equations (1) and (4), it is clear that
if $U(x;F_O)$ is increasing in x then the individual will prefer
all differential first order stochastically dominating shifts
from $F_O(\cdot)$,[7] and $U(x;F_O)$ will be concave in x if and only if
the individual is made worse off by all differential mean preserving spreads about $F_O(\cdot)$ (i.e. is locally risk averse in
the neighborhood of $F(\cdot)$).

Of course, as with any linear approximation to a differentiable function, the ranking determined by the first order
linear term (i.e. by the local utility function $U(\cdot;F_O)$) will
typically not correspond exactly to the ranking determined by
$V(\cdot)$ over any open neighborhood of $F_O(\cdot)$ in $D[0,M]$. However,
and again by analogy with standard calculus, it is possible to
completely and exactly reconstruct the preference functional
from knowledge of what its linear approximations (i.e. derivatives) look like at every point in the domain, by use of the
Fundamental Theorem of Integral Calculus. To do this, we take
any path of the form $\{F(\cdot;\alpha)\,|\,\alpha \in [0,1]\}$ from $F_O(\cdot)$ to $F(\cdot)$
(not necessarily "near" $F_O(\cdot)$), so that $F(\cdot;0) = F_O(\cdot)$ and
$F(\cdot;1) = F(\cdot)$, and use the fact that $V(F) - V(F_O)$ will be
simply the integral of $dV(F(\cdot;\alpha))/d\alpha$ as α runs from 0 to 1.
In the case of the "straight line" path $F(\cdot;\alpha) \equiv \alpha F(\cdot) +$
$(1-\alpha)F_O(\cdot)$, for example, we have

$$V(F) - V(F_O) = \int_0^1 \frac{dV(F(\cdot;\alpha))}{d\alpha}d\alpha =$$

$$= \int_0^1 \{\int U(x;F(\cdot;\alpha))[dF(x)-dF_O(x)]\}d\alpha, \tag{5}$$

since the derivative of the higher order term in (4) as α increases will be zero (see Machina(1982a) for details).

Besides yielding a way to completely reconstruct the preference functional $V(\cdot)$ from knowledge of the local utility functions, equation (5) yields insight on how generalized expected utility analysis may be used to obtain *global* characterizations of behavior in terms of "expected utility" type conditions on the local utility functions. For example, say that $F_1(\cdot)$ differs from $F_0(\cdot)$ by a "large" mean preserving spread. If the local utility functions $U(\cdot;F)$ are concave in x at each $F(\cdot)$, then it follows that the term in curled brackets in (5) will be nonpositive for each α, so that $V(\cdot)$ will weakly prefer $F_1(\cdot)$ to $F_0(\cdot)$. Indeed, it is shown formally in Machina(1982a) that the "expected utility" condition of concavity of (all) the local utility functions is *equivalent* to the individual being averse to all mean preserving spreads, or in other words, to the individual being globally risk averse.

A similar method was used in Machina(1982a) to prove two other extensions of "expected utility" analysis to the case of individuals with preference functionals which do not necessarily satisfy the independence axiom. Using straight line paths as in the previous paragraph, it is straightforward to show that the individual's preferences will exhibit "monotonicity," i.e. preference for first order stochastically dominating distributions, if and only if all the local utility functions are increasing in x. The second result extends the well known "Arrow-Pratt theorem" of comparative risk aversion: if we form the natural analogue to the Arrow-Pratt measure in our more general setting, i.e. $-U_{11}(x;F)/U_1(x;F)$ (where subscripts denote successive partial derivatives with respect to x), we have that one individual will be everywhere more risk averse than another in the standard behavioral senses (see Machina(1982a)) if and only if the "generalized Arrow-Pratt term" of the first individual is everywhere higher than that of the second, or equivalently, if and only if the first individual's local utility functions are everywhere more concave than the second's.

Note that while these types of extended expected utility theorems might seem "more complex" than those of expected utility theory since they involve checking all the local utility functions rather than a single von Neumann-Morgenstern utility function, they are in fact "less complex" in that the expected utility theorems may be thought of as derived from the more general theorems with the *additional* restriction that all of the local utility functions are identical.

The above algebraic arguments admit of a nice graphical interpretation in terms of the unit triangle diagram of Section 2 above. Since we are now considering preferences over the subset $D\{x_1,x_2,x_3\}$ of $D[0,M]$, we shall use the symbol P_0 = $(p_{1,0},p_{2,0},p_{3,0})$ instead of $F_0(\cdot)$ to denote the probability distribution about which we expand the preference functional. Figure 2 illustrates the general principle that if preferences (and hence indifference curves) are smooth, then there will exist a "tangent" (i.e. linear approximating) expected utility preference field to the individual's indifference curves at each distribution, as illustrated by the parallel straight lines which are tangent to the individual's actual (nonlinear) indifference curves at P_0. Figure 3 illustrates the above result that global risk aversion is equivalent to all the local utility functions being concave. Graphically, it is clear that what is necessary and sufficient for all mean preserving spreads (i.e. all northeast movements along iso-expected value lines) to make the individual worse off is not that the in-difference curves necessarily be linear, but rather that they be everywhere steeper than the (dashed) iso-expected value lines. Of course, this is equivalent to the condition that the tangents to the indifference curves be everywhere steeper, which from the analysis of Section 2 is seen to be equivalent to the condition that all the *local* utility functions are con-cave in x. Finally, we could illustrate the above generalized Arrow-Pratt theorem on comparative risk aversion by a pair of

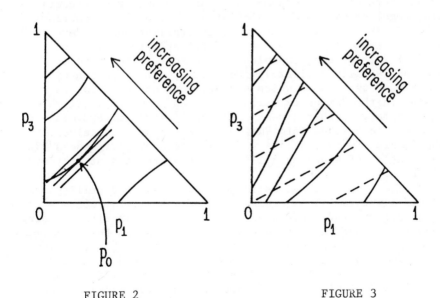

FIGURE 2   FIGURE 3

nonlinear preference fields, one of whose indifference curves
always intersected the other's from below (i.e. were everywhere steeper).

Having developed the above results for the case of general differentiable preference functionals, it is useful to
see how they might be applied to specific special cases, i.e.
to specific nonlinear functional forms. Pursuing the Taylor
expansion analogy further, we see that the simplest generalization of "linearity in the probabilities" is "quadratic in
the probabilities," or in other words, a functional form such
as

$$V(F) \equiv \int R(x)dF(x) + \frac{1}{2}[\int S(x)dF(x)]^2, \qquad (6)$$

whose local utility function can be calculated to be

$$U(x;F) = R(x) + S(x)[\int S(z)dF(z)]. \qquad (7)$$

Thus, if $R(\cdot)$ and $S(\cdot)$ are both positive, increasing, and concave it follows that $V(\cdot)$ will exhibit both monotonicity and
global risk aversion, and conditions under which one preference
functional of this form was everywhere more risk averse than
another could similarly be determined. Table 1 presents several specific functional forms which have been suggested by
researchers which are examples of smooth preference functionals, together with their calculated local utility functions.

It is clear that many more generalizations of "expected
utility" type results to non-expected utility maximizers can
be derived, for some examples, the reader is referred to
Machina(1982a,1982b,1982c). We conclude this section with
remarks on two issues which seem to have caused a lot of confusion in the "expected utility vs. non-expected utility" debate, namely whether non-expected utility maximizers can necessarily be tricked into "making book against themselves," and
the nature of "cardinality vs. ordinality of preferences" in
the context of expected utility vs. non-expected utility maximization.

There are two senses in which non-expected utility maximizers might make book against themselves (i.e. violate a preference for first order stochastic dominance in either a single
choice or a sequence of choices). The first is that in *certain
types* of non-expected utility models, most notably the "subjective expected utility" or "prospect theory" model (Edwards
(1955), Kahneman & Tversky(1979)), it is *necessarily* true that
the individual will strictly prefer some prospects to others

which stochastically dominate them (see Kahneman & Tversky
(1979,pp.283-284)).   Such a property of a model is clearly undesirable, and in the present author's view, makes such models
unacceptable as descriptive theories (it is straightforward to
show that this model is *not* a special case of a general differentiable preference functional).   The second sense is that if
an individual has a differentiable preference functional and
the local utility functions are not all increasing, then the
individual will prefer some distributions to others which stochastically dominate them.   Of course, the analogous result is
also true of expected utility maximizers: to achieve a preference for first order stochastic dominance, we must posit utility functions, von Neumann-Morgenstern *or* local, which are increasing in x.   It is clear that the *real* issue is whether
there can exist non-expected utility maximizing individuals
who will not make book against themselves, or whether making
book against oneself is an *intrinsic* property of non-expected
utility maximizers.   The answer is easy- we know from above
that individuals with increasing local utility functions always
prefer stochastically dominating distributions in pairwise
choices, and the transitivity which follows from the maximization of $V(\cdot)$ ensures that such individuals will never violate
stochastic dominance preference in a sequence of choices
either.

        The final issue is the apparent confusion that going
from expected utility to non-expected utility involves going
from "cardinal" preferences to "ordinal" preferences.   This is
not true.   There are two related, though distinct, functions
for the expected utility maximizer: the preference functional
$V(\cdot)$ over $D[0,M]$ (which happens to be linear) and the von
Neumann-Morgenstern utility function $U(\cdot)$ over $[0,M]$.   The
first of these is ordinal in that any monotonic transformation
of $V(\cdot)$ will represent the same preference ranking over $D[0,M]$,
and the second is cardinal in that another von Neumann-
Morgenstern utility function $U*(\cdot)$ will represent the individual's preferences if and only if $U*(x) \equiv aU(x) + b$ $(a > 0)$.
Precisely the same is true of non-expected utility maximizers:
clearly the preference functional $V(\cdot)$ of a non-expected utility maximizer is ordinal, and in Machina(1982a) it was shown
that the *local* utility functions $U(\cdot;F)$ are cardinal in that
another set of local utility functions will represent the same
preferences if and only if they are a positive linear transformation of the original set.   Thus, the *preference functionals* of all individuals, expected utility maximizing or otherwise, are always ordinal, and the *utility functions,* von

TABLE 1 - LOCAL UTILITY FUNCTIONS

Mathematical Form	Reference*
Linear (i.e. expected utility)	von Neumann & Morgenstern (1944)
Mean & variance of utility (special case of simple & general quadratic)	Allais(1952,p.108)
Simple quadratic (special case of general quadratic)	Machina(1982a,p.295)
General quadratic	Machina(1982a,fn.45)
First three moments of utility	Hagen(1979,p.272)
Rational (i.e. ratio of two linear forms)	Chew & MacCrimmon(1979) Fishburn(1981b) Bolker(1967)

* The reference cited for each functional form is not necessarily the first appearance of that form, nor should it be
  inferred that the respective author necessarily "prefers"
  that form over others they may have presented. In some instances I have slightly changed the exact form as given in
  the reference for greater simplicity.

FOR VARIOUS FUNCTIONAL FORMS OF $V(\cdot)$

$V(F)$	$U(x;F)$
$\int U(x)dF(x)$	$U(x)$
$\bar{u} - \lambda \int (U(x)-\bar{u})^2 dF(x)$ $(\bar{u} = \int U(x)dF(x))$	$U(x) - \lambda U(x)^2 + 2\lambda U(x)\bar{u}$
$\int R(x)dF(x) \pm \frac{1}{2}[\int S(x)dF(x)]^2$	$R(x) \pm S(x)\int S(z)dF(z)$
$\int\int T(x,z)dF(x)dF(z)$ $(T(x,z) \equiv T(z,x))$	$2\int T(x,z)dF(z)$
$\bar{u} + f(s^2,m^3)$ $(\bar{u} = \int U(x)dF(x),$ $s^2 = \int (U(x)-\bar{u})^2 dF(x),$ $m^3 = \int (U(x)-\bar{u})^3 dF(x))$	$U(x) + f_1 \cdot [U(x)^2 - 2U(x)\bar{u}]$ $+ f_2 \cdot U(x)[U(x)^2 - 3U(x)\bar{u}$ $\qquad + 3\bar{u}^2 - 3s^2]$
$\dfrac{\int w(x)dF(x)}{\int \alpha(x)dF(x)}$	$\dfrac{w(x) - V(F)\alpha(x)}{\int \alpha(z)dF(z)}$ **

** I am indebted to Kenneth MacCrimmon (private correspondence)
for the derivation of the local utility function of the
rational form. The expression in the Table differs from
his due to a difference in notation.

Neumann–Morgenstern or local, are always cardinal. Whether or not the independence axiom is satisfied is irrelevant.

4. THE NATURE OF SYSTEMATIC VIOLATIONS OF THE INDEPENDENCE AXIOM

One of the most important points made by the defenders of expected utility theory is that dropping the independence axiom (i.e. linearity) and retaining only transitivity and completeness (and possibly smoothness) results in a model which possesses almost no predictive power. We have seen in the previous section how generalized expected utility analysis, while not *requiring* strong behavioral assumptions in order to apply, nevertheless still admits of refutable hypotheses such as monotonicity and risk aversion, via assumptions on the local utility functions which are analogous to the expected utility conditions. In the present section we review the evidence on the four known types of systematic violations of the independence axiom, and show that they will all follow from a *single* assumption on the shape of the individual preference functional $V(\cdot)$, which we term "Hypothesis II."[8] Thus, in addition to the usual hypotheses of monotonicity and risk aversion, generalized expected utility analysis admits of an evidently quite powerful refutable hypothesis on precisely how individuals violate the independence axiom, and one which has been substantially confirmed by the evidence so far.

4.1. The common consequence effect

As an example of the first type of systematic violation of the axiom, the common consequence effect, we shall consider the first, and still most famous, specific example of this effect, namely the so-called "Allais Paradox" (see Allais(1952, p.89), Morrison(1967), Moskowitz(1974), Raiffa(1968), and Slovic & Tversky(1974), for example). First proposed by Allais in 1952, this example consists of obtaining the subject's preference ranking over the two pairs of risky prospects

a_1: {100% chance of \$1M   versus a_2: {10% chance of \$5M
                                                   {89% chance of \$1M
                                                   { 1% chance of \$ 0

and

a_3: {10% chance of \$5M   versus a_4: {11% chance of \$1M
        {90% chance of \$ 0   {89% chance of \$ 0

where \$1M = \$1,000,000. While it is easy to show that an expected utility maximizer would prefer either a_1 and a_4 (if $[.10U(5M) - .11U(1M) + .01U(0)] < 0$) or else a_2 and a_3 (if $[.10U(5M) - .11U(1M) + .01U(0)] > 0$), experimenters such as those listed above have repeatedly found that the modal if not majority choice of subjects has been a_1 and a_3, which violates the independence axiom.

The common consequence effect is really a generalization of the type of violation exhibited in the Allais Paradox, and involves choices between pairs of prospects of the form:

prospect	probability $\quad p$	$1-p$
b_1	k	C*
b_2	a*	C*
b_3	k	c*
b_4	a*	c*

where a*, C*, and c* are (possibly) random prospects with C* stochastically dominating c*, and k is a sure outcome lying between the highest and lowest outcomes of a*, so that, for example, b_2 is a prospect with the same ultimate probabilities as a compound prospect yielding a p chance of a* and a 1-p chance of C*. It is clear that an individual satisfying the independence axiom would rank b_1 and b_2 the same as b_3 and b_4: whether the "common consequence" was C* (as in the first pair) or c* (as in the second) would be "irrelevant." However, researchers such as Kahneman & Tversky(1979), MacCrimmon(1968) and MacCrimmon & Larsson(1979) as well as the five listed on the previous page have found a tendency for individuals to violate the independence axiom by preferring b_1 to b_2 and b_4 to b_3 in problems of this type (this is the same type of behavior as exhibited in the Allais Paradox, since the prospects a_1, a_2, a_3, and a_4 there correspond to b_1, b_2, b_4, and b_3, respectively, with k = C* = \$1M, c* = \$0, and a* a 10/11:1/11 chance of \$5M or \$0). In other words, the better (in the sense of stochastic dominance) the "common consequence," the more risk averse the choice (since a* is riskier than k).

4.2. The common ratio effect

A second type of systematic violation of the independence
axiom, the so-called "common ratio effect," also follows from
an early example of Allais' (Allais(1952,p.91)) and includes
the "Bergen Paradox" of Hagen(1979) and the "certainty effect"
of Kahneman & Tversky(1979) as special cases. This effect
involves rankings over pairs of prospects of the form:

$$c_1: \begin{cases} p & \text{chance of } \$X \\ 1-p & \text{chance of } \$0 \end{cases} \quad \text{versus} \quad c_2: \begin{cases} q & \text{chance of } \$Y \\ 1-q & \text{chance of } \$0 \end{cases}$$

and

$$c_3: \begin{cases} \alpha p & \text{chance of } \$X \\ 1-\alpha p & \text{chance of } \$0 \end{cases} \quad \text{versus} \quad c_4: \begin{cases} \alpha q & \text{chance of } \$Y \\ 1-\alpha q & \text{chance of } \$0 \end{cases}$$

where $p > q$, $X < Y$, and $0 < \alpha < 1$ (the term "common ratio"
derives from the equality of $\text{prob}(X)/\text{prob}(Y)$ in c_1 vs. c_2 and
c_3 vs. c_4). Once again, it is clear that an individual satisfying the independence axiom would rank c_1 and c_2 the same as
c_3 and c_4, however, researchers have found a systematic tendency for subjects to depart from the independence axiom by
preferring c_1 to c_2 and c_4 to c_3. Thus, Kahneman & Tversky
(1979) found, for example, that while 86% of their subjects
preferred a .90:.10 chance of $3,000 or $0 to a .45:.55 chance
of $6,000 or $0, 73% preferred a .001:.999 chance of $6,000
or $0 to a .002:.998 chance of $3,000 or $0. Besides Kahneman
and Tversky, other researchers who have found this effect are
Hagen(1979,pp.285-296), MacCrimmon & Larsson(1979,pp.350-359),
and Tversky(1975).

4.3. Oversensitivity to changes in small probability-outlying events

A third type of systematic violation of the independence
axiom is that, relative to the "linearity" property of expected
utility, individuals tend to exhibit what may be termed an
"oversensitivity to changes in the probabilities of small probability-outlying events." While the formalization of this
notion requires both a precise definition of what it means
for an individual to become "more sensitive" to changes in the
probability of an event (relative to changes in the probabilities of certain other events) as well as what it means for an
event to become "more outlying" relative to other events, we
begin with an intuitive discussion of this notion, using the

Allais Paradox of Section 4.1 as an example.

Note that, in the Allais example, the changes from prospects a_1 to a_2 and from a_4 to a_3 both consist of a (beneficial) shift of .10 units of probability mass from the outcome $1M to the outcome $5M and a (detrimental) shift of .01 units from $1 to $0. Since the typical individual prefers a_1 to a_2, we see that when the initial distribution is a_1, i.e. when the outcome $0 is a low probability event, the increase in its probability (at the expense of the preferred outcome $1M) is not compensated for by the beneficial shift of mass up to $5M. However, when the initial distribution is a_4, we see that the event $0 is no longer such a low probability-outlying event (since its probability is now .89) and we find that the individual is no longer as sensitive to the increase in its probability, in the sense that the beneficial shift from $1M to $5M is now enough to compensate and the change to a_3 is preferred. In other words, when the initial distribution changed in a manner which made the outcome $0 "less outlying," the individual became less sensitive to changes in its probability relative to changes in the probabilities of $5M and $1M.

There is an alternative way to view this example which helps bring out another aspect of the notion of "outlyingness." Note that the change in the initial distribution from a_1 to a_4 may be thought of as making the event $5M "more outlying" relative to the events $1M and $0 since, although the probability of the event $5M itself hasn't changed, the bulk of the distribution has moved *farther away* from the event $5M. And in response, the individual has become more sensitive to changes in the probability of $5M, since the beneficial increase in its probability (at the expense of $1M) which was not enough to outweigh the detrimental shift when the initial distribution was a_1 is now enough to outweigh it when the initial distribution is a_4.

The above discussion serves as motivation for our formalizations of the notions of "changes in sensitivity" and "outlyingness." Noting that any change in a probability distribution must consist of one or more "shifts" of probability mass from one event to another, we define the marginal rate of substitution $MRS(x_2 \rightarrow x_3, x_2 \rightarrow x_1; F)$ as the amount of probability mass which must be shifted from payoff level x_2 to x_3 per unit amount shifted from x_2 to x_1 in order to leave the individual indifferent, when the amounts shifted are infinitesimally small and the initial distribution is $F(\cdot)$ (in the following discussion, we assume $x_1 < x_2 < x_3$). Then, the notion of increased sensitivity in the above discussion of the Allais Paradox may be

formalized by saying that a change in the initial distribution
$F(\cdot)$ makes the individual *more sensitive to changes in the
probability of* x_1 *versus changes in the probabilities of* x_2
and x_3 *(and equivalently, less sensitive to changes in the
probability of* x_3 *relative to changes in the probabilities
of* x_1 *and* x_2*)* if the change serves to raise the value of
$MRS(x_2 \rightarrow x_3, x_2 \rightarrow x_1; F)$ (i.e. the individual is more sensitive to
changes in the probability of x_1 if a shift of probability
mass from the intermediate value x_2 to x_1 now requires more
of a compensating shift of mass from x_2 up to x_3, and similarly for the case of a decreased sensitivity to changes in the
probability of x_3 relative to changes in the probabilities
of x_1 and x_2).

Again using the discussion of the Allais Paradox as motivation, we will say that any rightward shift of mass within
the interval $[x_2, \infty)$ serves to change the initial distribution
in a manner which makes the event x_3 *less outlying relative to
events* x_1 *and* x_2, since rightward shifts of mass within the
interval $[x_2, x_3]$ clearly move the distribution away from x_1
and x_2 and toward x_3, and rightward shifts within the interval
$[x_3, \infty)$ also serve to make x_3 less of a "large" outcome relative to the bulk of the distribution, since they result in x_3
being farther from the "right edge" of the distribution. Similarly, leftward shifts of mass within the interval $(-\infty, x_2]$
serve to make the event x_1 *less outlying relative to the events
x_2 and x_3.* Thus, our formalization of the "oversensitivity
condition" is:

> "any change in the initial distribution which serves
> to make an event more (less) outlying relative to a
> pair of other events serves to change the relevant
> marginal rate of substitution so as to make the indi-
> vidual more (less) sensitive to changes in the proba-
> bility of that event relative to changes in the pro-
> babilities of the other two events."

While using a notion (the marginal rate of substitution)
which is not typically seen in the analysis of preferences
over probability distributions, the above condition is very
much in the spirit of the Hicks-Allen "diminishing marginal
rate of substitution" assumption of nonstochastic demand
theory, in that it relates changes in a fundamental marginal
rate of substitution to changes in the "current consumption
bundle" (in this case, the initial distribution). Furthermore, this condition may be shown to be equivalent to the

common consequence effect and to imply the common ratio effect
(see Machina(1982a)), and in Section 4.5 below will be shown
to possess a nice graphical interpretation in terms of the indifference curves in the unit triangle diagram.

4.4. The utility evaluation effect

The final type of systematic violation of the independence
axiom may be termed the "utility evaluation effect." It is
well known that there are several ways of evaluating or "assessing" the von Neumann-Morgenstern utility function of an
expected utility maximizer, all of which, according to the
theory, will yield the same function subject to positive linear transformations (see, for example, Farquhar(1982)). However, in actual practice different techniques have "recovered"
utility functions from the same individual which differ in
systematic ways.

    One of the most frequently used assessment methods is
termed the "fractile method" (see McCord & de Neufville(1982)).
This method begins by arbitrarily defining $U(0) = 0$ and $U(M)$
$= 1$ for some positive M, and picking some fixed probability $\bar{p}$
between zero and unity. The first step in the method then
consists of determining the individual's certainty equivalent
of a $\bar{p}:1-\bar{p}$ chance of M or 0. If we term this certainty equivalent c_1, it follows from the equation $U(c_1) = \bar{p}U(M) +$
$(1-\bar{p})U(0)$ that $U(c_1)$ will have the value $\bar{p}$. The second and
third step consist of finding the certainty equivalent c_2 of a
$\bar{p}:1-\bar{p}$ chance of c_1 and 0 (so that $U(c_2) = \bar{p}U(c_1) + (1-\bar{p})U(0) =$
$\bar{p}^2$) and the certainty equivalent c_3 of a $\bar{p}:1-\bar{p}$ chance of M or
c_1 (so that $U(c_3) = \bar{p}U(M) + (1-\bar{p})U(c_1) = \bar{p} + (1-\bar{p})\bar{p}$). Further
points on the utility curve are determined by finding the cer-
tainty equivalents of a $\bar{p}:1-\bar{p}$ chance of c_2 or 0, a $\bar{p}:1-\bar{p}$ chance
of c_1 or c_2, a $\bar{p}:1-\bar{p}$ chance of c_3 or c_1, a $\bar{p}:1-\bar{p}$ chance
of M or c_3, etc., always interpolating by letting $\bar{p}$ be the probability of the higher of the two payoffs. Thus, if $\bar{p} = 1/2$,
the first step would find that monetary value whose utility
was $1/2$, the second and third steps would find the values with
utility levels $1/4$ and $3/4$, and so on through $1/8$, $3/8$, $5/8$,
$7/8$, $1/16$, $3/16$, etc. Let $U^{\bar{p}}(\cdot)$ denote the utility function
derived in this way, for a given value of $\bar{p}$.

    Of course, if the individual is an expected utility maxi-
mizer, this method ought to recover the same utility function
for each value of $\bar{p}$ used, i.e. the functions $U^{1/2}(\cdot)$ and
$U^{1/3}(\cdot)$ ought to be identical, since both would have the same
normalization $U(0) = 0$ and $U(M) = 1$. However, Karmarkar(1974)

discovered an almost universal tendency for the recovered $U^{\bar{p}}(\cdot)$
curve to lie above the $U^{p^*}(\cdot)$ curve whenever $\bar{p}$ was higher than
p^*.[9] This same effect was found (though less markedly) by
McCord & de Neufville(1982) and can also be recovered from the
experimental data presented by Allais(1979).[10] Once again,
individuals are seen to be evidently departing from the expected utility hypothesis of linearity in a systematic manner.

4.5. Hypothesis II

The previous subsections have presented four types of systematic violations of the independence axiom that have been found
by empirical researchers. Needless to say, if these four types
of behavior were entirely unrelated (or even mutually contradictory), then supporters of expected utility theory would have
a valid point in maintaining that any generalization of expected
utility designed to accomodate them would be nothing more than
an *ad hoc* extension of the model in each of these four directions.

However, it turns out that not only are each of the above
four aspects of behavior compatible, but they all follow from
a *single* assumption on the shape of the preference functional
$V(\cdot)$. Thus, the data are telling us that not only do individuals' preferences depart from linearity, but they do so in a
single systematic manner, which in addition may be modelled
quite easily and which (expected utility theorists note:) leads
to further refutable restrictions on behavior.

As in standard calculus, one particularly compact way of
specifying the nature of a nonlinearity in a preference functional is to specify how the derivative (i.e. the local utility function) of the functional varies as we move about the
domain $D[0,M]$. Our formal hypothesis, termed "Hypothesis II,"[11]
basically states that as we move from one probability distribution in $D[0,M]$ to another which (first order) stochastically
dominates it, the local utility function becomes more concave
at each point x, or stated formally in terms of the Arrow-Pratt
ratio $-U_{11}(x;F)/U_1(x;F)$:

Hypothesis II: If the distribution $F^*(\cdot)$ first order
stochastically dominates $F(\cdot)$, then

$$-U_{11}(x;F^*)/U_1(x;F^*) \geq -U_{11}(x;F)/U_1(x;F)$$

for all $x \in [0,M]$.

Hypothesis II possesses a straightforward graphical inter-

pretation in terms of the indifference curves in the unit triangle diagram. Note first that the set of all probability distributions in the triangle which stochastically dominate a
given distribution correspond to all the points which are
northwest of the point representing the distribution.[12]   According to Hypothesis II, therefore, the local utility functions
at these northwest distributions will be more concave. However, we know from Section 3 that the more concave the (von
Neumann-Morgenstern or local) utility function, the steeper
the slope of the indifference curves through the point. Accordingly, Hypothesis II implies that indifference curves in
the unit triangle are "fanned out" as in Figure 4, with steeper
curves lying to the northwest and flatter curves lying to the
southeast.

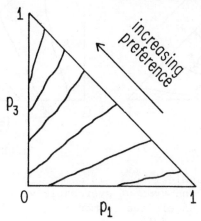

FIGURE 4

To get an idea of how Hypothesis II implies the common
consequence effect, let us refer back to its general formulation (the table in Section 4.1) and consider the special case
when the value k and the payoff levels of the prospects c*,
C*, and a* are all elements of $\{x_1, x_2, x_3\}$ for some $x_1 < x_2 <$
x_3, so that the prospects b_1, b_2, b_3, and b_4 are all in the
set $D\{x_1, x_2, x_3\}$ and hence may be plotted in the unit triangle
diagram. In such a case it is straightforward to show that
the four prospects will always form a parallelogram with b_2
and b_4 to the northeast of b_1 and b_3 respectively, and the
segment $\overline{b_1 b_2}$ parallel to and to the north and/or west of $\overline{b_3 b_4}$,
e.g. as shown in Figure 5. In this case it is easy to see

how the "fanning out" property of indifference curves implied
by Hypothesis II would lead an individual to violate the independence axiom by preferring b_1 to b_2 and b_4 to b_3, which is
precisely the common consequence effect. In Machina(1982a) it
was shown that Hypothesis II is in fact *equivalent* to the common consequence effect in the more general case when c*, C*,
and a* may be arbitrary (possibly continuous) prospects.

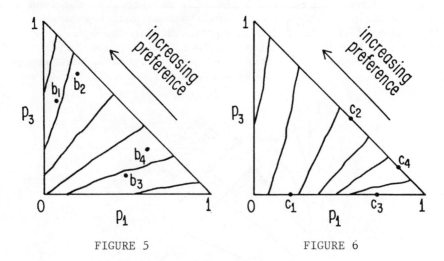

FIGURE 5   FIGURE 6

     A similar graphical analysis demonstrates how Hypothesis
II implies the second type of systematic violation of the independence axiom, namely the common ratio effect. Letting x_1
= 0, x_2 = X, and x_3 = Y in the formulation of Section 4.2 and
plotting the prospects c_1,c_2,c_3,c_4 in the unit triangle diagram, we once again find that c_2 and c_4 are northeast of c_1
and c_3 respectively and that $\overline{c_1c_2}$ is parallel to and northwest
of $\overline{c_3c_4}$, as seen in Figure 6. And similarly, it is clear how
the "fanning out" property implied by Hypothesis II would lead
the individual to violate the independence axiom by preferring
c_1 to c_2 and c_4 to c_3, i.e. exhibit the common ratio effect.
     Hypothesis II's implication that the individual will be
systematically oversensitive to changes in the probabilities
of low probability-outlying events may be seen quite simply
from Figure 4 above. We begin by noting that, just as in non-
stochastic demand theory, the marginal rate of substitution
MRS$(x_2{\to}x_3,x_2{\to}x_1;F)$ is precisely equal to the slope of the indifference curve through the point corresponding to the distribution F$(\cdot)$ in the diagram, since rightward and upward

movements in the diagram correspond to the shifts $x_2 \rightarrow x_3$ and
$x_2 \rightarrow x_1$ respectively. Under the fanning out implication of Hypothesis II, we find that the individual is most sensitive to
changes in the probability of x_1 relative to changes in the
probabilities of x_2 and x_3 (i.e. $\mathrm{MRS}(x_2 \rightarrow x_3, x_2 \rightarrow x_1; F)$ is the
highest) near the left edge of the triangle, or in other words
precisely when x_1 is a low probability event (i.e. p_1 is low).
Note also that moving straight up in the triangle, which does
not change p_1 but increases p_3 at the expense of p_2, also
serves to make the event x_1 more outlying (since it moves probability mass further away from x_1) and indeed is seen to also
increase the individual's sensitivity to changes in p_1, as
measured by the slope of the indifference curves. An analogous
argument applies to the individual's sensitivity to changes
in p_3 relative to changes in p_1 and p_2.

Finally, we may also use the unit triangle diagram to illustrate how Hypothesis II implies the utility evaluation effect. If we were to take an individual satisfying Hypothesis
II and try to "evaluate" his or her $U^{1/2}(\cdot)$ curve, the first
step (as in Section 4.4) would be to determine the certainty
equivalent c_1 of a $1/2{:}1/2$ chance of M or O. Consider now
Figure 7, where we pick $x_1 = 0$, $x_2 = c_1$, and $x_3 = M$, so that
the origin (i.e. the sure prospect c_1) is seen to lie on the

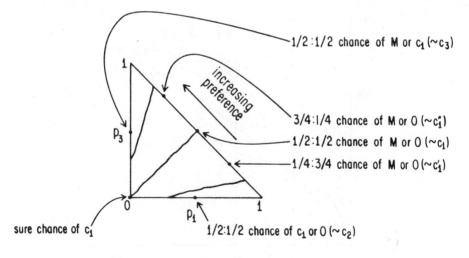

$1/2{:}1/2$ chance of M or $c_1 (\sim c_3)$

increasing preference

$3/4{:}1/4$ chance of M or O $(\sim c_1'')$

$1/2{:}1/2$ chance of M or O $(\sim c_1)$

$1/4{:}3/4$ chance of M or O $(\sim c_1')$

p_3

p_1

sure chance of c_1'

$1/2{:}1/2$ chance of c_1 or O $(\sim c_2)$

("$\sim$" denotes indifference)

FIGURE 7

same indifference curve as the prospect which offers a $1/2:1/2$ chance of M or 0. We then find the sure amount c_2 which is indifferent to a $1/2:1/2$ chance of c_1 or 0, and the amount c_3 which is indifferent to a $1/2:1/2$ chance of M and c_1 (see Figure 7). These three points, with their associated $U^{1/2}(\cdot)$ values of $1/4$, $1/2$, and $3/4$, are plotted in Figure 8 as points on the $U^{1/2}(\cdot)$ curve.

Now, to evaluate the first point on the $U^{1/4}(\cdot)$ curve, we find the certainty equivalent c_1' of a $1/4:3/4$ chance of M or 0. However, if we note where this latter prospect lies in Figure 7, we see that it will be preferred to a $1/2:1/2$ chance of c_1 or 0, so that its certainty equivalent c_1' will be higher than c_2. This of course implies that $U^{1/2}(\cdot)$ will attain a value of $1/4$ before $U^{1/4}(\cdot)$ does, so that $U^{1/2}(\cdot)$ lies above $U^{1/4}(\cdot)$ in this region. Similarly, the first point on the $U^{3/4}(\cdot)$ curve will be the value c_1'' which is indifferent to a $3/4:1/4$ chance of M or 0, and again it is seen from Figure 7 that since this prospect will be less preferred than a $1/2:1/2$ chance of M or c_1, c_1'' must be less than c_3, which implies that $U^{3/4}(\cdot)$ lies above $U^{1/2}(\cdot)$ in this range (see Figure 8). This analysis may be extended to a further evaluation and comparison of the three "evaluated utility functions" in a manner which continues to exhibit the utility evaluation effect.

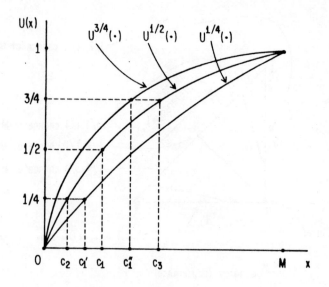

FIGURE 8

Accordingly, it is *not* true, as some expected utility defenders might suppose, that the violations of the independence axiom which researchers have found are random and unsystematic departures from expected utility, but rather, individuals have been found to depart from expected utility in a systematic and unified manner, as captured by Hypothesis II in general and by the "fanning out" property in the special case of preferences over three-outcome distributions.

4.6. Further predictions and policy implications of Hypothesis II

It is easy to see that Hypothesis II possesses that final required property of any replacement of the expected utility hypothesis, namely the ability to generate further refutable predictions and policy implications. Of course, since each of the four types of systematic violations of expected utility discussed above is a general principle rather than a specific example, each admits of an infinite number of specific examples which serve as refutable predictions. As a new type of example, I would like to consider a problem posed by Professor Arrow in his superb and thought provoking Plenary Talk in this Conference. Arrow noted that one of the canonical problems in choice under uncertainty involves the tradeoff between the probability and the outcome value of an unfortunate event, and offered the specific example of an individual with initial wealth $\$W$ facing a p probability of a loss of $\$X$ (with a 1-p probability of no loss). A natural question to ask here is how does the individual's marginal rate of substitution between p and X depend upon their existing values. Defining expected utility $\Phi(p,X;W) \equiv pU(W-X) + (1-p)U(W)$, we get that this marginal rate of substitution is

$$MRS_{p,X} = \left.\frac{dp}{dX}\right|_{\Phi} = \frac{-pU'(W-X)}{U(W) - U(W-X)} \qquad (8)$$

In his talk, Arrow noted that this expected utility formulation implied a possibly quite useful restriction on behavior, namely that, fixing X and W, the marginal rate of substitution between p and X is proportional to p, i.e. to the probability of the unfortunate event. He quite rightly noted that it would be possible to exploit this property to make important predictions *as well as policy suggestions*, say in determining the tradeoff between the probability and severeness of a nuclear accident, and also noted that any acceptable alternative to expected utility would have to possess this same type of ability.

To see how generalized expected utility analysis, and more particularly Hypothesis II, might be applied to this problem, we replace the expected utility maximand $\Phi(p,X;W)$ with the more general maximand $V(pG_{W-X}+(1-p)G_W)$, where G_c stands for the distribution with unit mass at c, so that $pG_{W-X}+(1-p)G_W$ represents the distribution in question. We then have from equation (4) that

$$MRS_{p,X} = \left.\frac{dp}{dX}\right|_V = \frac{-pU_1(W-X;pG_{W-X}+(1-p)G_W)}{U(W;pG_{W-X}+(1-p)G_W) - U(W-X;pG_{W-X}+(1-p)G_W)} =$$

(after some manipulation)   (9)

$$= -p\left[\int_{W-X}^{W}\exp\left[-\int_{W-X}^{z}\left\{-\frac{U_{11}(\omega;pG_{W-X}+(1-p)G_W)}{U_1(\omega;pG_{W-X}+(1-p)G_W)}\right\}d\omega\right]dz\right]^{-1}.$$

As usual in generalized expected utility analysis, we see the formal analogy with the expected utility case: the marginal rate of substitution in (9) is identical to that in (8) with the von Neumann–Morgenstern utility function $U(\cdot)$ replaced by the local utility function $U(\cdot;F)$ when $F = pG_{W-X}+(1-p)G_W$. However, since the local utility function in (9) now depends on the precise distribution $pG_{W-X}+(1-p)G_W$, the marginal rate of substitution is no longer strictly proportional to p as before. However, this is not to say that Hypothesis II is without implications in this case. Noting that an increase in p induces a first order stochastic worsening of the distribution $pG_{W-X}+(1-p)G_W$, we see that under Hypothesis II an increase in p will lower the term in curled brackets in (9) (the Arrow-Pratt term) for each value of ω, so that Hypothesis II implies that the marginal rate of substitution between p and X varies less than proportionately with p. The replacement of the expected utility prediction of exact proportionality with a weak inequality on proportionality reflects the fact that Hypothesis II is a weak inequality which includes the expected utility case (i.e. the independence axiom) as a borderline case, just as, geometrically, "fanning out" includes parallel linear indifference curves as a borderline case. Nevertheless, weak inequalities are still refutable restrictions on behavior (we use them all the time in economics) and this result is clearly not without policy implications which, if not as strong as the ones generated by expected utility, are at least more accurately tied to what we have observed about individual's actual preferences. While this is just a single example, it should be clear that

Hypothesis II can be used to derive other important behavioral predictions and policy implications.

5. CONCLUSION

Defenders of the expected utility approach are quite correct in insisting that any alternative to expected utility not only be consistent with the data, but also be at least on the order of elegance of the expected utility theory, and capable of easily derived behavioral restrictions and implications for policy analysis. The technique of generalized expected utility analysis seems to fit these requirements. Specifically,

> while making virtually no requisite assumptions on preferences other than completeness, transitivity, and smoothness, it allows us to retain the elegant set of concepts, tools, and techniques of expected utility analysis,

> it admits of refutable restrictions on preferences and hence on behavior, with the concepts of monotonicity and risk aversion, for example, modelled almost exactly as in expected utility analysis, and

> it admits of a restriction (Hypothesis II) which implies the four known types of observed systematic violations of the independence axiom, and which generates both additional refutable behavioral predictions as well as policy implications.

Whether the future will yield empirical observations which contradict Hypothesis II, or even the underlying assumption of smooth preferences, is really not the issue at hand.[13] The present point is that generalized expected utility analysis seems to offer a theoretically powerful and empirically supported generalization of the expected utility model. Indeed, if generalized expected utility analysis and other related models lead to the type of empirical work which will require still newer models to replace them, they will have served us well.

Department of Economics
University of California, San Diego

NOTES

1. I am indebted to Maurice Allais, Kenneth Arrow, John
   Harsanyi, and Ed McClennen for discussions of this material during the Conference, and to Beth Hayes, Joel Sobel,
   and Halbert White for helpful comments on the manuscript.
   All errors and opinions, however, are my own.
2. See for example Chew & MacCrimmon(1979), Fishburn(1981a,
   1981b), Handa(1977), and Kahneman & Tversky(1979).
3. Of course, any comparison of the refutable implications of
   two competing models should be followed immediately by a
   discussion of which of these implications have and have
   not in fact been refuted.
4. For a more complete and rigorous treatment of much of the
   material in Sections 3 and 4, see Machina(1982a,1982b,
   1982c).
5. The indifference curves here are the loci of solutions to
   the equation $p_1U(x_1) + (1-p_1-p_3)U(x_2) + p_3U(x_3) = k$ for
   different values of the constant k. Northwest movements
   make the individual better off since they consist of either
   increases in p_3 at the expense of p_2, increases in p_2 at
   the expense of p_1, or a combination of the two.
6. See for example Kahneman & Tversky(1979,pp.271-273), Tversky
   (1969,1975), Grether(1978), and Grether & Plott(1979).
7. See Hadar & Russell(1969) for the definition of first order
   stochastic dominance.
8. "Hypothesis I" is a separate hypothesis on the typical
   shape of the local utility function which, in conjunction
   with Hypothesis II, serves to generate behavior of the
   type observed by Friedman & Savage(1948) and Markowitz
   (1952) (see Machina(1982a)).
9. Of Karmarker's four subjects, three exhibited fitted $U^p(\cdot)$
   curves which strictly and markedly increased with p. The
   fourth ("Subject B") exhibited $U^{9/10}(\cdot)$ and $U^{3/4}(\cdot)$ curves
   which were both above the $U^{1/2}(\cdot)$ curve, but which crossed
   each other at one point. Since the curves of this subject
   were much closed to each other than the curves of the other
   subjects, it is possible that this crossing is due to the
   slightly random character of responses which is typically
   found in studies of this type.
10. McCord & de Neufville found that the great majority of their
    subjects exhibited $U^{1/4}(\cdot)$ curves which were below their
    $U^{1/2}(\cdot)$ curves in the region where the curves had a value
    of 1/4. However, an equal number of their subjects had
    $U^{3/4}(\cdot)$ curves above and below their $U^{1/2}(\cdot)$ curves,

indicating no average departure from linearity in either direction in this region. McCord & de Neufville also found that whether the $U^{1/4}(\cdot)$ and $U^{3/4}(\cdot)$ curves lay above or below the $U^{1/2}(\cdot)$ curve seemed to be correlated with the subject's degree of risk aversion, with the $U^{1/2}(\cdot)$ curve typically lying higher relative to the other curves for risk averters and lower for risk lovers. However, since their method of classifying individuals as risk averse or risk loving was based on the concavity or convexity, and hence *height*, of the $U^{1/2}(\cdot)$ curve, this finding may in part be a statistical artifact introduced by their method of catagorizing the observations. Finally, since Allais' method of constructing his "$B_{1/2}$" curves differed slightly from the fractile method, his data may only be used to compare $U^{1/2}(\cdot)$ with $U^p(\cdot)$ for $p < 1/2$, where it exhibits the utility evaluation effect described in this section (see Allais(1979,pp.611-654)).

11. See Note 8.
12. Stochastically dominating shifts in $D\{x_1,x_2,x_3\}$ are shifts which increase p_3 at the expense of p_2 and/or increase p_2 at the expense of p_1, which correspond respectively to upward and/or leftward (i.e. northward and/or westward) shifts in the unit triangle diagram.
13. See Note 6.

REFERENCES

Allais, M.: 1952, 'The Foundations of a Positive Theory of Choice Involving Risk and a Criticism of the Postulates and Axioms of the American School', (Translation of 'Fondements d'une Théorie Positive des Choix Comportant un Risque et Critique des Postulats et Axiomes de L'Ecole Americaine', Paris, CNRS), in Allais & Hagen(1979).

Allais, M.: 1979, 'The So-Called Allais Paradox and Rational Decisions Under Uncertainty', in Allais & Hagen(1979).

Allais, M. and O. Hagen: 1979, Expected Utility Hypotheses and the Allais Paradox: Contemporary Discussions of Decisions under Uncertainty with Allais' Rejoinder, D. Reidel, Dordrecht, Holland.

Bolker, E.: 1967, 'A Simultaneous Axiomatization of Utility and Subjective Probability', Philosophy of Science 34, 333-40.

Chew, S.H. and K. MacCrimmon: 1979, 'Alpha-Nu Choice Theory: A Generalization of Expected Utility Theory', University of British Columbia Faculty of Commerce and Business Administration Working Paper No.669.

Debreu, G.: 1959, Theory of Value: An Axiomatic Analysis of General Equilibrium, Yale University Press, New Haven.

Dreze, J.: 1974, 'Axiomatic Theories of Choice, Cardinal Utility and Subjective Probability: A Review', in J. Dreze (ed.), Allocation Under Uncertainty: Equilibrium and Optimality, John Wiley & Sons., New York.

Edwards, W.: 1955, 'The Prediction of Decisions Among Bets', Journal of Experimental Psychology 50, 201-14.

Farquhar, P.: 1982, 'Utility Assessment Methods', University of California, Davis, Graduate School of Administration Working Paper No. 81-5.

Fishburn, P.: 1981a, 'Nontransitive Measurable Utility', Bell Laboratories Economics Discussion Paper No. 209, forthcoming in Journal of Mathematical Psychology.

Fishburn, P.: 1981b, 'Transitive Measurable Utility', Bell Laboratories Economics Discussion Paper No. 224, forthcoming in Journal of Economic Theory.

Friedman, M. and L. Savage: 1948, 'The Utility Analysis of Choices Involving Risk', Journal of Political Economy 56, 279-304. Reprinted in G. Stigler and K. Boulding (eds.), Readings in Price Theory, Richard D. Irwin, Chicago, 1952.

Grether, D.: 1978, 'Recent Psychological Studies of Behavior Under Uncertainty', American Economic Review Papers and Proceedings 68, 70-74

Grether, D. and C. Plott: 1979, 'Economic Theory of Choice and the Preference Reversal Phenomenon', American Economic Review 69, 623-38.

Hadar, J. and W. Russell: 1969, 'Rules for Ordering Uncertain Prospects', American Economic Review 59, 25-34.

Handa, J.: 1977, 'Risk, Probabilities, and a New Theory of Cardinal Utility', Journal of Political Economy 85, 97-122.

Hagen, O.: 1979, 'Towards a Positive Theory of Preferences Under Risk', in Allais & Hagen(1979).

Herstein, I. and J. Milnor: 1953, 'An Axiomatic Approach to Measurable Utility', Econometrica 21, 291-97.

Kahneman, D. and A. Tversky: 1979, 'Prospect Theory: An Analysis of Decision Under Risk', Econometrica 47, 263-91.

Karmarkar, U.: 1974, 'The Effect of Probabilities on the Subjective Evaluation of Lotteries', Massachusetts Institute of Technology Sloan School of Management Working Paper No.698-74.

MacCrimmon, K.: 1968, 'Descriptive and Normative Implications of the Decision Theory Postulates', in K. Borch and J. Mossin (eds.) Risk and Uncertainty, MacMillan & Co., London.

MacCrimmon, K. and S. Larsson: 1979, 'Utility Theory: Axioms Versus "Paradoxes"', in Allais & Hagen(1979).

Machina, M.: 1981, '"Rational" Decision Making vs. "Rational" Decision Modelling?: A Review of Expected Utility Hypotheses and the Allais Paradox, Edited by Maurice Allais and Ole Hagen', Journal of Mathematical Psychology 24, 163-75.

Machina, M.: 1982a, '"Expected Utility" Analysis Without the Independence Axiom', Econometrica 50, 277-323.

Machina, M.: 1982b, 'A Stronger Characterization of Declining Risk Aversion', Econometrica 50, 1069-79.

Machina, M.: 1982c, 'Temporal Risk and the Nature of Induced Preferences', University of California, San Diego, manuscript.

Markowitz, H.: 1952, 'The Utility of Wealth', Journal of Political Economy 60, 151-58.

McCord, M. and R. de Neufville: 1982, 'Fundamental Deficiencies of Expected Utility Decision Analysis', Massachusetts Institute of Technology, manuscript.

Morrison, D.: 1967, 'On the Consistency of Preferences in Allais' Paradox', Behavioral Science 12, 373-83.

Moskowitz, H.: 1974, 'Effects of Problem Representation and Feedback on Rational Behavior in Allais and Morlat-Type Problems', Decision Sciences 5, 225-42.

Pratt, J.: 1964, 'Risk Aversion in the Small and in the Large', Econometrica 32, 122-36.

Raiffa, H.: 1968, Decision Analysis: Introductory Lectures on Choice under Uncertainty, Addison-Wesley, Reading, Mass.

Rothschild, M. and J. Stiglitz: 1970, 'Increasing Risk: I. A Definition', Journal of Economic Theory 2, 225-243.

Savage, L.: 1972, Foundations of Statistics, Dover Publications, New York. (Revised and enlarged version of the work originally published by John Wiley & Sons, New York, 1954).

Slovic, P. and A. Tversky: 'Who Accepts Savage's Axiom?', Behavioral Science 19, 368-73.

Tversky, A.: 1969, 'Intransitivity of Preferences', Psychological Review 76, 31-48.

Tversky, A.: 1975, 'A Critique of Expected Utility Theory: Descriptive and Normative Considerations', Erkenntnis 9, 163-73.

von Neumann, J. and O. Morgenstern: 1944, Theory of Games and Economic Behavior, Princeton University Press, Princeton (Second Edition, 1947, Third Edition, 1953).

Wold, H.: 1952, 'Ordinal Preferences or Cardinal Utility?', Econometrica 20, 661-63.

PART VI

GAME THEORY AND RATIONAL BHAVIOR

John C. Harsanyi

USE OF SUBJECTIVE PROBABILITIES IN GAME THEORY

ABSTRACT

Classical game theory used only objective probabilities
(for characterizing random moves and mixed strategies).
Subjective probabilities were first introduced in modelling
games with incomplete information. More recently,
Reinhard Selten and the present writer have used subjective
probabilities in our solution theory for noncooperative
games. The paper will discuss some of the methodological
problems associated with this work. It will also comment
on the economic meaning of von Neumann-Morgenstern utility
functions.

1. SUBJECTIVE AND OBJECTIVE PROBABILITIES AND THE THEORY OF
   RATIONAL BEHAVIOR

Since game theory is part of the general theory of rational
behavior, I will first outline its place in this wider
setting. But before doing so, I will comment on the somewhat
controversial distinction between subjective and objective
probabilities.[1]

Most writers dealing with the foundations of the
probability concept follow Ramsey [1926], de Finetti [1937],
and Savage [1954] in reducing all probabilities to
subjective probabilities (usually interpreted in a
behavioristic manner). Others, such as von Neumann and
Morgenstern [1947], Luce and Raiffa [1957], and Anscombe
and Aumann [1963], admit objective probabilities as an
independent source of our probability concept. As Anscombe
and Aumann have shown, this latter approach has important
advantages:

(1) It enables us to base decision theory on simpler
and intuitively much more convincing rationality axioms
than is possible under the Ramsey-de Finetti-Savage approach
[see Harsanyi 1977, pp.41-46; also Harsanyi, 1978]; and

(2) It substantially simplifies the proof of the
expected-utility maximization theorem [ibid.]

B. P. Stigum and F. Wenstøp (eds.), Foundations of Utility and Risk Theory with Applications,
297–310.
© *1983 by D. Reidel Publishing Company.*

Moreover, as Popper has pointed out:

(3) If we want to make sense of modern physics, in particular of thermodynamics and of quantum mechanics, we need the concept of objective probability, interpreted as an objective propensity (or tendency) of some physical systems to produce various outcomes with numerically specifiable long-run frequencies.

Once we admit both subjective and objective probabilities, we have to divide individual decision theory (utility theory) into three branches, dealing with rational decision making under certainty (with known outcomes), risk (with outcomes having known objective probabilities), and uncertainty (with the objective probabilities of some or all outcomes being unknown or even undefined). Yet, in all three cases we find that rational behavior, i.e., human behavior satisfying appropriate rationality requirements, will amount to utility maximization or to expected-utility maximization.

In order to obtain a comprehensive definition of rational behavior, the theory of individual rationality (decision theory) must be supplemented by two further disciplines, both studying rational behavior in social settings. One is game theory, which deals with the rational behavior of two or more individuals trying to promote their own, often more or less conflicting, interests in cooperation and/or competition with another. (These conflicting interests need not be selfish interests: there may be a very intensive conflict also between two altruists who are trying to pursue incompatible altruistic objectives.) The other discipline is ethics (so defined as to include welfare economics), which deals with the question of how the various individuals can rationally promote the common interests (the common good) of society as a whole.

Finally, any analysis of rational behavior, i.e., of practical rationality, must be supplemented by a study of theoretical rationality, both in its deductive and in its inductive branches.

2. USE OF SUBJECTIVE PROBABILITIES IN ANALYZING GAMES WITH INCOMPLETE INFORMATION

Game theory, ever since it was founded by von Neumann and Morgenstern [1944] as a systematic discipline, has always made essential use of the probability concept. But at first it used only objective probabilities, for the purpose of characterizing random moves and various types of mixed

strategies. (In fact, as is well known, von Neumann's
axiomatic theory of rational behavior under risk was a by-
product of his work on game theory.)

As far as I know, subjective probabilities were first
used in game theory in analyzing games with incomplete
information [Harsanyi, 1967-68]. We say that a given game
involves incomplete information if some or all players are
uncertain about some important parameters defining the game,
such as the payoff functions of and/or the strategies
available to the other players. (It is assumed, however,
that each player will entertain a subjective probability
distribution about the parameters unknown to him.)
Classical game theory was unable to deal with such games
involving incomplete information.

Yet, we have found that we can easily bring these games
under the scope of the common analytical tools of game theory
if we model the players' uncertainty about the relevant
parameters of the game as an uncertainty about the outcomes
of certain fictitious random moves within the game. By making
appropriate assumptions about which player can or cannot
observe the outcomes of various random moves, we can model
any desired distribution of knowledge and/or ignorance among
the players and can study its effect on the game. We can
also study the question of how any given player can optimally
infer information, originally unavailable to him, by
observing the moves of those players who possess this
information. This in turn leads to the question of how to
conceal information optimally from the other players by
choosing strategies which otherwise would be nonoptimal; and
how to convey information optimally to them in a credible
manner when they know that one may have an interest in
misleading them.

This theory of games with incomplete information is now
used extensively in economics in studying bargaining, auctions,
competitive bidding, oligopolistic competition with and
without free entry and/or free exit, etc. [For a survey of
some of this literature, see Engelbrecht-Wiggans, 1980].

3. THE HARSANYI-SELTEN SOLUTION THEORY AND THE PROBLEM OF EQUILIBRIUM-POINT SELECTION

Another use of subjective probabilities is in a solution
theory for noncooperative games developed by Reinhard Selten
and the present writer. [This theory will be presented in a
forthcoming book by the two of us. For a preliminary

discission, see Harsanyi, 1981, Parts I-II.]

The distinction between cooperative and noncooperative games was proposed by Nash [1951]. He defined cooperative games as games with free communication and with enforceable agreements, and defined noncooperative games as games without these properties. It is now generally admitted that the crucial criterion is the possibility of enforceable agreements. Thus, cooperative games are now commonly defined simply as games with enforceable agreements, and noncooperative games as games without such agreements. Nash has also pointed out that the solution of any noncooperative game must be an equilibrium point, which can be defined as follows:

I will denote player i's payoff function by H_i, and his strategy set (which includes both his pure and mixed strategies) by Q_i (i = 1,...,n). Let $q = (q_1,...,q_n)$ be a strategy comibiantion for the n players, and q_{-i} be the (n-1)-tuple $q_{-i} = (q_1,...,q_{i-1}, q_{i+1},...,q_n)$ which remains if we remove player i's strategy q_i from this n-tuple q. I will call q_{-i} an "i-incomplete strategy combination".

I will say that a given strategy q_i** of player i is a best reply to the i-incomplete strategy combination q_{-i} if

$$H_i(q_i^{**},q_{-i}) \geq H_i(q_i^*,q_{-i}) \tag{1}$$

for all $q_i^* \varepsilon Q_i$ and $\neq q_i^{**}$. Thus, q_i^{**} is a best reply to q_{-i} if it does at least as well against q_{-i} as any other strategy q_i^* of player i does. I will say that q_i^{**} is a strong best reply if it satisfies (1) also with a strong inequality sign >, i.e., if it does clearly better than any other strategy.

A strategy combination q is called an equilibrium point if the q-strategy q_i of every player i is a best reply to the other (n-1) player's strategy combination q_{-i}. It is called a strong equilibrium point if every player's strategy q_i is a strong best reply to q_{-i}.

Though the concept of equilibrium points is a very convincing solution concept for noncooperative games, Reinhard Selten discovered in the early sixties that it must

be narrowed down to the concept of perfect equilibrium points
if we want to exclude some obviously irrational "imperfect"
equilibrium points [Selten, 1975]. But, for lack of space,
I must refer the reader to Selten's paper.

Yet, even if we restrict ourselves to perfect
equilibrium points, we are faced with a major difficulty:
Almost all interesting games have many very different
equilibrium points, possibly even infinitely many of them.
This may be called the multiplicity problem.

The main purpose of the Harsanyi-Selten solution theory
is to overcome this multiplicity problem by appropriate
criteria for equilibrium point selection, i.e., for
selecting one specific equilibrium point as the solution for
the game.

As will be clear from even this very short discussion,
our theory is formally a solution theory for noncooperative
games only. But, in actual fact, it does define a solution
for every finite game (and can be extended also to all
sufficiently regular infinite games), both cooperative and
noncooperative. This is so because every cooperative game
can be remodelled as a noncooperative bargaining game. Thus
our solution theory provides a uniform approach for defining
solutions for all games and achieves a remarkable unification
of game theory as a whole, extending to both its cooperative
and its noncooperative subdivisions.

4. USE OF SUBJECTIVE-PROBABILITY CONSIDERATIONS IN OUR SOLUTION THEORY

Our solution theory makes essential use of subjective
probabiliites because it is an attempt to formalize our
common-sense thinking about rational behavior in game
situations, which itself always makes extensive use of
subjective-probability considerations.

For example, if a given person A wants to sell his car,
he will choose his asking price always on the basis of such
probabilistic considerations. He will realize that the higher
he sets his asking price, the more money he will make if he
can find a buyer at this price -- but also the lower the
probability that he will actually find a buyer. Thus he
must always set a possibility of a higher payoff against a
lower probability of actually obtaining this payoff.

Any person B who wants to buy a car must go through the
same sort of probabilistic argument, though in his case it
will work in the opposite direction: the higher the price he

offers for a given car, the higher the probability that the
seller will accept it.

Again, if we assume that there are more potential buyers
than one -- say, that there are k such individuals, $B_1, B_2 \ldots$,
B_k -- then, as common sense tells us, the likely selling price
of the car will be higher than it would be with just one
potential buyer. This is again a result of probabilistic
reasoning. For instance, the seller, A, will decide he can
now afford to hold out for a higher price because, even if
the probability that any given potential buyer should accept
this higher price may be the same as it would be in the one-
buyer case, the probability that at least one buyer will
accept it is now much higher. Thus, let ρ be the probability
that any given buyer will accept this high price. Then, the
probability that at least one of the k buyers will accept it
is

$$\rho^* = 1 - (1-\rho)^k. \tag{2}$$

Even if ρ is a very low probability, ρ^* may be quite high a
probability (if k is large enough).

Similar probabilistic considerations can be used to show
that in the case of k potential buyers, the expected
competition by the other buyers will force each buyer to offer
a relatively high price. [For details, see Harsanyi, 1981,
Part II, pp.3-11.]

Formally, our solution theory uses these probabilistic
considerations in choosing between any given pair of
equilibrium points. More exactly, we first choose a specific
subset of all perfect equilibrium points (according to
criteria I cannot discuss here) and call it the set of
primitive equilibrium points. In many games, including most
bargaining games, the set of primitive equilibrium points
will coincide with the set of strong equilibrium points; and
the latter in turn will coincide with the set of all pure-
strategy perfect equilibrium points.

Except for some rather special cases, our theory will
select one of these primitive equilibrium points as the
solution. The selection process itself will be based on
pairwise comparisons between such primitive equilibrium points.

Thus, we will always ask the question: If our choice were
restricted to two primitive equilibrium points, say, to q^1
and q^2, which of these two would be the preferable solution
for the game? Expressed in our terminology, which (if either)
of these two equilibrium points will dominate the other?

Dominance, in turn, is defined in terms of two concepts, called payoff-dominance and risk-dominance. We say that equilibrium point q^j payoff-dominates equilibrium point $q^k(j,k = 1,2$ and $j \neq k)$ if it yields every player a strictly higher payoff, i.e., if

$$H_i(q^j) > H_i(q^k) \text{ for every player i.} \tag{3}$$

(Thus, payoff-dominance is the same thing as strong Pareto superiority.)

On the other hand, the concept of risk-dominance is meant to formalize the intuitive idea that one equilibrium point is preferable over the other because it represents the player's best response, in some appropriate sense, to the risks they are facing in trying to choose between these two equilibrium points.

At a more formal level, we proceed as follows: The hypothetical situation where the players feel sure that the outcome will be either q^1 or q^2 but are unsure which of these it will actually be, will be called a situation of q^1/q^2 uncertainty.

We assume that in this situation each player h will formulate his expectations about the behavior of any other player i ($i \neq h$) by assigning a subjective probability distribution p_i to the set ϕ_i of all pure strategies ϕ_i available to player i. Our theory provides an algebraic formula for computing this subjective probability distribution (subjective probability vector) numerically from the payoff functions and the strategy sets of the game. Since this algebraic formula is the same for all players $h \neq i$, all these players h are assumed to use the same probability distribution p_i to formulate their probabilistic expectations about player i's behavior. For convenient reference, we call this probability vector p_i the bicentric prior probability distribution for player i, generated by the two equilibrium points q^1 and q^2. (The term bicentric refers to the fact that it is generated by these two equilibrium points.)

Of course, our theory defines such a bicentric prior p_i for every player i. If we put them together, we obtain the n-tuple

$$p = (p_1,\ldots,p_n), \tag{4}$$

called the bicentric prior combination p, summarizing the n players' mutual expectations about one another's behavior.

On the other hand, if we omit the one prior p_i from this n-tuple p, we obtain the (n-1)-tuple.

$$p_{-i} = (p_1,\ldots,p_{i-1}, p_{i+1},\ldots,p_n), \tag{5}$$

which is called an i-incomplete bicentric prior combination. This vector p_{-i} will be assumed to summarize player i's probabilisitc expectations about the other (n-1) players' likely behavior.

Now, two cases are possible.

(A) It may happen that all n incomplete prior combinations $p_{-1}, p_{-2},\ldots,p_{-n}$ have unique best replies $q_1^0, q_q^0,\ldots,q_n^0$, and these best-reply strategies form an equilibrium point $q^0 = (q_1^0,\ldots,q_n^0)$ of the game.

(B) The conditions stated under (A) fail to be fully satisfied.

In case (A), we will say that the equilibrium point q^0 just defined represents the players' best response to the assumed situation of q^1/q^2 uncertainty. Accordingly:

(A_1) If $q^0 = q^1$, then we will say that q^1, being the players' best reponse to the assumed uncertainty situation, risk-dominates q^2.

(A_2) If $q^0 = q^2$, then we will say, by similar reasoning, that q^2 risk-dominates q^1.

(A_3) If $q^0 \neq q^1$ and $\neq q^2$, then we will say that neither of the two equilibrium points q^1 and q^2 risk-dominates the other.

In case (B), it will not be immediately clear what the players' best response should be to the assumed situation of q^1/q^2 uncertainty. Intuitively, this will represent a situation where the original uncertainty could not be resolved as yet by the preliminary analysis so far undertaken.

In such situations, our theory uses the tracing procedure [see Harsanyi, 1975], which is meant to model a reasoning process by which the players' expectations will converge to a specific equilibrium point if originally these players had non-equilibrium expectations about each other's behavior, represented by any arbitrary n-tuple $p = (p_1,\ldots,p_n)$, where each $p_i (i = 1,\ldots,n)$ is an arbitrary subjective probability distribution over the pure strategies of one particular player i, expressing the other players' probabilistic expectations about this player i's likely behavior.

Let me denote the <u>outcome</u> of this tracing procedure,
if applied to the bicentric prior combination $p = (p_1,\ldots,p_n)$,
as $q^{00} = T(p)$. Given our intuitive interpretation of the
tracing procedure, this equilibrium point q^{00}, which is the
outcome of the tracing procedure, can be regarded as the
players' "generalized" <u>best response</u> to the assumed situation
of q^1/q^2 uncertainty. Accordingly, in case (B) we define
risk-dominance as follows:

(B_1) If $q^{00} = q^1$, then q^1 <u>risk-dominates</u> q^2.

(B_2) If $q^{00} = q^2$, then q^2 <u>risk-dominates</u> q^1.

(B_3) If $q^{00} \neq q^1$ and $\neq q^2$, then <u>neither</u> of these two
equilibrium points risk-dominates the other. Note that
mathematically our definitions in case (A) are special cases
of those in case (B).

We are now in a position to define the concept of
dominance as follows: Equilibrium point q^j <u>dominates</u>
equilibrium point $q^k (j,k = 1,2$ and $j \neq k)$ if

(i) q^j <u>payoff-dominates</u> q^k; or if

(ii) neither equilibrium point payoff-dominates the
other, but q^j does <u>risk-dominate</u> q^k.

Thus, payoff-dominance is given precedence over risk-
dominance: the latter counts only if payoff-dominance is
absent. Our reasoning is that if one equilibrium point payoff-
dominates the other, none of the players will press for
acceptance of this latter equilibrium point. Consequently,
there will be <u>no risk</u> for the players in moving to the payoff-
dominating equilibrium point, and any risk-dominance
relationship that may formally exist can safely be disregarded.

In many games, there is <u>one</u> primitive equilibrium point
dominating <u>all</u> other primitive equilibrium points. If this
is the case, this equilibrium point will be selected by our
theory as the <u>solution</u>.

If there is no such globally dominating equilibrium
point, the situation will be more complicated; and, for lack
of space, I will not here describe the construction procedure
our theory uses in such cases to select a solution for the
game. [But see Harsanyi, 1981, for a partial description of
this construction procedure.]

5. CONCLUSION

I have argued that the distinction between <u>subjective</u> and
<u>objective</u> probabilities and, therefore, between <u>risk</u> and

uncertainty is a valid distinction. I have discussed two
uses of subjective probabilities in game theory: their use
in analyzing games with incomplete information, and their
use in our solution theory. In the latter case, they are
used to define risk-dominance relationships between primitive
equilibrium points. I have argued that their use in this
context is merely a formalization of the probabilistic
arguments we all use at a common-sense level in thinking
about strategical problems in real-life game situations.

APPENDIX

A NOTE ON RISK TAKING AND ON VON NEUMAN-MORGENSTERN UTILITIES

In the second edition of their famous book, Theory of Games
and Economic Behavior, von Neumann and Morgenstern [1947]
have shown that, if any given decision-maker's preferences
among lotteries satisfy certain rationality axioms, we can
always construct for him or for her a utility function U
possessing the expected-utility property. That is, let

$$L = (A,p; B,1-p) \qquad\qquad\qquad (*)$$

denote a lottery yielding prize A with probability p and
yielding prize B with probability 1-p. Then the utility
of this lottery to the decision-maker will be

$$U(L) = pU(A) + (1-p)U(B). \qquad\qquad\qquad (**)$$

A utility function U possessing this expected-utility
property is often called a von Neumann-Morgenstern (vNM)
utility function.
    Of course, operationally such a utility function will
be defined in terms of the decision-maker's perferences among
lotteries and, therefore, can be said to express his or her
attitude toward risk taking: the more concave this utility
function (i.e., the stronger its tendency toward decreasing
marginal utility for money), the stronger his or her risk
aversion; and the more convex this utility function (i.e.,
the stronger its tendency toward increasing marginal utility),
the stronger his or her risk preference.
    Yet, people's attitudes toward risk are themselves in
need of explanation. In principle, this explanation could
lie either in the outcome utilities or in the process
utilities of risk-taking behaviour (or in both).

By outcome utilities, I mean the utilities and disutilities the decision-maker expects to derive from the outcomes -- i.e., from the gains and the losses -- that may arise from his risk-taking behavior.   For example, suppose that a given lottery ticket provides a 1/1,000 probability of winning $2,000, which gives it the actuarial value of $2. Nevertheless, some people may be willing to pay as much as (say) $10 for this lottery ticket.   The explanation may be that they assign a very high utility (a very high relative importance) to winning $2,000 (e.g., because this money would buy them a badly needed car), whereas they assign a very low disutility (a very low relative importance) to losing the $10 they pay for the lottery ticket (because this loss would not significantly lower their standard of living).

In contrast, by process utilities I mean all the psychological utilities and disutilities associated with the act of gambling itself -- such as those derived from the nervous tension and the excitement produced by gambling; those derived from the feelings of pleasure and of self-satisfaction if one wins and from the feelings of disappointment and of self-reproach if one loses; etc.

Even though risk-taking behavior in the real world in many cases will involve both types of utilities, it is clear from von Neumann and Morgenstern's own words [op.cit., p.28] that their theory is meant to abstract from all process utilities (which they call the "specific utility of gambling") and is meant to apply only to situations where these process utilities are unimportant.   In fact, it is only in such situations that the vNM axioms represent acceptable rationality requirements.   (In particular, whenever process utilities are important, their compound-lottery axiom and their independence axiom lose their plausibility.)

Accordingly, as I have argued elsewhere [Harsanyi, 1978], the von Neumann-Morgensterm theory (and Bayesian decision theory in general) must be restricted to situations where the decision-maker is under a moral obligation, or is under a prudential requirement, to take a purely result-oriented attitude, paying attention only to outcome utilities and disregarding all process utilities.   For example, it is natural to expect a business executive to do his very best to achieve optimal results for his shareholders, rather than worry about his own psychological costs and benefits during the decision-making process.   Likewise, a political leader is expected to do his very best to achieve optimal results for his constituents rather than be preoccupied with his own

personal process utilities, etc. In contrast, when people
gamble for entertainment in a casino, we cannot expect them
to obey the vNM axioms or to be guided by the criterion of
maximizing the expected values of their vNM utility functions.

Thus, we reach the conclusion that, in those situations
where vNM utility functions are applicable at all, these
utility functions are restricted to expressing the decision-
makers' outcome utilities and have nothing to do with their
process utilities and, therefore, have nothing to do with
their like or dislike for gambling as such.

This means that, contrary to prevailing opinion, if,
e.g., a given person has a highly convex vNM utility function
and, therefore, shows a high willingness to take risks, this
is not due to his liking for gambling per se. Rather, it is
due to the fact that his or her utilities for the prizes he
or she might win are relatively large as compared with his or
her disutilities for the losses he or she might suffer. In
other words, it is due to the mathematical structure of his
utilities and disutilities, i.e., to the mathematical form
of his or her vNM utility function. Thus, in ultimate
analysis, a person's attitude toward risk is determined by
his von Neumann-Morgenstern utility function, and not the
other way around.

Yet, if a person's attitude toward risk taking is
explained by his vNM utility function, how can we explain
the mathematical form of this utility function itself? The
answer is that, as long as we lack a full-fledged analytical
theory of utility functions, we cannot provide more than a
very partial explanation. But a partial explanation we can
provide in terms of the concepts of substitute and of
complementary commodities.

The greater the importance of substitution relationships
among the commodities consumed by a given individual, the
stronger tendency his or her vNM utility function will show
toward decreasing marginal utility for money; and the greater
the importance of complementarities among these commodities,
the stronger the tendency it will show toward increasing
marginal utility. Since most commodities are mild
substitutes for each other, most individuals' vNM utility
functions will display decreasing marginal utility at most
income levels. But it is quite possible that, over some
limited ranges of income, complementarities will become
sufficiently important to generate regions of increasing
marginal utility. (The consumer of our example was induced
to gamble at unfavorable odds, i.e., to display increasing

marginal utility for money, because he wanted to buy a car,
i.e., because of his interest in a large and indivisible
commodity. But note that, from a mathematical point of view,
indivisibilities can be regarded as special cases of
complementarities.)

                    University of California, Berkeley

NOTE

1. The author wants to express his thanks to the National
   Science Foundation for supporting this research through
   grant SES77-06394-A02 to the University of California,
   Berkeley, administered by the Center for Research in
   Management.

REFERENCES

Anscombe, F.J. and R.J. Aumann: 1963, 'A Definition of
   Subjective Probability', Annals of Mathematical Statistics
   34, 199-205.
de Finetti, B.: 1937, 'La prévision: ses lois logiques, ses
   sources subjectives', Annals de l'Institut Henri Poincaré 7,
   1-68.
Engelbrecht-Wiggans, R.: 1980, 'Auctions and Bidding: A
   Survey', Management Science 26, 119-142.
Harsanyi, J.C.: 1967-68, 'Games with Incomplete Information
   Played by "Bayesian" Players', Parts I-III, Management
   Science 14, 159-182, 320-334 and 486-502.
_____: 1975, 'The Tracing Procedure', International
   Journal of Game Theory 4, 61-94.
_____: 1977, Rational Behavior and Bargaining
   Equilibrium in Games and Social Situations, Cambridge
   University Press, Cambridge, England.
_____: 1978, 'Bayesian Decision Theory and
   Utilitarian Ethics', American Economic Review 68, 223-228.
_____: 1981, 'Solution for Some Bargaining Games
   Under the Harsanyi-Selten Solution Theory', Parts I-II,
   Working Papers CP-431 and 432, Center for Research in
   Management, University of California, Berkeley, California
   94720, U.S.A.
Luce, R.D. and H. Raiffa: 1957, Games and Decisions, Wiley,
   New York.
Nash, J.F.: 1951, 'Non-cooerative Games', Annals of
   Mathematics 54, 286-295.

Ramsey, F.P.: 1931, The Foundations of Mathematics and Other
    Logical Essays, Kegan Paul, London.
Savage, L.J.: 1954, The Foundations of Statistics, Wiley,
    New York.
Selten, R.: 1975, 'Reexamination of the Perfectness Concept
    for Equilibrium Points in Extensive Games', International
    Journal of Game Theory 4, 25-55.
von Neumann, J. and O. Morgenstern: first edition 1944,
    second edition 1947, Theory of Games and Economic Behavior,
    Princeton University Press, Princeton, N.J..

Knut Midgaard

BARGAINING AND RATIONALITY:
A DISCUSSION OF ZEUTHEN'S PRINCIPLE AND
SOME OTHER DECISION RULES

1. INTRODUCTION

Rational bargainers will, unless context gives rise to
special considerations, aim at an agreement which is better
to both or all parties than no agreement, and Pareto-
optimal. For quite long, economists generally held the
view that within the set of possible agreements indicated
above, which we shall call the negotiation set, the solution is indeterminate. In his book Problems of Monopoly
and Economic Warfare, however, which appeared in 1930,
Frederik Zeuthen argued that the fundamental tendency will
be that a party who is known to be less willing to risk
conflict than his opponent (or equally willing), must yield
or make a concession. (See Zeuthen, 1975, pp. 145 ff.)
    Zeuthen's principle has gained a central place in bar-
gaining theory. Different objections have been raised,
however. Thomas C. Schelling's theory, presented in The
Strategy of Conflict (1960), forms an interesting contrast.
Schelling, in addition to emphasizing the significance of
commitments, points out that a successful coordination of
expectations and choices is necessary to avoid breakdown
in bargaining; and he emphasizes that widely different factors, such as precedents, qualitative limits, etc., may
contribute to giving one particular possible outcome the
prominence or uniqueness which makes it the focal point of
the coordination process.
    In the view of the present author, Schelling's point
is an important one. On the other hand, in remarking, "One
has to have a reason for standing firmly on a position,"
Schelling (1960, p. 70) has himself given us a reason for
asking whether there might exist kinds of reasons that are
good, or have weight, across all kinds of bargaining situations, or at least within a wide class of bargaining
situations.
    Zeuthen's principle, it seems, deserves special atten-

B. P. Stigum and F. Wenstøp (eds.), Foundations of Utility and Risk Theory with Applications,
311–325.

tion in this connection. Intuitively, a bargainer seems to
give a good or strong reason for not yielding if he says,
"I choose to insist on my demand, expecting my opponent to
yield, because we both know that I am willing to run a higher
risk of conflict than he does." However, as soon as we try
to explain why this is a good reason, problems arise.

   In the present paper a few words will be said about
Zeuthen's justification of the principle later to be called
by his name, and about related lines of thought. Our discussion will first of all, however, take John C. Harsanyi's
rationality postulates, formulated in his book Rational Behavior and Bargaining Equilibrium in Games and Social Situations (1977), as its points of departure. I conclude that
these postulates narrow down the set of acceptable or relevant 'clues' or 'decision rules' in an interesting way. Contrary to Harsanyi's claim, however, I find that there are
also other decision rules than Zeuthen's which, in the classes of simple bargaining games specified by Harsanyi, meet
Harsanyi's postulates.

   I have been made aware that Harsanyi and Reinhard Selten are working on a theory which will supersede the one
presented in Harsanyi's book. The postulates of rational
behaviour and rational expectations will here be given more
precise formulations. It is impossible for me to judge
whether my objections to the present version of the theory
will apply to the more precise version. The considerations
elicited by the present version, however, do not necessarily
lose their interest if that is not the case. The present
version of the theory seems to be a fruitful point of departure within a broader approach to bargaining, where different
game rules and different assumptions concerning the players'
rationality are taken into account. Being a political scientist, I find that both empirical research and studies with a
practical purpose require that a wide range of such possibilities be taken into account.

   The significance of empirical relevance may justify an
example from real-life bargaining before we engage in rather
abstract discussions. As the prospects associated with the
different possible outcomes, in particular that of breakdown,
are central inputs in the decision rules to be discussed,
the following quotation from an earlier study (Midgaard,
1976, pp. 131 f.) might be of interest.

      After the four-power whaling conference between Japan,
      Holland, Norway and the United Kingdom in London in
      February 1961, which broke down because Holland insisted
      upon a quota of 7 per cent while the other countries

would not agree to giving her more than 6 per cent,
Norway sent a note to the Dutch government saying that
6 per cent ought to be enough for Holland as she had
only one expedition and the average per expedition for
the other countries was 4.35 per cent. In its reply to
this note, the Dutch government made three points.
  (i) The Netherlands could not accept a quota of 6 per
cent because the Dutch whaling industry, with its one
expedition, could not, in case of a reduced global
quota, maintain a reasonable profitability by reducing
the number of expeditions.
  (ii) The Dutch government was prepared to contribute
to the bridging of the gap of one per cent still remaining.
  (iii) 'A failure of the Vancouver meeting (to be held
shortly after) would have grave and far-reaching consequences, certainly for the Netherlands but particularly
for those countries that were to an even greater extent
interested in whaling in Antarctica.'

2. ZEUTHEN'S ANALYSIS

It is not possible, within the frame of this paper, to carry
out a detailed analysis of Zeuthen's discussion. It should
be pointed out, however, that Zeuthen explained the significance of the parties' risk-willingness by referring to the
importance of threats or commitments in bargaining. More
specifically, he pointed out that it may prove difficult or
impossible for the leadership of an organization to back down
from its commitment to a certain bargaining position because
the reactions of the common members of the organization would
make backing down a very bad alternative (Zeuthen, 1975,
pp. 146-153). The possibility of such a situation gives
rise to the following line of reasoning:
  Suppose an escalation of public threats or commitments
takes place. Then the risk that one will not be able to
yield or make a concession even if one wants to, will sooner
or later pass one's critical risk, i.e. the risk of conflict
that one is willing to accept. If the situation is symmetric in all other respects, the critical risk of the party
with the lower risk-willingness will be passed first. Fore-
seeing this, this party should therefore yield or make a
concession right at the outset, before any escalation of
threats has taken place. He has no reason to expect the
other party to back down before him.

The basic premiss in this line of reasoning, suggested
by Zeuthen's comments, seems to be the <u>principle of suffici-</u>
<u>ent reason</u>. The party with the lower risk-willingness should
yield or make a concession, because he has no reason to believe that his opponent should do so first. It is not until
this has been accepted that the party's expected utility of
yielding or making a concession will be higher than that of
insisting on his demand.

Threat escalation – or, the foreseen possibility of it
– is not the only kind of dynamics that may prompt behaviour
according to Zeuthen's principle. Thus, the increasing
likelihood that communication will not be sufficiently effective as deadline comes close, may also make risk-willingness the decisive factor.

The intuitive appeal of Zeuthen's principle seems, to
a large degree, to be due to a more or less clear recognition
of specific kinds of processes such as those suggested above.
Further inquiries are necessary, however, to tell whether
the conditions for bargaining behaviour according to Zeuthen's
principle – or according to other well-defined decision
rules – can be delimited in a clear and transparent way. In
order to better come to grips with this question we have to
consider Harsanyi's bargaining theory.

3. HARSANYI'S ANALYSIS

3.1. Bilateral restricted bargaining

Harsanyi distinguishes between what he calls 'ultimatum
games' and what he calls 'bargaining games'. He argues that
a rational player, before a bargaining game takes place, can
in a credible way commit himself to ignoring any commitment
(of the ultimatum type) during the bargaining process (Harsanyi, 1977, p. 187). In a study of rational bargaining,
one can therefore limit oneself to games where commitments
are assumed not to be made. Our discussion will, more specifically, be limited to Harsanyi's analysis of 'simple'
bargaining games, i.e. bargaining games where "the players
have essentially only one conflict strategy, viz., simple
non-cooperation" (Harsanyi, 1977, p. 141).

The concept of decision rule plays a central part in
Harsanyi's analysis. The question to be answered is which
decision rules might be consistent with rationality.

Harsanyi's analysis is characterized by a specification
of the rules of the bargaining game and by a specification

of rationality postulates that a decision rule has to meet.

The rules of the bargaining game formulated by Harsanyi implies the following for restricted bargaining: The players move simultaneously. In the first move, player 1 proposes A_1 and player 2 proposes A_2. In the second move, either has the choice between insisting on his own proposal (α) and accepting that of his opponent (β). If both insist, there will be conflict, C, i.e. no agreement. If one player insists while the other yields, the outcome will be the one proposed by the former. If both players express willingness to concede, then player 1 will obtain $U_1(A_2)$, i.e. the value to him of player 2's proposal, and player 2 will obtain $U_2(A_1)$.

The essence of Harsanyi's rationality postulates can be summarized in the following way.

There are eight postulates: first, five postulates A1 – A5 of rational behaviour for game situations and, second, three postulates B1 – B3 of rational expectations. Two postulates, A3 and B3, are crucial in Harsanyi's discussion of the bargaining game. The former reads as follows (Harsanyi, 1977, pp. 116 and 153 f.):

A3. <u>Subjective-best-reply postulate (Bayesian expected-utility maximization postulate)</u>. In a bargaining game $B(G)$ associated with a game G profitable to you, as far as your binding agreements with other players allow, always use a bargaining strategy β_i representing your <u>subjective</u> best reply to the mean bargaining-strategy combination β^i that you expect the other player to use.

It should be noted here that a player's mean bargaining-strategy combination in bilateral bargaining is the mixed strategy that corresponds to his opponent's subjective probabilities associated with the first player's pure bargaining strategies.

Postulate B3 reads as follows (Harsanyi, 1977, pp. 118 and 154):

B3. <u>Expected-independence-of-irrelevant-variables postulate</u>. You cannot expect a rational opponent to make his bargaining strategy β_j dependent on variables whose <u>relevance</u> for bargaining behaviour <u>cannot be established</u> on the basis of the present rationality postulates.

Harsanyi explains that the purpose of postulate B3, which may for short be called the 'relevance postulate,' is "to exclude some completely arbitrary decision rules, e.g. making the players' payoffs proportional to their telephone number" (Harsanyi, 1977, p. 118) or "to the logarithm of

their waist measurements, and so forth" (ibid., p. 160).
Excluding such possibilities, the relevance postulate certainly reduces the set of pertinent clues or decision rules
in an interesting way. The question is exactly which set is
left. Before going into Harsanyi's argument, I would like
to suggest three types of rules which in my opinion would
satisfy Harsanyi's relevance postulate, as formulated in his
book:

first, decision rules based only on the values of utility associated with the possible outcomes of the bargaining
game;

second, decision rules based on objectively measurable
quantities which occur as inputs to the utility functions,
the typical example being monetary values;

third, decision rules that include a first-order criterion of one of these kinds and a second-order criterion
of some other kind, the second-order criterion being relevant where two possible agreements are equally strong candi-
dates according to the first-order criterion.

Zeuthen's principle is of the first type because, as
we shall shortly see, a party's risk-willingness is a function of his values of utility only. Why does Harsanyi conclude that this is the only decision rule that satisfies his
relevance postulate?

In his analysis Harsanyi introduces the subjective probability p_{ji}, which is player i's assessment of the likelihood that player j will insist on his proposal A_j, besides
player i's critical risk r_i, i.e. the maximal p_{ji}^j for which
i is willing to insist on his proposal A_i. Using this
notation he states the following conditions - (8.4) and
(8.5) - for rational behaviour in the restricted bargaining
game (Harsanyi, 1977, pp. 150 f.):

... if player i wants to maximize his expected utility,
then he can choose alternative α, i.e. he can stand on
his last offer A_i, only if

$$(1 - p_{ji}) \cdot U_i(A_i) + p_{ji} \cdot U_i(C) \gtreqqless U_i(A_j) \qquad (8.4)$$

that is, if

$$p_{ji} \lesseqgtr r_i = \frac{U_i(A_i) - U_i(A_j)}{U_i(A_i) - U_i(C)} \qquad (8.5)$$

Zeuthen's principle can be formulated in these terms:
Player i will insist on his proposal A_i if, and only if,
$r_i > r_j$.

Now, in Harsanyi's argument the formulation of a specific form of postulate B3 plays a central role (Harsanyi,
1977, p. 155):

B3*. Expected-independence-of-irrelevant-variables
postulate - specific form. In restricted two-person
bargaining, we cannot expect a rational opponent to make
his choice between alternatives α and β dependent on any
other variables than the four quantities r_1, r_2, p_{12},
and p_{21}.

Postulate B3* is justified in this way (Harsanyi, 1977,
p. 154):

We have already seen that if player i is a Bayesian
expected-utility maximizer - i.e., if he follows our
Postulate A3 - then he can choose alternative α only if
Condition (8.4) is satisfied. This means that his bargaining behavior will depend only on the quantity r_i
and on the subjective probability p_{ji}. Thus player 1's
behavior will depend on r_1 and on p_{21}^{ji}, while player 2's
behavior will depend on r_2 and on p_{12}. In other words,
Postulate A3 makes these four variables relevant for
the two players' bargaining behavior. Careful reading
of our rationality postulates will show that none of
our postulates establish the relevance of any other
variables.

Suppose, for a moment, that we accept Postulate B3*.
Then we must accept Harsanyi's conclusion: that Zeuthen's
principle is the only decision rule which meets the rationality postulates submitted by Harsanyi. There seems to be
no flaw in the mathematical deduction of this result. A
central question therefore is whether B3* follows from the
other postulates.

My discussion of Harsanyi's claim that B3* follows from
the other postulates, and his claim that only Zeuthen's principle meets these postulates, will be linked to a discussion
of a decision rule which, in my view, is as plausible as
Zeuthen's principle. This decision rule, which I shall call
the gain/loss rule, reads as follows:

If a party in bilateral bargaining is known to have
less to gain than his opponent, as compared to what he
can lose, by insisting on his own proposal, then he must
yield or make a concession.

In order to be able to discuss this decision rule in a
satisfactory way, the rule must be made more precise on two
points:

First, what a party can gain from insisting on his own

proposal is the value difference to him between this proposal
and the kind of compromise that will result from both expressing willingness to yield; in restricted bargaining we may
assume that the compromise consists in a lottery with equal
chance for A_1 and A_2 (cf. Ståhl, 1972, p. 235).

Second, what a party can lose is the value difference
to him between his opponent's proposal and no agreement.

Now, two interesting variants of the gain/loss rule can
be distinguished (cf. the types of decision rules introduced
earlier):

first, a variant where gains and losses are measured in
von Neumann-Morgenstern values of utility;

second, a variant where gains and losses are measured
in objectively measurable quantities that occur as inputs to
the players' utility functions, the typical example being
monetary values.

Suppose, now, that two players who are known to act
according to the same variant of the gain/loss rule, succeed
in arriving at an agreement on this basis. Then their behaviour satisfies postulate A3, Subjective-best-reply-postu-
late, and, more specifically., Condition (8.4). Moreover,
their behaviour is based on variables which are clearly
relevant for Bayesian expected-utility maximizers. Altogether, both variants of the gain/loss rule seem to satisfy
Harsanyi's rationality postulates A1 – A5 and B1 – B3. We
have therefore shown, it might seem, that players who satisfy
rationality postulates A1 – A5 and B1 – B3 need not behave
in accordance with Zeuthen's principle.

The question arises, however, whether the gain/loss rule
yields the same behaviour and outcome as Zeuthen's principle.
If this is the case the players can be said to act in accordance with Zeuthen's principle even if critical risks play no
role in their considerations.

Let us first consider the variant where gains and losses
are measured in values of utility.

If the ratio between the possible gain and the possible
loss for player i is denoted by q_i' we get:

$$q_i' = \frac{U_i(A_i) - \frac{1}{2}(U_i(A_i) + U_i(A_j))}{U_i(A_j) - U_i(C)}$$

It is more convenient to introduce a parameter $q_i = 2q_i'$.
After some rearrangement we get:

$$q_i = \frac{U_i(A_i) - U_i(A_j)}{U_i(A_j) - U_i(C)}$$

According to the gain/loss rule, then, player i must yield (or make a concession) to his opponent j if $q_i < q_j$ (or: $q_i \leqq q_j$). Which outcome will this decision rule lead to?

Harsanyi has shown that according to Zeuthen's principle player i must yield (or make a concession) if the Nash product $(U_i(A_i)-U_i(C)) \cdot (U_j(A_i)-U_j(C))$ associated with his proposal A_i is smaller than, or equal to, the Nash product associated with his opponent j's proposal A_j; from this follows that the players will end up in the Nash solution, i.e. the outcome which maximizes the Nash product. It is easily seen that for the decision rule associated with the fractions q_i and q_j the same condition holds; so, the players will end up in the Nash solution under this decision rule, too.

We must therefore conclude that players who act on the first variant of the gain/loss rule, where gains and losses are measured in values of utility, can be said to act in accordance with Zeuthen's principle. It is obvious, however, that the same does not generally hold true for the second variant of the gain/loss rule, where gains and losses are measured in objectively measurable quantities which occur as inputs in the players' utility functions, e.g. monetary values. As utility functions are not generally linear in such quantities, there will be cases, perhaps many, where bargaining according to this variant of the gain/loss rule will lead to a behaviour and an outcome which are not in accordance with Zeuthen's principle. This implies, as a secondary point, that the specific form B3* of Harsanyi's relevance postulate does not follow from the other rationality postulates.

A final note should be made on the gain/loss rule. It can be reformulated in the following way:

If a party in bilateral bargaining is known to make a smaller relative sacrifice than his opponent by yielding, i.e. make a smaller sacrifice as compared to the possible loss associated with insisting on his proposal, then he must yield or make a concession.

This variant of the decision rule could be called the relative sacrifice rule. It should be noted that the two variants need not be equivalent in real-life bargaining cf. Kahneman and Tversky, 1979).

3.2. Bilateral non-restricted bargaining

Both Zeuthen and Harsanyi move quite swiftly from their conclusion as to what constitutes rational behaviour in restricted bargaining, to their conclusion on rationality in non-
restricted bargaining.

Harsanyi (1977, p. 158) presents the following argument:

> ... let us assume that the two players' last offers A_1
> and A_2 have been such that $r_1 > r_2$. Then it still will
> be true that, <u>as long as neither player makes a new of-</u>
> <u>fer</u>, our rationality postulates will require player 2 to
> make a concession, accepting player 1's last offer in
> full. But now player 2 can avoid this extreme move by
> making a new offer A_2', representing a concession going
> beyond player 2's last offer A_2, yet falling short of
> full acceptance of player 1's last offer A_1. Because
> player 2 will prefer making a small concession rather
> than making a large one, making such a new offer A_2'
> will be the rational thing for him to do.

Harsanyi is obviously right in pointing out that making a
full concession is not rational as long as there is a possibility of making a smaller concession. It is not immediately
obvious, however, that players who meet Harsanyi's rationality postulates will act upon Zeuthen's principle in cases
where they approach each other through a sequence of unilateral concessions. They may of course act upon the gain/
loss rule (relative sacrifice rule). They might also base
themselves on what I shall call the <u>minimal concession rule</u>:

> If a party by making a minimal concession will make a
> smaller relative sacrifice than the other party, or
> parties, would do by making a minimal concession, then
> the former shall make a minimal concession.

It can be objected that within a given description of a
simple bargaining game there may be nothing that tells us
what a minimal concession would be. If the payoff vectors
associated with the possible agreements are assumed to form
a convex set, there could be nothing of the kind: one would
have to add a more or less precise convention as to what
should be considered the least <u>acceptable</u> concession. In
the case of a discrete set of potential bargaining outcomes,
however, the concept of minimal concession is meaningful.
In many real-life cases the set of alternatives will indeed
be rather limited.

If values are measured in von Neumann-Morgenstern utilities the minimal concession will under reasonable assumptions yield the same outcome as Zeuthen's principle.

The decision rules dealt with so far all presuppose a sequence of unilateral concessions. The notion of compromise, however, can help us see another possibility, viz., that of simultaneous concessions. We shall consider two decision rules which permit simultaneous concessions.

The equal relative sacrifice rule reads as follows:
That outcome shall be accepted as a compromise which is such that the relative sacrifice involved in moving from the best possible agreement in the negotiation set to this point, is the same for both or all parties.
The equal risk-willingness rule reads as follows:
That outcome shall be accepted as a compromise which is such that each party is equally willing to risk conflict when considering this outcome as a counter-proposal to that possible agreement in the negotiation set which he considers best.

Note that the term 'relative sacrifice' in the first definition means the value or utility loss involved in moving from the best element of the negotiation set to the compromise point, as compared to the value or utility loss involved in moving from the compromise point (or, alternatively, the best element of the negotiation set) to no agreement.

Harsanyi's relevance postulate is obviously met by the equal risk-willingness rule. Not only does this decision rule presuppose von Neumann-Morgenstern values of utility. It even exploits the notion of critical risks, just like Zeuthen's principle. The equal relative sacrifice rule can make choices dependent either on utility functions or on quantities which occur as inputs to utility functions. So, Harsanyi's relevance postulate is satisfied in both cases. It should be noted that the two compromise rules, due to the role played by the best element of the negotiation set, do not meet Nash's condition of independence of irrelevant alternatives (cf. Luce and Raiffa, 1958, p. 127).

Our two compromise rules will yield an outcome in cases where the alternatives form a convex set. In other cases an unambiguous measure of closeness to equality may be necessary. The equal relative sacrifice rule will of course yield different outcomes according to what measures of value are used. If von Neumann-Morgenstern values of utility are used the equal relative sacrifice rule will yield the same outcome as the equal risk-willingness rule. Normally, this will not be the Nash solution.

The two compromise rules are particularly but not exclusively relevant to situations where the players have committed themselves so strongly to their primary positions
that neither can make a unilateral concession. In this connection I will make the claim that such commitments, because
simultaneous concessions constitute a way out, are not incompatible with rationality in non-restricted bargaining.

We may now wonder whether these two rules are 'natural'
decision rules. Do they have an intuitive appeal similar to
that of Zeuthen's principle? To me the equal relative sacrifice rule has such an appeal, just like the gain/loss rule
(the relative sacrifice rule) and the minimal concession
rule. The equal risk-willingness principle is more proble-
matic in this respect.

3.3. Multilateral bargaining

Zeuthen limited his analysis to bilateral bargaining. Harsanyi, however, has adapted Zeuthen's principle to a subset
of multilateral negotiations, viz. simple bargaining games.
It should be noted that in such games the payoff vectors are
supposed to form a convex set.

Harsanyi's concept of a solution for n-person simple
bargaining games (Harsanyi, 1977, p. 196) is expressed in
the following passage:

> In a simple game G, a given payoff vector $u=\bar{u}$ will repre-
> sent the equilibrium outcome of bargaining among the n
> players only if no pair of players i and j has any in-
> centive to redistribute their payoffs between them as
> long as the other players' payoffs are kept constant.
> Thus we can define multilateral bargaining equilibrium
> among the n players by the requirement that there should
> be bilateral bargaining equilibrium between any two
> players i and j.

Having introduced this solution concept, Harsanyi proposes a way in which the multilateral bargaining equilibrium
can be reached. His point of departure is the idea of a
provisional agreement which the players have somehow arrived
at. If this provisional agreement is not identical with the
multilateral bargaining equilibrium, at least one (rational)
player will find that he can challenge another player, pro-
posing another payoff distribution between the two, the payoffs of the other players being kept constant. Suppose a
player i does so. If, according to the Zeuthen principle

for bilateral bargaining, he has a stronger position than the
player challenged, j, the latter must make a concession, and
the two players will end up in a bilateral bargaining equilibrium, viz. the point which maximizes their Nash product.
If the modified provisional agreement which is thereby arrived at is not identical with the multilateral bargaining
equilibrium, there will again be a player who can challenge
another player, and so on. For any such round of bilateral
bargaining the Nash product for all n players will increase,
or at least not decrease; and under appropriate procedural
rules the players will in the end arrive at the multilateral
bargaining equilibrium, which maximizes the Nash product for
all n players.

    Although Harsanyi's adaptation of Zeuthen's principle to
the n-person case corresponds to the two-person principle in
central respects, there are significant differences. First,
the n-person principle does not take as its point of departure the proposals submitted by the various players, determining who shall first make a concession, and so on; instead,
a jump is made to a provisional agreement, from where starts
a sequence of bilateral bargaining games in accordance with
some procedural rule. Second, while the two-person Zeuthen
principle works whenever there are at least two possible
agreements that are better to both players than conflict,
Harsanyi's n-person principle may fail to yield a result if
the set of payoff vectors is not convex.

    These limitations, of course, are due to the complexi-
ties of multilateral bargaining. They should be kept in mind,
however, when considering other possible decision rules. Let
us first consider the minimal concession rule.

    As was noted in Section 3.2, the notion of a minimal
concession is not a vacuous one. The set of possible agreements may very well be not only finite but rather limited,
and in the continuous case there may be a convention to the
effect that only concessions above a certain size are acceptable.

    The first point I would like to make is that the minimal
concession rule may be viewed as an equally natural adaptation of Zeuthen's principle to the multilateral case as Harsanyi's adaptation. It has the advantage that it requires
no jump to a provisional agreement. Instead, it indicates
a way in which the players may move smoothly from their original positions to an agreement.

    The problem is of course under what conditions players
will be able to reach an agreement through such a process of

convergence. The difficulties may indeed be great, or even
insurmountable (cf. Midgaard and Underdal, 1977). Shortcuts
may be possible, however, if the players are able to foresee
the outcome of the process.

On this point it should be recalled that the minimal
concession rule will under reasonable assumptions lead to the
Nash solution. Possibly, the players might act upon a combination of this decision rule and Harsanyi's adaptation of
Zeuthen's principle.

On the other hand, it does not go without saying that
this is a workable procedure. There may be a need for another
kind of rule for working out a compromise. In different contexts and for various reasons the equal relative sacrifice
rule or the equal risk-willingness rule may prove more effective in producing an acceptable solution. These decision
rules require relatively few calculations and relatively few
steps. As multilateral bargaining often requires a chairman
in order to prevent deadlock, the institutional framework is
likely to be such that a compromise can easily be put on the
table without any party thereby weakening its position.

4. CONCLUSION

Our discussion of Zeuthen's principle and other decision
rules has to a large extent taken place within the framework
established by Harsanyi in his theory of bargaining games.
Our comments on Zeuthen's own analysis, however, suggested
somewhat different frameworks, and in our discussion of
Harsanyi's analysis the significance of psychological factors
like framing and of institutional elements like the role of
a mediator or a chairman, was indicated.

It seems to be in line with Harsanyi's approach to proceed, in the analyses of negotiations, by systematically
inquiring into the consequences of different kinds of assumptions. The conditions of real-life negotiations should be
focused this way. More specifically, in the further discussion of Zeuthen's principle and decision rules like the gain/
loss rule (the relative sacrifice rule) and the equal relative sacrifice rule, the consequences of different kinds and
degrees of uncertainty related to their 'use' in real-life
negotiations, should be dealt with in a systematic manner.

Institute of Political Science
University of Oslo

ACKNOWLEDGEMENTS

I am indebted to Aanund Hylland for most valuable comments and advice during my work on this paper. Arild Underdal and Bjørn Erik Rasch have made useful comments on earlier versions. Comments by John C. Harsanyi, Kenneth J. Arrow and Reinhard Selten during the discussion at the conference were clarifying, and elicited further thinking about the topic of my paper. All remaining deficiencies are of course my own responsibility.

REFERENCES

Harsanyi, J.C.: 1977, Rational Behavior and Bargaining in Games and Social Situations, Cambridge University Press, Cambridge.

Kahneman, D. and A. Tversky: 1979, 'Prospect Theory: An Analysis of Decision Under Risk', Econometrica 47, 263-91.

Luce, R.D. and H. Raiffa: 1958, Games and Decisions: Introduction and Critical Survey, John Wiley, New York.

Midgaard, K.: 1976, 'Co-operative Negotiations and Bargaining: Some Notes on Power and Powerlessness', in B. Barry (ed.), Power and Political Theory: Some European Perspectives, John Wiley, London, 1976.

Midgaard, K. and A. Underdal: 1977, 'Multiparty Conferences', in D. Druckman (ed.), Negotiations: Social-Psychological Perspectives, Sage, Beverly Hills, pp. 329-345.

Schelling, T.C.: 1960, The Strategy of Conflict, Harvard University Press, Cambridge, Mass.

Ståhl, I.: 1972, Bargaining Theory, The Economic Research Institute at the Stockholm School of Economics, Stockholm.

Zeuthen, F.: 1975, 'Economic Warfare', in O.R. Young (ed.), Bargaining: Formal Theories of Negotiation, University of Illinois Press, Urbana, pp. 145-163. Reprinted from F. Zeuthen: 1930, Problems of Monopoly and Economic Warfare, Routledge and Kegan Paul, London.

PART VII

UTILITY AND RESOURCE ALLOCATION

Sten Thore

HOTELLING UTILITY FUNCTIONS

ABSTRACT

A class of utility functions is distinguished, tentatively
associated with the name of H. Hotelling. The definition
requires the marginal utility of income to be identically
equal to a constant. The class of utility functions which
satisfies this condition is not uniquely given. The nature
of the mathematical constraint which the definition imposes
on the utility function depends upon the way prices are being normalized.

If for instance there is a numeraire, the price of which
is put equal to unity, the indifference hypersurfaces must
be equiform to each other in the direction of the axis of
the numeraire. Again, if prices are so-called "real" prices,
(so that income equals unity) then the utility function must
be homothetic, etc.

Hotelling utility functions generate demand functions
which have an integrating factor equal to a constant. Given
the indirect demand functions, the Hotelling utility function
can therefore be written down right away by explicit integration of these functions. Hotelling functions would
therefore seem attractive for applied utility models.

1. Motivation

The present paper discusses a particular class of cardinal
utility functions, which is here tentatively associated with
the name of H. Hotelling [1,2].[1] They are defined as cardinal utility functions for which the marginal utility of
income is identically equal to a positive constant, say
unity.[2] Thus, writing a utility function $U(q_1, q_2, \ldots, q_n)$
(for the notation and the mathematical assumptions see the
formal presentation in Section 2), one has

$$U_1 / p_1 = U_2 / p_2 = \ldots = U_n / p_n \equiv 1 \qquad (1.1)$$

B. P. Stigum and F. Wenstøp (eds.), *Foundations of Utility and Risk Theory with Applications*,
329–346.
© 1983 *by D. Reidel Publishing Company.*

or, with common notation

$$\mu \equiv 1. \tag{1.2}$$

In a well-known paper from 1942 entitled "Constancy of the Marginal Utility of Income," [6] Samuelson set out to "examine ... exhaustively ... the rigorous implications of the constancy of the marginal utility of income."[3] The opening point of his analysis is the observation that the marginal utility of income is not invariant to a monotonic transformation of the utility index.

The present investigation is written under a slightly different perspective. The issues of cardinal versus ordinal utility, which were still inflaming the minds 40 years ago, should by now be settled. Instead, the economic profession has moved on to the practical empirical estimation of utility functions. Utility functions are needed in many areas of applied economic work, in particular in applied general equilibrium theory. This practical need may motivate the present reexamination.

The class of utility functions to be discussed here are attractive for applied work because these utility functions can be formed directly by explicit integration of the indirect demand functions $p_1 (q_1, q_2, ..., q_n)$, $p_2 (q_1, q_2, ..., q_n) ..., p_n (q_1, q_2, ..., q_n)$. These indirect demand functions have an <u>integrating factor equal to unity</u>. Samuelson's doctrine of revealed preference can then be effected empirically in the following manner: (i) estimate the indirect demand functions, (ii) integrate these functions and form the utility function.

Section 2 provides a formal definition of Hotelling utility functions. Section 3 gives some examples of Hotelling utility functions. The condition (1.2) imposes conditions on the mathematical form of $U (q_1, q_2, ..., q_n)$, but the precise nature of these conditions depends upon how prices are normalized. Different normalizations generate different mathematical forms for the utility function.

Section 4 presents the corresponding indirect utility functions. Both direct and indirect utility can be written as line integrals, and there is a simple relationship between the two which obtains as an application of integration by parts.

The Appendix reviews some work by Hotelling, Samuelson and Takayama and Judge.

2. Hotelling Utility Functions Defined

Let the index $j = 1, 2, \ldots, n$ represent an enumeration of all consumer goods. The quantities of these goods purchased by the consumers are represented by the vector $q \; \varepsilon \; R^n$. The (non-negative) vector of prices of these goods is denoted $p \; \varepsilon \; R^n$.

The indirect demand functions will be written $p\,(q)$.[4] They are defined on the positive orthant of q-space. These functions assign a set of demand prices to each point in their domain. Let these functions be given and known. Assume that they are single-valued; the normalization of prices will be treated later. Assume further that the indirect demand functions are positive and differentiable on their domain.

Assume that the matrix

$$\left[\frac{\partial p_j\,(q)}{\partial q_k}\right] \qquad\qquad j, k = 1, 2, \ldots, n \qquad\qquad (2.1)$$

is symmetric and negative semidefinite.

Define the Hotelling utility function[5]

$$U\,(q) = \int_L \sum_{j=1}^{n} p_j\,(a)\; da_j. \qquad\qquad (2.2)$$

The path of integration L is defined in the space R^n. The vector of integration is denoted a, and the path runs from some fixed initial point to the point $a = q$. The symmetry of the matrix (2.1) ensures that the line integral exists and is independent of its path. Further, $U\,(q)$ is a concave function; the Hessian is given by the matrix (2.1), which is negative semidefinite.

At this initial point of the argument, it is important to make the distinction between (i), the underlying (ordinal) utility index which would generate the indirect demand functions p (q) and (ii), the function (2.2) itself.

Theorem 1. The underlying utility index and the Hotelling utility function have the same indifference map. Hence, the one must be a monotonic transformation of the other.

For differentiation shows that

$$U_j = P_j (q)$$

and hence the slope element of an indifference curve of U (q) is

$$\left(\frac{dq_k}{dq_j}\right)_{U = const.} = \frac{U_j}{U_k} = \frac{P_j(q)}{P_k(q)}$$

which is identical to the slope element of an indifference curve of the underlying utility function.

Remembering Theorem 1, I shall from now on refer to U (q) simply as "the" utility function. It is a cardinal function.

The utility maximization problem of one consumer can then be written

$$\max \quad U (q) \tag{2.3}$$

subject to

$$q^T p \leq y$$

$$q > 0$$

where p is the vector of market prices and the scalar y is nominal income.

Theorem 2. The dual of the budget constraint (the "marginal utility of income"), say the scalar μ, equals unity.

To prove this, write down the Kuhn-Tucker conditions[6]

$$P_j (q) = \mu p_j \qquad\qquad j = 1, 2, \ldots, n.$$

In words, p_j (q) and p_j are proportional to each other. Further, since they must be normalized in the same manner, it follows that they must actually be equal. Hence $\mu = 1$.

Theorem 3.   Consider any well-defined differentiable cardinal utility function. If the dual of the budget constraint equals unity, then the utility function must be of the Hotelling form (2.2).

For any differentiable utility function can be written[7]

$$U(q) = \int \sum_{j=1}^{n} \frac{\partial U}{\partial q_j} \, dq_j$$

or, inserting $\dfrac{\partial U}{\partial q_j} = \mu p_j$

$$U(q) = \int \sum_{j=1}^{n} \mu(q) \, p_j(q) \, dq_j.$$

Putting $\mu(q) = 1$, this expression collapses into (2.2)

3.   Some Examples of Hotelling Utility Functions

The substantive content of the path independency condition depends upon the particular system of normalization of prices. Once the normalization has been specified, the mathematical constraints on the utility function are also laid down, and a particular class of utility functions emerges satisfying these constraints.

(i)   If one particular good is elected to serve as a numeraire, say the nth good with $p_n = 1$, then the indifference hypersurfaces in n dimensions must be equiform to each other in the direction of the axis of the numeraire. In other words, the entire indifference map can be generated by shifting one arbitrary indifference hypersurface parallel to itself in the direction of the axis of the numeraire.[8] (This result may be thought of as to reflect the "neutrality" of the numeraire.)

For consider the case of three consumer goods $j = 1, 2,$ 3. Let the indirect demand functions be $p_1(q)$, $p_2(q)$, $p_3 \equiv 1$.

The matrix (2.1) reads

$$
\begin{bmatrix}
\dfrac{\partial p_1}{\partial q_1} & \dfrac{\partial p_1}{\partial q_2} & \dfrac{\partial p_1}{\partial q_3} \\[2ex]
\dfrac{\partial p_2}{\partial q_1} & \dfrac{\partial p_2}{\partial q_2} & \dfrac{\partial p_2}{\partial q_3} \\[2ex]
0 & 0 & 0
\end{bmatrix}
\tag{3.1}
$$

and the path independency conditions require that

$$
\frac{\partial p_1}{\partial q_2} = \frac{\partial p_2}{\partial q_1}
\tag{3.2}
$$

$$
\frac{\partial p_1}{\partial q_3} = \frac{\partial p_2}{\partial q_3} = 0.
$$

The first of these two relations states the path independency condition for the n - 1 first variables. The second states the property which was to be demonstrated.

The conditions (3.2) are satisfied if the indirect demand functions are of the form

$$
p_1 (q) = p_1 (q_1, q_2)
\tag{3.3}
$$

$$
p_2 (q) = p_2 (q_1, q_2)
$$

$$
p_3 (q) = 1
$$

yielding the utility function

$$
U (q) = (\smallint\, p_1 (q_1, q_2)\, dq_1 + p_2 (q_1, q_2)\, dq_2) + q_3
\tag{3.4}
$$

The line integral can be recognized as the "quasi-welfare" of all consumer goods (except the numeraire). (The term was introduced by Takayama and Judge [7], for a discussion see the Appendix.) In words, the utility function equals "quasi-welfare" plus the holding of <u>numeraire</u>.

The formula (3.4) belongs to Samuelson.[9] But Samuelson also dismissed this case out of hand, noting that it implies that any increase in income is allocated entirely to increased holdings of the <u>numeraire</u>.[10] And he goes on to say: "It need hardly be said that all empirical budgetary studies show this hypothesis to be absurd."[11]

With some extension of notation, however, the same result may appear perfectly sensible. Let the consumer have a preference field which spans both consumer goods and primary resources such as labor. Let q be a vector with both positive and negative entries, where the demands for consumer goods are entered with a positive sign and the supplies of primary resources with a negative sign. The left hand side of the budget constraint $q^T p \leq y$ will then contain both positive terms (consumption expenditure) and negative terms (income obtained from primary resources sold). The symbol y may be identified with initial holdings of the <u>numeraire</u> (money).

The result which seemed so absurd to Samuelson then only states that any increase in initial holdings of money will be entirely absorbed in the financial portfolio of the consumer and will affect neither his demand for consumer goods nor his supply of resources. Neutral money.

(ii) If prices are so-called "real prices" measured in relation to nominal income, nominal income being held constant (e.g., Lau [5]), then the utility function must be homothetic.

This result seems to belong to Silberberg.[12] Its roots can be traced back to Samuelson.[13]

Silberberg's indicated proof essentially goes via the route of the corresponding direct demand functions. This means, however, that some mathematical generality is lost because the assumptions of the implicit function theorem must then be fulfilled so that the indirect demand functions can be inverted. An alternative proof is provided below, which does not require the existence of the direct demand functions.

For the purpose of the proof, it is sufficient to consider the case of just two consumer goods, $j = 1, 2$. Consider the indirect demand functions $p_1 (q)$ and $p_2 (q)$. The matrix (2.1) reads

$$
\begin{bmatrix}
\dfrac{\partial p_1}{\partial q_1} & \dfrac{\partial p_1}{\partial q_2} \\[2ex]
\dfrac{\partial p_2}{\partial q_1} & \dfrac{\partial p_2}{\partial q_2}
\end{bmatrix}
\tag{3.5}
$$

Path independency requires that

$$
\frac{\partial p_1}{\partial q_2} = \frac{\partial p_2}{\partial q_1} .
\tag{3.6}
$$

Normalize prices so that $p_1 q_1 + p_2 q_2 = 1$. After differentiating this relation, some manipulation shows that

$$
\frac{\partial (p_1 / p_2)}{\partial q_1} \, q_1 + \frac{\partial (p_1 / p_2)}{\partial q_2} \, q_2 = 0.
\tag{3.7}
$$

Using Euler's theorem, it follows that the relative price ratio p_1 / p_2 is a homogenous function of order zero in the variables q_1, q_2. The utility function must then be homothetic (cf Lau [5], Lemma 1).

(iii) Let us take a look at the case when prices are normalized so that they add up to unity, $\Sigma \, p_j = 1$.

The form of the utility function can then be found in the following manner. In the case of three goods, one must have

$$
\frac{U_1}{p_1} = \frac{U_2}{p_2} = \frac{U_3}{p_3} = \frac{U_1 + U_2 + U_3}{1} = 1
\tag{3.8}
$$

and the differential equation $U_1 + U_2 + U_3 = 1$ has the general solution

$$
U = q_1 + \phi(q_2 - q_1) + \psi(q_3 - q_1)
\tag{3.9}
$$

where ϕ and ψ are arbitrary differentiable functions.[14]

Differentiating (3.9) and inserting into (3.8) one finds the indirect demand functions

$$p_1(q) = 1 - \phi'(q_2 - q_1) - \psi'(q_3 - q_1) \qquad (3.10)$$

$$p_2(q) = \phi'(q_2 - q_1)$$

$$p_3(q) = \psi'(q_3 - q_1).$$

They add up to unity.

The matrix (2.1) reads

$$\begin{bmatrix} \phi'' + \psi'' & -\phi'' & -\psi'' \\ -\phi'' & \phi'' & 0 \\ -\psi'' & 0 & \psi'' \end{bmatrix} \qquad (3.11)$$

which is symmetric. Negative semidefiniteness requires

$$\phi'' + \psi'' \leq 0$$

$$\phi''(\phi'' + \psi'') - \phi''^2 \geq 0$$

$$\phi''\psi''(\phi'' + \psi'') - \phi''\psi''^2 - \phi''^2 \psi'' \leq 0$$

which boils down to ϕ'', $\psi'' \leq 0$, i.e., the two arbitrary functions ϕ and ψ must be concave.

(iv) As a curiosity, one might mention the possibility of normalizing prices at each point in the preference field so that by construction μ always equals unity.[15] Since

$$U_1 / p_1 = U_2 / p_2 = \ldots = U_n / p_n = \mu$$

this normalization at each point would involve dividing all nominal prices p_j by the factor μ.

The path-independency condition then follows from the existence of U, and the negative semidefiniteness condition simply expresses that U be concave. In other words, _any_ well-behaved utility function will do.

4. Indirect Hotelling Utility Functions

In this section, it will be assumed that prices have been normalized so that prices are so-called "real" prices (see Section 3).

Assume that the assumptions of the implicit functions theorem are fulfilled, so that p (q) can be inverted to yield the <u>direct demand functions</u> q (p). They are defined on the positive orthant of p-space. These functions will then also be differentiable and the matrix

$$\left[\frac{\partial q_j(p)}{\partial p_k}\right] \qquad\qquad j, k = 1, 2, \ldots, n \qquad\qquad (4.1)$$

will be symmetric and negative semidefinite.[16]

Consider the line integral

$$V(p) = -\int_{L'} \sum_{j=1}^{n} q_j(b)\ db_j. \qquad\qquad (4.2)$$

The path of integration L' is defined in the space R^n. The vector of integration is denoted b, and the path runs from some fixed initial point to the point b = p. The symmetry of (4.1) ensures that the line integral exists and is independent of its path. Further, the negative semidefiniteness of (4.1) means that the line integral V (p) is convex.

V (p) will be called the <u>indirect Hotelling utility function</u>.

Theorem 4. Changing independent and dependent variables in the demand functions, the direct Hotelling utility function inverts into the indirect Hotelling utility function. Mathematically,

$$U(q(p)) \equiv V(p). \qquad\qquad (4.3)$$

Equation (4.3) is proved in the following manner. Integration by parts gives[17]

$$U(q(p)) = \int\limits_{q_0(p_0)\to q(p)} \sum_{j=1}^{n} p_j(a)\, da_j =$$

$$= p^T q(p) - p_0^T q(p_0) - \int\limits_{p_0\to p} \sum_{j=1}^{n} q_j(b)\, db_j$$

The notation $q_0(p_0)\to q(p)$ indicates an arbitrary path in q-space from the fixed initial point q_0 to the point q. Preparing for the change of independent and dependent variables, these two points are written $q_0(p_0)$ and $q(p)$, respectively, where $p_0 = p_0(q_0)$ and $p = p(q)$. Similarly, the notation $p_0\to p$ denotes an arbitrary path in p-space from p_0 to p.

Inserting the definition of V (p)

$$U(q(p)) = p^T q(p) - p_0^T q(p_0) + V(p).$$

However, $p^T q(p) = p_0^T q(p_0) = 1$, and one is left with $U(q(p)) = V(p)$, as stated.

5. Conclusions

In 1938, H. Hotelling wrote down and discussed a general expression ((2.2) cf also eq. (ii) in the Appendix) which he called "total benefit." Hotelling himself never identified "total benefit" as a utility function.

"Total benefit" was formed by integrating the indirect demand functions over an arbitrary path in the quantity space. In order for "total benefit" to exist, the integral has to be independent of the path of integration.

As a matter of fact, "total benefit" is a cardinal utility function. Furthermore, it is the very utility function which would generate the indirect demand functions which were used in defining it in the first place (more precisely: the underlying ordinal utility index is a monotonic transformation of the integral).

The path-independency condition is in general a quite strong one, laying down conditions on the mathematical form of the utility function. It turns out that the specific mathematical nature of the utility function depends upon the fashion in which prices are being normalized.

The Hotelling benefit function therefore turns out to be not one but several different utility functions--it is an entire class of utility functions. The mathematical forms of these functions differ, but they have one thing in common: they can all be written as a line integral (2.2) where the value of the integral is independent of the path.

The Hotelling utility functions share another common feature: they all have a constant marginal utility of income. Indeed, any utility function for which the marginal utility is constant is a Hotelling utility function.

(i)   If there is a numeraire, say good n, the price of which is put equal to unity, the Hotelling utility function reads

$$\int \sum_{j=1}^{n-1} p_j (q) \, dq_j + q_n$$

where q_n is the amount of numeraire demanded, and the line integral is evaluated over the domain of the $n-1$ first variables.

(ii)   If prices are real prices, so that nominal income is always put equal to unity, the Hotelling utility function is homothetic.

(iii) If prices are normalized, so that they sum to unity, the Hotelling utility function is of the form eq. (3.9). As noted, this form may be attractive in intertemporal applications.

The list above displays some of the alternatives available. Suppose now that in a given applied modelling situation one desires to explore the possibility of characterizing utility as a Hotelling function, computing it by straight forward explicit integration of the indirect demand functions. Then there exists a choice to be made regarding the normalization of prices and the nature of the underlying assumptions regarding the form of U (q). In any given situation, one may try to select the set of assumptions which would appear to be more realistic.

APPENDIX

In a paper published in 1933 [1], H. Hotelling introduced the concept of "total benefit" w which was defined so that[18]

$$\frac{\partial w}{\partial q_i} = h_i \qquad\qquad\qquad (i)$$

where q_i denotes the quantity bought of the ith commodity, and $h_i = h_i (q_1, q_2 ..., q_n)$ is the excess of demand price over marginal cost for a fixed set of q's.

In this first paper, Hotelling never took the step of integrating the differential equation (i); hence "total benefit" was not identified as a line integral.

In 1938, however, Hotelling develops the same ideas further. He now writes total benefit[19]

$$w = \int \Sigma\, h_i\, dq_i \qquad\qquad\qquad (ii)$$

and he also notes the integrability conditions

$$\frac{\partial h_i}{\partial q_j} = \frac{\partial h_j}{\partial q_i} . \qquad\qquad\qquad (iii)$$

He goes on to say: "...there is a good reason to expect these integrability conditions to be satisfied, at least to a close approximation, in an extensive class of cases."[20]

He also points out that "the surpluses belonging to different persons...may be added to give a meaningful measure of social value."[21]

As is clear from the title of his 1938 paper, Hotelling was vividly concerned with practical applications of his work. As an example, he mentions: "The change in w that will result from a proposed new public enterprise, such as building a bridge, may fairly be set against the cost of the bridge to decide whether the enterprise should be undertaken."

And he goes on to explain in some detail how such cost-benefit analysis should be carried out in practice.

P. A. Samuelson. In 1952 [7], Samuelson showed how a simple partial equilibrium problem for spatially separated markets could be solved by maximizing "net social pay-off."

Illustrating his analysis by some simple diagrams for the case of two regions and two prices, Samuelson noted that, "an economist looking at these figures would naturally think of some kind of consumer's surplus concept."[22] He went on to warn: "However, the name consumer's surplus has all kinds of strange connotations in economics. To avoid these and to underline the completely artificial nature of my procedure, I shall simply define a 'net social pay-off' function..."[23] Net social pay-off was defined as the sum in all markets of the algebraic area between the demand curve and the supply curve (but deducting transportation costs).

T. Takayama and G. G. Judge. Extending Samuelson's work to the case of several commodities, Takayama and Judge noted that the concept of "social pay-off" could be traced back to Hotelling.[24] They formed for each region i the expression

$$\int_0^{y_i} p_i(n_i)\, dn_i - \int_0^{x_i} p_i(\xi_i)\, d\xi_i$$

where $p_i(n_i)$ = demand price

$p_i(\xi_i)$ = supply price

y_i = demand

x_i = supply

and called this expression "quasi-welfare."

Takayama and Judge also defined "quasi-indirect welfare" by integrating the excess demand function over the quantity domain.[25]

The Institute for Constructive Capitalism, The University of Texas at Austin.

NOTES

1
An account of Hotelling's work is provided in the Appendix.

2
The constant can always be brought equal to unity by a
suitable normalization of cardinal utility.

3
Ibid. p. 37.

4
On the terminology, see Hurwics and Uzawa [3].

5
For references to Hotelling's work, see the Appendix.
Hotelling himself called the expression (2.2) "total benefit."

6
Equality is obtained because q is restricted to be positive.

7
In line with conventional practice, I am here making no
distinction between the vector of integration and the upper
limit of the integral. The explicit notation is like in
(2.2).

8
The geometrical property explained in the main text is
illustrated in Figure a in the case of just two goods,
j = 1, 2 where q_2 is the numeraire.

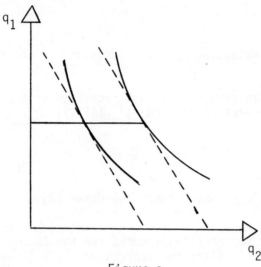

Figure a

9
[6], eq. (50).

10
A look at Figure a will convince the reader of the truth of this statement. For a rigorous proof, see Samuelson, _ibid_.

11
Ibid., p. 85.

12
Silberberg [8], see p. 946.

13
Samuelson [6], pp. 80-81, cf also Lau [5], Theorem XI.

14
An equivalent symmetric but more cumbersome notation would be

$$U = 1/3(q_1 + q_2 + q_3) + \phi(q_2 - q_1) + \psi(q_3 - q_2) + \chi(q_1 - q_3)$$

where ϕ, ψ and χ are arbitrary differentiable functions. A possible application of (3.9) which immediately comes to one's mind is the case of an intertemporal utility function where 1, 2 and 3 are three consecutive time periods. The utility (3.9) then equals consumption in the first period plus functions of the increase of consumption over the two subsequent time periods.

15
I am grateful to Dr. G. Debreu for pointing out this case to me.

16
See e.g., Hurwics and Uzawa [3].

17
For the general formula for integration by parts of a line integral, see Kortanek and Pfouts [4], mathematical appendix.

18
[1], p. 605.

19
[2], p. 247.

20
[2], p. 247.

21
Ibid.

22
[7], p. 287.

23
Ibid., p. 288.

24
[9], p. 108.

25
[9], p. 187.

REFERENCES

[1] Hotelling, H., "Edgeworth's Taxation Paradox and the Nature of Demand and Supply Functions," The Journal of Political Economy, Vol. 40, No. 5, October 1932, pp. 577-616.

[2] Hotelling, H., "The General Welfare in Relation to Prob-
     lems of Taxation and of Railway and Utility Rates,"
     Econometrica, Vol. 6, No. 3, July 1938, pp. 242-269.

[3] Hurwicz, L. and H. Uzawa, "On the Integrability of Demand
     Functions," in Preferences, Utility and Demand; a
     Minnesota Symposium; edited by J. S. Chipman, L. Hurwicz,
     M. Richter and H. S. Sonnenschein; Jovanovich, New York,
     1971.

[4] Kortanek, K. O. and R. W. Pfouts, "A Biextremal Principle
     for a Behavioral Theory of the Firm," Journal of Mathe-
     matical Modelling, in press, 1982.

[5] Lau, L. J., "Duality and the Structure of Utility
     Functions," Journal of Economic Theory, Vol. 1, No. 4,
     December 1969, pp. 374-396.

[6] Samuelson, P. A., "Constancy of the Marginal Utility of
     Income," in Lange et. al. eds., Studies in Mathematical
     Economics and Econometrics, in memory of Henry Schultz,
     University of Chicago Press, Chicago 1972, pp. 75-91.

[7] Samuelson, P. A., "Spatial Price Equilibrium and Linear
     Programming," American Economic Review, Vol. 42, 1952,
     pp. 283-303.

[8] Silberberg, E., "Duality and the Many Consumer's Sur-
     pluses," American Economic Review, Vol. 62, No. 5,
     December 1972, pp. 942-952.

[9] Takayama, T. and G. G. Judge, Spatial and Temporal Price
     and Allocation Models, North-Holland, Amsterdam, 1971.

A. Camacho

CARDINAL UTILITY AND DECISION MAKING
UNDER UNCERTAINTY

1. INTRODUCTION

In the expected utility theory developed by von Neuman and
Morgenstern (1947) (See also Marschak, 1950), cardinal utility indices for an individual corresponding to a finite
set of prizes $\{x_1,\ldots,x_i,\ldots,x_n\}$, are derived from the
ordering by the individual of the probability distributions
over the set of prizes. It is shown that if the ordering
of these probability distributions satisfies certain, so
called, rationality conditions or rules,[1] then cardinal
utility indices u_i^v, constant up to positive affine transformations, can be assigned to the prizes x_i such that the
individual orders the probability distributions as if he or
she were maximizing the expected value of the utilities u_i^v.
According to some interpretations of the expected utility
theory, the cardinal utility function $u_i^v(x_i) = u_i^v$ represents a joint effect of the attitude toward risk of the
individual and his or her "utility" or satisfaction of the
prizes. There is no need, therefore, according to these
interpretations of the theory, to assume the actual reality
of utility as a cardinal magnitude under riskless condi-
tions, thus by-passing the controversy of cardinality versus ordinality where the existence in riskless conditions
of utility as cardinal magnitude and the need to use it in
economic theory are the main issues.

Allais' theory of cardinal utility and decision under
uncertainty (1979), on the other side, assumes that cardinal utililty indices s_i giving the psychological values,
under riskless conditions, of the prizes x_i do exist.
These cardinal utility indices s_i can be determined by considering either psychologically equivalent variations, or
minimum perceptible thresholds (Weber-Fechner). It further
assumes that individuals in choosing among lotteries may
take into account without violating rationality not only
the expectation of the psychological values s_i but also the
variance and even higher moments. Indeed, the only constraints that rationality, according to Allais' Theory,

B. P. Stigum and F. Wenstøp (eds.), Foundations of Utility and Risk Theory with Applications,
347–370.
© 1983 by D. Reidel Publishing Company.

imposes on preferences over lotteries are <u>transitivity</u> and <u>absolute preference</u> (1979, p. 69).

In the theory of cardinal utility and decision under uncertainty presented in this paper it is assumed like in Allais' that, <u>under riskless conditions</u>, cardinal utility indices u_i^c of the prizes x_i do exist and can be precisely defined. [1] These cardinal utility indices u_j^c are not derived like Allais' s_i by considering "equivalent variations" or "minimum perceptible thresholds." They are derived by considering what I have called a <u>choice situation</u> and <u>(imagined) identical repetitions of the choice situation.</u> By using the cardinal utility indices u_i^c, the law of large numbers and the <u>rule of long run success</u>, a rationality argument is developed to justify, in choosing among lotterries, applying the rule of maximizing the expected value of the utilities u_i^c. It should be stated, however, that the <u>normative force</u> attributed to this rule by this writer is not as strong as that attributed to the <u>rationality axioms</u> by some of the advocators of the expected utility theory,[2] and that the conclusions derived from this theory are closer to those derived from Allais' theory than to those of the expected utility theory.

The notions of <u>choice situation</u> and <u>(imagined) identical repetitions of a choice situation</u> are <u>basic</u> to the theory of cardinal utility presented here. Section 2 of this paper is devoted to discussing these notions and how they are used in precisely defining <u>intensity</u> of <u>preference</u> and in deriving the <u>cardinal utility indices</u> u_i^c for the prizes x_i.[3] In section 3, the discussions of section 2 are formalized and a system of axioms is presented from which the cardinal utility indices u_j^c are rigorously derived. These cardinal utility indices, the <u>law of large</u> numbers and the rule of long run success are then used in Section 4 to develop an argument in favor of the <u>rule</u> that prescribes, in choosing among lotteries, maximizing the expected value of the indices u_i^c. In section 5, the theory considered in this paper, Allais' theory of cardinal utility and decision under uncertainty and the expected utility theory are further discussed and compared with each other. Finally, section 6 contains some general concluding remarks.

2.   INTENSITY OF PREFERENCE AND CARDINAL UTILITY

As stated in the <u>Introduction</u>, the notions of <u>choice situation</u> and <u>(imagined) identical repetitions of a choice</u>

situation are basic to our theory of cardinal utility.
They are used in precisely defining intensity of preference, and in rigorously deriving a cardinal utility index
under riskless conditions. Although the notions were
stated explicitly for the first time in the paper
"Approaches to Cardinal Utility" (Camacho, 1980) and
further developed in the monongraph Societies and Social
Decision Functions: A Model with Focus on the Information
Problem (Camacho, 1982), they constitute the basis
justifying the system of axioms leading to the cardinal
utility functions used in my previous work on cardinal
utility and social choice (see for instance Camacho, 1974).

2.1. Choice Situation.

A decision maker facing a set of available actions and going
through the process of mentally evaluating or imagining the
consequences of each of the alternative possible actions
that he can take constitutes a choice situation.
     Thus, a consumer, at a given moment, in possession of
a given amount of money, facing n commodities whose prices
are given, and trying to mentally determine, in order to
decide what bundle to buy, the satisfaction that he may
derive from each of the alternative bundles of these commodities that he can buy (given their prices and the amount of
money that he possesses) is an example of a choice situation.
     A person, after dinner, facing a set of three possible
drinks, say, coffee, tea and camomile, imagining the consequences (pleasure, etc.) to be derived from each one of
these possible drinks in order to determine what drink to
take, is another example of the notion of a choice situation.
     The chairman of the board of directors of a company,
evaluating possible alternative investment plans in order
to decide what plan his company should adopt; and the
president of a country trying to imagine the consequences
of alternative tax programs in order to decide which one to
propose, are further examples of the notion of choice
situation stated above.
     The decision maker facing a choice situation ranks
first, according to his preferences, the available alternatives and then chooses one with the highest rank. It is
assumed here that the decision maker in the process of ranking the available alternatives proceeds as follows: He or
she supposes choosing an action, imagines the consequenses
that follow from having taken that action and records those

imagined consequences in his or her memory; then, as if
facing the choice situation for the first time, the decision
maker assumes he or she chooses a different action, imagines
the consequences of having taken that action, and records
those imagined consequences in his or her memory; then, as
if again facing the choice situation for the first time, he
or she repeats the process with a third action and continues
until all the available actions have been considered.
Finally, by comparing the memories of these imagined consequences of the different available actions, he reaches an
order of preference or ranking of the available alternative
actions.

2.2 (Imagined) Identical Repetitions of a Choice Situation.

Furthermore, it is assumed that the decision maker, when
facing a choice situation, can imagine having to face the
same (or an identical) choice situation not only one time,
but two times, or three times, or any number of times. That
is, the decision maker, when facing a choice situation, can
imagine: taking one action, living the consequences of
having taken that action, facing the same choice situation
anew, taking another action (not necessarily the same as
the one taken the first time), living through its consequences, facing the same choice situation a third time, etc.
     The decision maker, when imagining facing an identical
choice situation a certain number of times, can proceed to
rank, according to his or her preferences, the corresponding
sequences of actions. Let us assume, for the sake of
concreteness, that the decision maker imagines facing three
times a choice situation whose set of available actions $X =$
$\{x, x', x''\}$ contains three actions. There are then twenty-
seven possible sequences of three actions (one action for
each time that he or she faces the choice situation):
$(x,x,x,)$, (x,x,x'), ..., (x'',x'',x'').
     It is suggested that the decision maker, in determining
his or her rank of the twenty-seven possible sequences, of
size three, of actions is guided by the following mental
process: (i) He or she imagines: the choice situation,
taking one action out of the set of available actions $X =$
$\{x, x', x''\}$ and living the consequences of having taken that
action; he or she then records those consequences in his or
her memory. He or she imagines facing a second time the
same choice situation, taking one action out of the set
$X = \{x, x', x''\}$ of available actions and living the

consequences of having taken that action; then records
those consequences in his or her memory. He or she
imagines facing a third time the same choice situation,
taking one action out of the set of available actions
X = {x, x', x"} and living the consequences of having taken
that action; then records those consequences in his or her
memory. Finally, the decision maker records in his or her
mind the aggregate consequences of the three actions
considered. (ii) He or she applies the process described
in (i) to each of the twenty-seven possible sequences, of
size three, of actions, {x, x, x}, {x, x, x'}, ..., {x",
x", x"} and then proceeds to order, according to his or her
preferences, the twenty-seven possible sequences.

2.3. Intensity of Preference.

Let us see now how we can use the notion of (imagined)
identical repetitions of a choice situation to precisely
define intensity of preference.

That there is intensity of preference is universally
accepted. Thus, if in the choice set considered in subsection 2.2 above, to make the example more vivid, x
represents having coffee, x' having tea and x" having
camomile, and I prefer having coffee to having tea and
having tea to having camomile; at the same time I may feel
also that my preference for coffee over tea is more intense
than my preference for tea over camomile. The problem then
is not whether or not intensity of preference exists, but
how to precisely define and measure this magnitude.

I suggest that a decision maker facing a choice situation can state precisely his or her intensity of preference, given the choice situation, by considering sequences
of identical choice situations and his or her preference
orderings of the corresponding sequences of actions. Suppose the previous example and that the decision maker
prefers coffee to tea and tea to camomile. That is, he or
she prefers x to x' and x' to x". Then, if when considering three identical repetitions of the choice situation the
decision maker:

(i) Is indifferent between the sequence of action (x, x',
x") and (x', x', x'), the intensity of preference for x
over x' is equal to the intensity of preference for x' over
x".

(ii) Prefers the sequence (x, x', x") to the sequence
(x', x', x'), the intensity of preferences for x over x' is
greater than the intensity of preference for x' over x".

(iii) Prefers the sequence (x', x', x') to the sequence
(x, x', x"), the intensity of preference for x over x' is
smaller than the intensity of preference for x' over x".
        In case (i), the loss in satisfaction, by the decision
maker, by having tea (x') instead of coffee (x) in the
first choice situation is exactly compensated by having tea
(x') instead of camomile (x") in the third choice situation.   In case (ii), the loss of satisfaction, by the decision maker, by having tea (x') instead of coffee (x) in
the first choice situation is greater than the gain in
satisfaction by having tea (x') instead of camomile (x") in
the third choice situation.   In case (iii), the loss of
satisfaction, by the decision maker, by having tea (x')
instead of coffee (x) in the first choice situation is
smaller than the gain in satisfaction by having tea (x')
instead of camomile (x") in the third choice situation.
        And in general, if the decision maker, when consider-
ing a sequence of k+1 identical choice situations, is
indifferent between the sequence of size k+1 consisting of
1 coffee and k camomiles (x,x",...,x") and the sequence of
size k+1 consisting of k+1 teas (x',x',...,x'), then, we
say that the intensity of preference of the decision maker
for coffee over tea is k times his or her intensity of
preference for tea over camomile.[4]

2.4. Cardinal Utility.

Let, as above, the action "having coffee" be denoted by x,
the action "having tea" by x' and the action "having
camomile" by x". Thus the set of available actions, to be
denoted by X, is X = {x, x', x"}. Assume, as before, that
the decision maker prefers having coffee to having tea and
having tea to having camomile. That is, he prefers x to x'
and x' to x".
        The ordinal utility function, as is well known, is an
assignment of numbers to actions such that (i) if two
actions are indifferent to each other from the decision
maker's point of view, the numbers assigned to them must be
equal; and (ii) if one action is preferred by the decision
maker to another action, the number assigned to the prefer-

red action must be greater than the number assigned to the
other action.
    Thus, if the decision maker prefers, as stated above,
x to x' and x' to x":   u(x)=3, u(x')=1, u(x")=0; and
v(x)=2, v(x')=1, v(x")=0 are both ordinal utility functions.
    But if we want the assignment of numbers to actions,
that is, the utility function, to represent not only the
order of preference of the decision maker but also its
intensity of preference, and the intensity of preference of
the decision maker for x over x' is, say, twice as large as
his or her intensity of preference for x' over x", then we
should require that the difference between the numbers (the
utilities) assigned to x and x' be twice as large as the
difference between the numbers (utilities) assigned to x'
and x".   In this case u(x)=3, u(x')=1, u(x")=0 is a utility
function that satisfies such a requirement and is called a
cardinal utility function.   The function v(x)=2, v(x')=1,
v(x")=0 that indicates the preference ordering of the
actions by the decision maker but not the intensity of his
or her preference is called an ordinal utility function.   A
utility function which is required to represent only the
order of preference is called an ordinal utility function.
A utility function which is required to represent both the
order of preference and the intensity of preference is
called a cardinal utility function.

3.   A SYSTEM OF AXIOMS FOR CARDINAL UTILITY

3.1.   General Discussion.

In this Section we will formalize the ideas discussed and
illustrated in Section 2.   There we indicated that the
decision maker can determine the intensity of his or her
preference and a cardinal utility function representing not
only his or her preference but also the intensity of his or
her preference by considering sequences of identical choice
situations and proceeding to order, according to his or her
preferences, the corresponding sequences of available
actions.
    At the risk of tiring the reader, we want to insist
again on the two following points: (i) when the decision
maker faces a choice situation and imagines an identical
repetition of this choice situation, both the available
actions and the anticipated satisfactions from these
actions are the same in the original choice situation and

in the _imagined_ identical repetition; and (ii) that the
identical choice situation does not have to occur in
reality; it only needs to be _imagined_ by the decision
maker. Therefore our theory of cardinal utility may apply
also to those choice situations for which it is not
plausible to assume that identical repetitions will occur.
        We will thus assume that the decision maker can
imagine any number h of repetitions of the (_same_) choice
situation and order, according to his or her preferences,
the corresponding sequences, of size h, of available
actions. We will then state in the form of axioms the
natural properties that these preference orderings,[5] defined
on the set of h-tuples of actions, must satisfy. Finally,
from the stated axioms, the desired cardinal utility
function will be derived.
        The main result of this section is stated in the form
of two theorems that establish a one-to-one correspondence
between the elements of the set of all the classes of cardinal utility functions defined on the set of actions X and
the elements of the class of all the relational systems[6]
defined on X that satisfy the proposed axioms.
        The proposed axioms are: the _Permutation Axiom_, the
Independence Axiom, the _Repetition Axiom_ and the _Rate of
Substitution Axiom_.
        The _Permutation Axiom_ simply states that when consider-
ing a sequence of identical choice situations, the preferences of the decision maker regarding the available corresponding sequences of actions, do not depend on the order in
which the actions are taken.
        The reader that has not yet properly understood the
notion of (_imagined_) _identical repetitions of a choice
situation_ may object to this axiom (as well as to the
others). For instance, he or she may argue as follows:
suppose the choice situation in which I am sitting one
evening in a restaurant and trying to make a selection from
a menu containing a meat entry, a chicken entry and a fish
entry; consider now six consecutive evenings and six selections (one selection per evening), two meat selections, two
chicken selections and two fish selections; then he or she
may insist: I am not indifferent regarding the order in
which I take the six dinners; I certainly would prefer to
have meat the first evening, chicken the second, fish the
third, meat again the fourth, chicken the fifth, and fish
the sixth, than to have meat the two first evenings, then

chicken the following two evenings and finally fish the
fifth and the sixth evenings.

The answer to this objection is that our objector is
not considering six identical choice situations. He or she
is imagining having, for instance, meat the first evening
and then, having had meat the first evening, how he or she
would feel the following evening, etc. But if he or she
were considering identical choice situations, he or she
would feel the following evening exactly the same as the
first and the order in which he or she takes his or her
dinners would not matter.

The Independence Axiom asserts that the preference
ordering of two sequences of actions, of size $h = h_1 + h_2$,
where the h_2 last actions are the same in both sequences,
is determined only by the h_1 first actions of the sequence
and is, therefore, independent of whatever the last h_2
actions of the sequence may be.

The Repetition Axiom roughly says that if the decision
maker, when considering a choice situation, prefers, say,
action x to action x', then when considering h identical
choice situations he or she would prefer the sequence
consisting of h actions x to the sequence consisting of h
actions x'.

Finally, the Rate of Substitution Axiom postulates the
existence of intensity of preference determined in the way
illustrated in the previous section. For each quadruple of
actions x, x', x", x''' such that x is at least as preferred
as x' and x" is strictly preferred to x''', it postulates the
existence of a non-negative real number $R(x, x'; x", x''')$
which is precisely the intensity of preference of x over x'
with regard to the intensity of preference of x" over x'''.

Let us turn now in the following subsection to the
formal presentation of the axioms.

3.2. A System of Axioms.

Let X be any set containing at least two elements: the set
of available actions. The elements of X will be represented
by lower case x with sub indices and (or) super indices
attached when necessary.

Write $Y_1 = X$, and for any integer h greater than 1,
let $Y_h = X \times \ldots \times X$: the h-fold Cartesian product of X.
The elements of Y_h will be represented by y_h, y_h', etc.
We will write $y_h = (x_1,\ldots,x_h)$, $y_h' = (x_1',\ldots,x_h')$, etc. The
elements $x_1,\ldots,x_h$ are called entries or components of y_h.

Let Q_h be a preference ordering defined on Y_h. The relations P_h, I_h (strict preference and indifference, respectively) on Y_h are defined as follows for all y_h, y_h' εY_h, $y_h P_h y_h'$ iff $y_h Q_h y_h$ and not $y_h' Q_h y_h$; $y_h I_h y_h'$ iff $y_h Q_h y_h$ and $y_h' Q_h y_h$.

The Axioms. We assume that the preference orderings Q_h ($h = 1,2,\ldots,$) satisfy the following axioms:

PERMUTATION AXIOM. Let π and δ be any two functions from the set $\{1,\ldots,h\}$ onto itself. Then $(x_1,\ldots,x_h)$ $Q_h(x_1',\ldots,x_h')$ iff $(x_{\pi(1)},\ldots, x_{\pi(h)})$ $Q_h(x_{\delta(1)}',\ldots,x_{\delta(h)}')$.

INDEPENDENCE AXIOM. Let $h = h_1 + h_2$, where h_1 and h_2 are natural numbers greater than 0. For $y_{h_1} \varepsilon Y_{h_1}$, and y_{h_2} εY_{h_2}, write $(y_{h_1}; y_{h_2}) = y_h$, where the first h_1 components of y_h are those of y_{h_1} and the last h_2 components are those of y_{h_2}. Then, for all y_{h_1}, $y_{h_1}' \varepsilon Y_{h_1}$ and all $y^* \varepsilon Y_{h_2}$, $y_{h_1} Q_{h_1} y_{h_1}'$ iff $(y_{h_1};y^*_{h_2})Q_h (y_{h_1}';y^*_{h_2})$.

REPETITION AXIOM. For any positive natural number n, and any $y_h \varepsilon Y_h$, write $(n \times y_h) = (y_h;\ldots;y_h) \varepsilon Y_{nh}$: the sequence obtained by repeating n times y_h. Then

$$y_h Q_h y_h' \text{ iff } (n \times y_h) Q_{nh}(n \times y_h').$$

RATE OF SUBSTITUTION AXIOM. For each x, x', x", x''' ε X such that $xQ_1 x'$ and $x"P_1 x'''$, there exists a real and non-negative number $R(x,x';x",x''')$ such that the following is true for any natural h greater than 0:

(a) if $y^*_h = (x^*_1,\ldots,x^*_h)$ is obtained from y_h $= (x_1,\ldots,x_h)$ by

substituting in y_h r entries (r > 0) x by r entries x', and s entries (s $\geqslant$ 0) x''' by s entries x", then

$$y_h^* P_h y_h \text{ iff } \frac{s}{r} > R(x,x';x'',x'''),$$

$$y_h P_h y_h^* \text{ iff } \frac{s}{r} < R(x,x';x'',x'''),$$

$$y_h I_h y_h^* \text{ iff } \frac{s}{r} = R(x,x';x'',x'''),$$

(b) if $y_h^* = (x_1^*,\ldots,x_h^*)$ is obtained from y_h

$$= (x_1,\ldots,x_h) \text{ by}$$

substituting in y_h r entries (r > 0) x' by r entries x, and s entries (s ⩾ 0) x" by s entries x''', then

$$y_h^* P_h y_h \text{ iff } \frac{s}{r} < R(x,x';x'',x'''),$$

$$y_h P_h y_h^* \text{ iff } \frac{s}{r} > R(x,x';x'',x'''),$$

$$y_h I_h y_h^* \text{ iff } \frac{s}{r} = R(x,x';x'',x''').$$

The function R defined on the set of quadruples $(x,x';x'',x''')$ such that xQ_1x' and $x"P_1x'''$ is called the Rate of Substitution function.

The class of all the relational systems, with domain X, $(X,Q_1,\ldots,Q_h,\ldots,)$ satisfying the Permutation, Independence, Repetition and Rate of Substitution Axioms will be represented by $\mathcal{Q}$, and its elements by Q,Q', etc.

3.3. Two Theorems.

Let X, as already defined, be any set containing at least two elements. Let u be any function from X to the reals whose range contains at least two elements. Let U be the class of all the functions obtained from u by positive affine transformations. Call $\mathcal{U}$ the set of such classes. Let $\mathcal{Q}$, as defined before, be the set of all the relational systems, with domain X,Q = $(X,Q_1,\ldots,Q_h,\ldots,)$ which satisfy the Permutation, Independence, Repetition and Rate of Substitution Axioms.

The following two theorems establish a one-to-one correspondence between the elements of $\mathcal{U}$ and $\mathcal{Q}$.

THEOREM 1. (i) To each U $\varepsilon \mathcal{U}$ we can assign a Q $\varepsilon \mathcal{Q}$ such that for any h > 0 and any u ε U, $(x_1,\ldots,x_h)Q_h(x_1',\ldots,x_h')$iff

$$\sum_{i=1}^{h} u(x_i) > \sum_{i=1}^{h} u(x_i').$$

(ii) If u^* is any function from X to the reals such that for any $h > 0, (x_1,\ldots,x_h)Q_h(x_1',\ldots,x_h')$iff

$$\sum_{i=1}^{h} u^*(x_i) > \sum_{i=1}^{h} u^*(x_i'), \text{ then } u^* \varepsilon U.$$

THEOREM 2. (i) To each $Q \varepsilon \mathcal{Q}$ we can assign an $U \varepsilon \mathcal{U}$ such that for any $h > 0$ and any $u \varepsilon U$, $(x_1,\ldots,x_h)$ $Q_h(x_1',\ldots,x_h')$ iff

$$\sum_{i=1}^{h} u(x_i) > \sum_{i=1}^{h} u(x_i') .$$

(ii) If u^* is any function from X to the reals such that for any $h > 0, (x_1,\ldots,x_h)Q_h(x_1',\ldots,x_h')$iff $\sum_{i=1}^{h} u^*(x_i)$ $> \sum_{i=1}^{h} u^*(x_i')$, then $u^* \varepsilon U$.

The proofs of Theorem 1 and Theorem 2 are omitted here. The reader interested in the details of these proofs is referred to (Camacho, 1979a) or to (Camacho, 1982, chapter 4).

The cardinal utility indices obtained above will be represented in the coming sections by $u_i^c(x_i)$ or simply u_i^c, to distinguish them from the von Neuman and Morgenstern cardinal utility indices to be represented there by $u^v(x_i)$ or simply u_i^v.

4. MAXIMIZING THE EXPECTED VALUE OF THE UTILITIES u_i^c
        AND THE RULE OF LONG RUN SUCCESS

The approach followed in this section was presented by this writer in an earlier paper (Camacho, 1979b). It was suggested by the late Professor Marschak (1951, pp. 504-5), who proposed to start out with the intuitive very appealing common sense definition that "the best policy or rule is the one that succeeds in the long run" and then try to determine whether the rule of maximizing the expected value of some utility is a best rule according to this common sense definition.[7]

It is the feeling of this writer that if expected utility maximization has not been interpreted and justified more often in the past as a rule of long run success through the law of large numbers it is because an appropriate theory of cardinal utility as the one presented above, was lacking.

Let us try to see now how by using the cardinal utility indices u_i^c and the law of large numbers, maximizing the expected value of the utilities u_i^c, obtained in section 3, can be interpreted as a rule of long run success. To this end, we will proceed as follows: first, we will make some comments on the notion of probability used here; then the rule of long run success is precisely defined; finally, it will be shown that the rule that prescribes choosing among alternative probability distributions one that maximizes the expected value of the utilities u_i^c, satisfies the rule of long run success.

Probability. The word probability is used here in the objective or statistical sense. That is, the probability p_i assigned to an event E_i is taken here to be the limit to which the frequency of occurrence of the event E_i 'converges' when the random experiment generating E_i is repeated infinitely many times.

Consider a riskless choice situation whose set of available actions $X = \{x_1,\ldots,x_i\ldots,x_n\}$ contains $n \geqslant 2$ actions. Let $u_1^c,\ldots,u_i^c,\ldots,u_n^c$ be the cardinal utility indices obtained in section 3 by having the decision maker imagine (identical) repetitions of the riskless choice situation and proceed to order, according to his or her preferences, the corresponding alternative sequences of actions. As was shown there, these riskless cardinal utility indices have the property that, given k (identical) repetitions of the choice situation, the decision maker prefers the riskless sequence of corresponding actions $x_{h_1},\ldots,x_{h_i},\ldots,x_{h_k}$ to the riskless sequence $x'_{h_1},\ldots,x'_{h_i},$ $\ldots,x'_{h_k}$ if and only if $\sum_{i=1}^{k} u^c(x_{h_i}) > \sum_{i=1}^{k} u^c(x'_{h_i})$; the decision maker is indifferent between the two sequences if and only if
$$\sum_{i=1}^{k} u^c(x_{h_i}) = \sum_{i=1}^{k} u^c(x'_{h_i}).$$

Let us now bring risk into the choice situation. Let
be a random experiment whose set of possible outcomes
is partitioned into n events, $E_1,\ldots,E_i,\ldots,E_n$ with
corresponding <u>objective</u> probabilities $p_1,\ldots,p_i,\ldots,p_n$.
And consider alternative random experiments $\mathcal{E}$, $\mathcal{E}'$, . . .
generating corresponding <u>objective</u> probability distributions
$(p_1,\ldots,p_i,\ldots,p_n)$, $(p_1',\ldots p_i'\ldots,p_n')$, . . .

Assume that the decision maker is no longer able to
choose an action out of the set X; assume that the decision
maker is able to choose only among random experiments. If
he or she chooses random experiment $\mathcal{E}$, with outcomes
$E_1,\ldots,E_i,\ldots,E_n$, then this random experiment is performed
once and if E_1 obtains, action x_1 is adopted, . . ., if E_i
obtains, action x_i is adopted, . . ., if E_n obtains, action
x_n is adopted.

If the choice situation repeats itself k times and the
decision maker chooses random experiment $\mathcal{E}$, then each of
the k times that the choice situation occurs, the experiment   is performed and the event that obtains determines,
as was described in the previous paragraph, the action of
the set X that will be adopted.

<u>The rule of long run success.</u> Let $x_{h_1},\ldots,x_{h_i},\ldots,x_{h_k}$
and $x'_{h_1},\ldots,x'_{h_i},\ldots,x'_{h_k}$ be the sequences of the first k
actions generated by the random experiments $\mathcal{E}$ and $\mathcal{E}'$, or
equivalently by their corresponding probability distribu-
tions $(p_1,\ldots,p_i,\ldots,p_n)$ and $(p_1',\ldots,p_i',\ldots,p_n')$. Clearly,
the sequences $x_{h_1},\ldots,x_{h_i},\ldots,x_{h_k}$ and $x'_{h_1},\ldots,x'_{h_i},\ldots,x'_{h_k}$
are random and therefore we can calculate the probability
that, say, the sequence $x_{h_1},\ldots,x_{h_i},\ldots,x_{h_k}$ be preferred
to the sequence $x'_{h_1},\ldots,x'_{h_i},\ldots,x'_{h_k}$ by the decision maker.
In symbols, $\Pr[(x_{h_1},\ldots,x_{h_i},\ldots,x_{h_k}) > (x'_{h_1},\ldots,x'_{h_i},\ldots,x'_{h_k})]$.

Now, we say that the decision maker satisfies or follows
the <u>rule of long run success</u> if he or she chooses the
probability distribution $(p_1,\ldots,p_i,\ldots,p_n)$ over the
probability distribution $(p_1',\ldots,p_i',\ldots,p_n')$ whenever

$$\lim_{k\to\infty} \Pr\left[(x_{h_1},\ldots,x_{h_i},\ldots,x_{h_k}) > (x'_{h_1},\ldots,x'_{h_i},\ldots,x'_{h_k})\right] = 1.$$

It will be easy to prove now, using the law of large numbers, the proposition that a decision maker that chooses probability distribution $p = (p_1, \ldots, p_i, \ldots, p_n)$ over probability distribution, $p' = (p_1', \ldots, p_i', \ldots, p_n')$ whenever

$$\sum_{i=1}^{n} p_i u_i^c > \sum_{i=1}^{n} p_i' u_i^c$$ satisfies the rule of long run success.

That is, a decision maker that chooses probability distribution p over probability distribution p' whenever the expected value of the utilities u^c, given p, $E[u^c|p]$ is greater than the expected value, given p', $E[u^c|p']$, satisfies the rule of long run success.

Proof. As stated above, the cardinal utility indices u_i^c have the property that the sequence of actions $x_{h_1}, \ldots, x_{h_i}, \ldots, x_{h_k}$ is at least as good as the sequence $x_{h_1}', \ldots, x_{h_i}', \ldots, x_{h_k}'$ if and only if $\sum_{i=1}^{k} u^c(x_{h_i}) \geq \sum_{i=1}^{k} u^c(x_{h_i}')$.

If the sequences of actions $x_{h_1}, \ldots, x_{h_i}, \ldots, x_{h_k}$ and $x_{h_1}', \ldots, x_{h_i}', \ldots, x_{h_k}'$ are generated, respectively, by the probability distributions $(p_1, \ldots, p_i, \ldots, p_n)$ and $(p_1', \ldots, p_i', \ldots, p_n')$ then

$$Z_k = \frac{1}{k} \sum_{i=1}^{k} u^c(x_{h_i}) \quad \text{and} \quad Z_k' = \frac{1}{k} \sum_{i=1}^{k} u^c(x_{h_i}')$$

are random variables and by the law of large numbers we know that Z_k and Z_k' converge in probability, respectively, to $\sum_{i=1}^{n} p_i u^c(x_i)$ and $\sum_{i=1}^{n} p_i' u^c(x_i)$ as $k \to \infty$. Now, the rule of maximizing the expected value of the utilities $u^c(x_i)$ prescribes that the probability distribution $(p_1, \ldots, p_i, \ldots, p_n)$ be preferred over the probability distribution $(p_1', \ldots, p_i', \ldots, p_n')$ whenever $\sum_{i=1}^{n} p_i u^c(x_i)$ is greater than $\sum_{i=1}^{n} p_i' u^c(x_i)$, which implies that $\lim_{k \to \infty} \Pr[Z_k > Z_k']$

$= 1$. But $\Pr[Z_k > Z_k'] = \Pr[kZ_k > kZ_k'] =$

$$\Pr[\sum_{i=1}^{k} u^c(x_{h_i}) > \sum_{i=1}^{k} u^c(x'_{h_i})] =$$

$$\Pr[(x_{h_1}, \ldots, x_{h_i}, \ldots, x_{h_k}) > (x'_{h_1}, \ldots, x'_{h_i}, \ldots, x'_{h_k})].$$

Thus $\sum_{i=1}^{n} p_i u^c(x_i) > \sum_{i=1}^{n} p'_i u^c(x_i)$ implies that

$$\lim_{k \to \infty} \Pr[(x_{h_1}, \ldots, x_{h_i}, \ldots, x_{h_k}) >$$

$$(x'_{h_1}, \ldots, x'_{h_i}, \ldots, x'_{h_k})] = 1.$$

Q.E.D.

5.   THEORIES OF CARDINAL UTILITY AND DECISION MAKING UNDER UNCERTAINTY

This section is devoted to discussing and comparing Allais' theory of cardinal utility and decision under uncertainty, the expected utility theory and the theory considered in this paper.

First I shall try to summarize the views on cardinal utility contained in these theories, then the implications of these theories for decision making under uncertainty are considered.

5.1 Views on Cardinal Utility

According to the expected utility theory, there is no need to assume the existence of utility as a cardinal magnitude in riskless situations. The cardinal utility function $u^v(x_i)$, which is derived from the so called rationality axioms of this theory, is determined not only by the "utility" or satisfaction of the prizes to the individual but also by his or her attitude toward risk. Indeed, the concavity, convexity or linearity of the function $u^v(x_i)$ are taken to correspond to attitudes toward risk: with concavity corresponding to risk averse, convexity to risk loving and linearity to risk neutrality.[8]

According to Allais' theory of cardinal utility, (e.g. Allais, 1979, pp. 8, 46) cardinal utility representing

intensity of preferences in riskless situations does exist.
It can be given an operational definition by introducing
either the notion of equivalent psychological increments or
the notion (Fechner-Weber) of minimum perceptible thresholds.

The view adopted in this paper is, like Allais', that
a cardinal utility function $u^c(x_i)$ representing both the
order of preference of the prizes and the intensity of
these preferences in riskless situations does exist. It
appears to differ from Allais' view in the way that cardinal utility is operationally and precisely defined.

To this writer, intensity of preferences and cardinal
utility can precisely be defined by using the notions of
choice situation and (imagined) identical repetitions of a
choice situation as discussed in section 2 above.

The notion of minimum perceptible thresholds, which
appears appropriate in measuring sensation as a function of
the intensity of the stimulus, does not appear adequate, in
this writer's view, to determine intensity of preferences
and cardinal utility. If I am a diabetic, I may very well
strongly prefer a smaller to a larger amount of sugar in my
coffee even if the difference in sweetness is below my
minimum perceptible threshold. Other similar examples can
easily be suggested by the reader.

In determining preferences and intensity of preferences of alternative actions, the individual, in this
writer's view, takes (or should take) into consideration
not only sensation, whether it is pleasant or unpleasant,
but all the consequences of the actions under consideration. The sensation derived from an action is part of the
consequences of the action, but not necessarilly all.
Therefore, reference only to minimum perceptible thresholds
in determinig intensity of preferences and cardinal utility
for an individual seems unsatisfactory.

What Allais means by equivalent psychological increments is not clear to this writer. He tries to determine
the equivalent psychological increments of an individual by
asking him or her questions of the following type "for what
value of i is your intensity of preference for $i over $100
the same as your intensity of preference for $100 over $50?"
If this question were presented to me I would respond, as
Machina says he would (Machina, 1981, p. 169), by asking
what it meant. However, by using the notions of choice
situation and repetitions of a choice situation discussed in
section 2 above this question can be reformulated in a

meaningful way by telling the individual to _imagine_ that the
choice situation he or she is facing is going to repeat
itself two times and then try to determine the value of i
for which he or she is indifferent between "receiving $100
each of the three times that the choice situation occurs"
and "receiving $$i$ one of the three times, $100 the other and
$50 the other."

With the question formulated in this manner, the value
of i that makes the individual indifferent between the two
alternatives is the one whose intensity of preference over
$100 is the same as the intensity of preference of $100
over $50.

If Allais' equivalent psychological increments were
defined in this way, then his psychological indices s_i
should coincide, up to positive affine transformation,
with the cardinal utility indices u_i^c determined in section 3
of this paper.

Allais states (1979 , p. 8) that if an individual is a
von Neuman and Morgenstern expected utility maximizer (his
or her psychology is neo-Bernoullian), then his or her von
Neuman Morgenstern utility index $u^v(x_i)$ must coincide, up to
a positive affine transformation, with Allais' psychological
index $s(x_i)$.

If an individual is a von Neuman Morgenstern expected
utility maximizer and also satifies the axioms stated in
section 3 above that led to the existance of the cardinal
utility indices u_i^c, then, there may exists a function
$u_i^v = F(u_i^c)$ assigning to each value of u_i^c a value of u_i^v.
But, contrary to Allais', to this writer the function F, if
it does exist, does not have to be a positive linear
transformation.   Indeed, it was proposed elsewhere
(Camacho, 1979c, p. 216) to use the curvature of this
function to characterize the attitude toward risk, with the
individual being considered: risk neutral, if F is a
positive affine transformation; risk averse, if F is a
monotonic increasing and strictly concave transformation;
risk loving, if F is a monotonic increasing and strictly
convex transformation.

It can easily be seen, of course, that if F is not a
positive affine transformation, then the individual does
not follow the rule of long run success stated before in
section 4 and, in this sense, it can be considered that he
or she is not acting rationally. However, violating the
rule of long run success does not imply violating either
Allais' axiom of absolute preference (the principle of

stochastic dominance) or the transitivity of the preference ordering of the probability distributions. Since these are (aside from taking into account objective probabilities) Allais' only rationalty requirements, it follows that an individual can be rational in Allais' sense and risk averse or risk loving in our sense.

5.2   Implications for Decision Making Under Uncertainty

According to the expected utility theory (or to the neo-Bernoullians) rationality means adherence by the individual, in ranking probability distributions over a set of prizes $\{x_1,\ldots,x_i,\ldots,x_n\}$, to the axioms of the theory. This adherence, as is well known, implies the existence of the cardinal utility indices u_i^v and the ordering of probability distributions according to the corresponding expected values of the u_i^v. That is, a probability distribution $p=(p_1,\ldots,p_i,\ldots,p_n)$ is ranked equal to a probability distribution $p'=(p_1',\ldots,p_i',\ldots,p_n')$ if and only if $E[u^v|p] = E[u^v|p']$. It is ranked above if and only if $E[u^v|p] > E[u^v|p']$.

To Allais, rationality requires, besides that the individual takes into account objective probabilities, only that his or her ordering of probability distributions be transitive and that the axiom of absolute preference (or the principle of stochastic dominance) is not violated.

Let us consider two positions. One, take rationality as meaning satisfying the rule of long run success stated above. Two, take rationality in Allais' sense.

If we take rationality as meaning satisfying the rule of long run success, then it can be shown that the so called rationality axioms of the expected utility theory are neither necessary nor sufficient for rationality in this sense. They are not sufficient because the individual can satisfy the expected utility theory axioms and at the same time violate the rule of long run success. This would be the case if the utility indices u_i^v obtained from the rationality axioms of the expected utility theory do not coincide, up to a positive affine transformation, with the cardinal utility indices u_i^c. They are not necessary because the following lexicographic ordering of probability distributions:

rank p equal to p' if $E[u_i^c|p] = E[u_i^c|p']$ and $\sigma[u_i^c|p]$

$$= \sigma[u_i^c|p'],$$

$$\text{if } E[u_i^c|p] > E[u_i^c|p'],$$

rank p above p'   or if $E[u_i^c|p] = E[u_i^c|p']$, $\sigma[u_i^c|p]$

$$< \sigma[u_i^c|p'],$$

where $\sigma[u_i^c|p]$ represents the standard deviation of the
random utility u_i^c given p,
satisfies the rule of long run success but not the axioms
of the expected utility theory.

Although rationality in the sense of not violating the
rule of long run success allows for behavior that takes
into consideration not only the expected value but also the
dispersion of the cardinal utility indices u_i^c as Allais requires, this is so to an extend that, this writer is
convinced, would not satisfy Allais. The dispersion of
the cardinal utility indices u_i^c can affect the way in
which the probability distributions are ranked only if the
expected values corresponding to these probability distributions are the same. But if they are not the same, then the
probability distribution with the higher expected value is
always ranked above the probability distribution with the
lower expected value.

The rule of long run success is certainly compelling
if the choice situation were to repeat itself infinite
many times. But since in real life a choice situation,
although it may repeat itself many times, does not repeat
infinite many, this rule, it can be argued, may not be as
compelling as it looks. This criticism is correct.

More difficult to analyze is the criticism that the
rule of long run success does not take into consideration
the possibility of being ruined.[9] If being ruined is one
"prize" of the set of prizes over which the probability
distributions are defined, and there is a cardinal utility
index corresponding to this "prize" derived from the axioms
stated in section 3, then there is no reason for singling
out the "prize" "being ruined." If, on the other hand, a
cardinal utility index, in the sense defined in this paper,

does not exist for the "prize" "being ruined," then for those situations where this prize enters, our theory does not apply.

If, in view of these criticisms, we take rationality in the less restrictive Allais' sense, then certainly violating the rule of long run success does not imply violating rationality. However this writer feels that teaching the decision maker how to precisely define and determine the cardinal utility indices u^c, and how to use them, in conjunction with the law of large numbers, to prove that maximizing the expected value of the utility indices u^c satisfies the rule of long run success may be of value in helping him or her reach better decisions.

6.   CONCLUDING REMARKS

At the root of the thinking, in decision making under uncertainty, leading to rules prescribing the maximization of the expected value of some utility indices, seems to be the notions of cardinal utility and of long run success, and the application of the law of large numbers.

In this paper we have tried to make these notions precise and to use them, in conjunction with the law of large numbers, to show some implications of the rule that prescribes, in choosing among uncertain prospects, to maximize the expected value of the cardinal utility indices u_i^c. We think that the knowledge of these implications is of value in helping the decision maker choose among uncertain prospects.

In view of these implications, the decision maker may take into consideration, when choosing among probability distributions over prizes not only the corresponding expected values, dispersions, and even higher moments of the u_i^c, but also how many times he or she expects the choice situation may repeat itself.

Department of Economics
University of Illinois at Chicago

NOTES

1. Rules that according to Marschak (1950), any rational man should follow in ordering the probability distributions.

2. Pratt (1974, pp. 91-2) states "I am all in favor of any
    argument which will convince anyone not already convinced
    that maximizing expected utility is the only behavior
    worth rational consideration." And Marschak (1950 and
    1979) talks of the rationality rules leading to the maxi-
    mization of expected utility as if to follow them in
    making decisions under uncertainty were almost as compel-
    ling as to follow the rules of arithmetic in making
    calculations, or the rules of logic in reasoning.

3. The notions of <u>choice situation</u> and (<u>imagined</u>) <u>identical</u>
    <u>repetitions of a choice situation</u> underlie the theory of
    cardinal utility developed by this writer in previous
    publications (See, for instance, Camacho 1974). However,
    they do not appear explicitly stated until 1980 when they
    were presented in (Camacho, 1980).

4. It has been suggested in relation to the positionalist
    approach to social choice (Hansson, 1973, p. 44), that
    the number of alternatives ranked betwen two given alter-
    natives, say x and x', be considered as a measure of the
    intensity of preference for x over x'. Thus if we consider
    two pairs of alternatives x preferred to x' and x"
    preferred to x''' , and the number of alternatives ranked
    between x and x' is greater than the number of alternatives
    ranked between x" and x''' , the conclusion is that the
    intensity of preference for x over x' must be greater than
    the intensity of preference for x" over x''' . It must be
    emphasized that under the present approach, the number of
    alternatives ranked between two given alternatives, say x
    and x', is not an indicator of the intensity of preference
    for x over x'. Referring to the case with coffee, tea and
    camomile, it is conceivable to imagine one hundred
    different drinks ranked betwen tea and camomile and none
    between coffee and tea and still having the intensity of
    preference for coffee over tea greater than the intensity
    of preference for tea over camomile.

5. A <u>preference ordering</u> defined on a set is a reflexive,
    transitive and connected binary relation defined on the
    set.

6. A relational system is a non-empty set X, called the
    domain of the relational system, and a sequence, finite
    or infinite, of relations defined on X.

7. A related problem was also studied later by J. Marschak
    and R. Radner in the context of 'long run subjective
    probabilities.' See in particular (Marschak and Radner
    1972, chapter 4, sections 9, 10, 11).

8. According to Allais (1979, p. 8), to von Neuman and Morgenstern u_i^v is cardinal utility in Jevons' sense. It represents intensity of preferences. Without going into the argument regarding what each author thought of his proposed utility index, this writer feels that in present day interpretation of the expected utility theory, the indices u_i^v are taken to be the result of both the attitude toward risk and the intensity of preference.

9. See Allais (1979, p. 570, note 131).

REFERENCES

Allais, M.: 1979, 'The Foundations of a Positive Theory of Choice Involving Risk', in M. Allais and O. Hagen (eds.), Expected Utility Hypotheses and the Allais Paradox: Contemporary Discussions with Allais's Rejoinder, D. Reidel, Dordrecht, Holland, pp. 27-145.

Camacho, A.: 1974, 'Societies and Social Decision Functions', in W. Leinfellner and E. Köhler (eds.), Developments in the Methodology of Social Sciences, D. Reidel, Dordrecht, Holland, pp. 217-253.

Camacho, A.: 1979a, 'On Cardinal Utility', Theory and Decision 10, 131-45.

Camacho, A.: 1979b, 'Maximizing Expected Utility and the Rule of Long Run Success', in M. Allais and O. Hagen (eds.), Expected Utility Hypotheses and the Allais Paradox: Contemporary Discussions with Allais's Rejoinder, D. Reidel, Dordrecht, Holland, pp. 203-229.

Camacho, A.: 1980, 'Approaches to Cardinal Utility', Theory and Decision 12, 359-79.

Camacho, A.: 1982, Societies and Social Decision Functions: A Model With Focus on the Information Problem, D. Reidel, Dordrecht, Holland.

Hansson, B.: 1973, 'The Independence Condition in the Theory of Social Choice', Theory and Decision 4, 25-49.

Machina, M. J.: 1981, '"Rational" Decision making versus "Rational" Decision Modeling?' Journal of Mathematical Psychology, 24, pp. 163-75.

Marschak, J.: 1950, 'Rational Behavior, Uncertain Prospects and Measurable Utility', Econometrica 18, 11-41.

Marschak, J.:   1951, 'Why "Should" Statisticians and Business-
   men Maximize "Moral Expectation"'. Proceedings of the
   Second Berkeley Symposium on Mathematical Statistics and
   Probability, University of California Press, Berkeley, CA,
   pp. 993-506.
Marschak, J. and Roy Radner: 1972, Economic Theory of Teams,
   Yale University Press, New Haven, Conn.
Marschak, J.:   1979, 'Utilities, Psychological Values and
   Decision Makers', in M. Allais and O. Hagen (eds.), Expected
   Utility Hypotheses and the Allais Paradox: Contemporary
   Discussions with Allais's Rejoinder, Dordrecht, Holland,
   pp. 163-174.
Pratt, J. W.:   1974, 'Somme Comments on Some Axioms for Decision Making under Uncertainity', in M. Bach, D. McFadden,
   and S. Wu (eds.), Essays on Economic Behavior under Uncertainity. North-Holland, Amsterdam, Holland, pp. 82-92.
von Neuman, J. and Morgenstern, O.:   1947, Theory of Games
   and Economic Behavior, Second edition. Princeton, N.J.

Morris H. DeGroot

Decision Making with an Uncertain Utility Function

1.   INTRODUCTION

In this paper we shall consider sequential decision
problems in which the decision maker (DM) is uncertain about
his utility function. In problems of this type, learning
about the utility function from observations and experiences
realized during the sequential process is an important consideration when the DM tries to choose his decisions in an
optimal fashion. Such problems are known as problems of
adaptive utility.

One central purpose of this paper is to present a survey
and summary of the concepts of adaptive utility as they were
introduced and developed in Cyert and DeGroot (1975, 1980)
and DeGroot (1982). Several examples will be described which
illustrate and explicate these concepts.

The two central components of any decision problem under
uncertainty are the DM's subjective probabilities, which
characterize his knowledge and beliefs, and his subjective
utilities, which characterize his preferences and tastes.
In the usual developments of decision theory, it is assumed
that the DM can specify his utility function fully and precisely. Thus, although the mathematical model of decision
making recognizes that the DM will change and update his
probabilities in the light of new information and data
obtained during the sequential process, it is also assumed
that the DM has a known fixed utility function during that
process.

In models of adaptive utility, the notion of learning
is applied to utilities as well as probabilities. It is
assumed that the utility that the DM will receive from specific consequences that might result from his decisions are
uncertain to some extent, and the expected utility of these
consequences changes as the DM learns from experience. Once
it is recognized that utilities can change by experience in

B. P. Stigum and F. Wenstøp (eds.), Foundations of Utility and Risk Theory with Applications,
371–384.
© 1983 *by D. Reidel Publishing Company.*

this way, it becomes important to incorporate the likelihood
of such changes in the theory of decision. The DM must now
choose experiments and decisions at each stage of a sequential process that will maximize his overall expected utility
when he recognizes that his utility function may be different
from what he thinks it is and that he must·try to learn about
his utility function as an integral part of the decision
making process.

The economics literature contains various papers that
are more or less close to the spirit of the approach being
described here. Optimal sequential experiments where information is gained from decisions and consequences have been
studied by Grossman, Kihlstrom, and Mihrman (1977), Kihlstrom
(1974), and Kihlstrom and Mihrman (1975). Problems involving
learning about linear utility functions have explicitly been
considered by Manning (1971) and Long and Manning (undated
technical report). Notions of changing utilities and tastes
have been discussed by Witsenhausen (1974) and by Marschak
(1978), Pessemier (1978), and Pollak (1978). Simon (1955)
has expressed the fundamental idea underlying adaptive
utility very well: "The consequences that the organism
experiences may change the payoff function - it doesn't know
how well it likes cheese until it has eaten cheese." This
approach is rather different from that of Stigler and Becker
(1977) in which it is assumed that the DM's utility function
over the sequential process is completely known and there
are no stochastic variables present, either as observations
or parameters.

2.   COMMODITY BUNDLES

As an example of learning about one's utility function
by a Bayesian process, suppose that a DM must allocate his
income b in a given period among k commodities. Let
$p_1, \ldots, p_k$ denote the prices of these commodities and let
$x_1, \ldots, x_k$ denote the amounts of the commodities that are
purchased in a given period. Finally, let $U(x_1, \ldots, x_k)$
denote the DM's utility function in this context.

If the function U is completely known, then the DM
will choose $x_1, \ldots, x_n$ to maximize U subject to the
income constraint

$$\sum_{i=1}^{k} p_i x_i = b \ . \tag{2.1}$$

Under the usual assumptions regarding differentiability and first order conditions, the optimal choices $x_1, \ldots, x_k$ will satisfy the relations

$$\frac{1}{p_1} \frac{\partial U}{\partial x_1} = \ldots = \frac{1}{p_k} \frac{\partial U}{\partial x_k} \tag{2.2}$$

as well as (2.1).

If U is not completely known to the DM, then it may not be possible to implement the solution specified by (2.2) because these values will not be known. Suppose, for example, that it is known that U has the following form

$$U(\underset{\sim}{x} | \underset{\sim}{\alpha}) = \sum_{i=1}^{k} \alpha_i \log x_i \ , \tag{2.3}$$

where $\underset{\sim}{x} = (x_1, \ldots, x_k)$ and $\underset{\sim}{\alpha} = (\alpha_1, \ldots, \alpha_k)$ is a vector of parameters such that $\alpha_i > 0$ for $i=1, \ldots, k$ and $\sum_{i=1}^{k} \alpha_i = 1$. If $\underset{\sim}{\alpha}$ is known, then the optimal choice of x_i is

$$x_i = b\alpha_i/p_i \quad \text{for} \quad i=1, \ldots, k \ . \tag{2.4}$$

If the DM is uncertain about the value of $\underset{\sim}{\alpha}$, then in accordance with the Bayesian approach to learning he will represent his uncertainty by a prior distribution on $\underset{\sim}{\alpha}$. Since $\underset{\sim}{\alpha}$ enters (2.3) linearly, the DM will maximize his expected utility $E[U(\underset{\sim}{x}|\underset{\sim}{\alpha})]$ in any single period simply by choosing

$$x_i = bE(\alpha_i)/p_i \quad \text{for} \quad i=1, \ldots, k \ . \tag{2.5}$$

Suppose now that the DM must choose $x_1, \ldots, x_k$ in each period of an n-period sequential decision process, and suppose that the total utility of the DM over the entire process is a weighted or discounted sum of the utilities (2.3) in each period. If the DM can learn about α from the experience of consuming the amounts $x_1, \ldots, x_k$ of the k commodities in each period, then it may be possible for him to attain a higher overall expected utility than he would achieve by following the myopic decision rule (2.5) in which he simply maximizes his expected utility in each period without explicitly trying to gain information that would be helpful in future periods.

What kind of information about his utility function does the DM receive when he consumes the amounts $x_1, \ldots, x_k$ of the different commodities in a given period? In the context being considered here, this information is typically more of a qualitative nature rather than a quantitative nature. The experience of consuming $x_1, \ldots, x_k$ cannot typically be assessed by the DM in terms of a numerical utility. Rather, the DM will assess his experience as being satisfactory or unsatisfactory, better or worse than expected, etc. These ideas will now be described in terms of two explicit mathematical models of learning.

1. At the beginning of each period, the DM's expected utility from consuming $x_1, \ldots, x_k$ is

$$E[U(\underset{\sim}{x}|\underset{\sim}{\alpha})] = \sum_{i=1}^{k} E(\alpha_i) \log x_i . \qquad (2.6)$$

The actual utility that he will experience is given by (2.3). In this first model, it is assumed that the DM can determine whether the actual utility was greater or less than expected. In other words, after consuming $x_1, \ldots, x_k$, the DM can determine whether (2.3) or (2.6) is larger (or whether they are equal). Since the value of (2.6) is fixed and known in a given period, once $\underset{\sim}{x}$ has been chosen, the DM can actually learn in that period whether the particular linear combination of $\alpha_1, \ldots, \alpha_k$ given by (2.3) is larger or smaller than a constant. By an expeditious choice of the $\underset{\sim}{x}$'s sequentially over the n periods, the learning process can be facilitated.

2. In this second model, it is assumed that after he has consumed $x_1, \ldots, x_k$ in a given period, the DM can determine

whether he would have preferred slightly larger amounts of some of the commodities and correspondingly smaller amounts of others while still satisfying the income constraint (2.1). More explicitly, let x be any point in the hyperplane defined by (2.1) and let R be the family of all rays r that emanate from $\underset{\sim}{x}$ and lie in the hyperplane. Then it is assumed that after he has consumed $x_1, \ldots, x_k$ the DM can determine for every ray $r \in R$ whether the directional derivative of U at $\underset{\sim}{x}$ in the direction of r is positive or negative (or zero). It follows from (2.3) that this determination is equivalent to learning whether each linear function of $\alpha_1, \ldots, \alpha_k$ in a certain infinite family of linear functions is positive or negative.

Some further details of these two models are given in Cyert and DeGroot (1975). We now turn to a different example in which the concept of adaptive utility seems to capture the essential features of a familiar topic.

3.   SPECIAL MARKETING PROMOTIONS

In an effort to increase future sales of some product, a firm may introduce a special marketing promotion during which it offers the product for sale at a price significantly below the usual price and possibly even below the firm's unit cost. A promotion of this type, or trial offer, is introduced in order to give potential customers an opportunity to learn about the product and about the utility of the product to them.

Suppose that each consumer x in the population X of current and potential customers has a maximum price $y(x)$ that he would pay for the product in each period. For convenience, assume that one unit of the product is consumed by a customer in each period, and that if a consumer tries the product in a single period he will learn his value of $y(x)$.

Suppose that the current price of the product is p_0. Then the population X can be partitioned into the following three disjoint sets G_1, G_2, and G_3:

1.   The set G_1 consists of those customers who are purchasers at the current price p_0. Hence G_1 consists of those consumers x who know that $y(x) \geq p_0$.

2. The set G_2 consists of those consumers x who have tried the product at least once in the past and learned that $y(x) < p_0$. Hence, G_2 consists of consumers x who do not purchase the product because they know that $y(x) < p_0$.

3. The set G_3 consists of those consumers who have never tried the product. Although a consumer x in G_3 is uncertain about the value of $y(x)$, he has presumably never tried the product because he thinks it is likely that $y(x) < p_0$.

The set G_3 can be described in more technical detail if we make the usual assumptions that utility is proportional to money gained or lost and is additive over different periods. Consider a consumer x who is uncertain about the value of $y(x)$. If he tries the product once and learns that $y(x) \geq p_0$, then he will continue to purchase the product at price p_0 in future periods, and over an infinite horizon he will realize a gain of

$$\sum_{i=0}^{\infty} \beta^i [y(x) - p_0] = \frac{y(x) - p_0}{1 - \beta} , \qquad (3.1)$$

where β is a discount factor $(0 < \beta < 1)$. If the consumer learns that $y(x) < p_0$ when he tries the product the first time, then he will realize a loss of $p_0 - y(x)$ and will not purchase the product in future periods.

Suppose that the consumer's prior distribution function for the uncertain value of $y(x)$ is $F(y|x)$. Then it follows that the consumer will not try the product if

$$\int_{p_0}^{\infty} \frac{y - p_0}{1 - \beta} \, dF(y|x) < \int_0^{p_0} (p_0 - y) \, dF(y|x) \qquad (3.2)$$

and he will try the product if the inequality (3.2) is reversed. The set G_3 consists of those consumers x for which (3.2) holds.

If the firm lowers its price to p, and maintains the
new price in future periods, then (1) it will retain all of
its customers in G_1, (2) it will gain as new customers those
consumers x in G_2 such that $p \leq y(x) < p_0$, and (3) it
will get at least one trial from those consumers x in G_3
for which the inequality (3.2) is reversed when p_0 is
replaced by p. The firm will then retain as customers those
consumers x in G_3 who learn that $y(x) > p$.

The firm can attempt to set an optimal price p based
on its knowledge about the distribution of $y(x)$ in the
sets G_2 and G_3, or it can introduce a trial offer. There
are various possible forms that a trial offer might take.
It can lower the price to p for a single period, some fixed
number of periods, or a random number of periods that depends
on the response to the offer. It can subsequently raise the
price back to the original level p_0 or some other level p_1.
It can either announce or not announce what the length of the
trial period will be and what the subsequent price will be.

The purpose of the trial offer is to make it relatively
cheap for the consumers in G_3 to learn their values of
$y(x)$. If the firm believes that its product is of high
quality then it believes that consumers will discover that
$y(x)$ is larger than they expected it to be. Thus, special
promotions such as trial offers seem to be based strongly on
the concept of adaptive utility. Further details about this
example are given in Cyert and DeGroot (1980).

4.   CONTROL PROBLEMS WITH UNKNOWN TARGETS

In the remainder of this paper we shall consider some
problems of adaptive utility that fit quite naturally into
the standard framework of optimal sequential decision theory,
with the additional complication that some aspects of the
payoff function or loss function are unknown or uncertain.

As a simple example, consider an n-period control process in which the DM chooses the value of a control variable
v_j in period j and then observes the value of a state
variable Y_j in accordance with the relation

$$Y_j = \theta v_j + \varepsilon_j \quad \text{for} \quad j=1, \ldots, n \; . \qquad (4.1)$$

Here θ is an unknown coefficient and $\varepsilon_1, \ldots, \varepsilon_n$ are independent and identically distributed random errors with a specified common distribution. The values of $v_1, \ldots, v_n$ are to be chosen sequentially, with v_j being chosen after Y_{j-1} has been observed $(j=2, \ldots, n)$.

Suppose that the purpose of choosing $v_1, \ldots, v_n$ is to keep the observations $Y_1, \ldots, Y_n$ close to some fixed target t, and suppose as usual that a quadratic loss function is used so that the loss over the n periods is

$$L(Y_1, \ldots, Y_n | t) = \sum_{j=1}^{n} \beta_j (Y_j - t)^2 \; , \qquad (4.2)$$

where $\beta_1, \ldots, \beta_n$ are positive weights. The additional complication beyond those in the usual models of this type is that we assume here that the target t is unknown and that the experimenter can gain information about t as the process evolves.

In particular, we assume that after the control variable v_j has been chosen in period j, the experimenter can observe not only the state variable Y_j but also another random variable X_j whose distribution depends on the unknown target t. The description of this model is completed by the specification of a joint prior distribution for θ and t, and a joint distribution for Y_j and X_j given v_j, θ, t, and the choices and outcomes of periods 1, ..., j-1.

It is not surprising that under these general conditions, the optimal choices of $v_1, \ldots, v_n$ depend on the kind of information that the experimenter expects to obtain about t. It is somewhat surprising, however, that this dependence persists even when the process of learning about t is completely independent of the process of generating $Y_1, \ldots, Y_n$. We shall now illustrate this comment by considering in detail an example with just two periods ($n = 2$).

Suppose that θ and t have independent prior distributions, and also that the observation X_1 obtained at the end of the first period has a distribution that depends on t but is independent of Y_1, v_1, or θ. (The observation X_2 is irrelevant in this example since there are only two periods.) We shall show that the optimal choice of v_1 depends on the nature of the distribution of X_1, i.e., on the kind of information that the DM expects to receive about t. As usual, we must determine the optimal choice of v_1 by backward induction.

For given values of θ, t, and v_2, the expected quadratic loss in the second period is

$$E[(Y_2-t)^2|\theta,t,v_2] = Var(Y_2|\theta,v_2) + [E(Y_2|\theta,v_2) - t]^2$$

$$= \sigma^2 + (\theta v_2 - t)^2 , \qquad (4.3)$$

where $\sigma^2 = Var(\varepsilon_2)$. If we now take the expectation of (4.3) with respect to the posterior distribution of θ given Y_1 and v_1, we obtain

$$\sigma^2 + v_2^2 \, Var'(\theta) + [v_2 \, E'(\theta) - t]^2 , \qquad (4.4)$$

where E' and Var' denote the expectation and variance calculated with respect to the posterior distribution. Finally, if we take the expectation of (4.4) with respect to the posterior distribution of t given X_1, we obtain

$$E'[(Y_2-t)^2] = \sigma^2 + v_2^2 \, Var'(\theta) + Var'(t)$$

$$+ [E'(t) - v_2 \, E'(\theta)]^2 . \qquad (4.5)$$

The expression (4.5) is a quadratic function of v_2 and therefore the optimal value of v_2 is easily found by differentiation to be

$$v_2 = \frac{E'(\theta) \ E'(t)}{E'(\theta^2)} \ . \tag{4.6}$$

When this optimal value of v_2 is substituted into (4.5) we obtain, after some algebra

$$E'[(Y_2-t)]^2 = \sigma^2 + E'(t^2) - \frac{[E'(t) \ E'(\theta)]^2}{E'(\theta^2)} \ . \tag{4.7}$$

By (4.2), the total expected loss in this problem with two periods is

$$\beta_1 \ E[(Y_1-t)^2] + \beta_2 \ E[(Y_2-t)^2] \ , \tag{4.8}$$

where

$$E[(Y_2-t)^2] = E\{E'[(Y_2-t)]^2\} \ . \tag{4.9}$$

The expectation in (4.9) is taken, for any fixed value of v_1, with respect to Y_1 and X_1. In particular, since $E'(t) = E(t|X_1)$ depends only on X_1 and not on Y_1, and $E'(\theta)$ and $E'(\theta^2)$ depend only on Y_1 and v_1 and not on X_1, and since X_1 and Y_1 are independent, it follows from (4.9) and (4.7) that the total expected loss will depend on

$$E[E^2(t|X_1)] \ . \tag{4.10}$$

The expectation (4.10) depends on the nature of the observation X_1. As one extreme case, if we know that X_1 is not going to yield any information about t, then $E(t|X_1) = E(t)$, the prior mean of t which is a constant whose value does not depend on X_1. Hence the value of (4.10) is just $E^2(t)$. At the other extreme, if we know that X_1 will be fully informative and actually reveal the true value of t, then $E(t|X_1) = t$ and the value of (4.10) is $E(t^2)$.

In summary, since the expected total loss, for any given value of v_1, depends on the value of (4.10) and this value depends in turn on the nature of the distribution of X_1, it follows that the optimal value of v_1 will depend on the nature of the distribution of X_1.

5. STOCHASTIC OPTIMIZATION

Various problems of stochastic programming and stochastic optimization with an unknown objective function fall into the general class of problems being considered in this paper. In this section we shall describe one problem of this type.

Suppose that $\underset{\sim}{\theta} = (\theta_1, \ldots, \theta_k)'$ is a k-dimensional vector whose components are unknown, and that the DM must choose the vector $\underset{\sim}{v} = (v_1, \ldots, v_k)'$ from a specified set in order to maximize the expected value of $\underset{\sim}{\theta}'\underset{\sim}{v}$. If the DM assigns a prior distribution to $\underset{\sim}{\theta}$ with mean vector $\underset{\sim}{\mu} = (\mu_1, \ldots, \mu_k)'$, then $\underset{\sim}{v}$ must be chosen to maximize $E(\underset{\sim}{\theta}'\underset{\sim}{v}) = \underset{\sim}{\mu}'\underset{\sim}{v}$. Let S denote the k-dimensional unit sphere, i.e., S is the set of all vectors $\underset{\sim}{v}$ such that

$$\|\underset{\sim}{v}\|^2 = \underset{\sim}{v}'\underset{\sim}{v} \leq 1 . \qquad (5.1)$$

If $\underset{\sim}{v}$ must be chosen from S then it is well known that the optimal choice of $\underset{\sim}{v}$ is, for $\underset{\sim}{\mu} \neq 0$,

$$\underset{\sim}{v} = \underset{\sim}{\mu}/\|\underset{\sim}{\mu}\| \qquad (5.2)$$

and the maximum value of $\underset{\sim}{\mu}'\underset{\sim}{v}$ is simply $\|\underset{\sim}{\mu}\|$.

Now suppose that before choosing $\underset{\sim}{v}$, the DM has the opportunity to gain some information about $\underset{\sim}{\theta}$. In particular, suppose that the DM can choose a vector $\underset{\sim}{x}$ in S and observe the value of

$$Y = \underset{\sim}{\theta}'\underset{\sim}{x} + \varepsilon \qquad (5.3)$$

where ε is a random error with a known distribution. What vector $\underset{\sim}{x}$ should the DM choose?

Any choice of $\underset{\sim}{x}$ and any observed value of Y will lead to a posterior distribution for the parameter $\underset{\sim}{\theta}$ with some mean vector μ^*. It follows from the preceding discussion that the DM should choose $\underset{\sim}{x}$ in order to maximize $E(\|\mu^*\|)$, where the expectation is calculated with respect to the predictive distribution of Y. In the special case that we shall now describe, this maximization can be carried out without difficulty.

Let $N(a,B)$ denote the normal distribution with mean vector $\underset{\sim}{a}$ and covariance matrix $\underset{\sim}{B}$. Suppose that the prior distribution of $\underset{\sim}{\theta}$ is $N(\mu,\Sigma)$ and the distribution of the random error ε is $N(0, \sigma^2)$. Then the predictive distribution of Y will be $N(x'\mu, \sigma^2 + x'\Sigma x)$ and the posterior mean vector μ^* of $\underset{\sim}{\theta}$ will be [see, e.g., DeGroot (1970), Sec. 9.9]

$$\underset{\sim}{\mu}^* = (\sigma^2 \underset{\sim}{\Sigma}^{-1} + \underset{\sim\sim}{xx'})^{-1} (\sigma^2 \underset{\sim}{\Sigma}^{-1} \underset{\sim}{\mu} + \underset{\sim\sim}{xY}) . \qquad (5.4)$$

These calculations become greatly simplified if we now assume that $\underset{\sim}{\mu} = 0$. Then the predictive distribution of

$$Z = Y^2/(\sigma^2 + \underset{\sim}{x}'\underset{\sim\sim}{\Sigma x}) \qquad (5.5)$$

will be a chi-squared distribution with one degree of freedom. Thus,

$$E(Z^{\frac{1}{2}}) = (2/\pi)^{\frac{1}{2}} . \qquad (5.6)$$

We can now use the relation

$$(\sigma^2 \underset{\sim}{\Sigma}^{-1} + \underset{\sim\sim}{xx'})^{-1} = \frac{1}{\sigma^2} \left(\underset{\sim}{\Sigma} - \frac{\underset{\sim\sim}{\Sigma xx'}\underset{\sim}{\Sigma}}{\sigma^2 + \underset{\sim}{x}'\underset{\sim\sim}{\Sigma x}} \right) \qquad (5.7)$$

to obtain

$$\|\mu^*\| = Q(\underset{\sim}{x})\ Z , \qquad (5.8)$$

where

$$Q(\underset{\sim}{x}) = \frac{\underset{\sim}{x}'\underset{\sim}{\Sigma}^2\underset{\sim}{x}}{\sigma^2 + \underset{\sim}{x}'\underset{\sim\sim}{\Sigma x}} . \qquad (5.9)$$

Thus,

$$E(\|\mu^*\|) = [2Q(x)/\pi]^{\frac{1}{2}} . \qquad (5.10)$$

It follows from (5.10) that x must be chosen to maximize $Q(x)$. This maximization can be reduced to a standard problem in multivariate analysis.

First, it should be noted that the optimal choice of x will always be an extreme point of S, i.e., a vector such that $\|x\| = 1$, since the maximum information about θ is obtained at such points. Hence, the DM must choose x to maximize

$$\frac{x'\Sigma^2 x}{x'(\sigma^2 I + \Sigma)x} \qquad (5.11)$$

subject to the constraint that $\|x\| = 1$.

Let r^* denote the largest eigenvalue of Σ, and let x^* be the corresponding eigenvector with $\|x^*\| = 1$. Then, as is well known, the value of (5.11) will be a maximum when $x = x^*$ and this maximum value will be $r^{*2}/(\sigma^2 + r^*)$.

The particular problem that we have just described was relatively easy for the DM to handle because he could choose x solely to attain the maximum amount of informatin about θ and he could then choose y solely to attain the maximum expected value of the objective function. We can extend our considerations to problems in which n vectors $x_1, \ldots, x_n$ must be chosen sequentially for purposes of both learning about θ and maximizing the expected payoff simultaneously. In such problems, the optimal choices of $x_1, \ldots, x_n$ are not necessarily extreme points of the set S. Some simple problems of this type, along with the example that we have worked out in this section, are presented in DeGroot (1982).

ACKNOWLEDGMENT

This research was supported in part by the National Science Foundation under grant SES-8207295.

Morris H. DeGroot is a Professor of Statistics at
Carnegie-Mellon University, Pittsburgh, Pennsylvania.

REFERENCES

Cyert, R.M. and M.H. DeGroot: 1975, 'Adaptive Utility',
Adaptive Economic Models (R.H. Day and T. Groves, eds.),
New York: Academic Press, 223-246. Reprinted in Expected
Utility and the Allais Paradox (M. Allais and O. Hagen,
eds.), Dordrecht, Holland: D. Reidel Publ. Co., (1980),
223-241.

Cyert, R.M. and M.H. DeGroot: 1980, 'Learning Applied to
Utility Functions', Bayesian Analysis in Econometrics and
Statistics (A. Zellner, ed.), Amsterdam: North-Holland
Publishing Co., 159-168.

DeGroot, M.H.: 1970, Optimal Statistical Decisions, New York:
McGraw-Hill Book Co.

Grossman, S.J., R.E. Kihlstrom and L.J. Mirman: 1977, 'A
Bayesian Approach to the Production of Information and
Learning by Doing', Review of Economic Studies 44, 533-547.

Kihlstrom, R.E.: 1974, 'A Bayesian model of demand for information about product quality', International Economic
Review, 99-118.

Kihlstrom, R.E. and L.J. Mirman: 1975, 'Information and market equilibrium', Bell Journal of Economics 6, 357-376.

Long, N.V. and R. Manning: undated, 'Adaptive Demand Theory:
The Case With a Linear Utility Function', unpublished,
School of Economics, University of New South Wales.

Manning, R.: 1971, 'Adaptive Demand Theory', unpublished,
Second Conference of Economists, Sydney.

Marschak, T.A.: 1978, 'On the Study of Taste Changing Policies',
American Economic Review 68, 386-391.

Pessemier, E.A.: 1978, 'Stochastic Properties of Changing
Preferences', American Economic Review 68, 380-385.

Pollak, R.A.: 1978, 'Endogenous Tastes in Demand and Welfare
Analysis', American Economic Review 68, 374-379.

Simon, H.A.: 1955, 'A Behavioral Model of Rational Choice',
Quarterly Journal of Economics 69, 99-118.

Stigler, G.J. and G.S. Becker: 1977, 'De Gustibus non est
Disputandum', American Economic Review 67, 76-90.

Witsenhausen, H.S.: 1974, 'On the Uncertainty of Future Preferences', Annals of Economics and Social Measurement 3,
91-94.

Frank Milne and H. M. Shefrin

WELFARE LOSSES ARISING FROM INCREASED PUBLIC
INFORMATION, AND/OR THE OPENING OF NEW SECURITIES MARKETS:
EXAMPLES OF THE GENERAL THEORY OF THE SECOND BEST

The present paper treats two important problems in financial
economics, one relating to tradable securities and the other
to publicly held information.[1] Suppose it has been decided
that an (apparent) improvement will be made in the operation
of a particular financial market. This "improvement" will
take one of two possible forms:
1.   A new (tradable) security will be introduced; and/or
2.   Better public information will be made available.
It is now widely understood that neither of these so-called
improvements need lead to welfare gains, and in fact can
result in unambiguous welfare losses!

This last remark strongly suggests that financial markets
display puzzling, if not paradoxical behavior. Yet we
argue below that the features in question are hardly specific
to financial markets. Rather, we contend that they arise
because the underlying framework comprises a special case of
the general theory of the second best. In this regard it
is worth recalling the prophetic remarks with which Lipsey
and Lancaster began their pioneering work:

> There is an important basic similarity underlying a
> number of recent works in apparently widely separated
> fields of economic theory. Upon examination, it would
> appear that the authors have been rediscovering, in some
> of the many guises given it by various specific problems,
> a single general theorem. This theorem forms the core
> of what may be called The General Theory of Second Best.
> Although the main principles of the theory of second
> best have undoubtedly gained wide acceptance, no general
> statement of them seems to exist. Furthermore, the
> principles often seem to be forgotten in the context of
> specific problems and, when they are rediscovered and
> stated in the form pertinent to some problem, this seems
> to evoke expressions of surprise and doubt rather than of

B. P. Stigum and F. Wenstøp (eds.), Foundations of Utility and Risk Theory with Applications,
385–395.
© 1983 *by D. Reidel Publishing Company.*

immediate agreement and satisfaction at the discovery of
yet another application of the already accepted generalizations.

We regard the above remarks to be prophetic because both
of the issues with which the present paper is concerned turn
out to constitute "yet another application of the already
accepted generalizations".   Therefore it appears that here
too, the second best "principles" seem to have been "forgotten
in the context of specific problems".   From a historical
perspective it is equally interesting that the rediscovery
of the second best principles in the context of the specific
financial problems treated here, did "evoke expressions of
surprise and doubt rather than immediate agreement and
satisfaction." It is for this reason that we wish to stress
the following: The welfare loss result cited above should
not be attributed to idiosyncracies which characterize either
better public information or new securities in financial
markets.   Rather it is the second best elements imbedded
within the problem which account for the features in question.

The first of the two problems we address concerns the
welfare impact of increasing the number of securities in an
incomplete market system.   In particular, Hart (1975) has
produced an intriguing example which has the addition of a
security (to the set of tradable securities) inducing a
welfare reduction for _every_ single trader in the economy.
The second result concerns the welfare impact of
introducing finer (or "better") public information in a
system of security markets.   Examples by Hirshleifer (1971),
Breyer (1979) and others show that finer information can
make all consumers worse off.

As it turns out these two problems are closely related;
and a unified framework can be formulated showing that the
examples are applications of the well-known theory of the
second-best[2] in which additional constraints are imposed on
the set of resource-feasible allocations.   In order to make
our case, we proceed as follows.   In section I, we sketch
a stylized model in which there are three periods and two
states of nature.   Significantly, our formulation uses two
separate sets of (second best) constraints to capture the
critical elements which arise in both the tradable securities
problem and the publicly held information problem.   One set
pertains to the securities issue and the other to the

information issue.   This technique will enable us to make
quite transparent the driving force behind the second best
welfare results cited above.

In section II we discuss the implications of changing
the information structure for a particular variant of our
model, and emphasize the second-best nature of the example.
In section III we consider an example of our model where
increasing the number of securities decreases welfare - and
again the second best nature of the problem is emphasized.
The concluding section makes some general comments on
possible extensions and generalizations of the ideas in this
paper.

1.   A FORMAL MODEL

Consider a simple exchange economy with two households A and
B;   three time periods $t\varepsilon$ (1,2,3); and two states of the
world S_1 and S_2 where the information structure takes the
following form:

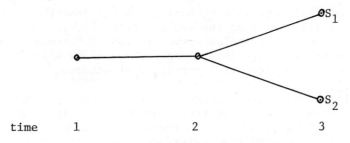

time   1   2   3

Figure 1.

In other words, at times 1 and 2 both households do not
know which state will occur;   but at 3 the true state is
revealed to them.   Notice that the definition of a state
of the world is sufficiently general to include the observation of some signalling mechanism.   (We will assume that
any signalling mechanism is not under the control of either
agent).   Assume that there are two commodities available in
states S_1 and S_2, but only one at times 1 and 2.   This is a
simplifying assumption of no great importance.

Assume that households are "rational", in the Radner
(1972) sense, such that they have identical point expectations

of prices; and these prices turn out to be market-clearing prices.

Now, in order to emphasize the distinction between information constraints and constraints on the use of assets, define primitive consumption $x_h(\ell, t, s)$ and endowments $w_h(\ell, t, s)$ where the arguments are: h-household, ℓ-commodity, t-time period, and s-state. Therefore the information structure illustrated in figure 1 effectively describes the constraints.

(1)   (a) $x_h(\ell, 1, S_1) = x_h(\ell, 1, S_2)$

       (b) $w_h(\ell, 1, S_1) = w_h(\ell, 1, S_2)$

       (c) $x_h(\ell, 2, S_1) = x_h(\ell, 2, S_2)$

       (d) $w_h(\ell, 2, S_1) = w_h(\ell, 2, S_2)$

In technical jargon, the constraints (1) describe a σ-algebra or filtration on the set of states S_1, S_2. Any variation in this information structure can be formulated as a change in these constraints. In section II we will illustrate such a change in information structure.

Households have preferences over contingent consumptions; and these preferences can be represented by utility functions of the form $U_h[<x_h(\ell, t, s)>]$. Notice that the constraints (1) are quite separate from the preferences over primitive contingent consumptions.[4] This allows us to change the information structure without changing the primitive preferences.

To transfer wealth over time and across states, consumers have available (potentially at least) a set of primitive securities such that $a_h(\ell, t, \tau, s)$ is a claim held by h, for one unit of commodity ℓ, in (τ, s), as negotiated at (t, s). $(\tau \varepsilon \{t+1, \ldots, 3\})$. We will assume that for various reasons (e.g. transactions costs, government regulations) that certain primitive securities or combinations of primitive securities are unavailable.[5] Given that both households face the same set of constraints, let us simply assume that $a_h \varepsilon C'$ where C' is a constraint set on the set of basic securities. This constraint set is sufficiently general to include short-sale restrictions; restrictions requiring trading in composite securities, and so on.

Of course assets should also be constrained by the σ-algebra. If we consider those constraints to be described by $a_h \varepsilon$ B then

(2) $a_h \varepsilon$ C' $\cap$ B $\equiv$ C.

Finally, in providing a formal statement of the household's problem, we specify a sequence of budget constraints, with asset holding providing the links between periods and states.   If there is a sufficiently complete set of markets, then the set of budget constraints collapses to a single budget constraint.

Formally, the budget constraint set for household h is:

(3)
(a) $\displaystyle\sum_{s=S_1}^{S_2} [p(1,s)x_h(1,s) + \sum_{t=2}^{3} \Pi(1,\tau,s)a_h(1,\tau,s)$

$-p(1,s)w_h(1,s)] \leqslant 0;$

(b) $\displaystyle\sum_{s=S_1}^{S_2} [p(2,s)x_h(2,s) + \Pi(2,3,s)a_h(2,3,s)$

$-p(2,s)w_h(2,s) - p(2,s)a_h(1,2,s)] \leqslant 0;$

(c) $p(3,S_1)x_h(3,S_1) - p(3,S_1)w_h(3,S_1)$

$-p(3,S_1)[a_h(1,3,S_1) + a_h(2,3,S_1)] \leqslant 0;$

(d) $p(3,S_2)x_h(3,S_2) - p(3,S_2) - p(3,S_2)w_h(3,S_2)$

$-p(3,S_2)[a_h(1,3,S_2) + a_h(2,3,S_2)] \leqslant 0.$

Note (a) The variables have the commodity argument suppressed and should be treated as vectors;

(b) The variable $\Pi(\ \ )$ is the price of an asset.

Therefore each household faces a problem of maximizing $U_h(<x_h(\ell,t,s)>)$ subject to the constraints (1), (2), and (3). To complete the description of the economy we have the market clearing conditions:

$$\sum_h x_h(\ell,t,s) - \sum_h w_h(\ell,t,s) \leqslant 0$$

$$\sum_h a_h(\ell,t,\tau,s) \leqslant 0.$$

With our problem formulated we turn now to an example where there is a finer information structure.

II.   A Finer Information Structure

Consider the following example, which is a special case of our model developed in Section 1.[6] Let the information structure be as illustrated in figure 1.   The asset constraint set C is assumed to be sufficiently flexible so that at time 1 there is a riskless bond paying 1 unit of the commodity at date 2; but there are no contingent securities available at time 1 for trading in S_1 and S_2.   At time 2 let there be Arrow–Debreu securities for the two states S_1 and S_2 at time 3.   For simplicity assume that there is only one commodity in states S_1 and S_2.   Given this structure it is clear that the optimality theorems of Debreu (1959) Chapters 6 and 7 apply, so that given the information structure (as in figure 1) the allocation is Pareto Optimal.

Now consider a change in the information structure such that the true state is revealed at time 2.   The information structure is said now to be finer; or in terms of the infor-mation constraints we have now:

(1')   (a) $x_h(\ell,1,S_1) = x_h(\ell,1,S_2)$

        (b) $w_h(\ell,1,S_1) = w_h(\ell,1,S_2)$

Clearly (1') is less restrictive than (1).   Also constr-aint (2) becomes

(2') $a_h \ \varepsilon \ C' \cap B'$,

where B' represents the constraints from the finer σ-algebra. Alternatively we can illustrate the structure diagramatically:

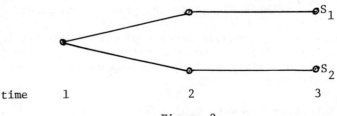

time   1   2   3

Figure 2.

Given the structure of the available securities consider the new equilibrium associated with the new information structure.   It is obvious that the Arrow-Debreu securities at time 2 are now redundant, and it is easy to provide numerical utility functions to show that both consumers will suffer a decline in utility from the introduction of finer information.[7]

Why does this apparent paradox occur ? Breyer (1979) has observed that by opening more security markets, so that contingent claims for S_1 and S_2 are available at time 1, then the new allocation is Pareto Optimal with respect to the finer information structure.   Therefore with these extra security markets, the introduction of finer information could not reduce welfare.

The crucial observation is that there is an interaction between the information and security constraints: by merely relaxing some of the combined constraints (1) and (2), but not the remainder, we have a second best situation.   Of course, we can discuss optimality given a particular information structure, as in Debreu (1959) Chapter 7. But when the information structure is a matter of choice this is merely a second best optimum.

We now turn to variations in the asset constraints, holding the information structure constant.

III.   Adding Securities to An Incomplete Market System

In an important contribution, Hart (1975) provided an example where in an incomplete market system adding a security made both households worse off.   We will slightly modify his example and give a simple interpretation showing the second best "paradox".   The example will be a certainty model, but it can be reinterpreted as an uncertainty model.

Consider three dates $t = 1,2,3$ with certainty where there are two commodities at each date.   We will have an exchange economy with two households A and B, who have utility functions:

$$U_A = U(x_A(1,1)) + f(x_A(1, 1);   x_A(1,2), x_A(2,2))$$

$$+ \beta^A g(x_A(1,3), x_A(2,3))$$

$$U_B = U(x_B(2, 1)) + \beta^B g(x_B(1,2), x_B(2,2))$$

$$+ f(x_B(2,1); x_B(1, 3); x_B(2,3))$$

Assume   (a) $U: R_+ \to R$; $g: R_+^2 \to R$; $f: R_+^3 \to R$;

(b) $U'(\ )$, $g_1, g_2, f_1, f_2, f_3 > 0$;

(c) $g(\ )$ and $f(\ )$ are quasi-concave;

(d) $f(1; x, y) = g(x, y)$, $\forall x, y \geq 0$;

(e)   given $f(z; 1, 1)$, $g(1,1)$ and $z \neq 1$

then $\dfrac{d}{dz} (f_2/f_3) \neq g_1/g_2$

Furthermore, we assume that

$$w_A(2,1) = w_A(\ell, t) = 1 \text{ for } \ell = 1,2; \quad t = 2,3;$$

$$w_A(1,1) = 0$$

$$w_B(1, 1) = w_B(\ell, t) = 1 \text{ for } \ell = 1,2; \quad t = 2,3;$$

$$w_B(2, 1) = 0.$$

Now with no security markets linking periods, and no trade in commodity (1,1), there is no trade at date 1, but trade at dates t = 2,3.   Notice the symmetry in trades between agents at dates 2 and 3.

If we relax the constraint on trade for the commodity (1,1), then the consumers will swap endowments. Because of the symmetry assumptions there will be no trade at dates 2 and 3. Consumer A will lose at date 3 because there is a loss of trade.   But consumer A will gain overall from dates 1 and 2, even though trade disappears at date 2.   The latter assertion can be proved as follows: at the new prices at date 2, consumer A could always have chosen $x_A(1,1) = 0$ and $\tilde{x}_A = \{\tilde{x}_A(1, 2), \tilde{x}_A(2,2) \}$.   Holding $x_A(1, 1) = 0$ then because the terms of trade have swung in A's favour, this allocation is preferred to the constrained allocation. But at the new prices $\{x_A(1, 1) = x_A(1,2) = x_A(2,2) = 1\}$ is revealed preferred to $\{x_A(1, 1) = 0; \tilde{x}_A \}$. Thus

$\{x_A(1,1) = x_A(1,2) = x_A(2,2) = 1 \}$ is revealed preferred to the constrained allocation at dates 1 and 2.

By choosing β^A sufficiently large, consumer A is made worse off. A symmetrical argument applies to consumer B. Therefore relaxing a single constraint in an economy with multiple constraints can make all consumers worse off.

Our example is a certainty economy, but it can be reinterpreted as an uncertainty problem in the following way. Consider there to be only two dates and two states S_1 and S_2. Translate the original example so that $t = 2$ becomes S_1 and $t = 3$ becomes S_2. Clearly the existence, or not, of uncertainty is immaterial to the general argument, which can be applied, for example, to a certainty International Trade model.

Conclusion
    It should be obvious to the reader that our argument generalizes to any number of finite households, commodities, states and time periods. Furthermore it is possible to prove some quite general propositions giving conditions which rule out the possibility of second best "paradoxes". These propositions will not concern us here.[8]

In this paper we have considered different information structures and asset constraints in a mechanical comparative static exercise. It is more realistic to consider these changes as arising from the choices of agents within the system. For example, take the information system as given, but allow asset market activity to be determined by the actions of agents, constrained by transaction costs. Although the set of asset markets is endogeneously determined, it is not necessarily true that the outcome will be a Pareto Optimum. So long as the budget constraints of households cannot be collapsed to a single budget constraint, it is possible to construct second-best examples where multiple equilibria can be Pareto ranked, (see Hart (1975)). Secondly, given a particular transaction cost structure, lowering a transaction cost can lower welfare. (Our example in section III is an extreme case).

Similarly, if the information structure is chosen by an agent, it is obvious that second-best considerations cannot be ignored in analyzing the opportunities facing that agent.

For example, if households had to choose between the two
information structures proposed in the example in section II,
then the coarser structure would have been chosen.   There
is nothing peculiar about this example, for it has parallels
in the International trade literature in the theory of
tariff reduction.[9]

FOOTNOTES

1.   This paper is a simple exposition of some results
     contained in a more technical paper - see Milne and
     Shefrin (1981).
2.   For a discussion of this problem as a second-best
     problem see Cornes and Milne (1981).
3.   See Lipsey and Lancaster (1956).
4.   There is no necessity for these preferences to satisfy
     the von Neumann-Morgenstern axioms.
5.   It is important to understand that the explicit intro-
     duction of transaction costs does not avoid the second-
     best problems discussed here.   Simply consider the
     asset constraints as arising from infinite, or extremely
     large, transaction costs on certain primitive securities,
     and our arguments follow unchanged.
6.   This example is based on the example in Arrow (1978) and
     Breyer (1979).
7.   See Arrow (1978) and Breyer (1979).
8.   See Milne and Shefrin (1981).
9.   Consider two countries (households), two commodities and
     an equal ad valorem tariff on both goods.   The equil-
     ibrium is an optimum - the tariffs effectively cancel
     out when the tariff revenue is paid as income to the
     tariff imposing country.   If one tariff is removed the
     new equilibrium is not an optimum, and it is not
     difficult to see situations where both countries would
     be worse off by removing merely one tariff.

REFERENCES

Arrow, K.J.   (1978)   "Risk Allocation and Information: Some
   Recent Theoretical Developments", The Geneva Papers on
   Risk Insurance,   8,   pp.5-19.
Breyer, F.   (1979)   "Can Additional Information Really Have
   Negative Welfare Effects ? - A note on Arrow's Risk

Allocation and Information", The Geneva Papers on Risk and Insurance, 12, pp.23-25.

Cornes, R. and Milne, R. (1981) "A Simple Analysis of Mutually Disadvantageous Trading Opportunities", mimeo, Australian National University.

Debreu, G. (1959) Theory of Value, Yale University Press.

Hart, O. (1975) "On the Optimality of Equilibrium in a Securities Market", Journal of Economic Theory, 11, pp.418-443.

Hirshleifer, J. (1971) "The Private and Social Value of Information and the Reward to Inventive Activity", American Economic Review, 61, pp.561-574.

Lipsey, R. and Lancaster, K. (1956) "The General Theory of the Second Best", Review of Economic Studies, 24, pp. 11-32.

Milne, F. and Shefrin, H. (1981) "On Efficient Constrained Equilibria with Changing Information and Security Structures", mimeo, Australian National University and University of Santa Clara.

Radner, R. (1972) "Existence of Equilibrium of Plans, Prices and Price Expectations in a Sequence of Markets, Econometrica, 40, pp.289-303.

PART VIII

DECISION MAKING IN ORGANIZATIONS

Andrew J. Mackinnon and Alexander J. Wearing [1]

DECISION MAKING IN DYNAMIC ENVIRONMENTS

Abstract

A matter of puzzlement is how, given their limited
cognitive processing abilities, people are able to manage
complex dynamic systems. In this paper we present a summary
of some experimental findings which indicate more precisely
the nature of the problems faced by human beings in managing
dynamic systems, informally relate these findings to aspects
of utility and risk, and also consider briefly some consequent
ergonomic policy implications.

Background

There is a well-known story about a Northern Hemispheric
sophisticate who happened to find himself in the back country
of Australia. He stops to ask a local farmer, "How do I get
to Weetulta from here?", and receives the reply, "If I were
going to Weetulta, I wouldn't start from here"! A series
of ill-chosen turns has left our traveller with no good
choices. He now has to go back the way he came, if indeed
he can find the way, and if he has also enough fuel and day-
light. If only, we can imagine him saying to himself, if
only I had realised sooner that I had made one (or more)
wrong turns, and if only I had studied the map more closely
before leaving. The hope of the morning is replaced by
despair, as night draws in.

What characterises our hero's problem? First, he made
a sequence of decisions, each decision intended to move him
towards a long term goal (Weetulta), even though its immediate effect may have been to move him away from it. Second,
his environment changed over time (it had grown darker).
Third, his decisions suffered because of a delay in feedback
about their quality. Too late he learned from the farmer
that his initial decisions were wrong. Fourth, as a result
of the route that he had taken, fuel was consumed (and
could not be replaced) and so future decisions about subsequent routes were constrained. Fifth, some roads were
so rough that to traverse them again would be impossible.

B. P. Stigum and F. Wenstøp (eds.), Foundations of Utility and Risk Theory with Applications,
399–422.
© 1983 *by D. Reidel Publishing Company.*

If one wanted to return, another way would have to be found. For our Weetulta-bound traveller, the places to which it was possible to go were constrained by decisions already made, that is, the implications of current and past decisions reached into the future. Sixth, he was gravely hindered by the lack of an adequate model of the situation, the map that he left at home. Seventh, as night approached, our university trained peregrinator found that intelligent action needs the presence of hope, and that despair subtly but but greatly alters expected utilities (Sjoeberg, 1979).

Sequential decision making is difficult enough when the situation is simple. Even though normally we might not expect to become lost, we could easily find ourselves in the position of our sophisticated hero, were we mapless in the Weetulta countryside. However when the task becomes one of managing a complex dynamic system, then surely the task should become virtually impossible.

Indeed, it is matter of puzzlement how people are able to manage complex systems at all, be the task one of managing a company, directing an economy or even finding Weetulta. Both in laboratory and practical situations, there are many studies that show either how little information people use, and how sub-optimally they treat (and mistreat) it (See e.g., Evans, 1982; Dawes & Corrigan, 1974; Faust, 1982; O'Connell & Wearing, 1978; Wearing and Wearing, 1975). Just as there is no shortage of evidence that human beings like to keep matters simple, there is equally no argument that the world is a complex place. Indeed, theoretical arguments based on computer simulations have been developed to show that, without assistance, homo sapiens finds that dynamic systems are virtually unmanageable (Brewer, 1975; Metlay, 1975; Mackinnon, 1977).

Much of the argument elaborating the nature and extent of human cognitive limitations has focused on the making of single decisions (Cesa, 1982; Hammond, McClelland & Mumpower, 1980). Tasks that involve system management entail sequences of decisions. If people cannot handle simple static systems then, a fortiori, they should not be able to handle complex systems (where complexity is defined in terms of the number of elements contained in a system, the connections between these elements and the extent to which the relationships are deterministic or stochastic) that are also dynamic.

Yet, although people may not manage dynamic systems well, they do manage them. It is then somewhat remarkable that apart from motor tasks such as operating an aircraft or driving a car they have received little empirical study (there are some exceptions, e.g., Rappoport, 1975; Rappoport & Wallsten, 1972).

Most empirical work has chosen one of two emphases. One emphasis is exemplified by decision theorists, who have been concerned with optimality, and so have interested themselves with formal (and often conveniently simplified) descriptions of tasks, and with optimal strategies for performing these tasks. The second emphasis is chosen by cognitive psychologists, military planners, and business executives (but not management scientists, who fall rather into the first group), who have been more concerned with processes, and have tended to study decision behaviour in richer but less well understood tasks (Estes, 1980; Lockhead, 1980). Work in the first tradition pays little attention to ecological validity, a possibly dangerous disregard, as it is not clear to what other situations the findings and speculations from narrowly drawn situations generalize (see e.g., Ebbesen & Konecni, 1980). The second emphasis, particularly when war and business games comprise the experimental environment, has problems of both analysis (the tasks cannot be easily analysed in any formal sense) and generalizability, which may be a particular problem in military settings. Such games are akin to clinical studies derived from a variety of single cases and are usually$_2$ richer in hypotheses than in wide ranging conclusions.

In our research we have followed a middle ground. We began by looking at a relatively complex dynamic (but still analytically decomposable) situation, identifying the factors that might affect decision making, and then attempted to examine these identified factors in relative isolation from one another.

Dynamic Decision Making in a Complex Environment

Our first experiment involved a 'decision maker' interacting with a computer model and controlling a system that was presented as a welfare management task. Each experimental subject or decision maker had to take the role of an administrator who was responsible for allocating a fixed quantity of resources to different geographical areas where the resources could affect various kinds of welfare,

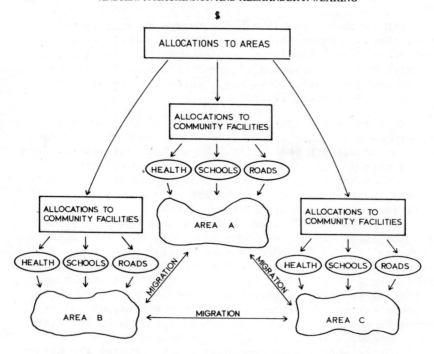

<u>Figure 1</u>
A diagrammatic representation of the MacKinnon & Wearing
(1980) task, showing the two allocation decision cycles
(first, to areas, & second to facilities) and the possible
interactions (through migration) between the areas.

such as health and education (see Figure 1). As a consequence of these allocations, welfare (here understood as
related to psychological well-being (Andrews & Withey, 1976;
Headey & Wearing, 1981))was generated and the amount of
well-being generated reflected the allocations of resources.
The experimental procedure is described in some detail in
Mackinnon & Wearing (1980) and in this paper we simply re-
capitulate their findings.

The Variables

    There were three independently manipulated variables[3];
each a component of complexity. The first was number; in
the experiment the number of elements in the system could

be either three or nine. This meant that each of the 3 geographical areas could possess either one kind of welfare
service, e.g., education (the 3 element condition), or three
kinds of welfare service, e.g., education, health and public
transport (the 9 element condition).

The second factor was whether or not the relationship
between the variables in the system was deterministic or
stochastic. A stochastic relationship was provided by
introducing a random error of $\pm$10% into each functional
relationship.

The third variable was whether or not the three geographical areas had an interactive relationship. Interaction occurred through migration. In the non-interactive
situation, the inhabitants of one area could not migrate to
any other area, no matter how unattractive their own area
might have become, perhaps as a result of the inequitable
allocation of resources, or of simple mismanagement. In the
interactive situation, population shifted from poorly served
to better served areas. Thus, the effect of pumping resources
into one area was to attract a large number of people from
the other areas, which would lead in time to the services
in that area being overloaded, leaving underutilized resources
languishing in the other two areas.

The Findings

We found that overall management of the three element
system was better, that its decision makers achieve more
well-being than those in the nine element systems. Second,
deterministic systems were easier to manage than stochastic
ones. Thirdly, interactive systems generated more well-being
than the non-interactive systems. These main effects are
qualified by the presence of interactions, the most notable
of which is mentioned below as the final finding.

A fourth finding was that the level of well-being in
nine element or complex systems was more variable over time
than in three element systems. A fifth finding was that,
over time, control or management of these systems steadily
improved in terms of the extent to which stability (redu-
ctions in short term fluctuations) of well-being across the
three areas was achieved.

Sixth, effective long term allocation policies were difficult to create and implement. Two results are relevant to this point. Notwithstanding the fifth finding mentioned above, fluctuations as a result of a previous allocation usually required a compensatory allocation the next time round, regardless of the overall allocationary policy. If decision makers chose to ignore small fluctuations, the possibility existed that the amplitude of the oscillations would increase, and if that happened, they found it very difficult to re-impose control over the system. Decision makers found themselves obliged to choose between small but frequent "adjustive" allocations that focussed only on the immediate situation, or ignoring fluctuations and attempting to pursue a longer term allocation policy, running the risk that an undamped fluctuation might suddenly burn out of control. Some decision makers used such an increment-alist strategy, others attempted to work to a systematic long term plan. This leads to a second result, which is that the ad hoc incrementalists in general produced better outcomes. In other words, incrementalists (in the Braybrooke & Lindblom (1963) sense) did better, on the average, than long range planners.

A seventh result was that the decision makers in this experiment were unable, in general, to describe with any precision the system which they had been managing. At the conclusion of the experiment they were asked to specify as precisely as possible the relationships shown in Figure 1. Even those who had proved effective system managers found the task difficult. Most worked by trial and error, arriving at the end of the experiment with only a dim notion about the existence of any general allocationary heuristics. When asked about strategies, most were conservative. They believed that the first task was to bring the system under sufficient control to avoid sudden adverse changes, and only then look to improve matters.

The eighth (and final) finding was foreshadowed above. The complexity of the interactions qualified all the main effects. For example the single worst group (with regard to the generation of well-being) was the complex (9 element) system with no interaction between these areas and stochastic (rather than deterministic) relationships between the variables, whereas the best single group was the nine element system with a stochastic relationship between the variables and an interactive relationship between che three areas.

Thus, one major finding of this study was that there is no simple relationship between the complexity of the system being managed and the behaviour or managability of that system. That is, an individual decision maker's ability to cope with the situation, although dependent upon the complexity of the system, does not depend upon that complexity in any obvious way.

A second major finding was that individuals were able to control the system, even though they were unable to comprehend its structure, by using 'rules of thumb' derived from experience in the task. This finding of control in the absence of comprehension raises the question of the component skills which are necessary in order to manage such a system. Of course, the finding itself is not surprising. Rational beings or not, most of the systems that we control more or less adequately, we do not really understand. Ask any Treasury official! These results also suggest that the most effective decisions were associated with low risk, and small but regular rewards. Indeed, if a decision maker loosened his or her control of the system (i.e. if welfare levels began to oscillate), control proved very difficult to regain.

The Next Step

Instead of finding that the three components of task complexity were related to behaviour in a simple fashion we found that the relationship (via the decision maker) was non-linear. Since it is well established that complex tasks are more difficult than simple ones because of the information processing limits of human beings[4], one is led to the conclusion that the decision makers were able to simplify the input so that they could either make or keep the task soluble.

In order to elucidate this relationship we needed a more particular analysis of the individual-system interaction. This involved identifying the important component processes involved in the management of a complex dynamic system.

The first fundamental operation that we identified was that of prediction. The ability to predict the value of Y given X where some relationship exists between X and Y is important in the management of any system. Accordingly, in order to understand the way in which human decision makers

manage complex systems we had to refine our understanding
of the way in which predicition occurs. Linked with prediction is the matter of the verification of that prediction.
Verification, particularly in socio-economic systems, is
frequently a troublesome task, as the number of auditors,
accountants and evaluators that encrust (particularly public
sector) programmes attests. However, in any verification
process a crucial systemic variable is feedback delay.
Given enough time, verification is always possible, but
managing a dynamic system demands feedback now, and the amount
of delay in feedback can affect substantially the management of a system. Thus the next question that we asked was
about the role of delay in feedback about a prediction.

   The second major fundamental operation was that of
control. Although the task in the first experiment was not
complicated, if it is compared with e.g., a business game,
the control activity did not directly steer the system
towards a greater level of well-being, but involved instead
making decisions about individual services and areas which in
turn contributed to the overall level of well-being. A
better starting point is to take the simplest possible
dynamic system, and then increase the level of complexity in
the structure of that simple system to determine how the
control process is acquired and managed. To parallel the
discussion of prediction, where, it was argued, the role of
delay is crucial, we considered the introduction of delay
into a simple feedback system. We began by looking at the ·
simplest possible dynamic system and then varying the level
of the complexity of structure in that system by introducing
a delay effect by adding another variable.

   We note in passing that the notions of prediction and
control are important not only in the context of systems
management, but also as psychological variables. The two
abilities to control and predict contribute independently
to the level of stress which a person undergoes. Thus
environments that are either unpredictable, uncontrollable,
or both are more stressful than those which can be predicted,
or controlled, or both (Perlmutter & Monty, 1977; Thompson,
1981; Miller, 1980). In addition a person's sense of competence and rationality is linked to their ability to predict
and/or control their environment, (Weiner, 1974, Perlmutter,
Scharf, Kersh & Monty, 1980).

The utility which a person derives from a situation may
be defined, not only in terms of monetary rewards, but also
in terms of variables like power, well-being, and satisfaction
(money, of course,may be a proxy for these). It follows that
both successful prediction and the exercise of control,
through their effects on both the level of stress, and the
sense of competence and rationality, affect the generation
of utility, perhaps as much or more than the achievement of
a particular target value of the system which the person may
be trying to reach. Of particular importance is the role of
utility generation (in psychological terms, reinforcement)
in rewarding, not only adaptive behaviour (in this case,
appropriate, or partly appropriate input), but the process
of creating that adaptative behaviour. People must continue
to have confidence in their own cognitive skills.

Thus one must view system management procedures not only
in terms of the extent to which they affect system behaviour,
but also in terms of their consequences for the decision maker.
To return to our example of the traveller lost in the outback,
once he yields to despair, he may become incapable of generating any adaptive decision strategy (Janis & Mann, 1977).

We remarked earlier that our 'decision makers' found it
difficult to comprehend the structure of the system that they
were managing. Nevertheless, to undertake these operations
implies an ability to generate at least some kind of model,
albeit simple, of the task. Even if the model were no more
than a set of "rules of thumb", some practical theory would
still be needed to provide consistency in the decisions.
Accordingly, we attempted to obtain process protocols from
our experimental 'decision makers'.

We thus ran several experiments. First, let us summarise
the important component processes listed or implied above.
We identified five. The first was the ability to predict
ordered functional relationships, that is, given X_n to
predict X_{n+1}; the second was the ability to manage delays
in feedback about the actual value of X_{n+1}; the third, was
the ability to control simple feedback systems; the fourth
was the ability to control simple feedback systems with delay
effects included and the fifth, the ability to develop or
generate models of the process involved.

Experiments on Prediction

Accordingly, the first experiments were directed towards
assessing the ability of people to predict simple exponential
growth (and decay) functions since there is some evidence that
even single tasks may not be trivial (Wearing, Kubovy & Thomas,
(1977). The experimental procedure was simple. Experimental
subjects (decision makers) were seated in front of a computer
terminal, a number (X_1) was displayed, and they were asked to
predict the next number X_2. Following their prediction, the
actual X_2 was shown, and the cycle was repeated, that is,
they were asked to predict the next number (X_3), given the
number (the correct answer to the first prediction problem)
that they had just seen.

The results are schematically summarized in Figure 2.
The data analysed were the errors made by the experimental
decision makers. While there was substantial variation
between them the basic mode of performance could be summarised
thus: For most people forecasting errors formed a nonsta-
tionary series. Errors were neglible when rates of change
were small but increased when the rate of change was large.
For many this series had an approximately exponential form
thus mirroring the function and its derivatives. More
interesting was the variance of the time series. While
the mean of the error series deviated only slightly from
zero, the variance increased greatly with increasing rate
of change. The change in variance followed an exponential
growth model in the majority of cases. The time constant
for the variance growth curve was greater than the growth
curve of the mean error.

Thus the overall picture of human beings as forecasters
shows them to be relatively accurate on average (with a
slight decline under increased rates of change) but decreasing in point by point accuracy as the rate of change increases.
In order for the variance to increase, while the mean remains
unchanged, the experimental subjects had to oscillate above
and below the actual value with inceasing amplitude, as
shown in Figure 2.

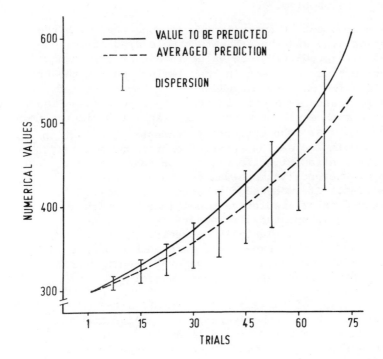

A schematic representation of performance in one-ahead
prediction of simple exponential growth functions, showing
both the average prediction and the dispersion.

   There exists classes of systems for which such input
would yield quite unstable behaviour. Thus, one particular
significance of this finding is that where a more complicated system is involved, fluctuation in judgements may be
fed through to its remoter parts where, depending on the
nature of the linkages between the variables, amplification
of the deviations may occur. From the point of view of a
manager, the appearance of perhaps quite rapidly changing
variable behaviour could present a major problem in controlling the system, a problem whose solution is made difficult
by the remoteness of its connection with the real primary

cause, and the apparent relative accuracy of the predictions generating the problem.

The second set of experiments was concerned with the effect of delays, and whereas with simple prediction, one is concerned with predicting one value in advance, in the delayed situation (at least in the simplest case), the prediction is being made two in advance. As was expected, less accurate forecasts were made in this experiment (see Figure 3). There was a much more pronounced exponential deviation from the actual values. The pattern of increased oscillation increasing with increasing rates of change was maintained. However, in contradistinction to the one-ahead prediction the mean of the oscillations was not an accurate forecast of the series. If smoothed forecasts were compared to a simple second order predictive model (one in which the rate of change is updated), forecasts in the first set of experiments would be relatively accurate. In contrast, the forecasts made in this experiment were much poorer than analogous ARIMA forecasts. Four general findings from these two sets of experiments may be noted:

1. The accuracy of forecasts was largely affected by their lead time. The decrement in performance was very marked in going from a lead time of one to two time periods ahead, even though the experimental subjects had their intermediate forecasts available to them.

2. 'Amount of change' led to decreased accuracy. In terms of mean forecasts, accuracy is only importantly reduced at larger lead times. Regardless of lead time, larger changes within a time period lead to greater point-to-point variation.

3. Forecasting occurred on a piecemeal basis. Few people were able to correctly identify the function that they had forecast.

4. Formal forecasting models do not adequately describe the behaviour of these human forecasters. Most 'non-intelligent' forecasting procedures produce errors consistently biased away from the direction of increasing change. In contrast the individuals in this experiment showed an ongoing pattern of point by point over-compensation, their estimates oscillating above and below the target value.

In summary we found that even a relatively short delay in feedback yielded fluctuations of both means and variances. Indeed, these fluctuations could become quite serious, and, where the values to be predicted were changing sharply, the judgements often wandered erractically away from the correct value.

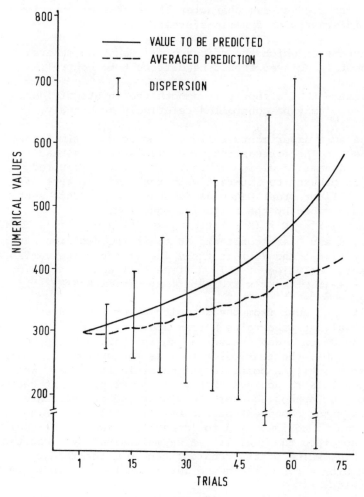

Figure 3

A schematic representation of performance in two-ahead prediction of simple exponential growth functions, showing both the average prediction and the dispersion.

Experiments on Control

    The two sets of experiments just discussed were not
dynamic in the true sense: While an ordered sequence of
consequent trials was presented, the experimental subjects'
'decisions' had no effect on subsequent trials. However
the results suggest two characteristics that might arise when
humans interact with dynamic systems.

1.   Systems in which the effect of a 'decision makers'
input is delayed should be difficult to control.

2.   Systems that effectively smooth the inputs of 'decision
makers' may be controlled relatively accurately.

    The next experiments followed a procedure similar to
that used in the forecasting experiments, but instead
involved dynamic decision making. They first required
'decision makers' to interact with the simplest type of
system, a first order negative feedback loop. This system
can be described by the following equation:
$$Y' = R \times (K - Y(t)) + Q \times U(t) \qquad (1)$$
where R, K and Q are constants, U(t) is the decision makers
input at time t and Y(t) is the value of the state variable
at time t. Solution of this differential equation yields
$$Y(t) = K + (Y(0) - K) \times EXP(-Rt) + Q \int_0^t U(t) \times EXP(R(\ -t)d \quad (2)$$

    With no input from the decision maker the system decays
exponentially to the value K from above or below. The decison
maker was given a goal value "g"(an integer, usually
$50 < g < 150$), the task being to make the system attain this
value as quickly as possible and maintain it there. While
it is possible to achieve this goal in one trial, it can only
be done with a knowledge of the system and its parameters.
Thus the major component of the task is to determine how the
system reacts to input and to 'steer' it towards the goal.
Having attained the goal it can be maintained by a constant
input. The value of the constant can be determined by
setting U(t) = c, Y(t) = g and letting t tend to infinity.
This yields:
$$c = (R/Q) \times (K - g) \qquad (3)$$
    Given this basic structure, the parameters in eqn (3)
may be varied experimentally to assess their effect on the
decision maker's performance. The interpretation of the
other parameters (K has been discussed above) is as follows:

Q is the boundary constant or parameter. Eqn (1) shows that the decision maker's input is multiplied by Q before it has any effect on the system.

R is the feedback parameter. It determines the rate at which the system attains equilibrium with no input. It also determines the effect of previous inputs to the system. Eqn (2) shows that all previous inputs are weighed according to how long ago they entered the system. If R is greater than zero the weight will decline to a negligible value as we move in time. Effectively the system will 'forget' what has been done to it and therefore is said to be stable.

There are thus five parameters capable of manipulation. To this time only Q and R have been systematically varied. The equilibrium parameter simply changes the origin of the process and so it is not inherently interesting. The actual value chosen for the goal has a similar status. The steady-state input required to maintain the goal arises from values chosen for the other parameters. This parameter and also K and g are of interest only if scaling characteristics are being investigated.

Two competing hypotheses can be formed concerning the (memory) parameter R: (1) As the 'short memory' system forgets inputs and thus the decision maker's previous errors more quickly than the long memory condition, better perform-ance should be exhibited in controlling it, or (2) whilst the long memory system retains errors it acts to smooth positive and negative errors in the manner described in the predictions experiments described above. Thus the long memory system may be easier to control.

Competing hypotheses can also be educed concerning the effect of different values of Q. The larger the value of this parameter the greater the effect of any input on the system. Brehmer's (see, e.g. Brehmer, Kuylenstierna & Liljegren,1974) work on learning to make inferences in bivariate relation-ships suggests the more visible a relationship the more accurate predictions become. Higher values of Q would make the effect of input more apparent and thus lead to better performance. However an additional complication, not present in Brehmer's experiments, occurs here. Because the decision maker's estimate has an effect on the behaviour of the system higher values of Q will make the system more sensitive to input. This may reduce performance. The relative importance of visibility versus sensitivity can only be determined experimentally.

The results may be summarized as follows: (1) The first quarter of the experiment consisted of a stage of learning and experimentation on the part of the decision maker during which time the average person did worse than even a minimally intelligent decision maker (one example of minimal intelligence would be to follow a rule which involves examining the difference between the present value and the goal, halving it, and using the result as input). The second quarter usually saw a great, even dramatic improvement. Whilst improvements in performance occurred in the remaining part of the experiment they were not as dramatic. This process of learning to manage the system usually occurred in the absence of any understanding of the formal structures of the system. (2) The boundary parameter had little observable effect on behaviour. (Note that both effects mentioned above may be operating and cancelling each other out.) (3) Systems with a longer 'memory' were controlled significantly better than systems with short information half-lives. When we consider these results in the light of findings from the prediction experiments, this suggests that these systems function as error smoothers, averaging decision makers' under and over compensations. (4) Control of the system was achieved by conservative 'rules of thumb'. People who changed strategies (and induced oscillations of increasing amplitude into the system), or who varied input (controlling) values rapidly, usually failed. A general inability to comprehend the nature of the system meant that the only successful strategy was one of jointed incrementalism, moving slowly and carefully towards the goal, avoiding large (and therefore high risk) input values which might on one hand move the system rapidly towards the goal, but on the other hand might lead to catastrophe.

These experiments dealt with the simplest possible dynamic system. Given that most of the people tested had a successful interaction with this type of system it seemed reasonable to determine the behaviour of the experimental subjects' interaction with systems that are analytically more complex, and in particular, included delays of effects.

The following approach was adopted. If a system is

expressed as a series of differential equations it can be
shown that the solution to equations given no input from
the decision maker (the homogeneous part of the system) and
to the weighting function is the sum of a number of exponential
terms:

$$Y(t) = EXP(-at) + EXP(-bt) \ldots.$$

where $\underline{a}$ and $\underline{b}$ are constants that may contain an imaginary
part. Three classes of solution exist: (1) Simple exponents
(as in the previous experiment), (2) exponential terms
multiplied by time, and (3) where $\underline{a}$ and $\underline{b}$ are complex numbers
they form complex conjugates and so may be transformed to the
real plane in the form $EXP(rt).Sin(wt)$.

The second and third class of solutions cannot arise
from the simple first order system. The simplest type of
system capable of yielding these solutions is a second order
system of the form:

$$y'' + dwy' = w \; y = QU(t) \tag{5}$$

The form of the solution of this equation depends on the
value of d. If it is greater than 1 only real exponents
will exist. This will give rise to solutions of the first
and second type. The sum of two exponents of the sum of
an exponent and an exponent multiplied by time are of much
of the same form as a simple exponent. Thus systems of this
kind were excluded from consideration as there appeared to
be a high probability of obtained results analogous to those
observed in the immediately previous experiment.

If d lies between 0 and 1 the solution will be of the
third type. While the importance of a particular input will
diminish exponentially just as in the first order system, this
effect will be modulated by the sinusoidal component so the
weighting will no longer be monotonic decreasing:At a certain
time inputs made further in the past will be more important
in determining the function of the system than more recent
inputs.

The introduction of an additional state variable has
effectively introduced a delay into the system. Whereas the
decision maker's input and the system's corrective feedback
were linked directly to the state variable in the first order
case, there is an extra state variable between these inputs
and the state variable in the second order system. This
means that by the time input and feedback is applied to the
output variable it may be 'out of date'. This leads to

oscillations described by the equation solutions described above.

This system appeared to represent an important, quantal jump in complexity: The behaviour of all other systems may be represented as sums of exponents and/or exponentially decaying sinusoids. While combinations of sinusoids may be more complex than a pure sine wave the resulting function is of a similar form.

Thus the next experiment was analogous to the previous one. The task given to the 'decision maker' was identical, i.e. to get the system to attain a given goal value and then to maintain it there. In the limit the task was identical as the system could be maintained at a given state with a constant input.

The 'memory' of the system (the rate of decline of the input weighing) was varied in exactly the same way as before. In addition the importance of the sinusoidal part of the weighting was also systematically varied. The combinations of these parameters meant that there were great differences in the input required to achieve the specified goal. To overcome this, the boundary parameter for each system was chosen so that the goal could be attained in each system with the same input.

The results were striking. Visual examination of decision makers' performance showed little if any goal directed performance. There were no differences between different experimental conditions. Typical patterns of performance resulted in the system drifting towards equilibrium as the decision makers alternated between positive and negative inputs. Most people also increased the magnitude of their input during the course of the experiment. This seemed to be an attempt to change the system's behaviour by brute force, a policy of desperation. It was not successful.

Thus when the feedback system included delays (at least, of the kind described above) people were quite unable to manage. Action at a temporal distance was beyond their capability. Even when we took graduates in mathematics as experimental subjects or informed our decision makers about the properties of the system, they still found it extraordinarily difficult. The action of a variable which changes sinusoidally over time was extremely difficult to incorporate into any decision function.

We come then to the question of the kind of models that people may be presumed to have in their heads. We attempted to obtain 'thinking aloud' protocols from our experimental subjects on the assumption that a rational and conscious decision maker should know what he or she is doing. Useful protocols were hard to get. Nevertheless, the following conclusions seem to hold: 1) Respondents used only the immediately preceding information, and delayed information was in general ignored; 2) Curves were treated as straight lines and where there were departures from linearity, linear fits were made. Where it was clear that a curve was not linear over its whole range, instead of treating it as a continuous function, be it sinusoidal, exponential or quadratic, people made piecewise linear fits by defining two (or more) kinds or rules, one applicable over one set of values, a second applicable over another. That is, one linear relation was observed in one range, another linear relation in another. Such an approach meant that no higher level organization or structural model emerged. People developed rules of thumb to apply in particular localities. This kind of procedure is quite ineffective in dealing with effects that are due to events coming from outside a particular locality, and so it proved.

Utility and Risk

Although this paper may appear to have wandered some distance from utility and risk, these two notions have been always implicit in the discussion, albeit not obtrusively and in any formal sense. We have seen that utility, operationally defined in our experiments in a very simple fashion, is probably more complicated than it seemed. It is interwoven proactively with the decision making process itself, the utility achieved at point p_n affecting the decision making at p_{n+1}. Hope does not always spring eternal in the human breast; its diminution affects subsequent decisions. Ends (goals) and means (processes) are not independent of one another (Locke, Shaw, Saari & Latham, 1981);the utility that one may rationally seek depends on the (cognitive) tools available, an observation which raises a question about the adequacy of formalisms intended to

capture the empirical reality of dynamic decision making
environments.

When we come to risk, we have seen that risk is something that our decision makers wish to control, and mostly
minimize. This is not surprising when we consider the
biologically defined limitation on human information processing. With a small working memory, both the retrospective
and forward planning horizons must be short. To proceed in
small increments is adaptive for such an organism. In
particular one would expect, with such creatures as human
beings, to find high discount rates, and minimization of
uncertainty. What is rational for homo economicus, is
overweeningly ambitious for homo sapiens.

Some Final Observations: Ergonomic Policy Implications

We began with the remark that people are only human.
Our experimental decision makers found it difficult to
construct models of the tasks with which they were engaged.
In addition they had to operate with a restricted working
(short-term) memory. As a consequence, they attempted
(if they were working adaptively) to minimize rates of
change in their environment. It also follows that effectiveness of system control depended on the presence of a fair
level of inertia in the system, and the absence of delayed,
or indirect non-linear variables. In short, the incrementalism described by Braybrook & Lindblom (1963) describes
not only what people actually do, but perhaps also what
they should do, if they are both to make effective decisions
in a dynamic environment, and maintain themselves in being
as effective decision makers.

If we ask ourselves how we can make things easier for
our common or garden human, then the answer must be that
we must give our systems a fair degree of inertia (on this
theory revolutions should always fail), provide timely
feedback about the effects of policy actions, and allow for
rapid, but small corrective movements. As it turns out,
most social and economic systems have sufficient inertia
to make the management problem one of the provision of
information. Because feedback loops (particularly if they
are short) are crucial to effective human functioning, both
at an individual and societal level (Carven & Scheier, 1982;
Wearing & Wearing, 1975), it is in the provision of rapid

policy information that it would be easiest to help the
human decision maker.

One implication of these results may appear to be that
long range planning is a waste of time. Such a conclusion
is an overgeneralization. It should also be noted that apart
from the fact that long range planning of some kind must
occur (e.g., planting trees, building roads), planning
serves significant psychological and mythical purposes. The
utility generated by long range planning is most (probably)
of a non-monetary kind. In any case, we have been discussing individual, not group or community decision making.

But our findings do suggest that if we have decision
makers who function best in an incrementalist environment,
then to function effectively they must have continuous
information in a usuable form (Pierce & Lovrich, 1982), and
focus on immediately and obviously adaptive responses. If
we are to eventually succeed in reaching Weetulta, and have
no map, we must ask directions often, and stop to check our
position at each cross-roads. It may be slower, but much .
less risky. If, of course, the system is a socio-economic
or biological one, and not in a state of equilibrium, but
going slowly downhill, such a prescription contains no long
term comfort. But that is another question, and for another
paper.

[1] We thank Anne Welfare, Jane Stuchberry, and Elizabeth
Mullaly for their assistance in the collection and analysis
of some of the data reported in this paper. We would like
to thank the Australian Research Grants Committee for their
assistance in funding this research.

[2] Perhaps an exception to this observation is the
research of Doerner and his associates (Doerner, Kreuzig,
Reither, & Staeudel, 1981; Doerner, 1980) who, over a period
of several years, have conducted a series of studies of
decision making in complex and uncertain environments.
However, the amount of work involved in conducting their
investigations means that it is unlikely that any other
group will be able to assemble the expertise and resources
to replicate it.

[3] The variables were embedded in models written in an
interactive continuous simulation language (Mackinnon, 1979),
and derived from the application of systems dynamics

(Forrester, 1968) to dynamic socio-technical problems (see, e.g. Batchman & Wearing, 1976; Henize, 1981; Thomas, Mackinnon & Wearing, 1978).

4
    We remind readers that an apparently simple term, 'information processing limits', conceals much subtle complexity, even in its application to decision making. See, e.g. Hammond & Brehmer (1973), and Shaw (1982).

REFERENCES

Andrews, F.M., & Withey, S.B. Social indicators of well-being. New York: Plenum, 1976.

Batchman, T.E., & Wearing, A.J. Applications of dynamic modelling to the social consequences of communications. IEEE Transactions on Systems, Men, and Cybernetic, 1976, SMB-6, 9, 605-622.

Braybrooke, D., & Lindblom, C.E. A strategy of decision: Policy evaluation and social process. New York: Free Press, 1963.

Brehmer, B., Kuylenstierna, J., & Liljgren, J. Effects of function form and cue validity on the subject's hypotheses in probabilistic inference tasks. Organizational Behaviour and Human Performance, 1974, 11, 330-354.

Brewer, G.D. Analysis of complex systems: An experiment and its implications for policy making. In T.R. La Porte (Ed.). Organized social complexity. Princeton: Princeton University Press, 1975, 175-219.

Carver, C.S., & Scheier, M.F. Control Theory: A useful conceptual framework for Personality-Social, Clinical, and Health Psychology. Psychological Bulletin, 1982, 92 111-135.

Cesa, I. Planning horizons in dynamic decision making. Final Honours Thesis, Department of Psychology, University of Melbourne, 1982.

Dawes, R.M., & Corrigan, B. Linear models in decision making. Psychological Bulletin, 1974, 81, 95-106.

Doerner, D. On the difficulties people have in dealing with complexity. Simulation and Games, 1980, 11, 87-106.

Doerner, D., Kreuzig, H.W., Reither, F., & Staeudel, T. Lohhausen: Vom Umgang mit Unbestimmtheit und Komplexitaet. Lehrstuhl Psychologie, Universitaet Bamberg, West Germany, 1981.

Ebbesen, E.B., & Konecni, V.J. On the external validity of
   decision-making research: What do we know about decisions
   in the real world? In Wallsten, T.S. (Ed.). Cognitive
   processes in choice and decision behaviour. Hillsdale:
   LEA, 1980, 21-46.
Estes, W.K. Comments on directions and limitations of
   current efforts towards theories of decision making. In
   Wallsten, T.S. (Ed.). Cognitive processes in choice and
   decision behaviour. Hillsdale: LEA, 1980, 263-274.
Evans, J. St. B.T. Psychological pitfalls in forecasting
   Futures, 1982, 14, 258-265.
Faust, D.A. Needed component in prescriptions for Science:
   Empiricalknowledge of human cognitive limitations.
   Knowledge: Creation, Diffusion, Utilization, 1982, 3,
   555-570.
Forrester, J.W. Principles of systems. Cambridge, Mass:
   Wright-Allen, 1968.
Hammond, K.R., & Brehmer, B. Quasi-rationality and distrust:
   Implications for international conflict. In Rappoport, L.,
   & Summers, D.A. (Eds.). Human Judgement and Social
   Interaction, New York: Holt, Rinehart & Winston, 1973,
   338-392.
Hammond, K.R., McClelland, G.H., & Mumpower, J. Human
   judgement and decision making. New York: Praeger, 1980.
Headey, B.M., & Wearing, A.J. Australians' priorities,
   satsifactions and well-being. University of Melbourne,
   Monograph in Public Policy Studies No. 4, 1981.
Henize, J. Can a shorter work-week reduce unemployment -
   A German simulation study. Simulation, 1981, 38, 145-156.
Janis, I.L., & Mann, L. Decision making. New York: Free
   Press, 1977.
Locke, E.A., Shaw, K.N., Saari, L.M., & Latham, G.P. Goal
   setting and task performance: 1969-1980. Psychological
   Bulletin, 1981, 90, 125-152.
Lockhead, G.R. Know, then decide. In Wallsten, T.S. (Ed.).
   Cognitive processes in choice and decision behaviour.
   Hillsdale: LEA, 1980, 143-154.
Mackinnon, A.J. Astudy of human interaction with complex
   systems employing interactive computer simulation
   techniques. Final Honours Thesis, Department of
   Psychology, University of Melbourne, 1977.
Mackinnon, A.J. A manual for ICONS. Department of
   Psychology, University of Melbourne, 1979.
Mackinnon, A.J., & Wearing, A.J. Complexity and decision
   making. Behavioural Science, 1980, 25, 285-296.

Metlay, D. On studying the future behaviour of complex
    systems. In T.R. La Porte (Ed.). Organised social
    complexity. Princeton: Princeton University Press, 1975,
    220-255.
Miller, S.M. Controllability and human stress: Method,
    evidence and theory. Behaviour Research and Therapy,
    1979, 17, 287-306.
O'Connell, M.A, & Wearing, A.J. Some factors affecting
    the choice of a home. Melbourne Psychology Reports,
    No. 47, 1978.
Perlmuter, L.C., & Monty, R.A. The importance of perceived
    control: Fact or fantasy? American Scientist, 1977, 65,
    759-765.
Perlmuter, L.C. Scharff, K., Karsh, R., & Monty, R.A.
    Perceived control: A generalised state of motivation.
    Motivation and Emotion, 1980, 4, 35-45.
Pierce, J.C., & Lovrich, N.P. Knowledge and politics: The
    distribution and consequences of policy-relevant inform-
    ation among citizens, activists, legislators, and experts.
    Knowledge: Creation, Diffusion, Utilization, 1982, 3,
    521-554.
Rappoport, A. Research paradigms for studying dynamic
    decision behaviour. In Vendt/Vlek (Eds.) Utility,
    probability and human decision making. Holland: Reidel,
    1975.
Rappoport, A., & Wallsten, T.S. Individual decision
    behaviour. Annual Review of Psychology, 1972, 23,
    131-176.
Shaw, M.L. Attending to multiple sources of information:
    1. The integration of information in decision making.
    Cognitive Psychology, 1982, 14, 353-409.
Sjoeberg, L. Strength of belief and risk. Policy Science,
    1979, 11, 39-58.
Thomas, S.A., Mackinnon, A.J. & Wearing, A.J. A simulation
    model of subscriber/system interaction in a telephone
    network. Melbourne Psychology reports, No. 51, 1978.
Thompson, S.C. Will it hurt less if I can control it? A
    complex answer to a simple question. Psychological
    Bulletin, 1981, 90, 89-101.
Wearing, A.J., & Wearing R.J. People in the cities.
    Canberra: AIUS, 1975.
Wearing, A.J., Kubovy, M., & Thomas, S.A. Heuristics in
    learning to make univariate linear predictions. Paper
    read to the Psychonomic Society, Washington, D.C., 1977.
Weiner, B. Cognitive views of human motivation. New York:
    Academic Press, 1974.

Hans W. Gottinger

THE ECONOMICS OF ORGANIZATIONAL DESIGN

1. INTRODUCTION

Which conditions must be fulfilled on the level of organizational decision making to construct a theory for bounded
rationality in organizations? We propose an information
processing model of an organization in which limits of decision making are generated by 'overload' such that the level of organizational performance decreases in probability.
This is a cooperative model of organizations as compared to
conflict theories of organizations where game theoretic
tools apply. It is probably close to the Japanese stereo-
type of organization or team-like organizational forms,
Marschak (1974), according to which harmony prevails and
implementation and incentive aspects are not the major problem. We adopt a designer's point of view, very much akin
to engineering science, which mixes normative and descriptive elements of decision making. It is hoped that the model has practical implications.

Two key functional elements underlie the design of any
organization: its structure and the set of behavioral rules
that make the organization work and perform. In general,
the structure of an organization is a directed graph, or
briefly, a _digraph_ that could be generated by a computing
machine. The graph is called 'directed' because each branch
has an origin or terminal indicating the direction in which
the information flow is to take place.

The other element is the set of behavioral or procedural rules which governs the relationship among the organization members and forms the 'standard operating routine'
(SOR) of the organization. In practice, these procedures
are sometimes laid down in elaborate detail embedded in a
systemic environment (say in an organizational handbook),
sometimes they are left entirely to tradition and common
sense among the members. In this paper we will be primarily
concerned about SORs which relate to the problem solving
aspect of the organizational forms, and which are of in-

B. P. Stigum and F. Wenstøp (eds.), Foundations of Utility and Risk Theory with Applications,
423–442.
© 1983 by D. Reidel Publishing Company.

trinsic interest to the designer. More precisely, the SOR
of an organization is a specification of exactly what pie-
ces of information should be transmitted from one member to
another. Applied to an organization member as a decision
maker this means that his sources must be specified for by
the SOR, and hence, also his input alphabet and symbol pro-
habilities. It furthermore means that his output alphabet
must be specified as well, along with the destination for
his output symbols and the assignment probabilities that he
is to use for them. The SOR will then in particular determine the load of every organization member, in the sense in
which this term will be defined in the next section.

2. ORGANIZATIONAL DESIGN: BASIC DEFINITIONS

We deal here with the major building blocks of the kind of
organization which has been described as 'task-oriented'.
The purpose of organizations appears to be best modelled as
a decision making task, so we start with an extremely simple decision making, or, 'computational' model. Assume that

(i)   the organization receives an input drawn from a
        certain set of inputs and is required to respond to
        it with an output,

(ii)   it is rewarded for such a response with a certain
        payoff which, in general, depends on the response, as
        well as the input,

(iii)   the goal of the organization is to maximize the ex-
        pected, or, 'average' payoff.

In information-theoretic terms we may speak of all inputs and outputs as being 'signals', the same term may also
be applied to transmissions among organization members. The
signal will be understood to be a sequence of symbols: a
symbol may be a single letter, a memo, a certain number of
resource costs, a job specification, a price quotation,
etc. The collection of different symbols that are used in
the signal are its 'alphabet'. All alphabets are assumed to
be finite but possibly quite large.

In this model, the organization member 'processes' input x_j into output y_k. This processing may be deterministic or stochastic. The probabilistic process simply re-

flects the <u>degree of reliability</u> of symbol processing, which is a crucial notion for determining failure rates in large message transferring mechanisms.

Beyond the degree of reliability it is essential to assume that a processing job can be more or less difficult for the organization member, depending on the nature of the task as well as on his competence for its execution. As a proxy measure for the <u>level of difficulty</u>, or, complexity of a task assigned to the organization member we could use the (average) processing time which he needs to perform a given task, i.e., the individual processing time times the respective probability with which the processing of the symbols is called for. We could visualize an organization member, a machine, as being composed of an <u>input</u> machine and an <u>output</u> machine - hooked in serial connection. The reason for this distinction is that an organization member may be called upon to do quite different tasks, and may have difficulties of different kinds in performing them. One is the acquisition and sorting out of input symbols, the other is the production and dispatching of output symbols.

As a weak normative requirement, we postulate that an organization is required to meet its schedule, and this is linked to the <u>average processing time</u> τ of each member not exceeding the average time between the arrivals of input symbols, namely one time unit.

Therefore,

$$\tau = \tau^{(i)} + \tau^{(o)} \leqq 1$$

must be assured for every member of the organization, where $\tau^{(i)}, \tau^{(o)}$ are the mean processing times of his input and output machines, respectively. If this bound is violated for some member, he will be considered 'overloaded', in an intuitive and technical sense.

<u>Example</u>. Take the simplest case of a single decision maker (or decision machine), labeled DM, how can he manage the processing task under a SOR. Suppose

$$x_j = \{x_j^1, x_j^2\} \quad \text{input symbols}$$

$$y_k = \{y_k^1, y_k^2\} \qquad \text{output symbols}$$

are processed in such a way that the (mean) payoff is largest. Then

$$\text{SOR:DM:} x_j \longrightarrow y_k \text{ with probability 1.}$$

Here, j and k range over the DM's input and output alphabets, respectively. If it develops that the DM can actually manage this SOR without overload, the designer's job is done. He has specified the organizational structure which is trivial in this case, namely a graph consisting of a single node (the DM), and has drawn up the SOR for it.

However, the designer may find that the DM is badly overloaded, and hence, that he is error-prone. In general, this will entail a deterioration of performance, in the sense that the mean-payoff is decreased by the incidence of error. The question is then how performance can be improved by using an organization of more than one member. In fact, there are quite a few options available to the designer, but if we confine ourselves to centralized, bureaucratic type organizations, the designer can basically do only two things: he can interpose an organizational unit between the DM and the sources, which is intended to reduce the <u>input load</u> of the DM somehow, and another one between the DM and the destination, intended to alleviate his <u>output load</u>.

The two units do quite different work. The first will be referred to as 'staff'. Its function is to preprocess information and to present it to the DM in a form to make further processing possible. The second is called the 'line' used in an analogous manner to accept signals and implement decisions which the DM is best capable of generating.

The load reduction can be achieved in the following way: The staff can, for instance, take on the job of searching for necessary inputs, and the line that of producing the outputs at appropriate locations. Both are often time-consuming tasks, involve long symbol processing times and result in high loads.

3. THE SIMPLEST CASE OF LINE ORGANIZATION

We start with a brief discussion of a one-man line, consisting of one buffer unit only, say γ, which accepts all instructions $d_1, d_2, \ldots, d_n$ from the DM, converts them to the desired outputs $y_1, y_2, \ldots, y_n$ and delivers them to a collecting agency, the Post Office, or else, directly to their destinations.

Then the SOR is specified by the table

$$\text{SOR:} \begin{cases} \text{DM:} x_k \longrightarrow d_k, d_k \text{ to } \gamma \text{ with probability 1,} \\ \gamma : d_k \longrightarrow y_k, y_k \text{ to P.O. with probability 1.} \end{cases}$$

Since the DM's input is unknown at this stage of organizational design the effectiveness of this arrangement can only be judged by the extent to which it reduces the DM's output load, without overloading γ. Avoidance of overload means that an organization is required to 'keep up with the schedule'. Applied to an individual organization member this means that his mean processing time τ must not exceed the average time, namely one time unit. If this is not done, i.e., if $\tau > 1$ for some member he will be said to be 'overloaded'.

The DM's <u>mean output processing time</u> amounts to

$$\tau_{DM} = \sum_k t_{DM,k} P_k.$$

Here $t_{DM,k}$ is the processing time of the DM for the directive d_k and P_k is the processing probability that he is doing that.

In order for this design to be effective the $t_{DM,k}$ must be smaller than they would be if the DM had to produce y_k himself.[1] Otherwise there would be no point in having a line unit. Also, overload must be avoided by γ. That is,

$$\tau_{\gamma k} = \sum_k t_{\gamma k} P_k \leqq 1,$$

where $t_{\gamma k}$ is γ's intrinsic processing time for the conversion of d_k to y_k.

This simple two-member organization, in effect, di-
vides the input and output loads between the DM and the
line unit γ. The arrangement, in other words, will avoid
overload on γ and will notably reduce the DM's output load.

4. THE ALTERNATELY PROCESSING LINE

If the designer finds that a one-member line is not sufficient to solve the problem he will expand it to include additional members. In that case, he must decide whether to
use the line for _alternative_ or _parallel_ processing. First,
we treat the alternately processing line. Under this option
the DM follows some procedural rule by which he issues directives to the various line members once at a time, each
instructing its addressee to produce a certain output.[2]
The basic idea is that in this way every line member can be
given more time to do his processing at least on the average, and therefore, is more likely to avoid overload than
one unit, γ, acting by itself.

Thus, consider a multiple member line, starting with γ
and δ and ending with μ, i.e., $s = \gamma, \delta, \ldots, \mu$. Let the DM,
once during each time interval, issue an instruction
$d_k, k = 1, 2, \ldots, n$ to one (and only one) of the line
members, directing him to produce the output symbol y_k.
The DM can act according to his SOR, the most general and
most flexible appears to be a stochastic or mixed rule
which prescribes that the directive be issued to s with a
certain probability P_{sk}.

The SOR for the DM and his line could thus be specified as follows:

$$\text{SOR:} \begin{cases} \text{DM:} x_k \longrightarrow d_k, d_k \text{ to s with probability } P_{sk} \\ s : d_k \longrightarrow y_k, y_k \text{ to P.O. with probability } 1. \end{cases}$$

The P_{sk} are the _assignment probabilities_, satisfying

$$P_{sk} \geq 0, \sum_s P_{sk} = 1.$$

The probability that an arbitrary line member s receives any assignment is given by

$$Q_s = \sum_k P_{sk} P_k.$$

This is the probability that a specific line unit gets assigned to a task and that this task is implemented. The probability for s receiving the specific assignment d_k, to be denoted by $Q(d_k|s)$, is obviously the conditional probability.

$$Q(d_k|s) = P_{sk} P_k / Q_s.$$

i.e., the probability that a specific task k is allocated to s. The SOR is considered to be successful if it reduces the output load on the DM and if it avoids overload on the line. Now the output load of the DM is represented by his mean processing time τ_{DM}. The line unit's load is

$$\tau_s = \sum_k t_{sk} P_{sk} P_k = Q_s \sum_k t_{sk} Q(d_k|s),$$

$$s = \gamma, \delta, \ldots, \mu.$$

The DM's individual processing time $t_{DM,k}$ for the directive d_k may no longer be constant, because, in view of his operating mode, if his output machine is load-dependent the $t_{DM,k}$ will be functions of the number μ of line members and the assignment probabilities P_{sk} prescribed for the DM by the SOR. On the other hand, s processes y_k to only one destination, e.g., the Post Office. Therefore, if there is any load-dependence it is due to his input machine. His mean processing time τ_s which comprises both his input and output processing will then depend on the probabilties with which he receives his inputs d_k.[3]

Let us see whether the expansion of the line has actually overcome the problem of the one-member line. Is it always possible to avoid overload on the line? It can be shown that the answer is yes, in general, provided the line is made large enough.

Theorem 1: Suppose that the input machines of the line members are load-dependent and that their processing times t_{sk} remain bounded, $t_{sk} \leq T$, as μ increases. The assignment probabilities can be chosen such that no member is overloaded, provided   is made sufficiently large.

Remark: The assignment probabilities can certainly be made equal, $P_{sk} = 1/\mu$. Overload will then be avoided if

$$\sum_k t_{sk} P_k /\mu \leq T/\mu \leq 1,$$

which certainly is possible if μ is made large enough. Load dependence would imply here - for a general definition see Gottinger (1981) - that the line units mean processing time is a function of the size n of his input alphabet and of the probabilities with which he receives his input symbols. - These probabilities may be interpreted in two ways here, namely as $P_{sk} P_k$ or as $Q(d_k|s)$. The second in effect assumes that his input machine adapts to the relative frequency with which d_k occurs among his assignments, while the first makes the machine adaptive to the relative frequency with which d_k is processed by him among all assignments.

Corollary 1: Let the input machine of the s-th line member be load-dependent:

(a)   if this dependence is on the probabilities $Q(d_k s)$
      Theorem 1 remains valid

(b)   if it is on the probabilities $P_{sk} P_k$, Theorem 1
      remains valid if also
      $\lim_{k \to \infty} P_k t_{sk}(P) = 0$ as P_k goes to zero.

Proof:

(a)   Let $Q_s = 1/\mu$ and $Q(d_k|s) = 1/n$.
      Since P_k can safely be assumed to be different from zero,

$$P_{sk} = Q(d_k|s)/P_k = 1/\mu n P_k$$

can be made less tha 1 in this way.

(b) t_{sk} depends on $P_{sk} P_k$, put $P_{sk} = 1/\mu$.

      Then

$$\lim_{\mu \to \infty} \tau_s = \lim_{\mu \to \infty} \textstyle\sum_k t_{sk}(P) P_k / \mu = 0$$

and $\tau_s \leq 1$ is there for assume when μ is large enough.

This proves the corollary.

The organization designer who sets up a line for alternate processing can thus fully expect to avoid overload among its members if he makes it large enough.

He cannot expect the same for the DM, however. In fact, if the DM's output machine is load-dependent he must be prepared for the opposite, for as the number μ of line members is increased, the DM is liable to become overloaded. The best the designer can do is to minimize his overload, while avoiding overload among the line members. - The solution of this design can then be visualized as a sequence of programming problems. For every $\mu \geq 1$ determine a set of assignment probabilities $P_{sk}, s = \gamma, \delta, \ldots, \mu$ such that

$$\tau_{DM} = \textstyle\sum_k t_{DM,k} P_k \longrightarrow \text{Min},$$

is subject to the constraints

$$P_{sk} \geq 0, \textstyle\sum_s P_{sk} = 1 \quad \text{and}$$

$$\tau_s = \textstyle\sum_k t_{sk} P_{sk} P_k = Q_s \textstyle\sum_k t_{sk} Q(d_k | s),$$
$$s = \gamma, \delta, \ldots, \mu.$$

If a smallest $\mu* = \mu$ is found at which the problem has a feasible solution, then the most economical line has been determined, as well as an SOR which minimizes the DM's overload while completely avoiding overload among its members.[4]

5. THE PARALLEL PROCESSING LINE

Consider again a multiple-line organization. The organization is again expected to produce n output symbols, $y_k, k = 1, 2, \ldots, n$. Each of these symbols is decomposable into m subsymbols

$$y_k^\sigma, \text{i.e.} \qquad y_k = [y_k^1, y_k^2, \ldots, y_k^m].$$

The procedural rule laid down for the output machine of the DM, first of all, will be a parallel processing rule of the following kind. This rule will first of all require him to issue a directive d_k^σ to a line member once on the average per unit time interval, instructing him to produce the subsymbol y_k^σ. The line member to which this is done, will also be prescribed by the rule. In particular, it will specify a permutation P_{uk} for the superscripts $\boxed{1,2,\ldots,m}$

$$\boxed{\sigma_1,\sigma_2,\ldots,\sigma_m} = P_{uk}\boxed{1,2,\ldots,m}$$

with the understanding that $d_k^{\sigma_1}$ is to be issued to $\gamma, d_k^{\sigma_2}$ to δ etc.[5] The rule will, furthermore, prescribe which among all (m!) possible permutations the DM may use, and finally with what assignment probability P_{uk} satisfying

$$P_{uk} \geq 0, \sum_u P_{uk} = 1(k = 1,2,\ldots,n)$$

it is to be used. The rule would constitute the SOR for the DM.

A line member, on receipt of his instruction d_k would turn out the subsymbol y_k and transmit it to the Post Office. There, the subsymbols would be packaged into the complete symbol y_k and dispatched to the proper destination. The SOR for this arrangement is tabulated as follows

$$\text{SOR:} \begin{cases} \text{DM}:x_k \longrightarrow P_{uk}\boxed{d_k^1,\ldots,d_k^m}d_k^\sigma \text{ to s with probability } P_{uk} \\ s:d_k^\sigma \longrightarrow y_k^\sigma, \ y_k^\sigma \text{ to P.O. with probability } 1 \end{cases}$$

$$\sigma = 1,2,\ldots,m, \ k = 1,2,\ldots,n$$

where u is the number of allowed permutations.

What can be said about the effectiveness of such an SOR. So far as the DM is concerned, it will be successful if it reduces his mean processing time as far as possible, with $t_{DM,k}$ now interpreted as the time needed by him to generate the m-triplet of instructions d_k^σ, and to address them to the proper line members with the prescribed proba-

bility. As far as the line members are concerned, the SOR
will be successful if it eliminates overload among them.
The conditions for that can be obtained as follows. Among
the permutations which the DM may use there will be a certain subset which assigns the subsymbol d_k^1 of d_k to
unit s, for example. The probability of this happening is

$$(*) \; P_{sk}^1 = \sum_u P_{uk},$$

with the sum extended over all u that belong to that subset. In analogous manner one defines $P_{sk}^2, \ldots, P_{sk}^m$. Then
if

$$(**) \; \tau_s = \sum_k \sum_\sigma t_{sk}^\sigma P_{sk}^\sigma P_k \leqq 1 \qquad \begin{array}{l} \sigma = 1,2,\ldots,m \\ k = 1,2,\ldots,n \end{array}$$

s is not overloaded. The factor t_{sk}^σ is his intrinsic processing time for the conversion of the instruction d_k^σ into his contribution y_k^σ to the line output. Under these
circumstances, the designer can approach the problem of the
design of a parallel processing line in several ways, most
naturally in two ways.

(1) He may try to increase the size of m on the line,
member by member, and for each m perhaps also increase the
number of allowed permutations. He may continue this process, if necessary, until he reaches the limit of the practical decomposability of the symbols y_k. At each such
step he could also attempt to minimize the mean processing
time τ_{DM}, subject to constraints (*) and (**). This procedure again would require the solution of a sequence of
programming problems very similar to (though a little mes-
sier than) that discussed in the previous section. Under
this set-up a line could be established which can avoid
overload, as well as an SOR that actually does so.

(2) A second possible approach for the designer is to
go directly to the limit of the decomposability of the symbols y_k. If that limit is m, he can enquire whether an m-
member line can avoid overload among its members if he allows u permutations in the assignment of subsymbols among
them. This will evidently be so if the largest among the
mean processing times τ_s is less than 1. He can determine
this by finding an SOR which minimizes the largest τ_s, on
the premise that this SOR will avoid overload on the line

if overload is avoidable there in the first place. Such an SOR will be called a Minimax SOR for reasons we will show next.

Theorem 2: Minimax SORs have the property that they equalize the mean processing times τ_s of the line members. Such SORs always exist, regardless of whether the input machines of the line members are load-dependent.

Proof: For simplicity consider a three-man line, consisting of γ, δ, ε. It will be shown first that a Minimax SOR, if it exists, is among those which equalizes the τ_s's = γ, δ, ε, the existence of equalizing SORs will be proven thereafter.

(1) Note that the constraints

$$P_{uk} \geq 0, \sum_{uk} P_{uk} = 1 \qquad (k = 1,2,\ldots,n)$$

define a convex polyhedron CP in the space of the variables P_{uk}. Consider the subset of CP on which $\tau_\gamma = \tau_\delta = \tau_\varepsilon$ and assume for the moment that it is non-empty. Select a point in that subset on which the common value assumes its minimum τ^*. It is claimed that this is a point at which the largest of the τ_s's = γ, δ, ε is as small as possible. For suppose not, one could find another point of CP at which the largest τ_s is smaller than τ^*. However, it would then also be larger than any other τ_s at that point for if they were all equal, τ^* would not have been the smallest. It follows that τ^* minimizes the largest τ_s.

(2) It now remains to be shown that there exist equalizing SORs, i.e., that the subset on which $\tau_\gamma = \tau_\delta = \tau_\varepsilon$ is non-empty. Here, we can use a line of reasoning by Nash as exposited by Luce and Raiffa (1957), p. 391. Suppose that some mixed SOR has been chosen by the designer but that τ_γ, τ_δ, and τ_ε are not equal. In that case he can choose a new SOR which is the same except for the assignment probabilities of two symbols, d_i and d_k, say. Consider the change in probabilities

$$P'_{ui} = \left[P_{ui} + \frac{|\tau_\gamma - \tau_\delta|}{u} \right] / \left[1 - |\tau_\gamma - \tau_\delta| \right]$$

$$P'_{uk} = \left[P_{ui} + \frac{|\tau_\gamma - \tau_\delta|}{u} \right] / \left[1 + |\tau_\gamma - \tau_\epsilon| \right]$$

The transformation from the P_{ui} and P_{uk} to the P'_{ui} and P'_{uk} is a continuous transformation, and it carries CP into itself. By Brouwer's fix-point theorem it has a fixed point, i.e., a set of assignment probabilities for which P_{ui} and P'_{ui}, as well as P_{uk} and P'_{uk} are the same. Evidently for this particular set,

$$|\tau_\gamma - \tau_\delta| = |\tau_\gamma - \tau_\epsilon| = .0,$$

it follows that there exist equalizing SORs.

Note that the proof is valid regardless of whether the input machines of the line members are, or are not, load-dependent. If they are not, the problem of determining the Minimax SOR is of a well-known type which is called an 'assignment problem', and more particularly, of the variety of 'bottleneck-assignment problems'. Algorithms exist by which pure SORs can be determined, at least in principle (e.g. Ford and Fulkerson (1974), p.57).

Pure SORs, however, may produce overload on the line in cases in which mixed ones still avoid it. The determination of a best mixed SOR, can be formulated as the following LPproblem: determine values for the assignment probabilities, subject to the probability constraints, and to $\tau_\gamma = \tau_\delta = \tau_\epsilon$, such that τ_γ, say is minimized.

This type of programming problem assumes u fixed, for instance, at u = m! The designer, on finding that the Minimax SOR avoids overload on the line, may wish to investigate the possibility of a smaller line or at least a smaller number u of permutations, on the expectation that the load on the DM will be reduced in this fashion. He can do this by solving a sequence of programming problems which is in some respect the reverse of the one discussed earlier in this section. He would proceed as follows: decrease u step-wise for every m until you find a pair (m,u), for which even the Minimax SOR no longer avoids overload.

6. LINE STRUCTURE AND SPAN OF CONTROL

In this section it will be shown that line structure and

the notion of span of control are a rather natural consequence of load-dependence. In the practice of organizational design there appear to be several reasons for the
existence of a limit on the number of line members who receive their instructions directly from another.

(i)   The addition of line members increases the wage
         bill, and the transition from m to (m + 1) may not
         be economically justified with regard to the pro-
         ductivity of the organization (see Beckmann (1978)).

(ii)   The job of the proper distribution of assignments
         among the line becomes more complex and more time
         consuming for the DM, as the overall size of the
         line increases.

(iii)   Each line member demands a certain amount of super-
         visory time and attention for 'personal' problems,
         i.e., for problems which are not directly related
         to the tasks assigned to him.

Referring to (i) involves a comparison of trade-offs
between marginal costs and marginal benefits of extending
the line: keeping it as it is could involve overload,
hence, a cost due to errors and loss of performance, but if
another member is added there will be an extra (wage) cost.
The latter cost may be greater than the former. If so, the
organization is better off without a new member. We will
not consider this situation further.[6] Items (ii) and
(iii), referring to job complexity and to the 'personel attention syndrome', respectively, though different in assessment, can be subsumed under the heading of 'load-dependence', as will be argued next.

First, consider the analytical handling of (iii) with
respect to mean output processing time. Assume that the DM
has to set aside a certain average proportion $c(m)$ of every
unit time interval for 'personal attention problems' of the
m line members to whom he assigns their tasks. It is then
reasonable to assume further that $c(m)$ is monotone non-de-
creasing in m. The time needed for 'personal attention problems', however, will then in effect merely be an addition
to the mean output processing time of the DM and will change
$\tau_{DM}(m)$ to $\tau_{DM}(m) + c(m)$. The requirements of load-dependence, as in Gottinger (1980), would be preserved, but

the factor $c(m)$ might as well have been included in the mean processing time $\tau_{DM}(m)$ to start with, and this will be assumed in what follows.

<u>Example</u>. In order to explain the connection between load-dependence and line structure, suppose that a line has been set up for alternate processing. Suppose further that it has been possible to solve the sequence of programming problems described previously (Sect. 5) and that a four-man line identified by γ, δ, ε, ϕ, has been found adequate. This would mean that an SOR has been derived which minimizes the mean output processing time τ_{DM} and which at the same time, avoids overload among the four line members. Suppose, finally, that it is intended to reduce τ_{DM} further, for whatever reason. In that case, an echelon of new line members, call them 'liaison managers', can be interposed between the DM and the existing four, such as i and j. LMi links the DM to γ and δ, LMj does it for ε or ϕ. A table of the SORs governing these operations looks as follows.

$$
\text{SOR} \left\{ \begin{array}{l}
\text{DM: } x_k \longrightarrow d_k, d_k \text{ to i or with prob.} P_{ik} \text{ or } P_{jk}, \\[2ex]
\text{i: } d_k \longrightarrow d_k, d_k \text{ to } \gamma \text{ or } \delta \quad " \quad " \quad P_{\gamma k}, P_{\delta k} \\[2ex]
\text{j: } d_k \longrightarrow d_k, d_k \text{ to } \varepsilon \text{ or } \phi \quad " \quad " \quad P_{\varepsilon k}, P_{\phi k} \\[2ex]
\gamma, \delta, \varepsilon, \phi: d_k \longrightarrow y_k, y_k \text{ to P.O.} \quad " \quad " \quad 1
\end{array} \right.
$$

$$(k = 1, 2, \ldots, n).$$

This SOR complicates the above mentioned programming problems in the following way. The largest possible reduction of the DM's output load can be achieved by solving a corresponding, newly structured problem: Minimize τ_{DM} w.r.t. assignment probabilities P_{ik} and P_{jk} subject to the constraints:

$$P_{sk} \geq 0 \quad (\bar{s} = \gamma, \delta, \varepsilon, \phi, i, j).$$

$$P_{ik} + P_{jk} = 1, \ P_{\gamma k} + P_{\delta k} = 1, \ P_{\varepsilon k} + P_{\phi k} = 1 \quad (k = 1, 2, \ldots, n)$$

$$\tau_i = \tau_i^{(input)}(P_i) + \tau_i^{(output)}(P_i, P_\gamma, P_\delta) \leq 1$$

$$\tau_j = \tau_j^{(input)}(P_j) + \tau_j^{(output)}(P_j, P_\varepsilon, P_\phi) \leq 1$$

$$\tau_s = \tau_s^{(input)}(P_s) + \tau_s^{(output)}(P_s) \leq 1 \quad (s = \gamma, \delta, \varepsilon, \phi).$$

The introduction of line echelons, such as i and j, of course, does not make sense if the DM's output is load-independent.

His mean processing time τ_{DM} is then unaffected by the member m of line members to whom he issues instructions. Issuing them to four is no more complex a task as issuing them to two. However, if his output is load-dependent there is every expectation that the introduction of new first echelon will be beneficial. Not only is the number m smaller for him by a factor of 2, there is also the possibility of his being able to use a pure SOR to i and j.

In general, i and j will suffer from load-dependence as badly as the DM, as indicated by the constraints. With reference to the programming problem it may be useful to have a simple sufficient condition which assures at least the existence of a feasible solution. For such a condition we prove

Theorem 3: Suppose that a single-echelon line of m members can execute an alternate processing task without overload. If the designer has at his disposal a sufficiently large pool of potential liaison managers, i, whose mean processing times satisfy

$$(*)\ \max \tau = \max \left\{ \tau_i^{(input)}(P_i) + \tau_i^{(output)}(P_i, P_\gamma, P_\delta, \ldots) \right\}$$
$$\leqq 1$$

where the maximum is extended over the symbol probabilities P_{ik} of the input alphabet and over the probabilities $P_{\gamma k}, P_{\delta k}, \ldots$ of assignments to r destinations, then the same processing tasks can also be performed by a line with e echelons, the first of which need not have more than two members, and where e is the smallest integer such that

$$(**)\ e \geqq \log_r m/2 + 1.$$

Proof: The sufficiency condition (*) is obvious: it says intuitively that there is no way of overloading the liaison managers as long as each has no more than r subordinates. If there are e echelons, if the first has two members each of whom makes assignments to r members in the second echelon, and each of the latter do the same, the last echelon has $m = 2r^{e-1}$ members. This implies the equality in (**). The inequality then holds if (m/2) is not a power of r. This completes the proof.

Condition (*) in general will be fulfilled by several values of r for any one liaison manager. However, one could expect there will be a maximum r for each. This maximum could be considered as a bound on his span of control since it is the upper limit on the number of subordinates he can have on the line. In order to determine the actual number, a series of programming problems of the type considered before would have to be solved.

The maximum number of r for the liaison managers, collectively, will also give the designer an indication of how many echelons he might have to provide on the line in order to bring about the greatest achievable reduction in the DM's output load. It appears that there is no more the organization designer can do for him by a suitable design of the line. Whatever additional measures are possible must be introduced through a proper design of the staff - to be taken up in a subsequent paper.

The discussion here has been limited to the alternately processing line. With suitable changes, it applies to parallel processing as well, although the argumentation becomes more involved.

7. SUMMARY AND CONCLUSIONS

The basic objective of the economics of organizational design as pertaining to line organizations is the reduction of the output load on the DM(s), without generating overload among the line members. As Arrow (1974, p. 37) has remarked, 'the scarcity of information-handling ability is an essential feature for the understanding of both individual and organizational behavior' and it is to be explicitly dealt with by the organizational designer.

The limit results on avoiding overload, or loss to the organization appear to agree, in principle, with other limit results on large teams obtained by Arrow and Radner (1979), particularly, in view of our Theorem 3 in the previous section, where it is shown that the performance of a centralized line is equivalent to a decentralized line, structured in e echelons, with a sufficiently large number of liaison managers assuming partial decision making functions.

The designer has two fundamental options of how to use the line. He can do its processing alternately or in parallel. He can also use mixtures of the two. If alternate processing is chosen, overload can always be avoided among the line by making the line large enough. Moreover, if the output (machine) of the DM is not load-dependent, all line members can receive their instructions from him directly without adverse effect on his output load. On the other hand, if his output is load-dependent, additional line echelons must be introduced as the size of the line is increased, to keep the DM's output load under control.

Similar remarks apply, in principle to a line that does its processing in parallel.

Overload among the line members however, may not be avoidable unless the production of the organizational output can be resolved into sufficiently many subtasks.

Here SORs have been established that require the optimal solution of programming problems to avoid overload.   -
In possibly more realistic situations, by setting up SORs for large organizations we may face difficulties in obtaining explicit analytical solutions. In these cases it might be advisable to establish more sophisticated SORs, namely those which are derived from 'allocation of effort' models or related models of bounded rationality (Radner (1975), Radner and Rothschild (1975)). For example, 'putting out fires' (damage control), or, 'staying with the winner' rules could be superimposed on such SORs and be more adequate for decision making in complex organizational environments

The choice between alternate and parallel processing, on the basis of this theory, should strictly be made after the programming problems have been solved. In practice, however, the choice often seems to be made on the basis of which mode enables a multiple-member line to get the job done faster. The comparison then frequently favors parallel processing because its processing times t_{sk} are typically shorter than their counterparts $P_{sk}t_{sk}$ for alternate processing. This will lead to shorter mean processing times, and, which appears to be even more important, in practice, to shorter delays in the delivery of the output products.

Neither processing mode is used in practice to the exclusion of the other. In many orgnizations parallel processing seems to be exploited as far as it can be, i.e., to the limit of decomposability of a task into subtasks. Beyond that alternate processing is applied, as the only remaining alternative.

This appears to be true for 'natural' as well as 'artificial' organizations, e.g., computer networks (Slotnick (1971)). In practice, organizations use 'pure' SORs most of the time. But occasionally supervisory reasonings lead to a mixing, such as considerations of justice and personal matters to equalize load among subordinates. The effect is an SOR resembling a (mixed) Minimax SOR.

MEDIS-Institut, GSF
8042 Neuherberg and Univ. Bielefeld
F.R.G.

NOTES

1. This relates to opportunity time. Sometimes you think it is better to do it yourself than to instuct someone who does it, in particular, if he does it wrongly.
2. In more concrete terms, this could be a rotational rule, a random rule without replacement, or, simply a rule to assign a task to anyone who is underloaded sufficiently.
3. Thus, input processing pertains to his cognitive limits of perception and comprehension, output processing to his ability to manipulate symbols.
4. Because of NP-related problems there may not be an optimal solution, and therefore, effective heuristic procedures may have to be found, see Gottinger (1983).
5. Thus, it is assumed that the task allocation permutes according to the number of receivers, and this in turn depends on to which extent the output symbols, and hence, the directives are decomposable.
6. In other considerations, such as security or safety issues, different organizational goals may require redundancy or duplication of existing personnel.

REFERENCES

Arrow, K.J.: 1979, The Limits of Organization, Norton, New York.

Arrow, K.J. and R. Radner: 1978 'Allocation of Resources in
    Large Teams', Econometrica 47, 361-385.
Beckman, M.J.: 1974, 'Rank in Organizations'. Lecture Notes
    in Economics and Mathematical Systems Vol. 161, Sprin-
    ger-Verlag, New York.
Ford, L.R. and D.R. Fulkerson: 1974, Flows in Networks
    Princeton University Press.
Gottinger H.W.: 1980, 'An Information-theoretic Approach to
    Large Organizations', Mathematical Social Sciences 1,
    223-233.
Gottinger, H.W.: 1983, Coping with Complexity, Reidel Publ.
    Comp., Dordrecht (to appear).
Luce, R.D. and H. Raiffa: 1957, 'Games and Decisions', Wil-
    ley-Verlag, New York.
Marschak, J.: 1974, 'Economic Information, Decision and Pre-
    diction', in Selected Essays Vol. III, Reidel Publ.
    Comp., Dordrecht.
Radner, R.: 1975, 'A Behavioral Model of Cost Reduction',
    Bell Journ. of Economics 6, 196-215.
Radner R. and M. Rothschild: 1975, 'The Allocation of Ef-
    fort', Journal of Economic Theory 10, 358-376.
Slotnick, L.: 1971, 'The Fastest Computer', Scientific
    American 224, 76-87.

Peter H. Farquhar and Peter C. Fishburn

INDIFFERENCE SPANNING ANALYSIS

ABSTRACT

The indifference spanning approach to assessing multiattribute utility functions is based on conditional indifference
relations. Such relations are used to derive multiadditive
representations that involve finite sums of products of
single-attribute conditional utility functions. This paper
reviews the multiadditive representation theorems of Fishburn and Farquhar (1982) and then provides a procedure for
constructing a set of basis elements to implement the indifference spanning approach. Several examples and directions
for further research are given also.

1. BACKGROUND

The consequences of many decisions can be evaluated on more
than one relevant attribute. For example, alternative modes
of personal transportation can be compared with respect to
convenience, travel time, cost, and safety. Ambient air
quality can be assessed in terms of constituent pollutants,
such as hydrocarbons, ozone, particulates, sulfur oxides,
etc. Computer time-sharing systems can be evaluated on the
basis of availability, reliability, and average response
times for editing, compiling, and other functions. Keeney
(1982) cites many more such applications in his overview of
decision analysis.

Since some decision problems are inherently multidimensional, there has been considerable interest over the past
several years in analyzing multiattribute expected utility
functions. This methodology provides systematic procedures
for examining preferences for consequences, attitudes towards
risk, and value tradeoffs among attributes. Because of the
practical difficulties in directly eliciting multiattribute
utility functions from individuals, research has focused on
the *decomposition approach*. This approach allows the assessment of a utility function over multiple attributes to be decomposed into several simpler tasks for the decision maker.

B. P. Stigum and F. Wenstøp (eds.), Foundations of Utility and Risk Theory with Applications,
443–459.
© 1983 *by D. Reidel Publishing Company.*

A key step in the decomposition approach is the testing of *independence properties* that characterize the relationship of tradeoffs among the attributes under conditions of risk. Given a particular independence property among the attributes, the decomposition approach prescribes how to represent the multiattribute utility function in terms of several marginal utility functions involving one or more attributes. In Section 3, we illustrate some of these independence properties and the corresponding multiattribute utility decompositions. Keeney and Raiffa (1976) describe numerous field studies and applications of the decomposition approach to multiattribute utility analysis. Fishburn and Keeney (1974), Farquhar (1977), and Fishburn (1977a) review various independence axioms and the corresponding multiattribute utility representation theorems used by the decomposition approach.

Even though decomposition methods require some effort to systematically test the reasonableness of different independence axioms, the overall approach is typically much easier to apply than a holistic analysis of preferences for risky decisions. Decomposition methods work well with additive, multiplicative, and other simple forms of utility representations (e.g., see Fishburn (1965a), Pollak (1967), Keeney (1968, 1971, 1972, 1974), Raiffa (1969), Meyer (1970), Nahas (1977), and others). On the other hand, Fishburn (1967, 1972), Farquhar (1978), and Keeney (1981) describe techniques for analyzing preference interdependencies and restructuring attribute sets to extend these simpler representations to somewhat more complicated situations.

As the degree of attribute interdependency increases, however, the effort needed to implement decomposition methods grows quickly. In cases where the only dependencies are between successive attributes, Fishburn (1965b, 1974), Meyer (1970), Bell (1977), and others provide relatively straightforward utility decompositions. Kirkwood (1976) gives a utility assessment procedure for parametrically dependent preference structures. Farquhar (1975, 1976) presents a general methodology for generating independence axioms and their corresponding multiattribute utility decompositions; his fractional hypercube methodology provides a hierarchy of utility models ranging from the additive model to forms that represent increasingly complicated preference interdependencies among attributes. These interdependencies are reflected by interaction terms in the

functional form of the utility decomposition. If the interaction terms are products of single-attribute functions,
then the decompositions are relatively easy to assess; on
the other hand, the presence of nonseparable interaction
terms complicates matters because functions over two or more
attributes need to be assessed.

A key disadvantage of the decomposition approach
appears in more complex decision problems when no independence axioms are verified. This situation can arise if for
some reason it is undesirable to conduct independence tests
or if certain axioms are tested and subsequently rejected.
Since each collection of independence axioms yields a particular multiattribute utility representation, in the absence
of any empirical verification one is forced to guess at the
form of the utility function or to employ some approach
other than decomposition. The former option is chosen in
many applications, though Camerer (1982) explains the many
pitfalls in not adequately accounting for attribute interdependencies in utility representations.

Recent advances in multiattribute utility analysis
provide alternatives to the decomposition approach discussed
above. Farquhar (1980) reviews three alternate approaches
based on (1) multivalent preference analysis, (2) approximation methods, and (3) indifference spanning analysis. After
a brief description of the first two approaches, the remainder of the paper is devoted to an exposition of spanning
methods for multiattribute utility analysis.

Unlike utility decompositions which rely on independence axioms defined on whole attributes, the *valence
approach* partitions the elements of each attribute into
classes on the basis of equivalent conditional preference
orders. In this way, one can derive various multivalent
independence axioms for which a particular independence
property holds on the restriction of an attribute to any of
its classes. At one extreme are the univalent independence
axioms of decomposition methods that require all elements in
an attribute be in the same equivalence class. At the other
extreme is complete utility dependence where each element
forms a distinct equivalence class. Thus there is an entire
spectrum of interdependencies that can be modeled by multivalent preference structures. Since preference interdependencies among attributes are reflected primarily by this
partitioning into equivalence classes, attribute interaction

effects are readily interpreted. The resulting multiattribute utility representations can be kept simple, because they are derived over a patchwork of subspaces defined by products of attribute equivalence classes.

Farquhar (1981) and Farquhar and Fishburn (1981) establish multivalent forms of additive, utility, and fractional independence axioms and the corresponding multiattribute utility representation theorems. They illustrate how the valence approach not only subsumes utility decomposition methods, but also produces representations for complex preference structures not covered by previous methods. Current research is directed at designing useful procedures to partition the elements of each attribute into equivalence classes and at analyzing the results of field studies to improve the applicability of multivalent preference structures.

When independence axioms are not checked, *approximation methods* can be used for multiattribute utility assessment. Keeney (1972), Nahas (1977), Tamura and Nakamura (1978, 1983), and Bell (1979a,b) examine approximations based on interpolation between single-attribute conditional utility functions. Fishburn (1977b, 1979) considers the degree of error involved in using various approximating forms, such as the additive, multiplicative, and others that yield exact results when particular independence axioms hold. He examines more general approximations using different types of linear interpolation and exact grid models.

Although these approximate representations are comparatively easy to assess, the goodness of the approximations remains a central issue in using these methods. Farquhar (1978), Keeney (1981), and Camerer (1982) note several situations where simple approximations yield poor representations of underlying preference structures and can thus contribute to serious misjudgments. Further applied research is needed on the use of utility approximations to avoid some of these problems.

2. INTRODUCTION

The purpose of this paper is to elaborate on a new approach for multiattribute utility assessment that appears to offer several advantages over other approaches. The *indifference spanning approach* provides (a) one functional representation for the entire outcome space (unlike multivalent preference

analysis), (b) a set of testable axioms to identify the form
of a multiattribute utility function (unlike approximation
methods), and (c) the assessment of only single-attribute
conditional utility functions (unlike utility decompositions
in complicated decision problems).

Using the indifference spanning approach, Fishburn and
Farquhar (1982) derive multiadditive utility representations
from axioms which use conditional indifference relations to
construct a so-called basis for each attribute. One such
multiadditive representation for a utility function u on the
two-attribute space X×Y is

$$u(x,y) = k + \sum_{i=1}^{n} a_i u(x_i,y) + \sum_{j=1}^{m} b_j u(x,y_j) \qquad (1)$$

$$+ \sum_{i=1}^{n} \sum_{j=1}^{m} c_{ij} u(x_i,y) u(x,y_j),$$

where k, a_i, b_j, and c_{ij} are scaling constants, and
$\{x_1,\ldots,x_n\}$ and $\{y_1,\ldots,y_m\}$ are bases for the attributes
X and Y, respectively. This multiadditive representation
requires $n+m$ single-attribute conditional utility functions
and at most $(n+1)(m+1)$ scaling constants to determine
$u(x,y)$.

The remainder of the paper is organized as follows.
Section 3 briefly reviews some definitions and the basic
multiadditive utility representation theorem from Fishburn
and Farquhar (1982). Section 4 describes a procedure for
finding basis elements by examining conditional indifference
relations on each attribute. The procedure is illustrated
with several examples. Section 5 comments on indifference
spanning analysis with more than two attributes, relates
it to work by Tamura and Nakamura (1983) on utility approximations using convex dependence, and concludes the paper
with some directions for further research.

3. MULTIADDITIVE REPRESENTATIONS

This section examines the multiadditive representations
introduced by Fishburn and Farquhar (1982) and further discussed in Fishburn (1982). We shall assume that u is a

von Neumann-Morgenstern utility function on X×Y, where both
attributes are essential to an individual's preferences.
Possible generalizations to more than two attributes are
covered in Section 5.

Let P_Y denote the set of all gambles or simple probability measures on Y, and let (x,p) be the gamble on X×Y
that gives $x \varepsilon X$ for sure and has a marginal gamble $p \varepsilon P_Y$ on Y.
If an individual's preferences for gambles in P_Y conditioned
on a fixed $x \varepsilon X$ do not depend on x, then by definition Y is
utility independent of X. In other words, if for all $p,q \varepsilon P_Y$
and all $x,x' \varepsilon X$, $(x,p) \succ (x,q)$ if and only if $(x',p) \succ (x',q)$,
then Y is utility independent of X.

Pollak (1967), Keeney (1968, 1971, 1972, 1974), Raiffa
(1969), Meyer (1970), and many others examine utility independence. One can show that Y is utility independent of X
if and only if there are real-valued functions f and h on X
and g on Y such that f is positive and

$$u(x,y) = f(x)g(y) + h(x), \qquad (2)$$

for all $x \varepsilon X$ and all $y \varepsilon Y$. An analogous result holds when X
is utility independent of Y. Thus, if X and Y are each
utility independent of the other, one can show that either
u has an additive form, $u(x,y) = u_1(x) + u_2(y)$, or u has a
multiplicative form, $u(x,y) = u_1(x) \cdot u_2(y) + k$.

Fishburn and Farquhar (1982) provide a fundamental
extension of utility independence. They show that Y is
"degree-n utility independent" of X if and only if u has a
multiadditive form

$$u(x,y) = \sum_{i=1}^{n} f_i(x)g_i(y) + h(x) \qquad (3)$$

with no restrictions on the signs of the functions.
This sum-of-products representation involves only single-
attribute functions, so practical assessment is straightforward. However, as the degree of preference dependency
of Y on X increases, the number of such functions to be
assessed increases accordingly.

The multiadditive representation above is derived from
conditional indifference relations. By conditioning on a
fixed $x \varepsilon X$, the indifference relation ~ for gambles on X×Y

induces an indifference relation $\sim_X$ on P_Y defined as follows for all $p,q \epsilon P_Y$.

$$p \sim_X q \quad \text{if and only if} \quad (x,p) \sim (x,q), \quad (4)$$

Similarly, for all nonempty sets $A \subseteq X$, define

$$p \sim_A q \quad \text{if and only if} \quad (x,p) \sim (x,q) \quad \text{for all } x \epsilon A. \quad (5)$$

We shall refer to $\sim_A = \bigcap \{\sim_X : x \epsilon A\}$ as the *indifference core* of A. For convenience, we define the indifference core of the empty set by $\sim_\phi \equiv P_Y \times P_Y$.

DEFINITION: A nonempty set $B \subseteq X$ is a *basis* of X if and only if

(i) B is *independent*: $\sim_{B \setminus \{x\}} \not\subseteq \sim_X$ for all $x \epsilon B$, and

(ii) B is *spanning*: $\sim_B = \sim_X$.

Thus B is a basis of X if $(x,p) \sim (x,q)$ for all $x \epsilon B$ implies that $(x,p) \sim (x,q)$ for all $x \epsilon X$, and if for every $x \epsilon B$ there is some pair $p,q \epsilon P_Y$ such that $(x,p) \not\sim (x,q)$ while $(x',p) \sim (x',q)$ for all $x' \epsilon B \setminus \{x\}$, provided that B has at least two elements. Otherwise, $B = \{x\}$ is a basis if $\sim_X \neq P_Y \times P_Y$ and if $(x,p) \sim (x,q)$ implies $(x',p) \sim (x',q)$ for all $x' \epsilon X$.

Since X is essential, it has a nonempty basis. Such a basis could be infinite, but we shall consider only finite bases and say that Y is *degree-n utility independent* of X if X has an n-element basis.

THEOREM (Fishburn and Farquhar, 1982): X has an n-element basis for finite $n \epsilon \{1,2,...\}$ if and only if there are real-valued functions $f_1, ..., f_n$, h on X and $g_1, ..., g_n$ on Y such that for all $(x,y) \epsilon X \times Y$,

$$u(x,y) = \sum_{i=1}^{n} f_i(x)g_i(y) + h(x),$$

and u does not have an analogous form for any n' < n.

When the multiadditive form in the above Theorem is viewed from the perspective of Y instead of X, it follows that if X has an n-element basis, then Y has an m-element basis where $m \epsilon \{n-1, n, n+1\}$. Using this fact, one can obtain the multiadditive representation in (1) that specifies the conditional utility functions on X and Y needed to assess u(x,y). As noted in the Introduction, this representation offers several advantages over alternate approaches to multiattribute utility assessment for complicated preference structures.

4. INDIFFERENCE SPANNING ANALYSIS

The practical assessment of multiadditive utility representations requires a simple procedure for determining an independent spanning set for each attribute. This section considers procedures for constructing bases and gives several examples to illustrate the use of such procedures.

We begin by noting several facts about the indifference spanning approach that are consequences of earlier definitions and results. First, every nonempty subset of an independent set is independent, and every finite spanning set includes a basis. Second, if A is a finite independent set and the indifference core of A is not included in $\sim_x$ for some $x \epsilon X \backslash A$, then $A \cup \{x\}$ is independent. Third, every finite maximal independent set is spanning and is therefore a basis. Fourth, if X includes a finite basis, then all bases of X have the same number of elements. And fifth, if X has an n-element basis, then Y has an m-element basis and $|n-m| \leq 1$.

Our procedure for constructing a finite basis on X when one exists is described as follows. Step 1 is to find any $x_1 \epsilon X$ for which $(x_1,p) \not\sim (x_1,q)$ for some $p,q \epsilon P_Y$. If no such x_1 exists, then $\sim_X = P_Y \times P_Y$, and X is not an essential attribute. (In this case, X can be deleted from the decision problem with no effect on the preference structure.) If such an x_1 is found, then $\{x_1\}$ comprises the initial independent set. Step 2 is an iterative one that searches for additional x_i to augment the existing independent set, call it B. One adds x_i to B if there are some $p,q \epsilon P_Y$ such that $(x,p) \sim (x,q)$ for all $x \epsilon B$ but it is not true that $(x_i,p) \sim (x_i,q)$. Thus, the indifference core of B is not included in $\sim_{x_i}$, so $B \cup \{x_i\}$ is an independent set. The successive iteration of this step ends when no more $x \epsilon X$ can be added; thus B is a maximally independent set and is therefore a basis.

EXAMPLE 1 (Generalized Utility Independence):

To illustrate our procedure for constructing a basis on X, suppose that an individual has the utility function $u(x,y) = (x - 1/2)y + 2x$ for $0 \leqslant x, y \leqslant 1$. In Step 1 of the procedure, we first consider $x_1 = 1/2$ as a possible initial independent set, but observe that $(1/2, p) \sim (1/2, q)$ for all $p, q \epsilon P_Y$ since u is constant. In searching then for another element, we let $x_1 = 0$ and observe that $(0,p) \sim (0,q)$ if and only if the expected values of p and q are equal. Thus, we have $B = \{0\}$ in Step 1, and $\sim_B = \{(p,q) \epsilon P_Y \times P_Y: E_p[y] = E_q[y]\}$. The next step is to search for an x_2 satisfying the following conditions: $E_p[y] = E_q[y]$ and not $(x_2,p) \sim (x_2,q)$. But these two conditions cannot be satisfied simultaneously for any $x_2 \epsilon X$. Therefore, the current independent set B is spanning, $\sim_B = \sim_X$, and is thus a basis for X.

Although $u(x,y) = f(x)g(y) + h(x)$ in the above example, Y is not utility independent of X because $f(x) \equiv x - 1/2$ is not positive for all $0 \leqslant x \leqslant 1$. One observes, however, that conditional preferences on P_Y depend on a fixed $x \epsilon X$ only through the sign of $f(x)$. This situation includes complete reversals of preference when f is negative and complete indifference when f is zero. Fishburn (1974) and Fishburn and Keeney (1974, 1975) say that Y is *generalized utility independent* of X in such cases and derive the representation $u(x,y) = f(x)g(y) + h(x)$ with no restrictions on the signs of the functions. Fishburn and Farquhar (1982) show that generalized utility independence is the same as degree-1 utility independence in the indifference spanning approach. Indeed, a basis for X in the above example has only one element, and any $x \neq 1/2$ forms a basis.

EXAMPLE 2:

Suppose that the attribute Y consists of distinct outcomes $y_1, y_2, \ldots, y_{n+1}$. Let p_i be the probability assigned to y_i by the gamble $p \epsilon P_Y$. In applying the basis procedure for the indifference spanning approach, suppose that the selection of the conditional element $x_1 \epsilon X$ directs an individual to focus exclusively on y_1 in comparing gambles on Y. For example, suppose that for all $p, q \epsilon P_Y$, $(x_1,p) \sim (x_1,q)$ if and only if $p_1 = q_1$. Thus, let $B = \{x_1\}$ for the initial independent set.

At the next step in the basis construction, there may be other elements in X that have the same conditional

indifference relation as $\sim_{x_1}$, but such elements cannot be
added to B. Instead, suppose there is an $x_2 \epsilon X$ such that
for all $p,q \epsilon P_Y$, $(x_2,p) \sim (x_2,q)$ if and only if $p_2 = q_2$.
Hence, the current independent set is expanded to B =
$\{x_1,x_2\}$, where $\sim_B = \{(p,q) \epsilon P_Y \times P_Y: p_1 = q_1$ and $p_2 = q_2\}$.
If $n = 2$, then B is a basis for X because $p_1 = q_1$ and $p_2 =$
q_2 together imply that $p = q$; obviously $(x,p) \sim (x,q)$ is
true for all $x \epsilon X$ if $p = q$, so $\sim_B = \sim_X$. If $n > 2$, then in
subsequent steps we assume that there are $x_i \epsilon X$ such that for
all $p,q \epsilon P_Y$, $(x_i,p) \sim (x_i,q)$ if and only if $p_i = q_i$ for i =
$1,\ldots,n$. A basis for X thus consists of n elements, B =
$\{x_1,\ldots,x_n\}$. Other bases can be constructed by different
pairings of conditional elements with n outcomes from Y.

This simple situation may be generalized in several
ways. Somewhat similar problems arise in multivalent
structures (Farquhar, 1978, 1981), in property fitting with
multidimensional scaling (Schiffman et al., 1981), and in
conjoint analysis (Green and Wind, 1973).

EXAMPLE 3:

Fishburn (1973) considers a two-period income example where
X and Y represent income received in a first and second period, respectively. The income amounts are transformed so that
$0 \leqslant x \leqslant 1$ and $0 \leqslant y \leqslant 1$, for convenience. Given $x = 0$ a particular
individual is risk averse for gambles on Y, but given $x = 1$
the individual is risk neutral for gambles on Y; an analogous
relationship holds with X and Y interchanged. With some additional scaling and preference information, a *bilateral* utility representation is derived for this situation.

$$u(x,y) = 1.8\sqrt{x} + 1.6\sqrt{y} - \left[1.8\sqrt{x} - 0.8x\right]\left[1.6\sqrt{y} - 0.6y\right] \quad (6)$$

$$= \left[-1.8\sqrt{x} + 0.8x + 1\right]\left[1.6\sqrt{y}\right]$$

$$+ \left[1.8\sqrt{x} - 0.8x\right]\left[0.6y\right] + 1.8\sqrt{x}$$

Since the latter expression is of the form $f_1(x)g_1(y) +$
$f_2(x)g_2(y) + h(x)$, Y is also degree-2 utility independent of
X. The conditional utility functions for extreme values of
x give $u(0,y) = 1.6\sqrt{y}$ and $u(1,y) = 0.6y + 1.8$, and (6) shows
how $u(x,y)$ is a linear combination of these two conditional
functions. In a similar way, several approximation results
use interpolation between two extreme conditional utility

functions (e.g., Schlaifer (1971), Fishburn (1977b, 1979),
Nahas (1977), Tamura and Nakamura (1978, 1983), and Bell
(1979a,b)).

In constructing a basis for X, we begin with any $x_1 \epsilon X$
and determine conditions for which $(x_1,p) \sim (x_1,q)$ for
$p,q \epsilon P_Y$. From (6), we note that $(x_1,p) \sim (x_1,q)$ implies that
$\alpha_1 E_p[\sqrt{y}] + \beta_1 E_p[y] = \alpha_1 E_q[\sqrt{y}] + \beta_1 E_q[y]$ for some constants
α_1 and β_1 that depend on x_1. The next step is to consider
$x_2 \epsilon X \backslash \{x_1\}$ and show that $(x_2,p) \sim (x_2,q)$ implies $\alpha_2 E_p[\sqrt{y}] +$
$\beta_2 E_p[y] = \alpha_2 E_q[\sqrt{y}] + \beta_2 E_q[y]$ for some constants α_2 and β_2
that depend on x_2. Therefore, $E_p[\sqrt{y}] = E_q[\sqrt{y}]$ and $E_p[y] =$
$E_q[y]$ whenever $(x,p) \sim (x,q)$ for $p,q \epsilon P_Y$. No further reduction is possible with additional $x \epsilon X$, so $B = \{x_1,x_2\}$ is a
basis for X. These conditions follow immediately from $x_1 =$
0 and $x_2 = 1$, but can be established with any $x_1 \neq x_2$ in X.

There are many generalizations of this two-period
income example. For instance, one can imagine a particular
individual who is risk neutral for gambles on Y given $x =$
x^*, risk averse given $x < x^*$, and risk seeking given $x > x^*$.
One can construct a three-element basis on X to model this
situation if, for example, $u(x,y)$ is a linear combination of
$u(0,y)$ and $u(x^*,y)$ for $0 \leq x \leq x^*$ and a linear combination
of $u(x^*,y)$ and $u(1,y)$ for $x^* \leq x \leq 1$. Other generalizations
are possible, too.

These examples illustrate the construction of bases
using the indifference spanning approach in a range of
problem settings. Because of the preference interdependencies between attributes, the procedure may appear somewhat
complicated, though it is straightforward to apply. Obviously, one will not have a specific utility function in
hand when determining conditional indifference relations, so
several comparisons of gambles will be needed to establish
these relationships; our examples employed utility functions
only as a shortcut to illustrate this process. More field
work and applications experience, however, can help to refine the process of determining conditional indifference
relations for basis construction in much the same way as
applications have improved the determination of conditional
preference relations in testing independence axioms for
utility decompositions.

5. FURTHER RESEARCH

There are two basic approaches for extending indifference
spanning methods to problems with more than two attributes.
Suppose that the outcome space is given by $X_1 \times \ldots \times X_N$.
One approach is to let $X = X_{\bar{i}}$ and $Y = X_i$, where $X_{\bar{i}} \equiv X_1 \times$
$\ldots \times X_{i-1} \times X_{i+1} \times \ldots \times X_N$. Thus an individual considers
gambles on a single attribute conditioned on all other at-
tributes being fixed at some value. A basis is constructed
for each $X_{\bar{i}}$, $i = 1,\ldots,N$. Following the development in
Farquhar (1975), Tamura and Nakamura (1983) use this
approach to derive a rather complicated N-attribute version
of the multiadditive utility representation in (1) by assuming convex dependence properties. Their work also includes
a set of inequalities relating the degrees of utility independence for different attributes. We suspect that these
results can be greatly simplified if a correlative structure
holds for the conditional indifference relations (e.g.,
Farquhar (1981) and Farquhar and Fishburn (1981)).

Another approach in extending the multiadditive utility
representation is to let $X = X_i$ and $Y = X_{\bar{i}}$. Now an individual considers gambles over N-1 attributes conditioned on a
fixed level of the remaining attribute. Since a basis is
constructed simply for each X_i, we expect that this generalization is relatively straightforward. The practical difficulty of considering gambles over N-1 attributes may be
alleviated by further developments along the lines of Keeney
(1974), where gambles over only two attributes at a time are
required.

Beyond the N-attribute generalizations of the multiadditive representation, there are a number of research issues associated with the determination of conditional indifference relations that can be addressed. Previous research
by MacCrimmon et al. (1969, 1974, 1977), Farquhar (1983),
and others is relevant to developing these aspects of the
indifference spanning approach for utility assessment.

Peter H. Farquhar   Peter C. Fishburn
Univ. of California, Davis Bell Telephone Laboratories
Davis, California, U.S.A.   Murray Hill, New Jersey, U.S.A.

ACKNOWLEDGEMENTS

This research was supported in part by the Office of Naval
Research under Contract #N00014-80-C-0897, Task #NR-277-258
to the University of California, Davis (Farquhar).

REFERENCES

Bell, D.E. (1977). "A Utility Function for Time Streams
having Inter-Period Dependencies," *Operations Research,*
Vol. 25, pp. 448-458.

Bell, D.E. (1979a). "Consistent Assessment Procedures using
Conditional Utility Functions," *Operations Research,*
Vol. 27, pp. 1054-1066.

Bell, D.E. (1979b). "Multiattribute Utility Functions:
Decompositions using Interpolation," *Management Science,*
Vol. 25, pp. 744-753.

Camerer, C. (1982). "Fitting Linear Models to Interactive
Data when Variables are Intercorrelated: Analytical
Results and Implications," unpublished manuscript, Kellogg
Graduate School of Management, Northwestern, University,
Evanston, Illinois.

Farquhar, P.H. (1975). "A Fractional Hypercube Decomposition Theorem for Multiattribute Utility Functions," *Operations Research,* Vol. 23, pp. 941-967.

Farquhar, P.H. (1976). "Pyramid and Semicube Decompositions
of Multiattribute Utility Functions," *Operations Research,*
Vol. 24, pp. 256-271.

Farquhar, P.H. (1977). "A Survey of Multiattribute Utility
Theory and Applications," in M.K. Starr and M. Zeleny
(eds.), *Multiple Criteria Decision Making,* TIMS Studies in
the Management Sciences, North-Holland, Amsterdam, Vol. 6,
pp. 59-89.

Farquhar, P.H. (1978). "Interdependent Criteria in Utility
Analysis," in S. Zionts (ed.), *Multiple Criteria Problem
Solving,* Lecture Notes in Economics and Mathematical Sys-
tems, Springer-Verlag, Berlin, Vol. 155, pp. 131-180.

Farquhar, P.H. (1980). "Advances in Multiattribute Utility
Theory," *Theory and Decision,* Vol. 12, pp. 381-394.

Farquhar, P.H. (1981). "Multivalent Preference Structures,"
Mathematical Social Sciences, Vol. 1, pp. 397-408.

Farquhar, P.H. (1983). "Utility Assessment Methods," *Management Science*, Vol. 29, to appear.

Farquhar, P.H. and P.C. Fishburn (1981). "Equivalences and Continuity in Multivalent Preference Structures," *Operations Research*, Vol. 29, pp. 282-293.

Fishburn, P.C. (1965a). "Independence in Utility Theory with Whole Product Sets," *Operations Research*, Vol. 13, pp. 28-45.

Fishburn, P.C. (1965b). "Markovian Dependence in Utility Theory with Whole Product Sets," *Operations Research*, Vol. 13, pp. 238-257.

Fishburn, P.C. (1967). "Interdependence and Additivity in Multivariate, Unidimensional Expected Utility Theory," *International Economic Review*, Vol. 8, pp. 335-342.

Fishburn, P.C. (1970). *Utility Theory for Decision Making*, Wiley, New York.

Fishburn, P.C. (1972). "Interdependent Preferences on Finite Sets," *Journal of Mathematical Psychology*, Vol. 9, pp. 225-236.

Fishburn, P.C. (1973). "Bernoullian Utilities for Multiple-Factor Situations," in J.L. Cochrane and M. Zeleny (eds.), *Multiple Criteria Decision Making*, University of South Carolina Press, Columbia, South Carolina, pp. 47-61.

Fishburn, P.C. (1974). "von Neumann-Morgenstern Utility Functions on Two Attributes," *Operations Research*, Vol. 22, pp. 35-45.

Fishburn, P.C. (1975). "Nondecomposable Conjoint Measurement for Bisymmetric Structures," *Journal of Mathematical Psychology*, Vol. 12, pp. 75-89.

Fishburn, P.C. (1977a). "Multiattribute Utilities in Expected Utility Theory," in D.E. Bell, R.L. Keeney, and H. Raiffa (eds.), *Conflicting Objectives in Decisions*, Wiley, New York, pp. 172-194.

Fishburn, P.C. (1977b). "Approximations of Two-Attribute Utility Functions," *Mathematics of Operations Research*, Vol. 2, pp. 30-44.

Fishburn, P.C. (1979). "Approximations of Multiattribute Utility Functions," *Journal of Approximation Theory*, Vol. 27, pp. 179-196.

Fishburn, P.C. (1982). *The Foundations of Expected Utility,* Reidel, Dordrecht, Holland.

Fishburn, P.C. and P.H. Farquhar (1982). "Finite-Degree Utility Independence," *Mathematics of Operations Research,* Vol. 7, pp. 348-353.

Fishburn, P.C. and R.L. Keeney (1974). "Seven Independence Concepts and Continuous Multiattribute Utility Functions," *Journal of Mathematical Psychology,* Vol. 11, pp. 294-327.

Fishburn, P.C. and R.L. Keeney (1975). "Generalized Utility Independence and Some Implications," *Operations Research,* Vol. 23, pp. 928-940.

Green, P.E. and Y. Wind (1973). *Multiattribute Decisions in Marketing: A Measurement Approach,* Dryden Press, Hillsdale, Illinois.

Keeney, R.L. (1968). "Quasi-Separable Utility Functions," *Naval Research Logistics Quarterly,* Vol. 15, pp. 551-565.

Keeney, R.L. (1971). "Utility Independence and Preferences for Multiattributed Consequences," *Operations Research,* Vol. 19, pp. 875-893.

Keeney, R.L. (1972). "Utility Functions for Multiattributed Consequences," *Management Science,* Vol. 18, pp. 276-287.

Keeney, R.L. (1974). "Multiplicative Utility Functions," *Operations Research,* Vol. 22, pp. 22-34.

Keeney, R.L. (1981). "Analysis of Preference Dependencies among Objectives," *Operations Research,* Vol. 29, pp. 1105-1120.

Keeney, R.L. (1983). "Decision Analysis: An Overview," *Operations Research,* Vol. 30, pp. 803-838.

Keeney, R.L. and H. Raiffa (1976). *Decisions with Multiple Objectives: Preferences and Value Tradeoffs,* Wiley, New York.

Kirkwood, C.W. (1976). "Parametrically Dependent Preferences for Multiattributed Consequences," *Operations Research,* Vol. 24, pp. 92-103.

MacCrimmon, K.R. and J.K. Siu (1974). "Making Trade-Offs," *Decision Sciences,* Vol. 5, pp. 680-704.

MacCrimmon, K.R. and M. Toda (1969). "The Experimental Determination of Indifference Curves," *Review of Economic Studies*, Vol. 36, pp. 433-451.

MacCrimmon, K.R. and D.A. Wehrung (1977). "Trade-Off Analysis: The Indifference and Preferred Proportion Approaches," in D.E. Bell, R.L. Keeney, and H. Raiffa (eds.), *Conflicting Objectives in Decisions*, Wiley, New York, pp. 123-147.

Meyer, R.F. (1970). "On the Relationship among the Utility of Assets, the Utility of Consumption, and Investment Strategy in an Uncertain, but Time-Invariant, World," in J. Lawrence (ed.), OR-69 -- *Proceedings of the Fifth International Conference on Operational Research - Venice 1969*, Tavistock Publications, New York, pp. 627-648.

Meyer, R.F. (1977). "State-Dependent Time Preference," in D.E. Bell, R.L. Keeney, and H. Raiffa (eds.), *Conflicting Objectives in Decisions*, Wiley, New York, pp. 232-243.

Nahas, K.H. (1977). "Preference Modeling of Utility Surfaces," unpublished doctoral dissertation, Department of Engineering - Economic Systems, Stanford University, Stanford, California.

Nakamura, Y. (1982). "Independence Conditions and Multi-additivity in Multiattribute Utility Theory," unpublished manuscript, Graduate School of Administration, University of California, Davis, California.

Pollak, R.A. (1967). "Additive von Neumann-Morgenstern Utility Functions," *Econometrica*, Vol. 35, pp. 485-494.

Raiffa, H. (1969). "Preferences for Multiattributed Alternatives," RM-5868-DOT/RC, The Rand Corporation, Santa Monica, California.

Schlaifer, R.O. (1971). *Computer Programs for Elementary Decision Analysis*, Division of Research, Graduate School of Business Administration, Harvard University, Boston, Massachusetts.

Schiffman, S., M.L. Reynolds, and F.W. Young (1981). *Introduction to Multidimensional Scaling: Theory, Methods, and Applications*, Academic Press, New York.

Tamura, H. and Y. Nakamura (1978). "Constructing a Two-Attribute Utility Function for Pollution and Consumption Based on a New Concept of Convex Dependence," in H. Myoken (ed.), *Information, Decision, and Control in Dynamic Socio-Economics,* Bunshindo, Tokyo, Japan, pp. 381–412.

Tamura, H. and Y. Nakamura (1983). "Decompositions of Multiattribute Utility Functions Based on Convex Dependence," *Operations Research,* Vol. 31, to appear.

von Neumann, J. and O. Morgenstern (1947). *Theory of Games and Economic Behavior,* 2nd. edition, Wiley, New York.

Fred Wenstøp

EVALUATION OF OIL SPILL COMBAT PLANS BY MEANS OF
MULTI-CRITERIA DECISION ANALYSIS

ABSTRACT

The exploration and development of the North Sea oil and gas
fields have increased significantly the potential for oil
pollution along the Norwegian coast. Pollution combat actions
are costly and their effectiveness questionable. In order
to evaluate different combat action strategies, it is
necessary to see action costs in relation to damage reduction. Damage involves several factors such as birds, fish,
other maritime life and recreational and industrial activities. This paper describes how multicriteria decision analysis is applied to the problem. Special emphasis is placed
on how the preference models were structured, the use of reference groups, problems of reliability and the relation between
willingness to pay and a multicriteria utility index.

1. BACKGROUND

The exploration and development of North Sea oil and gas
fields have increased the possibility of oil spills significantly. At the projected rate of development 1.7 accidental oil spills from tankers are expected per year near the
Norwegian coast. At the same time, a rate of approximately
2 blowouts from drilling and production activities are
expected. There has already been considerable damage from
accidental spills, making the need obvious for contingency
plans for how to handle various types of oil spills. As a
result, a four-year research program started in 1978: Oil
Pollution Control Research and Development Program (PFO).
Within this program the Central Institute of Industrial
Research (SI) has undertaken a project: "Cost/Benefit Analysis of Oil Pollution Control".

The goal of the project is to
- give an overall evaluation, with respect to costs and
   benefits (damage reduction) of both existing and alternative oil pollution contingency plans

B. P. Stigum and F. Wenstøp (eds.), Foundations of Utility and Risk Theory with Applications,
461–482.
© 1983 by D. Reidel Publishing Company.

- develop tools (models, data programs) for the future
  planning of oil pollution combat strategies, both region-
  ally and nationwide.

    Figure 1 shows the structure of our modelling efforts
to analyze specific oil spill scenarios and combat actions.
We distinguish between two decision levels: *Strategic decisions*
have to do with selection of the level of preparedness, how
much to spend on it, what type of equipment to acquire, where
to station it, etc. *Tactical decisions* are concerned with
selection of the best combat action when the oil spill scenario and the available resources are given. Figure 1 illustrates how we intend to go about measuring *the value* of a
combat action. The oil spill scenario describes where and
when the spill occurs, amount and type of oil and the rate
at which it is released and, finally, the weather conditions
including sea currents. The oil pollution combat action describes the positioning of oil skimmers, booms and ships near
the spill site or along the coast, and the eventual use of
artificial dispersants. The description is dynamic and includes time delays. The OPERATIONS MODEL calculates the
amount of oil which reaches the coast and the amount of oil
which evaporates or is naturally or artificially dispersed.
This model is FORTRAN implemented.

    The ENVIRONMENTAL MODEL calculates the resulting damage
to birds, shoreline and maritime life together with economic
loss to industrial activities, including fishery. This damage
depends heavily on local features such as the actual bird
life in the area. The VALUE MODEL is designed to compute the
value of the combat action in question by comparing estimates
of the incurred damage with and without the action. This
makes it possible to select the most "valuable" combat action
for the scenario under study. The *value of a combat action*
is the largest amount of money one would be willing to pay
for it (the extent of its damage reduction is assumed to be
known). Thus, the value model is a decision instrument on
the tactical level: A combat action which costs more (variable costs) than its value, should not be undertaken. But
figure 1 also is part of a decision instrument on the strategic level. Different levels of preparedness against oil
spills make different types of actions possible which will
be valued differently. This way one can study trade-offs
between preparedness costs and the value of actions for
different strategic decisions. To do this, it is of course

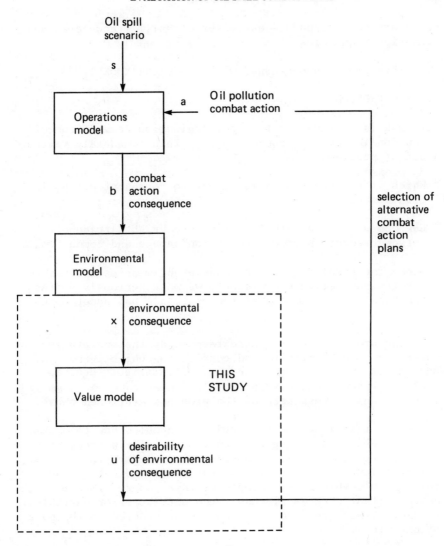

Figure 1. System of models which makes it possible to evaluate alternative oil pollution combat plans. The operations model calculates for a given oil spill scenario and combat action the resulting amounts of oil at sea and on shore. The environmental model calculates the corresponding physical damage. The value model assigns a utility index to the combination of action costs and physical damage, and calculates the willingness to pay for the action.

necessary to incorporate estimates of spill frequencies and
scenario frequencies.

  This paper is concerned with the VALUE MODEL.

2. THE PROBLEMS

Our task is to find a method for evaluation damage from oil
pollution in terms of combat costs. This immedately raises
a set of problems:

* Which attributes should we select to represent oil pollution damage?

* How can we find a method to find the "right" trade-off
  between reduction of oil pollution damage and combat cost?

* Since the resolution of the last problem necessarily incorporates subjective preferences, we must seriously address
  the question of *whose* preferences to use and under which
  premises.

  The problem area is characterized by the omnipresence of
uncertainty, subjectivity and conflicting objectives. This
has led us to adopt the method of multiattribute decision
analysis (Keeney and Raiffa [1976]. Under that paradigm
we shall now address each of the problems mentioned above.

  Note that I have not listed as a problem how to *estimate*
or *measure* factual oil pollution damage, only which attributes
we should use. That is of course also a major problem area,
but it belongs to the environmental model and not to the
value model, which is the topic of this paper. This means,
however, that when we discuss which attributes or variables
to use, we have to have the measurement problem in the back
of our minds.

3. SELECTION OF ENVIRONMENTAL CONSEQUENCE VARIABLES

The environmental consequence variables are of crucial importance for the analysis of alternative combat action plans.
A bad selection of variables will provide a poor foundation
for the evaluation of combat actions. Ideally, the set of
variables should be selected so that a realization of their
values:

- gives a complete description of the damage incurred

- is objectively measureable

- can be predicted for a given scenario and combat action
  through an operations model and an environmental model.

3.1 Objectives

After extensive discussions, the people participating in the
project agreed on the following:

   At the outset, we want to maximize the society's utility
in connection with oil spills. Oil spills are assumed to be
inevitable. This means that we both want to minimize pollution damage and combat action costs.

   Oil spill pollution damage we feel can be divided into
three categories; damage to the environment in general,
impairment of recreational areas and facilities and economic
loss to industrial enterprises such as fisheries.

   We have selected three areas of environmental concern;
the shoreline, the bird fauna and offshore maritime life
(benthic organisms).

   Together, these objectives form a goal hierarchy which
is shown on figure 2, where capital letters are used for
objectives and lower case letters are used for the variables.
For the sake of brevity, the variables are not discussed in
further detail. The important point is that we feel that
for a given oil spill, knowledge of the values of the 12
variables gives a complete account of the damage incurred
by that spill. For further discussion, see Fredrikson,
Ibrekk et al. [1982].

Figure 2.

Goal hierarchy	Description	variable name	domain and unit
PROTECT SHORE LINE	Average restitution time of affl. shore	SHORE-REST	.02-15 years
	Length of afflicted shoreline	LENGTH	.1-300 km
PROTECT THE ENVIRONMENT — PROTECT BIRD LIFE	Number of birds killed	DEATHS	3-270000 (birds)
	Restitution time of gull population	GULL-REST	.1-5 years
	Restitution time of duck population	DUCK-REST	.1-15 years
	Restitution time of auk population	AUK-REST	.1-50 years
PROTECT MARITIME LIFE·	Oil naturally dispersed in sea	NAT-DISP	.1-100000 tons
	Oil artificially dispersed in sea	ART-DISP	.1-33000 tons
PROTECT RECREATIONAL ACTIVITIES	Number of exposures to polluted shore	EXPOSURES	100-5M (times)
MINIMIZE ECONOMIC LOSS	Loss incurred to industry	INDUSTRY	0-500 M.NOK
	Loss incurred to fishery	FISHERY	0-500 M.NOK
MINIMIZE COMBAT COSTS	Cost of oil pollution combat action	COMBAT	0-1000 M.NOK

REDUCE DAMAGE

MAXIMIZE TOTAL UTILITY TO SOCIETY

A note on the domains of the variables
The domain of each variable is also shown in figure 2. The
domains are carefully selected so that most real oil spills
will fall within them. Only catastrophies will fall outside.
The domains are nothing else than a convenient specification
of our working area which we in principle are free to restrict
as we choose. The reason that we leave out catastrophies,
is that we feel that they would be evaluated differently
from more "regular" spills and therefore must be treated
separately. The maximum values are based on the "Amoco
Cadiz".

3.2 Goal formulation

Assume that an oil spill has occured. Several alternative
oil pollution combat actions are possible (including no action)
and one must be chosen. The estimated consequences of each
combat alternative is known and specified in terms of the
values of 12 variables. This set of 12 values is accordingly called a *consequence*. The goal of the combat action
leader is to select the action with the most desired consequence. This decision obviously involves conflicting objectives, where both economic and various environmental interests
must be weighted against each other. The decision thus
depends on subjective preferences.

Part of our task is to work out a method for consistent
evaluation of combat alternatives, so that it is possible
to study the effects of different preference structures.
This we shall do by modelling the decision process as maximization of (expected) utility. In this way we can work with
different utility functions representing different preference
structures. The utility index is assumed to be a function of
our 12 consequence variables. The function is of the von
Neumann-Morgenstern type.

4. THE UTILITY FUNCTION - THEORETICAL CONSIDERATIONS

4.1 The structure of the utility function

It is an infeasible task to identify the function

U_{Total} = U(SHOREREST, LENGTH, DEATHS, GULLREST, DUCKREST,
AUKREST, NATDISP, ARTDISP, EXPOSURES, INDUSTRY,
FISHERY, COMBAT)

unless it can somehow be decomposed. In Multi-Criteria
Decision Analysis the first step is usually to try to verify
that the condition of *mutual utility independence* among the
variables is satisfied to a reasonable approximation. In
that case U is a multiplicative utility function which only
demands the identification of 12 single-dimensional utility
functions and 13 constants. In our case, however, even this
is a rather taxing exercise where the reliability of the
results may be expected to be low.

There is a different approach. Look again at figure 2.
It is not unreasonable to expect little disagreement on the
relative weights of SHOREREST and LENGTH, and likewise on the
relative weights of the four BIRD-variables. On the other
hand, one might expect to find disagreement on the relative
importance of SHORELINE and BIRD LIFE and even more so on
ENVIRONMENT versus RECREATION and LOSS. The most controversial
issue would be the trade-off between DAMAGE and COMBAT COSTS.
We would like to separate the non-controversial issues from
the controversial ones, and thus make it more easy to study
them in isolation. This has led us to consider a hierarchic-
ally structured utility function molded after the tree structure of figure 2. Coded in algebraic forms, it looks like
this:

$$U_{Total} = U_{Total}\ (U_{Damage}, u_{Combat})$$

$$U_{Damage} = U_{Damage}\ (U_{Environ}, u_{Exposures}, U_{Loss})$$

$$U_{Loss} = U_{Loss}\ (u_{Industry}, u_{Fishery})$$

$$U_{Environ} = U_{Environ}\ (U_{Shore}, U_{Bird}, U_{Offshore}$$

$$U_{Shore} = U_{Shore}\ (u_{Length}, u_{Shorerest})$$

$$U_{Bird} = U_{Bird}\ (u_{Deaths}, u_{Gullrest}, u_{Duckrest}, u_{Aukrest})$$

$$U_{Offshore} = U_{Offshore}\ (u_{Natdisp}, u_{Artdisp})$$

The capital U's represent *components* of the total utility
function. They are multiplicative (or additive) utility
functions in several dimensions, i.e. of the form:

$$U(x_1, x_2, \ldots x_n) = k_1 x_1 + k_2 x_2 + k_n x_n + k k_1 k_2 x_1 x_2 + \ldots +$$

$$k k_{n-1} k_n x_{n-1} x_n + k^2 k_1 k_2 k_3 x_1 x_2 x_3 + \ldots + k^2 k_{n-2} k_{n-1} k_n x_{n-2} x_{n-1} x_n +$$

$$+ \ldots + k^{n-1} k_1 k_2 \ldots k_n x_1 x_2 \ldots x$$

which reduces to the *additive form* when $k = 0$:

$$U(x_1, x_2, \ldots x_n) \quad k_1 x_1 + k_2 x_2 + \ldots + k_n x_n$$

The lower case u's are utility functions with only one variable.

The utility (value of U_{Total}) attributed to a given scenario is computed in two steps.

Step 1: The value of each of the twelve lowercase utility functions is computed.

Step 2: The component utilities are computed sequentially, starting at the bottom.

The utility function is supposed to reflect the "true" preferences of the "decision maker". Since the concept of a decision maker is not well defined in this context, we are primarily concerned that the *structure* of the function should fit most decision makers, whereas its *content* (constants) should be adaptive to different sets of preference.

Is the structure reasonable? By structure we mean two things: The assumption that the component utility functions are multiplicative and that they can be linked together in a hierarchy. It is shown in Kenney and Raiffa [1976] that these questions are tied to the question of *utility independence*. More specifically, the structure holds theoretically if it is reasonable to assume that:

1. General damage and combat costs are mutually independent.

2. Environmental damage, number of exposures and economic loss are mutually independent.

3. Damages to shore, birds and pelagic life (offshore) are mutually utility independent.

4. Restitution time of gull-, duck- and auk-population and
   the number of birds killed are mutually utility dependent.

5. Length and restitution time of afflicted shore are
   mutually utility independent.

6. Amounts of oil which is naturally and artificially dispersed are mutually utility independent.

To say that attribute A is utility independent of
attribute B means that A's utility function is independent
of the value of B. Less technically, one could say that
preferences regarding situations where A's value is uncertain,
do not depend on the fixed value of B.

To say that a set of variables are mutually independent
means that every subset is utility independent of its complement.

We have considered the six assumptions above and concluded that, in light of the other uncertainties involved,
they are indeed reasonable approximations.

It should be added as a technical note that a hierarchy
of multiplicative functions is itself a *multilinear* utility
function.

4.2   The willingness to pay for a combat action

Suppose that we have identified a representative utility
function, U_{Total}. It expresses the degree of preference for
a given consequence in the form of a number between 0 and 1.
The domain of U_{Total} is the Cartesian product of the domains
of the 12 physical variables. Hence, $U_{Total} = 1$ when all
variables are at a minimum. $U_{Total} = 0$ when they are at a
maximum. Since these maximum values were arbitrarily chosen,
the value of U_{Total} for a given scenario obviously is not
absolute in any sense, but must be considered relative to
the chosen domain. This makes direct interpretation of
values of U_{Total} difficult and only compounds the traditional
communications problems which arise when one starts talking
about utilities. In addition, utilities do not automatically
add; an operation which becomes necessary when several spills
are to be considered simultaneously. It would, therefore,
be very convenient if it turned out to be possible *at this
point* to substitute money for utility.

First, two definitions: A *scenario* is the same as a consequence, i.e. set of values for the 12 consequence variables. A *damage scenario* is a set of values for the first 11 variables, leaving cost of combat out.

Let d be a damage scenario (the resulting damage after a combat action – if any – has been carried out). Let a be the cost of a combat action. Then we have

$$U = U_{Total} \ (d,a)$$

For a given oil spill incidence, d will be a function of a if we assume that the most efficient action which costs a is carried out:

$$d = d(a)$$

If no combat action is taken, we write

$$d(0) = d_0 \quad U_0 = U_{Total}(d_0, \ 0)$$

We now define *the amount we are willing to pay for an action which reduces the damage from d_0 to $d(a)$*, as the number $w(a)$ which satisfies the equation

$$U_0 = U_{Total}(d(a),w(a))$$

If $d(a)$ is thought of as a continuous function, this defines implicitly $w(a)$ as a function. It is our willingness to pay for a combat action which costs a and reduces the damage from d_0 to $d(a)$. The *net value* of the combat action is then

$$v(a) = w(a)-a$$

It is obvious that an action with a positive net value is cost effective. If it is the only available alternative to no action, it should be undertaken. This is seen from the fact that

$$w(a) > a \Rightarrow U_{Total} \ (d(a), \ w(a)) < U_{Total} \ (d(a),a)$$

But since $w(a)$ is defined so as to make $U_{Total} \ (d(a),w(a))$ equal to U_0 we have that

$w(a) > a \Rightarrow U_0 < U_{Total} \ (d(a),a)$

Thus, if the net value of an action is positive, the utility of no action is less than if the action were carried out. It does not follow, however, that the action which maximizes the net value necessarily also maximizes U_{Total}. Thus, we cannot uncritically substitute the theoretically correct maximization of (expected) utility with the more intuitively appealing maximization of (expected) net value. Figure 3 shows how these concepts are related. The parallel lines (which for simplicity are drawn straight) are isoutiles of U_{Total} which is assumed to be a multiplicative utility function.

$$U_{Total}(d,a) = k_1 U_{Damage}(d) + k_2 u_{Combat}(a) +$$
$$kk_1 k_2 U_{Damage}(d) u_{Combat}(a)$$

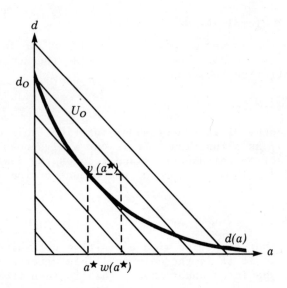

Figure 3. Determination of an optimal action a^* by two methods: Maximizing the net value $w(a)-a^*$ and maximizing utility. They do not always coincide.

The curved line $d(a)$ gives the relation between the cost of combat action a and the resulting damage d. Let us first find the optimal action a^* by maximizing U_{Total}. This corresponds to the point of tangency between $d(a)$ and the isoutiles:

$$d'(a^*) = - \frac{\partial U_{\text{Total}}(d(a^*),a^*) / \partial a}{\partial U_{\text{Total}}(d(a^*),a^*) / \partial d} \equiv$$

$$- \frac{k_2 u'_{\text{Combat}}(a^*) + kk_1 k_2 U_{\text{Damage}}(d(a^*)) u'_{\text{Combat}}(a^*)}{k_1 U'_{\text{Damage}}(d(a^*)) + kk_1 k_2 U'_{\text{Damage}}(d(a^*)) u_{\text{Combat}}(a^*)}$$

Next, let us find the action a^0 which maximizes net value. Graphically, this corresponds to sliding the line segment $v(a)$ which lies between the curve $d(a)$ and the isoutile passing through $(d_0,0)$ up and down until it reaches its maximal length. Its intersection with $d(a)$ then determines a^0. It is readily seen that whether $a^* = a^0$ depends on the shape of the isoutiles and therefore on the form of the function U_{Total}. We find that a^0 must satisfy:

$$d'(a^0) = - \frac{\partial U_{\text{Total}}(d(a^0),w(a^0)) / \partial a}{\partial U_{\text{Total}}(d(a^0),a^0) / \partial d} \equiv$$

$$- \frac{k_2 u'_{\text{Combat}}(w(a^0)) + kk_1 k_2 U_{\text{Damage}}(d(a^0)) u'_{\text{Combat}}(w(a^0))}{k_1 U'_{\text{Damage}}(d(a^0)) + kk_1 k_2 U'_{\text{Damage}}(d(a^0)) u_{\text{Combat}}(w(a^0))}$$

It is obvious that a sufficient condition for the two expressions to be identical and thus always give the same solution for a, is that

$$k = 0 \text{ and } u'_{\text{Combat}}(a) \equiv constant$$

In other words, U_{Total} must be an additive utility function and its second argument a linear utility function of combat cost. There are also other solutions, but they are of little practical significance.

All this means that when we are actually determining
our utility function U_{Total} in detail, it will be of special
importance to check whether this is a reasonable approximation
or not. If it is, we can safely use the *net value* of combat
actions as our decision criterion. If it is not, we have to
continue to work with utilities, or if we still want to work
with net values, investigate the magnitude of possible errors
we then might make. Note, however, that the value of a
combat action $w(a)$, is in all cases derived from the utility
function.

5.   THE UTILITY FUNCTION - PRACTICAL AND METHODOLOGICAL
CONSIDERATIONS

Before discussing the utility function, some issues regarding the research process itself must be clarified. A utility
function is supposed to represent the decision maker's
preference. Decisions which maximize expected utility are
considered rational. In this paper we are primarily concerned
with *operational decisions* which is the selection of the
most appropriate combat action plan when an actual oil spill
has occured and the available resources (level of preparedness) are given. The utility function also makes it possible
to estimate the benefit derived from combat actions (e.g.
net value) and since this depends on the level of preparedness, it is further possible to find out which level of preparedness is most suitable. This is a *strategic decision*.

But who is the decision maker whose utility function we
are trying to identify? Obviously, no single decision maker
can be found. What we really want to do, is to find a
reasonable expression for how much money Norwegians in general
are willing to spend to protect natural resources. A natural
idea would be to make some kind of a statistical survey and
figure out some kind of an average. This idea appears impractical for at least two reasons. First, the subject
matter is very complicated, so that it would take at least
six hours, at a terminal, to make one interview. Second,
people's preferences would most likely fluctuate wildly,
not only because of uncertainty, but mainly because of
regional differences. Why should a farmer who has never seen
the ocean care about polluted beaches? Our approach has,
therefore, been to rely on *expert groups* with special insight
into the subject matter. With the help of interactive software we try to chart down the opinions of people from such

groups in the form of a utility function. The software is constructed along the lines proposed by Keeney and Raiffa [1976].

Estimation of multidimensional utility functions always raises a series of questions of various kinds for the uniniti-ated. We have found it practical to try to establish group utility functions for two to three people. This effectively instigates critical questioning and debate. This in turn clarifies matters and lessens the possibilities of misunder-standings. It is symptomatic for this application, however, that this seldom has been a problem. One reason is that our groups are relatively homogeneous. So far, we have worked independently with two groups: One from the Board of Directors of the Program and one from the State Pollution Control Authority. The procedure has been as follows:

1. Terminal session with initial direct estimate of the utility function.

2. Feedback to the group: Implicit consequences of the utility function in terms of willingness to pay for selected oil pollution combat actions.

3. Terminal session with adjustment of the utility function.

4. New feedback of implicit consequences.

5. Final adjustments without terminal session and feedback.

Based on our experience with the two groups and previous experience with in-house reference groups, we have developed a keen feeling for the amount of uncertainty involved in the final result. We can say that it is not so large as to render the results useless, but to say that we are approximating factually pre-existing preference structures would be false. The degree of uncertainty as to one's own preferences with regard to the subject matter and the inconsistency over time, is certainly too large to make such a concept meaningful. One example was the form of the 12 one-dimensional utility functions. Although the concepts of probability and utility were well understood, it turned out very difficult to decide whether the functions representing environmental damage should be concave or convex. It is easy to argue for both viewpoints. Consequently, most of our utility functions were chosen to

be linear as some sort of a compromise. What we think we
are doing, therefore, is to construct utility models which
are *possible* representations of unclear preference structures.
Accordingly, we cannot employ the utility functions we estimate to find an "optimal" or "right" solution to the oil spill
combat problem. Instead, we use them as guidance towards a
recommendation of a reasonable combat policy.

6. SCENARIO ANALYSIS

In this chapter, selected scenarious are studied by means of
two different utility functions: Function A is informally
associated with the Board of Directors of the Oil Pollution
Control Research and Development Program, appointed by the
Ministry of Environmental Protection. Function B is informally
associated with the State Pollution Control Authority.

    In section 4.2 we defined "the willingness to pay for a
combat action" and derived the condition which ensures that
this measure is consistent with the utility measure, with
regard to choice among combat options. It turned out that
the conditions were indeed satisfied by both functions.
Thus, "willingness to pay" is the vehicle for the scenario
analysis. We calculate both the total willingness to pay
for a specified damage reduction (involving all 11 damage
variables) and how much one is willing to pay to reduce each
damage factor separately. Because the total utility function
is non-additive, the components do, in general, not sum to
the total.

6.1 Brislingfeltet scenario

Brislingfeltet is a fishing bank west of Stavanger. The
scenario portrays an accidental underwater blowout
(Fredrikson [1982]):

Spill rate: 4-6000 tons/day
Total amount: 26000 tons
Spill duration: 5 days

    For medium wind and wave conditions and typical wind and
sea current direction, the oil would reach the coast after
appr. 170 hours.

Combat action alternatives:

AO: No action   Cost: 0

A1:   Standard action   Cost: 15 mill. NOK
      This action includes mechanical collection near the
      spill site with 8 tug boats, 4 seagoing booms, 2
      skimmerboats and two large skimmers. In addition, one
      supply/repair ship and three tankers were needed.

A2:   Directing and leading the oil without collecting at
      the spill site.
                            Cost: 10 mill. NOK
      This is a strategy totally different from the one usually
      employed. We assumed that it was possible to reduce the
      length of the affected coastline with 30-35% by directing
      the oil towards a part of the shore.

A3:   Hypothetical action which virtually eliminates all
      damage.

      The effect of the actions depends on the weather condi-
tions and the damage on the season. The analysis is summed
up on the following page.

Action	A0	A1			A2			A3		
Function			A	B		A	B		A	B
Damage variable	D	D	W	W	D	W	W	D	W	W
SHOREREST (years)	3	3	0	0	2.5	1.43	0.94	0	8.58	5.6
LENGTH (km)	201	201	0	0	135	2.82	2.12	0	8.6	6.4
DEATHS (*birds)	9450	9450	0	0	6835	0.05	0	0	.19	.02
GULLREST (years)	3.1	3.1	0	0	3.1	0	0	0	.38	0
DUCKREST (years)	6	6	0	0	6	0	0	0	2.56	0.94
AUKREST (years)	12	12	.06	0	12	0	0	0	17.9	4.74
NATDISP (tons)	9500	8000	0	.3	4600	.06	.3	0	.35	1.88
ARTDISP (tons)	0	0	0	0	0	0	0	0	0	0
ESPOSURES (people · days)	200'	200'	0	0	100'	20.1	7.13	0	40.1	14.26
INDUSTRY (mill.NOK)	2.1	2.1	0	0	1.4	.72	0.35	0	2.17	1.04
FISHERY (mill.NOK)	1.5	1.5	0	0	1.3	.21	0.11	0	1.55	0.82
Total willingness to pay (mill.NOK)			.06	.3		25.0	10.7		71.0	28.5

D = resulting damage after combat action
W = willingness to pay for damage reduction (mill. NOK)

Table 1.   Brislingfeltet scenario, summer.   Weather: average.   Willingness to pay for oil spill combat actions A1, A2 and A3 according to the utility functions A and B.

The low evaluations of action 1 mean that the action
costs are around 100 times more than one appears to be willing
to pay for it. Action 1 is the kind of action one normally
would put into operation today for this kind of accident.
The result is primarily due to the consequence model which
predicts that the damage reduction is insignificant if only
a small part (10%) of the oil slick is picked up at sea.
This is so because local damage rapidly saturates when the
oil slick drifts ashore.

6.2 Real accidents

February 14, 1976, M/S "Drupa" let out 2400 tons of oil near
Sola at the south-west coast of Norway. Combat cost was
10 mill. NOK.

January 1981 M/S "Stylis" let out limited amounts of oil
in Skagerak, which polluted the coast from Hankø in Norway
far down into Bohuslän, Sweden. The effect on birds was
extensive, and got wide publicity. 500 000 NOK were spent
on pollution combat (Fredrikson et al. [1982]).

The damage scenarios are shown on the following page
with A's and B's willingness to pay to avoid the accidents
altogether.

		DRUPA			STYLIS		
Damage		D	W		D	W	
			A	B		A	B
Variable							
SHOREREST	(years)	5	8.8	6.14	2	1.59	0.98
LENGTH	(km)	120	8.5	6.02	50	1.45	1.15
DEATHS	(birds)	2000	0.1	0	250000	5.96	0.51
GULLREST	(years)	0.5	0.2	0.0	3	0.55	0.16
DUCKREST	(years)	2	.33	.16	6	3.0	1.15
AUKREST	(years)	5	6.35	1.7	14	26.54	5.85
NATDISP	(tons)	800	.03	.16	20	0	0.00
ARTDISP	(tons)	0	0	0	0	0	0
EXPOSURES	(peoples· days)	5000000	100.34	35.68	10000	2.0	0.7
INDUSTRY	(mill. NOK)	10	10.3	5.11	0.1	0.13	1.05
FISHERY	(mill. NOK)	2	2.07	1.08	0	0	0
Willingness to pay to avoid the damage (mill.NOK)			128.0	50.0		30.43	8.16

Table 2. Real oil spill scenarios with estimated damage and
calculated willingness to pay to avoid the accidents according to the utility functions A and B.
D = damage scenario
W = willingness to pay

7. CONCLUSIONS

Application of multi-criteria decision analysis as an aid in
the study of alternative oil spill combat tactics and strategies has turned out effective. The method has served as a
decisive problem structuring instrument among the participants in the project.

The participants included the model builders at the
Central Institute for Industrial Research in Oslo, where
operations researchers, chemists, biologists and economists
worked together. Adaption of multi-criteria decision analysis
led to a natural conceptual disctinction between the size of
the oil spill (tons of oil) and actual physical damage,

where willingness to pay for combat actions is linked to
damage reduction and not to the bulk of collected oil.
This conceptualization proved useful at the model building
stage, since the different sub-models could be made independently of each other.

The participants also included experts involved in
factual oil spill combat in Norway at the strategic level.
These were used as references with regard to value trade-
off considerations. Here again, multi-criteria decision
making turned out useful in highlighting the fact that all
decisions, both on a strategic and a tactical level with
regard to oil spill combat, necessarily involve conflicting
objectives and value trade-offs. The preference of the
experts were modelled in the form of hierarchical multiplicative utility functions in 12 variables. According to
our experience, the *validity* of the models were good. This
was enforced by repeated interactive terminal sessions with
accompanying discussions. On the other hand, the *reliability*
of the estimates were low. Very roughly, one can say that
the reference groups would feel comfortable with utility
functions which varied as much as ± 40% from the one we
arrived at with regard to willingness to pay. We believe
this not to be a consequence of the method we use, but
rather that it is due to an inherent uncertainty, even among
experts, of how much a society really should spend to protect the environmental resources. Consequently, in this project the estimated preference models were used as guiding
reference indicators rather than as estimates of fixed
opinions.

Although the project is not yet quite finished, our
results so far indicate that to keep the present level of preparedness for the next ten years will cost from 80 to 600
times more than either group is expected to be willing to
pay for it.

Norwegian School of Management
Hans Burums vei 30
1340 Bekkestua
Norway

REFERENCES

G. Fredrikson: Cost-Benefit Analysis of Oil Pollution
   Combat Alternatives, SI Report No. 810227-1, 1982.
   Central Institute of Industrial Research, P.O. Box 350,
   Blindern, Oslo 3, Norway.
G. Fredrikson, H. Ibrekk, K. Johannessen, K. Kveseth, H.M.
   Seip, K.L. Seip and F. Wenstøp: Oil Spill Combat:
   Damage Assessment Using Multiattribute Utility Functions.
   SI Report No. 820225-1, 1982.
R.L. Keeny and H. Raiffa: Decisions with Multiple
   Objectives: Preferences and Value Trade-offs,
   John Wiley and Sons, 1976.

NAME INDEX

Alberoni, F. 243
Allais, M. 16, 22, 31, 92,
    116, 131, 134, 174, 182,
    186, 187, 198, 206, 209,
    214, 248, 249, 250, 258,
    261, 263, 264, 274, 276,
    291, 292, 347, 365, 369
Allen, R.G.D. 280
Amihud, Y. 16
Andrews, F.M. 420
Arrow, K. 22, 31, 123, 134,
    174, 287, 394, 441

Batchman, T.E. 420
Baumol, W. 174
Becker, G.M. 134
Becker, G.S. 384
Beckman, M.J. 442
Bell, D.E. 174, 444, 453,
    455
Bernard, G. 16, 174
Bernoulli, J. 31, 230
Bertrand, J. 42
Blatt, J.M. 116, 174
Bolker, E. 274, 291
Borch, K. 150, 174, 292
Borel, E. 58
Borsch, K. 116
Braybrooke, D. 420
Brehmer, B. 420
Brewer, K.R.W. 134
Breyer, F. 394
Broglie, L. de 35
Brown, R.W. 103, 230, 243

Cagan, P. 31
Camacho, A. 175, 369

Camerer, A. 445, 455
Carver, C.S. 420
Cesa, I. 420
Charnes 174
Chernoff, H. 135
Chew, S. 175, 274, 291
Clarkson, J.K. 243
Coady, T. 175
Coombs, C.H. 135, 250
Cornes, R. 395
Corrigan, B. 420
Cournot, A. 35, 63
Cronbach, L.J. 93
Cyert, R.M. 371, 384

Daneshyar, R. 199
Davidson, D. 28, 31
Dawes, R.M. 420
Dean, G.W. 199
Debreu, G. 22, 32, 265, 292,
    395
De Groot, M.H. 134, 371, 384
Doerner, D. 420
Dreyfus, H.L. 135
Dreyfus, S.E. 135
Dreze, J. 264, 292
Dupuit, J. 19, 32
Dyen, J.B. 199
Dyer, J. 175

Ebbesen, E.B. 421
Eddy, D. 32
Edwards, W. 26, 30, 175, 230,
    243, 292
Einstein, A. 35, 63
Ellsberg, D. 98, 103, 131, 135,
    175, 243

483

SUBJECT INDEX

THEORY AND DECISION LIBRARY

An International Series in the Philosophy and Methodology
of the Social and Behavioral Sciences

Editors:

Gerald Eberlein, *University of Technology, Munich*
Werner Leinfellner, *University of Nebraska*

21. Maurice Allais and Ole Hagen (eds.), *Expected Utility Hypotheses and the Allais Paradox: Contemporary Discussions of Decisions Under Uncertainty With Allais' Rejoinder*. 1979, vii + 714 pp.
22. Teddy Seidenfeld, *Philosophical Problems of Statistical Inference: Learning from R. A. Fisher*. 1979, xiv + 246 pp.
23. L. Lewin and E. Vedung (eds.), *Politics as Rational Action*. 1980, xii + 274 pp.
24. J. Kozielecki, *Psychological Decision Theory*. 1982, xvi + 403 pp.
25. I. I. Mitroff and R. O. Mason. *Creating a Dialectical Social Science: Concepts, Methods, and Models*. 1981, ix + 189 pp.
26. V. A. Lefebvre, *Algebra of Conscience: A Comparative Analysis of Western and Soviet Ethical Systems*. 1982, xxvii + 194 pp.
27. L. Nowak, *Property and Power: Towards a Non-Marxian Historical Materialism*. 1983, xxvii + 384 pp.
28. J. C. Harsanyi, *Papers in Game Theory*. 1982, xii + 258 pp.
29. B. Walentynowicz (ed.), *Polish Contributions to the Science of Science*. 1982, xii + 291 pp.
30. A. Camacho, *Societies and Social Decision Functions. A Model with Focus on the Information Problem*. 1982, xv + 144 pp.
31. P. C. Fishburn, *The Foundations of Expected Utility*. 1982, xii + 176 pp.
32. G. Feichtinger and P. Kall (eds.), *Operations Research in Progress*. 1982, ix + 520 pp.

DATE DUE